Ramanujan:
Journey of a Great Mathematician

Ramanujan : Journey of a Great Mathematician

Arun Singhal
Devendra Kumar Sharma

राष्ट्रीय अभिलेखागार
वयं अभिलेखान् रक्षामः
NATIONAL ARCHIVES OF INDIA

यात्रा
YATRA BOOKS

vaniprakashan.com

Peparback First Edition : 2025

YATRA BOOKS
An imprint of Vani Prakashan Group
Head Office

4695, 21-A, Daryaganj, New Delhi 110 002, India
Phone : +91 11 23273167, 23275710

Registered Bookstores and Offices
Ashok Rajpath, Patna-800 004, Bihar
Coffee House Campus, Mahatma Gandhi Marg, Prayagraj-211 001, Uttar Pradesh
Mahatma Gandhi Antarrashtriya Hindi Vishwavidyalaya, Wardha-442 001, Maharashtra

sales@vaniprakashan.in
vaniprakashan@gmail.com

Ramanujan : Journey of a Great Mathematician

by
Arun Singhal
Devendra Kumar Sharma

ISBN : 978-93-48235-57-2
History/Biography

Price : ₹ 799

Printed and bound in India at Thomson Press (India) Ltd.

Contents

Acknowledgements

Srinivasa Ramanujan (22nd December 1887- 26th April 1920) was an Indian mathematician whose contribution to the theory of numbers has itself created history. He lasted only thirty two springs and his life was full of ups and downs, like the puzzles of mathematics.

The Theorems of mathematics have always attracted me and some times troubled me during my IIT Kanpur days, especially the theorems of Ramanujan. I was fortunate to get a chance to work in the National Archives of India. Perhaps the theorems of Ramanujan were calling me. I was excited to see original papers of S. Ramanujan and decided to work on them.

Working on the repertoire of a mathematical genius is very challenging and complicated, due to the complexity of the mathematical documents. We looked at documents available in the National Archives of India, Madras Port Trust, Ramanujan Museum and Math Education Center Chennai, his birthplace Kumbkonam, and also some documents in the custody of private persons.

I discussed the writing of a book and the idea that was in my mind with my colleague Dr. Devendra Kumar Sharma, and he happily accepted to collaborate in this journey. He made the tough task of writing this book look easy. I appreciate his dedication and hard work as a co-author.

I am thankful to the team Publication division of NAI specially Shri Limasashi Aier Archivist, Ms. Shrutakirti Rajan, Consultant, Ms. Monika Bansal, Consultant and Ms. Divyanshi Shrivastava Consultant for their valuable assistance in the selection of documents.

I am also thankful to Shri Sunil Paliwal, IAS, Chairman of Chennai Port Trust, Shri A.T.B.Bose, Secretary, Ramanujan Museum & Math Education Center and Professor S. Elumalai, Registrar, Madras University for providing important documents from their collection and granting us permission to use the documents in the book.

Most importantly I must thank my wife Mrs. Shalini Singhal who shared with me the travails and tributions which a researcher has to face during the course of his arduous work.

I am also thankful to Ms. Aditi Maheshwari, Managing Director, Vani Prakashan and Yatra Books whose wholehearted support has resulted in our work being published in the shape of a book.

28 February, 2025 **Arun Singhal**

Introduction

Srinivasa Ramanujan stands out as an extraordinary and brilliant mathematician from India, whose mathematical discoveries have left an indelible mark on the discipline. Born in the town of Erode on December 22nd, 1887, Ramanujan exhibited exceptional mathematical prowess from a young age. Despite his lack of formal higher education in mathematics, he formulated theories that have profoundly shaped the field[1].

His pioneering work encompassed areas such as number theory, infinite series, and continued fractions, and was truly revolutionary. As a teenager, he came across a book by George Shoobridge Carr filled with numerous theorems, which intrigued him and propelled him to further explore and expand upon these concepts, eventually leading to the formulation of his innovative theorems and ideas.

Starting his educational journey in October 1892, he displayed little interest in sports during his formative years.He was known for his quiet demeanour and penchant for inquiry. Over the ensuing two years, Ramanujan transitioned between schools in both his paternal and maternal hometowns, adapting to changes in language and location. Despite familial disputes and relocations, he remained committed to his education, navigating through various educational institutions. After several shifts, he found himself at Kangayan Primary School in Kumbakonam[2].

He excelled in his primary examinations, achieving top honours in the district by the age of ten. In January 1898, he enrolled in Town High School in Kumbakonam, an English-language institution, where he found a more fulfilling academic experience under the guidance of Headmaster S. Krishnaswami Iyer. Throughout his tenure there, Ramanujan's exceptional mathematical abilities garnered attention from both faculty and peers, elevating him to a sort of celebrity status.

During his schooling, Ramanujan consistently challenged his teachers,

1. Ram Suresh, Srinivasa Ramanujan, NBT Delhi, 1971, pp 5
2. Burce C Berndt & Robert A. Rankins, Ramanujan Letters and Commentary, Vol 9, American Mathematical Society, London Mathematical Society 1995, pp 1

showcasing his aptitude for mathematics. His inquisitive nature was exemplified by his enquiry into mathematical concepts, such as dividing zero by zero. Despite excelling in mathematics and receiving accolades such as the K. Ranganatha Rao prize in 1904 during his schooldays, Ramanujan faced challenges in other subjects after joining Government College, Kumbakonam in 1904, leading to his eventual failure in English composition and subsequent loss of scholarship[1].

The withdrawal of his scholarship, coupled with his unwavering focus on mathematics and a desperate need for financial support, drove Ramanujan to a state of misery. With his family's financial situation precarious and his passion for mathematics undiminished, he found himself at a crossroads. Eventually, in August 1905, at the age of seventeen, Ramanujan took the drastic step of running away from home, seeking opportunities in Vizagapatnam and later Rajahmundry.

At the age of eighteen, Ramanujan attempted to resume his education at Pachaiyappa's College in Madras. Impressed by his mathematical prowess, the college granted him a partial scholarship. Despite support from teachers like N. Ramanujachariar and P. Singaravelu Mudaliar, Ramanujan encountered setbacks, failing the First Arts (F.A.) examination in both 1906 and 1907. By 1908, he found himself directionless, without a job, and dependent on his family's patience, which gradually waned as his circumstances remained unchanged.

In late 1908, Ramanujan's life took an unexpected turn when his mother encountered a nine-year-old girl named Janaki during a visit to Rajendram village. They were married on July 14, 1909, though Janaki did not join Ramanujan until three years later[2].

Marriage changed the situation for Ramanujan. Now he began to earnestly search for some sort of employment. He even took up tuitions for a while. He was no longer in pursuit of a scholarship or the ambition to become a mathematician. Instead, he sought a job, an opportunity for a future, and a fresh start in life. Over the next two years, driven by sheer desperation, he travelled extensively across South India, seeking employment despite lacking a formal degree, while actively engaging in independent mathematical research.

1. Kanigal Robert, The Man who knew infinity, A life of the Genious Ramanujan, Rupa & Co, 1991 pp 47.
2. Govil Narendra Kumar and Sharma Bhudev Adbut Ganitagya Srinivasa Ramanujan, (Hindi) Prabhat Prakashan 2022, pp 45.

During this time, Ramanujan faced a medical issue as well—an abnormal swelling known as a hydrocele. The family lacked the funds for the surgery until January 1910 when one Dr. Kuppuswami volunteered to operate free of charge[1].

Sometimes later in 1910, Ramanujan, ailing from the effects of the operation, arrived at the doorstep of R. Radhakrishna Iyer, a friend from his Pachaiyappa days. Radhakrishna provided him with care, arranged for proper nourishment, and summoned a doctor. Recognizing Ramanujan's need for constant nursing, Radhakrishna put him on a train bound for his family in Kumbakonam. Before he left, Ramanujan, in a moving gesture, gave Radhakrishna two large notebooks containing his mathematical work. Ramanujan asked him to pass them on to Professor Singaravelu Mudaliar or to the British professor, Edward B. Ross at Madras Christian College, if anything happened to him, as he believed that his work should not die with him[2].

During that year, he also temporarily resided with Viswanatha Sastri, a former student he had tutored in Kumbakonam, who was now studying at Presidency College in Madras. Subsequently, Ramanujan took up residence on the Venkatanarayana Lane, in Park Town near the red buildings of the Central Railway Station. During this period, he relied on the support of two old friends from Kumbakonam, K. Narasimha Iyengar and his brother, K. Sarangapani Iyengar, who had previously assisted him with clothing and rail fares.

Having learned about the Indian Mathematical Society established by Prof V. Ramaswamy Aiyar in 1907, Ramanujan discovered that Prof. Aiyar, had contributed mathematical articles to the Educational Times in England while he was a student at Presidency College. Despite being informally referred to as Professor, he held the position of Deputy Collector in the Madras Civil Service and served as the ex officio President of the Local Body in his division. Ramanujan considered him a possible patron and travelled to Tirukkovilur, the headquarters of Ramaswamy Aiyar.

When Ramanujan reached Tirukkovilur, Ramaswamy Aiyar asked him to meet P. V. Seshu Aiyar, at Presidency College, and wrote a letter of recommendation. Ramanujan, who had been Seshu Aiyar's student at Government College, Kumbakonam, had not seen him since 1906. Now,

---

1. Kanigel Robert : The Man who Knew Infinity, a life of the Genius Ramanujan, Rupa, 1991, pp 72.
2. Ibid 74, 75.

four years later, Seshu Aiyar had moved to Presidency College in Madras. Armed with Ramaswamy Aiyar's recommendation and notebooks in hand, Ramanujan met Seshu Aiyar, obtaining leads and additional notes of introduction.

In December, Ramanujan sought an audience with R. Ramachandra Rao, a prominent figure well-versed in both the administrative and mathematical spheres. Educated at Madras's Presidency College, Rao had joined the provincial civil service at the age of nineteen in 1890. He was posted as the Collector of Nellore District, a town approximately a hundred miles north of Madras. Bestowed with the title 'Dewan Bahadur" earlier in the year, similar to a British knight, Rao was also a mathematician, serving as the President of the Indian Mathematical Society founded by Ramaswamy Aiyar four years earlier[1].

It remains unclear how Ramanujan secured an audience with Rao, but accounts converge on the role of Rao's nephew, R. Krishna Rao, as the final intermediary. Prof Seshu Aiyar also claimed to have paved the way, while Ramanujan's English friend, E. H. Neville speculated that Seshu Aiyar provided a letter of introduction that Ramanujan was hesitant to use due to timidity and shyness, possibly needing an extra push to meet Rao.

Anyhow, perhaps armed with a note of introduction from Prof Seshu Aiyar, Ramanujan journeyed to Nellore in December 1910 to meet Dewan Bahadur R. Ramachandra Rao. Ramanujan appeared before him with a frayed notebook under his arm, clearly reflecting his impoverished state. Living at Summer House, Sami Pillai Street, Triplicane, Madras, during this period, Ramanujan conveyed his simple desire for seeking basic sustenance and also some leisure to pursue his studies.

Following their conversation, Rao instructed Ramanujan to return home and assured him of financial support. Subsequently, Ramanujan received a monthly money order to cover his expenses[2]. During this period in 1911, Srinivasa Ramanujan's first paper appeared in the Journal of the Indian Mathematical Society, representing his initial step onto the stage of mathematics. He went on to share quite a few mathematical problems in the journal and also presented a second paper.

---

1. Govil Narendra Kumar and Sharma Bhudev Mathematics Wizard Srinivasa Ramanujan, Some Glimpses into his Life and Work, Prabhat Prakashan 2021 pp 45.
2. Bruce C Berndt and Robert A Rankins, Ramanujan letters and Commentary, American Mathematical Society, London Mathematical Society 1995, pp 1.

Ramanujan was reluctant to take money from R. Ramachandra Rao and he wanted to start working and earn a livelihood. He also worked for a few weeks at the Accountant General's office in Madras, in a temporary job. Seshu Aiyar and Ramaswamy Aiyar admired and respected Ramanujan's reluctance to depend on a monthly donation for sustenance. They endeavoured to support Ramanujan in realizing his desire to earn a living through his own efforts.

Eventually, they successfully convinced S. Narayana Aiyar, the Manager of the Port Trust in Madras, who had an active and keen interest in mathematics and was the Treasurer of the Indian Mathematical Society, to induct Ramanujan into his staff. Following their recommendation, on February 9, 1912,[1] Ramanujan applied to the Chief Accountant of the Madras Port Trust, seeking an appointment as a clerk and successfully secured a clerkship position in the accounts department. This opportunity, facilitated by Ramachandra Rao's influence, not only provided him with a job, but also afforded him the time and freedom to further explore his passion for mathematics. His application for the position was endorsed by E.W. Middlemast, a mathematics professor at the Presidency College[2].

Janaki joined Ramanujan sometime in late 1912. After their marriage, she had stayed on with her parents, often shuttling between her parents' and in-laws' place and learning everything that had to be learned regarding how to manage a household as a dutiful wife and daughter-in-law. When she came to stay with her husband, he had started working at the Madras Port Trust.

Summer House in Triplicane was about three miles from Ramanujan's workplace at the offices of the Port Trust opposite the harbour complex north of Fort St. George. A few months after starting his job, Ramanujan decided to move closer to his office, joining his grandmother in a little house on the Saiva Muthiah Mudali Street, in the district known as Georgetown. Ramanujan's mother Komalatammal joined him here. Janaki and Ramanujan had little contact at that time, both of them totally busy and immersed in their daily routines. His responsibilities at the Madras Port Trust likely involved verifying accounts and establishing cash

1. Letter from S.Ramanujan to Chief Accountant Madras Port Trust, Feb 9, 1912, PA Section, NAI New Delhi.
2. File No. 50-63/50 A2 NAI New Delhi.

balances. After a few months, he also stepped in for another clerk who was on leave, taking on the role of the "pilotage fund clerk."

The work wasn't particularly demanding, and eventually, he found himself working independently on mathematical tasks. Much later, Janaki would reminisce about her late husband, how he would keep working on mathematics, in whatever free time he had, in the morning before he left for office, and after coming back from work in the evenings.

Although Ramanujan's tenure at the Madras Port Trust lasted only around one year, his superiors, including the Chairman, Francis Spring, and the Chief Accountant, S. Narayana Aiyar, who had been trained as a mathematician, maintained a keen interest in him throughout his life. They actively advocated for him, ensuring he received necessary resources and support as a mathematical talent. Subsequently, they continued to track his academic and professional journey at the Universities of Madras and Cambridge with unwavering attention[1].

Ramanujan was gaining recognition among professors at various colleges in Madras, all eager to support his academic pursuits and nurture his exceptional talent. The initial initiative came from C.L.T. Griffith, a civil engineering professor at Madras Engineering College and a University College London graduate. Griffith contacted his former mathematics professor, M.J.M. Hill, sharing some of Ramanujan's work. Additionally, Griffith reached out to Francis Spring following Ramanujan's employment at the Port Trust. Other influential figures like Sir Gilbert Walker, a former Senior Wrangler, (Senior Wrangler is the person who achieves the highest overall marks among the Wranglers – the students at Cambridge who gain first-class degrees in mathematics) were also approached.

Spring corresponded with A. G. Bourne, Madras's Director of Public Instruction, who suggested referring Ramanujan to prominent Madras mathematicians. Acting on this advice, Ramanujan met with J. F. Graham, two weeks later[2].

Simultaneously, Ramanujan reached out in January 1913 to three distinguished Cambridge mathematicians: Professor H.F. Baker, Professor E.W. Hobson, and Professor G.H. Hardy, a Cayley Lecturer in Mathematics and Trinity College Fellow. Hardy's reply was positive and

1. File No. 50-63/50 A2 NAI, New Delhi
2. Ibid

supportive[1]. Upon receiving Ramanujan's letter with the one hundred and twenty theorems, Hardy immediately consulted his close colleague and fellow mathematician, J.E. Littlewood, with whom he had collaborated previously. Together, they were astounded by Ramanujan's work, recognizing his exceptional brilliance in mathematics.

Towards the end of February, Gilbert Walker was shown Ramanujan's work. Walker was a former Senior Wrangler, a former fellow and mathematical lecturer at Trinity, and at this time, head of the Indian Meteorological Department in Shimla. He was asked by Francis Spring to go through Ramanujan's work and Walker wrote to the Madras University the very next day, asking the University to appoint and support Ramanujan as a research student. In February 1913, Dr. Arthur Davies met Ramanujan and Narayan Aiyar and asked whether Ramanujan was ready to go to England. On behalf of Ramanujan S. Narayan Aiyar declined and the matter was dropped.[2]

In March 1913, Professor B. Hanumanta Rao, from the Government College of Engineering, extended an invitation to S. Narayana Aiyar for a meeting of the Board of Studies in Mathematics, aimed at discussing potential avenues of support for Ramanujan[3]. On the 19th of that month, the board convened and proposed to the university's governing body, the Syndicate, that Ramanujan be granted a research scholarship of seventy-five rupees monthly for the following two years—more than double his salary at the Port Trust. However, in April, during the subsequent Syndicate meeting, Ramanujan encountered a setback due to his incomplete degree status; as such scholarships typically required a Master's degree. Despite this setback, the Vice-Chancellor, P. R. Sundaram Ayyar, championed Ramanujan's cause as an exceptional circumstance, presenting it to the Syndicate for reconsideration. He personally advocated for Ramanujan to be awarded a research scholarship, prompting the university to seek the Chancellor's approval for an exception to be made. Consequently, Ramanujan was appointed as a Research Scholar at the University of Madras, effective 1st May, 1913, with a stipend of 75 rupees per month.

The Madras University Library, housed in a wing of the Connemara Public Library Buildings, had just then begun to function. Trivikrama

1. Letter from G.H. Hardy to Ramanujan PA Section NAI, New Delhi.
2. Kanigel Robert : The Man who Knew Infinity, a life of the Genius Ramanujan, Rupa, 1991, pp 185
3. Letter from B. Hanumata Rao to S. Narayan Aiyar, 1913 PA Section NAI, New Delhi.

Rao was then in charge of it. Ramanujan used to spend much of his time here. This was the first academic setting secured for Ramanujan. During this period, he used to spend the morning hours and the early hours of the night in the house of S. Narayana Aiyar. They would be working together on the Elliptic Integrals or other problems in Mathematics, till late in the night.

In September, Narayana Aiyar submitted some theorems to the Journal of the Indian Mathematical Society, attributing or giving credit to Ramanujan for one of the theorems. In October, he took Ramanujan to meet Richard Littlehailes, professor of mathematics at Presidency College and who soon thereafter became Madras's Director of Public Instruction. Littlehailes was intrigued by Ramanujan's work and said that he looked forward to studying Ramanujan's results[1].

As a research scholarship holder, Ramanujan was obligated to prepare reports every three months detailing his progress. He delivered three of them all on time in late 1913 and early 1914, before departing for Cambridge.

During all this time, he had been in correspondence with G. H. Hardy. In early January 1914, Hardy wrote to Ramanujan asking him to meet E. H. Neville, who was in Madras giving a series of lectures at the University. In fact, Hardy had entrusted Neville with the task of getting Ramanujan to agree to come to Cambridge[2]. An able mathematician and a Fellow of Trinity College, Hardy asked him to somehow convince Ramanujan to leave India and come to England. They met a few times, and Neville managed to gain Ramanujan's trust. Ramanujan was even willing to give Neville one of his precious notebooks to take away and to peruse at leisure. This was indeed a big thing, with Neville saying that it was the "the most astounding compliment ever paid to me."

When finally, Neville asked Ramanujan whether he was willing to come to England, he was pleasantly surprised to know that Ramanujan was indeed willing. All opposition that had been raised earlier were gone. By one account, many of Ramanujan's well-wishers including K. Narasimha Iyengar, a close friend, managed to persuade Komalatammal to give permission, and Seshu Aiyar, and Ramachandra Rao played a role in convincing Ramanujan.

1. File No. 50-63/50 A2 NAI, New Delhi
2. Hardy GH, Aiyar P.V. Seshu & Welson B.M. (Ed) Collected Papers of Srinivasa Ramanujan, Cambridge University Press (First Paper Book ed.) 2015 pp 16.

According to another account, Ramanujan's mother had a vivid dream in which she saw her son among Europeans and Goddess of Namakkal commanding her to let her son go and fulfil his dreams and his life's purpose. The details differ but the crux remains the same - it was the Goddess who granted permission to Ramanujan and that was why he acquiesced. Yet another version suggests that Ramanujan, his mother, Narayana Aiyar and his son went to Namakkal to pray and seek the blessings of the Goddess. It is mentioned in some documents that Ramanujan and Narayana Aiyar spent three nights at the temple. On the third night, Ramanujan rose from a dream and woke Narayana Aiyar with word that he had received command from the Goddess herself to go to England.

Neville was gratified and set about removing all other doubts that Ramanujan had regarding his travel to England. Ramanujan had quite a few queries regarding the finances to travel and live in England, and his vegetarianism, among others. Neville managed to assuage Ramanujan's doubts and immediately wrote to Hardy regarding the financial matters at hand. Neville planned to find money in Madras. But should he fail, he wanted that money be somehow found in England, so that financial difficulties should not become a hindrance for Ramanujan.

Hardy seemed to have forwarded Neville's letter to the India Office, because he soon received from C. Mallet, Secretary for Indian students, a worried reply. He told Hardy that money couldn't be obtained from the India Office for this purpose. He also doubted whether Trinity or Cambridge would come up with any, and even Madras for that matter. His pessimistic letter worried Hardy as well and he dashed off a letter to Neville.

Thankfully, Neville had managed the situation. Littlehailes had introduced him to influential people in the university or government, and everywhere he went, Neville praised Ramanujan. He wrote to Francis Dewsbury stating that the discovery of the genius of S. Ramanujan was definitely promising and one of the most interesting events during this time in the mathematical world. Littlehailes also formally requested Dewsbury to grant Ramanujan a 250-pound-per-year scholarship, coupled with a 100-pound grant to buy Western clothes and book passage to England. Francis Spring wrote a letter to Lord Pentland's Secretary, E. B.

Cotterell[1], since Spring had come to learn that the University was prepared to set aside ten thousand rupees, to secure Ramanujan's visit for two years in England. The decision was subject to approval from higher authorities and hence the rationale for his letter. Lord Pentland, the Governor of Madras[2], interceded on Ramanujan's behalf and so finally, Ramanujan was set to go to England.

Ramanujan's journey to England required significant preparations. Overcoming the societal and orthodox hurdles and barriers against overseas travel was the initial challenge. Adapting to English attire posed another obstacle. Ramanujan had to acquaint himself with Western clothing styles and, under Ramachandra Rao's insistence he abandoned the traditional South Indian practice of maintaining a long hair tuft. Despite these major changes and upheavals, Ramanujan remained steadfast in his vegetarianism and refused to give that up. On March 11th, 1914, Francis Spring made arrangements with the shipping company to ensure Ramanujan would have access to vegetarian meals during his long sea journey[3]. Fulfilling his familial responsibilities was also paramount. Ramanujan arranged for the University of Madras to allocate £50 annually from his scholarship to support his parents.

Ramanujan departed from Madras on March 17th, 1914, aboard the S.S. Nevasa, finally arriving in England on April 14th. Carrying the good wishes of his friends and colleagues from Madras, Ramanujan was welcomed warmly by the academic community in Cambridge.

Awaiting Ramanujan's arrival at the dock were E. H. Neville and his elder brother. Together, they proceeded by car to 21 Cromwell Road, located in London's South Kensington district, which served as a welcoming centre for newly arrived Indian students[4]. On April 18th, Ramanujan accompanied Neville to Cambridge, where he quickly found a new home at Neville's residence on the Chestertown Road. After spending a few weeks there, Ramanujan moved into rooms in the Whewell's Court, Trinity College, Cambridge.

Upon arriving in Cambridge, Ramanujan naturally needed some time to adjust to his new surroundings. The kindness of Hardy and Littlewood

1. File No. 50-63 A2 NAI New Delhi.
2. Singh Manoj; Srinivasa Ramanujan, Akshay Books, Delhi, 2024, PP 60.
3. Ranganathan SR; Ramanujan : The Man and the Mathematician, Asia, Publishing House, 1967. pp 37.
4. Kanigel Robert, The man who knew infinity, a life of the Genius Ramanujan, Rupa & Co. 1991, pp 199.

helped smoothen out this process. Administrative matters, such as fees and paperwork, were mostly efficiently handled by Hardy and Neville.

Before Ramanujan's arrival, Hardy had already examined the one hundred and twenty theorems that Ramanujan had sent him in January 1913. These theorems revealed both strengths and weaknesses in Ramanujan's mathematical work. Collaborating with Hardy and Littlewood, Ramanujan worked diligently and earnestly on improving them.

Although Ramanujan hadn't come to Cambridge for formal education, he attended some lectures during the Easter term. These included lectures not only by Hardy and also by others such as Arthur Berry.

Over the next few years, Ramanujan and Hardy met frequently. Ramanujan demonstrated the mathematical methods he had developed in India, which he had been reluctant to describe through international correspondence. Meanwhile, Hardy had Ramanujan's notebooks in front of him and could study them alongside the author.

Hardy faced a dilemma: he didn't want to subject Ramanujan to systematic instruction, fearing it might dampen his inspiration. However, he also couldn't let Ramanujan remain unaware of his mistakes. So, Hardy opted for a collaborative approach, learning from Ramanujan while also guiding him simultaneously.

Hardy had taken a significant risk in bringing Ramanujan to Cambridge, and after immersing himself in Ramanujan's notebooks, he most likely felt a mix of relief and pride. In his own words, "Ramanujan was my discovery. I did not invent him - like other great men, he invented himself - but I was the first really competent person who had the chance to see some of his work, and I can still remember with satisfaction that I could recognize at once what a treasure I had found."

It didn't take Hardy long to realize that Ramanujan's notebooks held valuable content worthy of publication. However, editorial work was necessary: shaping his results, translating them into clear English, and making the notation more familiar. Hardy, with his journalistic approach to mathematics, took on this task. He meticulously edited Ramanujan's manuscripts, even rewriting a few of the earlier ones. Remarkably, Hardy refrained from claiming any mathematical contribution, even after spending ample time with Ramanujan on them.

As a result, Ramanujan's raw notebook entries transformed into well-crafted mathematical papers, ready to be shared with the world. By June 1914, he and Hardy had laid the groundwork for two papers, one of which was presented by Hardy at the London Mathematical Society's meeting room, near Piccadilly, on June 11th. Among the audience were esteemed mathematicians like Hobson, Bromwich, and Littlewood. However, intriguingly, Ramanujan himself was absent.

In early August 1914, England declared war. In September, Ramanujan wrote to his mother, assuring her that England remained untouched by the conflict[1]. However, the reality was quite different. The war had a profound impact on Cambridge. Parts of the prestigious university were converted into temporary headquarters for the Officers Training Corps, an open-air hospital, and even an operating theatre. Cambridge, once bustling with undergraduates, now housed only a fraction of its usual population. College students and faculty members served in various capacities related to the war effort.

Until the outbreak of war, Hardy, Littlewood, and Ramanujan collaborated tirelessly on several of Ramanujan's conjectural results. Littlewood, now a second lieutenant in the Royal Garrison Artillery, eventually left the group due to war duty, but Hardy and Ramanujan continued their intense collaboration from the summer of 1914 to the summer of 1917[2].

Despite recognizing Ramanujan's superior natural mathematical ability, Hardy harboured no envy. Their relationship remained unwavering—Hardy was Ramanujan's steadfast friend and advocate. His main aim was to nurture Ramanujan's genius and push it to its limits.

The subsequent year, 1915, witnessed many papers published by Ramanujan, including the one that Hardy presented to the London Mathematical Society that memorable June evening. During his initial year in England, Ramanujan's work primarily consisted of Indian contributions. His twenty-three-page paper, titled "Modular Equations and Approximations to Pi," which appeared in the Quarterly Journal of

1. Letter from S.Ramanujan to his mother (written in Tamil) Smt. Komlata Ammal dated 11 Sept. 1914, Ramanujan Museum and Math Edu. Centre Chennai.
2. Rangnathan S.R, Ramanujan: The Man and the Mathematician, Asia Publishing House 1967, pp 41-42.

Mathematics, explored alternative paths to approximating pi. Remarkably, this work would later serve as the foundation for the fastest-known algorithm for determining the value of pi via computers.

Upon arriving in Cambridge, Ramanujan's initial shyness was sometimes misinterpreted as unfriendliness, leading to occasional taunts from fellow students. However, over time, he became a popular and legendary figure. He became the pride of Indian students—a mathematical genius whom the English had gone to great lengths to bring to Cambridge.

During the extended breaks between terms, Ramanujan mostly stayed in Cambridge. By mid-October 1915, he had moved to new rooms in Bishop's Hostel, closely situated behind Great Court. The layout resembled his previous accommodations in Whewell's Court, but now, Hardy was even closer.

At Cambridge, each student had a tutor overseeing their progress. Ramanujan's tutor was E. W. Barnes, who considered him amongst the most brilliant of all top Trinity students. Barnes, later a bishop, was a respected mathematician with significant contributions to his name.

In late 1915, Ramanujan's pivotal paper on highly composite numbers—the culmination of his work during his initial year in Cambridge—appeared in the Proceedings of the London Mathematical Society. Introduced by Hardy the previous June, the manuscript underwent revisions and finally reached its definitive form in March 1915, and was immortalized in print.

In November 1915, E. W. Barnes corresponded with Francis Dewsbury, the registrar of the University of Madras, praising Ramanujan's progress[1]. As his two-year scholarship approached its end, Barnes recommended extending it until Ramanujan could be elected as a Fellow at the College. Barnes confidently anticipated the outcome of this election was to occur later in October 1917, positioning Ramanujan for Trinity Fellowship.

Shortly thereafter, Hardy also communicated with Dewsbury, unequivocally declaring Ramanujan as "the best Indian mathematician of modern times." In Hardy's estimation, Ramanujan stood out as the most remarkable mathematician he had ever encountered.

In Madras, Sir Francis Spring echoed the sentiment, specifically

1. Govil Narendra Kumar and Sharma Bhudev Mathematics Wizard Srinivasa Ramanujan, Some Glimpses into his Life and Work, Prabhat Prakashan 2021 pp 123.

advocating for a two-year extension of Ramanujan's scholarship. The debate within Madras authorities centered on whether to extend it for one year or two. If the extension was only for a year, Ramanujan expressed a reluctance to return to India during the summer of 1916, considering that his scholarship would end in spring 1917, bringing him back home just nine months later.

The University administration grappled with the potential overlap between the Trinity fellowship and their scholarship. Eventually, they settled on a one-year arrangement, with the possibility of extensions. His 250-pound annual scholarship was further supplemented by 60-pounds per year from Trinity College.

Free from official college duties, Ramanujan could fully immerse himself in mathematics. Yet, despite his scholarly pursuits, a lingering desire gnawed at him and kept troubling him—the lack of a formal degree. For him, it was a mere formality, but he yearned for it nonetheless.

Typically, admission as a research student required a prior university diploma or certificate. However, in Ramanujan's exceptional case, this requirement was waived. In March 1916, he was awarded a B.A. degree 'by research' based on his extensive paper on highly composite numbers. He paid the five-pound dissertation fee and gave each of his examiners two pounds[1]. After a journey spanning a dozen years and two college setbacks since leaving Town High School, he finally possessed his degree.

Ramanujan chose not to return to India that summer. Perhaps it was due to the scholarship extension for just one year. Instead, he dedicated much of the following year to collaborating with Hardy on a mathematical journey that would forever intertwine their names in the annals of mathematics.

Ramanujan, despite being in a foreign country with an alien life, appeared to have adjusted splendidly. Mathematically, he exceeded the fondest hopes of Hardy, Littlewood, Neville, and his other English friends. Initially, he seemed socially adaptable as well. However, the pursuit of mathematics demanded immense personal energy, just as adapting to his new life in England did.

---

1. Bruce C Berndt and Robert A. Rankins, Ramanujan letters and Commentary, American Mathematical Society, London Mathematical Society, 1995 pp 137.

In October 1916, Ramanujan's paper was presented to the Cambridge Philosophical Society—but it was Hardy who read it, not Ramanujan. Similarly, when Hardy presented a joint paper at a meeting of the London Mathematical Society on January 18th, 1917, Littlewood, Neville, and Bromwich were present, but Ramanujan was absent.

In late 1916, Hardy penned an early account, attributing it to both himself and the distinguished Indian mathematician, Mr. S. Ramanujan. This joint work was presented at the Quatrieme Congres des Mathematiciens Scandinaves in Stockholm. The following year, a concise joint paper titled 'Une Formule Asymptotique Pour Ie Nombre Des Partitions Den' appeared in Comptes Rendus. Additionally, a one-paragraph reference to the French journal article surfaced in the Proceedings of the London Mathematical Society in March. However, the comprehensive forty-page paper detailing their collaborative efforts didn't materialize until 1918.

For Ramanujan, this mathematical expedition was utterly intoxicating. A decade earlier, his encounter with Carr had rendered him single-mindedly devoted to mathematics, to the point where he could no longer function as an ordinary college student pursuing all his subjects with the same passion and dedication. Now, a similar fervour consumed him, but with even greater intensity. It wasn't solely his personal delight in mathematics that propelled him forward; it was also the encouragement he received from Hardy. To Ramanujan, Hardy was the ideal colleague and mentor—one who recognized the breathtaking originality in him. This recognition only fuelled Ramanujan's eagerness to continue their collaborative work.

In late December 1916, the Indian Mathematical Society had held its first conference, in Madras. Lord Pentland himself opened the proceedings, being met on the steps of Presidency College by R. Ramachandra Rao, the society's fourth president. Lord Pentland, in his address mentioned "...a young Indian student, Mr. S. Ramanujan studying at Cambridge whose career we in Southern India are watching with keen interest and high anticipation. You know the story of the discovery of his unusual talent and all here will be glad to hear how entirely he is justifying the efforts which were made to give it full scope."

However, during his years in England, Ramanujan experienced considerable emotional strain. Two factors contributed to this: the sudden absorption into English society with totally distinct values from his own, and the totally unfamiliar cultural environment. The abruptness of this change caused him immense misery. Unfortunately, there were few individuals in Cambridge with whom he could openly discuss his feelings, leaving him without any outlet for relief.

His dietary habits posed additional challenges. Having always lived with family or close relatives in a familiar home environment, his bodily system had become rigidly attuned to specific food and habits. His taste preferences, meal times, and other related matters were firmly established. However, when he found himself in a society with different culinary customs, he realized the powerful grip that food habits had on him. Throughout his years in England, Ramanujan rarely had the opportunity to taste his habitual Indian cuisine, all the more because of the challenging conditions of the First World War.

Indeed, it is well-documented that Ramanujan faced challenges related to food habits during his time in England. Cooking his meals, often eating at odd times, and the lack of a diverse range of Indian food materials, to which he was accustomed, contributed to his continuous undernourishment[1].

Despite these emotional and physical hardships, Ramanujan's intellectual vigour remained unwavering. In the company of esteemed and eminent mathematicians in Cambridge, he passionately pursued his passion for mathematics.

In May 1917, the University of Madras received word from Hardy that Ramanujan was unwell, and it was suspected that he had contracted some incurable disease. The recommendation was for him to return immediately to the tropics. However, several obstacles stood in the way. The submarine threat during wartime made sea voyages risky, and India faced a shortage of capable English medical practitioners due to war demands. Taking all these unhelpful circumstances regarding physical and emotional comfort into consideration, it was decided that Ramanujan should remain in England. He entered a nursing home in Cambridge

1. Rangnathan S.R., Ramanujan The Man and the Mathematician, Asia Publishing House, 1967 pp 76.

during the summer of 1917 and was later moved to various sanatoria in Wells, Matlock, and London. By the end of 1918, it was confirmed that tuberculosis had taken hold[1].

Initially, Ramanujan's condition was dire, so much so that Hardy urgently sought assistance from the master of Trinity to relay the news to Ramachandra Rao in India via a special dispatch. Later, when Ramanujan showed slight improvement, Hardy sent news reassuring Ramachandra Rao and to alleviate any concerns that had been raised by the earlier report. There exists some evidence suggesting that Hardy himself took on the role of Ramanujan's caregiver for a brief period, calling him a 'difficult patient' in one of his letters.

A picky eater, Ramanujan defied medical advice, was very stubborn and he harboured little trust in conventional medicine. Ramanujan consulted at least eight doctors and entered five English hospitals and sanatoria over the next two years. Around October, he found himself at the Mendip Hills Sanatorium near Wells in Somerset. There, under the care of Dr. Chowry Muthu, an Indian physician who had coincidentally accompanied Ramanujan on the Nevasa three years prior, he grappled with his health. However, his stay was brief, and by November, he was transferred to the Matlock House Sanatorium in Derbyshire[2].

Ramanujan's health journey involved a series of diagnostic twists and turns. Initially, a gastric ulcer was suspected, but opinions on this fluctuated during his treatment. At one point, exploratory surgery was even considered. Interestingly, one doctor speculated that Ramanujan's hydrocele operation in India had been to remove a malignant growth, suggesting that cancer might be spreading. However, since Ramanujan's condition didn't worsen, most physicians dismissed this notion. Ultimately, it was tuberculosis that became the consistent focus of his treatment at Mendip Hills, and it would continue to be the primary concern in the years ahead.

However, as the year drew to a close, it wasn't just his physical well-being that troubled him; his mind was equally affected. Ramanujan was far from content at that time. To make matters worse, domestic tensions also sprouted. Ramanujan's mother, Komalatammal, shared an intense bond with her son—a child she had long yearned for and prayed to receive.

1. Rangnathan S.R., Ramanujan The Man and the Mathematician, Asia Publishing House, 1967 pp 496.
2. Bruce C Berndt and Robert A Rankins, Ramanujan letters and Commentary, American Mathematical Society, London Mathematical Society, 1595 pp 173.

Their similarities ran deep: they shared physical resemblance, thought patterns, and even their temperament. His mother,who was nearing fifty, possessed a formidable presence. In contrast, Ramanujan's wife, Janaki, remained meek and inexperienced, still in her teenage years. The intricate dynamics of this family played out against a backdrop of personal struggles and emotional complexities.

While Ramanujan was in India, Komalatammal apparently prevented Ramanujan and Janaki from having a great relationship. Once he departed for England, Janaki was made to do a lot of work and received no words of gratitude or encouragement from her mother-in-law. Eventually, correspondence between Ramanujan and Janaki was intercepted by his mother. At one juncture, Ramanujan wrote to his mother, urging her to bring Janaki to England. Unbeknownst to Janaki, her mother-in-law replied that such a move was out of the question. Komalatammal's perspective remains somewhat elusive, but according to some accounts, she attributed Ramanujan's ill health to Janaki's horoscope. In her view, had he married someone else, he would not have fallen sick[1].

The turmoil within Ramanujan's household had spilled over, distorting his relationship with his entire family. Initially, he wrote letters home frequently, then they began to dwindle and eventually, they ceased altogether. In 1914, Ramanujan corresponded with his family three or four times a month. By 1916, several months would pass before he wrote. During 1917, there was no communication from him at all[2].

For a considerable duration, perhaps burdened by the sense of abandonment by his own kin, Ramanujan remained silent about this matter. However, while in the Cambridge nursing home, he could no longer contain it. He confided in Hardy, and he also shared his feelings with a close friend of his.

In late 1917 or early 1918, Ramanujan tried to take his own life by hurling himself onto the train tracks as an approaching train bore down on him. Fortunately, a vigilant guard spotted this and swiftly pulled a switch, bringing the train to a screeching halt just a few feet away.

1. Vekantswaran TV, Kanitha Medhai Ramanujan, Bharthi Puspkalogam Chennai, Dec. 2017 pp 118.
2. Ibid 274-275.

Subsequently, he was apprehended and taken to Scotland Yard. Hardy, summoned to the scene, used his charm and academic standing to assert that the great Mr. Srinivasa Ramanujan, a Fellow of the Royal Society, could not possibly be arrested. However, the truth was that Ramanujan was not yet an F.R.S., and his immunity from arrest was illusory. The police were not deceived, but upon investigation, they recognized Ramanujan's reputation as an eminent mathematician and chose not to pursue charges. The officer in charge is later said to have stated that Scotland Yard did not want to spoil his life[1].

The exact trigger for Ramanujan's desperate leap onto the tracks remains unknown. Most likely, this was a rash and impulsive act and not something done deliberately to take his own life.

In 1916, Ramanujan's tutor Barnes had written to the University of Madras, expressing the belief that given Ramanujan's remarkable achievements, he would likely be elected a Fellow of Trinity College in the following October. However, October 1917 came and went without Ramanujan's election to that prestigious position. The disappointment was keenly felt, especially since he had also missed out on becoming a Fellow of the Royal Society.

The rejection by Trinity College continued to bother him, and his ill health prevented him from making significant mathematical contributions—which became an additional source of distress. The attending doctors did not suit his needs, and the available food was not satisfactory for him. Moreover, emotional support from home was scarce, and even Hardy, his close friend, couldn't provide much comfort.

Undeterred by the Trinity setback, Hardy embarked on a mission to boost Ramanujan's morale. On December 6, 1917, Ramanujan was elected to the London Mathematical Society. Just two weeks later, on December 18, Hardy and eleven other esteemed mathematicians—including Hobson, Baker, Bromwich, Littlewood, Forsyth, and Alfred North Whitehead (Bertrand Russell's collaborator on Principia Mathematica)—nominated him for an honour far more prestigious than any Cambridge college fellowship: the Certificate of a Candidate for Election to become a Fellow of the Royal Society[2].

Ramanujan's name was proposed for the Fellowship of the Royal

1. Govil Narendra Kumar and Sharma Bhudev, Mathematics Wizard, Srinivasa Ramanujan, Some Glimpses into his Life and Work, Prabhat Prakashan 2021, pp 124.
2. Ibid 126.

Society at the remarkably young age of thirty. His nomination was accepted—an unprecedented occurrence in modern times. Niel Bohr, the esteemed Danish physicist, is believed to be the only other person similarly elected[1].

Out of 104 candidates vying for election that year, Ramanujan was one of the only 15 who succeeded. Ramanujan expressed his profound gratitude to Hardy, in a letter, writing, "My words are not adequate to express my thanks to you. I did not even dream of the possibility of my election." In May, he would officially become S. Ramanujan, F.R.S. However owing to his fragile health, he wrote to the Royal Society from Matlock, explaining that he was currently too unwell to travel to London for his formal induction into the society.

News of his achievement enthralled India. Members of the Indian Mathematical Society in Madras conveyed their gratitude to Hardy for the guidance and support he extended to S. Ramanujan in his work. P. V. Seshu Aiyar added a personal note of thanks for the care provided during the months when Ramanujan's health was precarious.

In the autumn of 1918, Ramanujan's name resurfaced for consideration for a Trinity fellowship. Hardy, closely associated with Ramanujan and entrenched in Trinity's internal politics, was advised against nominating him this time. Instead, Littlewood (who had returned to Cambridge after being overwhelmed by work and a concussion) took up the task. Various issues flared up such as the issue of Ramanujan's race, and his suicide attempt. Despite his illness preventing him from attending in person, Littlewood authored a report refuting the rumours and provided two medical certificates affirming Ramanujan's mental soundness.

On October 13th, 1918, Ramanujan was elected a Fellow of Trinity College, Cambridge. He became the first Indian to receive this honour. The fellowship carried an annual honorarium of £250 for six years, without any attached duties or conditions[2].

As anticipated by Hardy, the honours bestowed upon Ramanujan, particularly his election as an F.R.S., significantly lifted his spirits. This positive turn of events marked what Neville would later describe as "a brief period of brilliant invention," commencing around the spring of

1. Rangnathan S.R., The Man and the Mathematician, Asia Publishing House, 1967 pp 41.
2. Ibid 44.

1918. The paper Ramanujan had presented at that time to the Cambridge Philosophical Society represented the pinnacle of this creative surge.

On November 26th, Hardy corresponded with Francis Dewsbury in Madras, providing an update on Ramanujan's condition. He expressed that it was now time to reconsider the matter of Ramanujan's temporary return to India and his overall future.

Ramanujan's health had improved, and Hardy informed Dewsbury that he was "on the road to a real recovery." Mindful of Ramanujan's sensitivities, Hardy suggested that the proposal should be made officially, and simultaneously addressed to both Ramanujan and himself. The proposition was straightforward: offer Ramanujan a university position that allowed him the freedom to pursue research and occasionally visit England. Hardy was confident that Ramanujan would welcome such an opportunity.

While Ramanujan was at the Colinette House, he got some good news. Throughout the war, the authorities in Madras had kept up with him through Hardy, periodically extending his leave of absence from the Port Trust and his fellowships from the University. In 1918, Ramanujan's mother came to Madras and learned that her son would be named University Professor, earning at least 400 rupees per month. Now, in the wake of his F.R.S., the Madras authorities were more or less falling all over themselves to see what they could do for him. And in late December 1918 or early in the New Year, he learned the university had granted him a 250-pound-per-year fellowship. This was on top of a like amount awarded to him by Trinity. And it was good for six years. He was also permitted periodic trips back to England.

Ten weeks before Ramanujan's arrival in Bombay, the Indian Mathematical Society met there for its second conference. Ramanujan's "brilliant career," his "very humble origin," and his elevation to the Royal Society were on every speaker's lips. He was returning at a bad time, though, at the height of a flu epidemic that would kill millions of people; among the mathematical society's small membership alone, it had claimed lives of five people. Others who had died during Ramanujan's time abroad were E. W. Middlemast, the Presidency College mathematics professor and Singaravelu Mudaliar, his mathematics professor at Pachaiyappa's College. The leading page of the society's journal, dated April 1, 1919, gave the news of Ramanujan's return, but that he was coming back, "in somewhat indifferent health."

Ramanujan left England, aboard the SS Nagoya, and landed in Bombay, in March 1919. The city of Madras cheered and supported Ramanujan. Back in May 1914 after Ramaujan had landed in England, he was already being heralded in the Madras papers. When he received his degree, they heard about it and celebrated it. When he was named an F.R.S., Madras had honoured him by convening a meeting at Presidency College. When it became known that Ramanujan was returning to India, the city of Madras was ready to welcome the country's famed son back.

He was greeted by his mother and brother, Lakshmi Narasimhan, but not his wife, Janaki. His heart sank at her absence, and he questioned his mother as he disembarked, only to be met with a brusque reply. Domestic discord had marred his years in England, and the divide between families had widened, leaving Janaki's whereabouts a mystery, lost amidst familial rifts and miscommunications. On Ramanujan's return, letters were dispatched, seeking Janaki's presence in Madras. Meanwhile, Janaki, unaware of her husband's return, resided in Rajendram, guided by her brother's counsel to steer clear of past conflicts. Upon learning of Ramanujan's return, she went to meet her husband, with her brother by her side[1].

To mitigate the perceived taint and stigma attached to travelling overseas by the orthodox Brahmins, Komalatammal had initially intended to escort her son straight to Rameswaram for purification rites at the temple, a place of spiritual significance for their family. However, upon seeing his frail condition in Bombay, she abandoned the plan; the arduous journey to Rameswaram was deemed too taxing for Ramanujan's weakened state. Thus, after a brief stay in Bombay, they embarked on the overnight journey to Madras aboard the Bombay Mail.

Arriving in Madras, Ramanujan found himself reunited with his wife a few days later, albeit his health deteriorating rapidly. His once robust frame was now withered and frail, causing concern among his loved ones and admirers.

As news of his arrival spread, the local papers began to recount his remarkable life story, prompting Sir Francis Spring to call for a more comprehensive biography. Narayana Aiyar was tasked with compiling a

1. S.R. Ranganathan, The Man and the Mathematician, Asia Publishing House, 1967 pp 49.

detailed account, which was published on April 6th, shedding light on Ramanujan's humble origins and unparalleled mathematical prowess.

Ramanujan was extended a university professorship, an offer he expressed his intent to accept once his health became better. Esteemed figures and notable personalities visited the recuperating genius and over the ensuing months, they generously covered his medical bills and other expenses, opening their homes to him. Among them were Ramachandra Rao, Sir Francis Spring, and Narayana Aiyar, all eager to support him in his recovery.

Later, in April, Ramanujan corresponded with Dewsbury, seeking a breakdown of his expenses during his time in England and his journey back, while also requesting that his fellowship payments be dispersed in monthly instalments. It was a sign that he was preparing for an extended period of convalescence and adjustment.

To provide Ramanujan with some respite from visitors, his doctor arranged for him to be relocated about a half mile south to a serene spot known as the Venkata Vilas on the Luz Church Road. It was here that Janaki and her brother finally caught up with him, followed shortly after by Ramanujan's father, grandmother, and younger brother from Kumbakonam[1]. For three months, Ramanujan resided here, during which time he and Janaki began to cultivate some semblance of a genuine relationship. Janaki had been just thirteen when he had departed; now she was eighteen.

As the sweltering Madras summer approached, Ramanujan's doctors advised him to seek refuge inland to escape the oppressive heat and humidity. Ramanujan's mother decided on Kodumudi, a tranquil place known for its Magudeswara temple. Through arrangements facilitated by the university, Ramanujan found lodging on the East Agraharam Street, close to the town registrar's office—a location denoting the Brahmin quarter. It was here, in August, that Ramanujan openly challenged his mother's authority.

Tensions had been simmering between them for weeks, even preceding their arrival in town. One day, as Ramanujan prepared to head to the river, Janaki expressed her desire to accompany him. Despite Komalatammal's objections, Ramanujan asserted that Janaki would indeed accompany him[2].

1. Kanigal Robert, The Man who knew Infinity, a life of the Genius Ramanujan, Rupa & Co, 1991 pp 317.
2. Ibid 320.

This moment marked a significant shift. Years of pent-up hostility, diverted communications, and incessant quarrels culminated in this rebellion. Though Ramanujan remained respectful, his stance was unwavering: Janaki would be by his side.

In the ensuing months, Janaki assumed a greater role in her husband's life. Ramanujan became more open and reliant on her, expressing regrets that her absence during his time in England may have contributed to his illness. As Ramanujan's health declined, Janaki increasingly took on the role of caregiver, tending to him day and night. When Komalatammal suggested sending Janaki back to her parents, Ramanujan adamantly refused.

For two months, Ramanujan remained in Kodumudi. Every Sunday, Dr. C. F. Fearnside, the Divisional Medical Officer, made visits. Dr. Fearnside suggested Coimbatore or Thanjavur as alternative locations for Ramanujan's care, but Ramanujan, with a play on words, dismissed the latter as "the place of my death." With the summer waning, pressure mounted to choose a more accessible location. Komalatammal decided on Kumbakonam.

On September 3, Ramanujan and the rest of the family left Kodumudi, and by dusk the following day, they arrived in Kumbakonam. Ramanujan was now under the care of a new doctor, P. S. Chandrasekar, specially brought down from Madras. Hardy, through the Royal Society, had intervened with the Madras authorities, who enlisted Chandrasekar, a fifty-year-old professor of hygiene and physiology at Madras Medical College and a renowned tuberculosis specialist. Accompanied by one of Ramanujan's oldest friends, Sarangapani, Chandrasekar visited Ramanujan at the house on Bhaktapuri Street. After a thorough examination, he concluded that Ramanujan's ailment was tuberculosis, despite earlier conjectures of blood poisoning.

When Ramanujan embarked on the SS Nagoya to return to India earlier that spring, the outlook for his recovery, particularly in Hardy's estimation, had been optimistic. However, the sanatoria where he had been treated over the past two years were deficient in curing tuberculosis. Chandrasekar now determined that Ramanujan's tuberculosis had progressed to an advanced stage, with his fate resting more on divine intervention than medical intervention.

Since falling ill two and a half years earlier, Ramanujan had endured a relentless cycle of medical consultations, conflicting diagnoses, and shifts between hospitals and nursing facilities, both in England and India. Despite these efforts, his condition steadily deteriorated, with the decline hastening in Kumbakonam. Due to the health condition Ramanujan decided to shift Madras in september 1919.

Towards the end of 1919, Ramanujan resided in one of the substantial stucco houses constructed for the British in a western suburb of the city, Harrington Road, Chetput, Madras, around the turn of the century. 'Kudsia' was among them, though Ramanujan's stay there appears to have been brief. Subsequently, he was accommodated in a notably larger residence, 'Crynant'. Eventually, he would be relocated once more, this time to another house known as 'Gometra'.

During his final months, Ramanujan often confided in his doctor, expressing the loss of interest and will to live. Despite earlier indications of accepting a university position once his health improved and his recent interest in subscribing to new mathematical journals in January 1920, there was a darker, more superstitious side to him. He had long interpreted his own horoscope as foretelling his demise before the age of thirty-five. Even upon arriving at Harrington Road in the Madras suburb of Chetput, he playfully remarked on the name's Tamil meaning, "chat-pat," signifying "it will happen soon."

As his end drew near, Ramanujan grew closer to Janaki. Despite occasional moments of cheerfulness or equanimity, there was laid a deep-seated despair underneath. The most distressing change for his friends was the alteration in his personality. The once cheerful and affectionate friend was now distant, subdued, bitter, and impatient. His once unshakeable faith appeared tarnished by his ordeal.

Talking about his health at that time, Janaki recalled, "he was only skin and bones," plagued by excruciating pain. Yet, amidst the agony, household conflicts, and his inner turmoil, Ramanujan persisted in his work. Even while confined to his bed, supported by pillows, he continued to work on his mathematics. Janaki would place his slate before him when he requested it, and later gather up the sheets of paper filled with his calculations, placing them in the large leather box he had brought from England. Even a few days before his death, he was busy scribbling, as his wife Janaki recalled later.

On the early morning of April 26th, 1920, Ramanujan slipped into unconsciousness. Around mid-morning, or perhaps a bit earlier, he passed away. Beside him were his wife, parents, two brothers, and a few close friends. He was thirty-two years old[1].

At the funeral later that day, most of his orthodox Brahmin relatives abstained from attending. Ramanujan, having crossed the seas and unable to travel to Rameswaram for the purification ceremonies his mother had intended due to his illness, remained tainted in their eyes. Ramachandra Rao coordinated the cremation, facilitated by his son-in-law and Ramanujan's childhood friend, Rajagopalachari, at the cremation ground near Chetput.

The following day, his death was officially recorded by a government clerk, assigned Registration No. 228.

At the time of Ramanujan's passing in April 1920, the editor of the Journal of the Indian Mathematical Society had fallen significantly behind schedule, with the issue bearing the news dated December 1920 announcing the untimely death of Mr. S. Ramanujan, B.A., F.R.S., on Monday, the 26th of April 1920, at his residence in Chetput, Madras. The journal promised to publish an account of his life and work in a subsequent issue. Seven months later, the journal carried two obituary notices, written by P. V. Seshu Aiyar, and Ramachandra Rao.

Even before his passing, Ramanujan had been hailed as a symbol of India's intellectual capabilities, with his mathematical talents elevating India's standing in the eyes of the world. Though his extraordinary abilities were seen as somewhat of an anomaly, he was celebrated as a quintessentially Indian genius, representing the nation's prowess in the field of science.

This book is an attempt to present authentic documents related to Ramanajn along with their sources. Each document is generally preceded by its transcript to make it easier for the reader to understand the contents.

1. Govil Narendra Kumar and Sharma Bhudev; Adbhut Ganitagya Srinivasa Ramanujan, (Hindi) Prabhat Prakashan 2022, pp 125.

Transfer of documents to the National Archives of India

In 1950, Mr M. S. Venkataraman, who was the son-in-law of S. Narayana Aiyar and had previously served as the Traffic Manager of the Madras Port Trust, held the position of Chairman of the Port Trust. This was the institution where Ramanujan himself had worked for approximately one year.

Recognizing the historical significance of the Ramanujan Papers, Mr. Venkataraman took the initiative to ensure their preservation. On June 19th, 1950, he formally requested Mr. K. Santhanam, the Minister of State for Transport and Railways in the Government of India, to oversee the preservation of the Ramanujan Papers at the National Archives of India.

Subsequently, on July 14th, 1950, the Government of India officially agreed to take control of the Ramanujan Papers, signifying their commitment to preserving this valuable collection. The transfer of the Papers to the Indian National Archives was completed on July 22th, 1950. In a Press Release dated October 17th, 1950, it was stated that the file encompassed 103 folios of varying sizes, starting with Ramanujan's application in February 1912 for the position of a clerk at the Madras Port Trust with a monthly salary of Rs 25. The file concluded with the report of Ramanujan's premature demise at the age of 32. Notably, the file contained intricate mathematical observations, showcasing Ramanujan's remarkable ability to solve complex abstract problems accurately[1].

Necessary arrangements were made to preserve this significant historical document within the National Archives. Simultaneously, a micro-film positive copy was planned to be provided to the Madras Port Trust for record-keeping. It's worth mentioning that we have lost several documents of Ramanujan due to lack of knowledge of the value

1. File No. 50-60/50 A2, M/o Education NAI, New Delhi

of Ramanajun Papers. He lived in rented house and shifting also a became a major reason of destroying some of his heritage. Despite this, some institutions, individuals and made serious efforts to protect them. Some documents and picture were protected by Ramanujan Museum and Math Education Centre Chennai. Some documents are available in university of Madras, Cambridge University and Royal Society of London.

[Copy of D.O: letter No. G1468 dated the 19th June 1950 from the Chairman, Madras Port Trust, Madras, to the Honourable Shri K. Santhanam, Minister of State for Transport Railways, New Delhi.]

……

While you were down here, I mentioned to you about the personal file of the late Sri S. Ramanujam, F.R.S., the great Mathematician. It has been preserved in the records of our office. If the Government of India are interested in having it kept at the National Museum, I shall obtain the sanction of the Board for removing it from our records.

Copy of D.O. letter No. G1468 dated the 19th June 1950 from the Chairman, Madras Port Trust, Madras, to the Honourable Shri K. Samthanam, Minister of State for Transport and Railways, New Delhi.

....

While you were down here, I mentioned to you about the personal file of the late Sri S. Ramanujam, F.R.S., the great Mathematician. It has been preserved in the records of our office. If the Government of India are interested in having it kept at the National Museum, I shall obtain the sanction of the Board for removing it from our records.

New Delhi,
June 21st, 1950.

Dear Maulana Saheb,

उन्हें लिखे कि इसपे कार्यवाही की जा रही है और सेक्रेटरी साहब भेजने के लिए यह फाइल यहाँ मँगवा कर नेशनल आर्काइव को दें
आज़ाद
5.7.50

I am herewith enclosing a copy of a letter I have received from the Chairman, Madras Port Trust. As you know, the late S. Ramanujam was perhaps the greatest mathematician of this century and is ranked as a great mathematician of all time. He was originally employed in the Madras Port Trust.

I wish, therefore, to suggest to you that the personal file of Ramanujam may be obtained from the Port Trust and kept as the property of the Government of India in the National Archives of India.

Yours sincerely,
K. Santhanam
Minister of State Transport & Railways

The Hon'ble
Maulana Abul Kalam Azad
Education Minister

The Hon'ble Minister has been informed that necessary action is being taken in the matter.

M. N. Masud
6.7.50

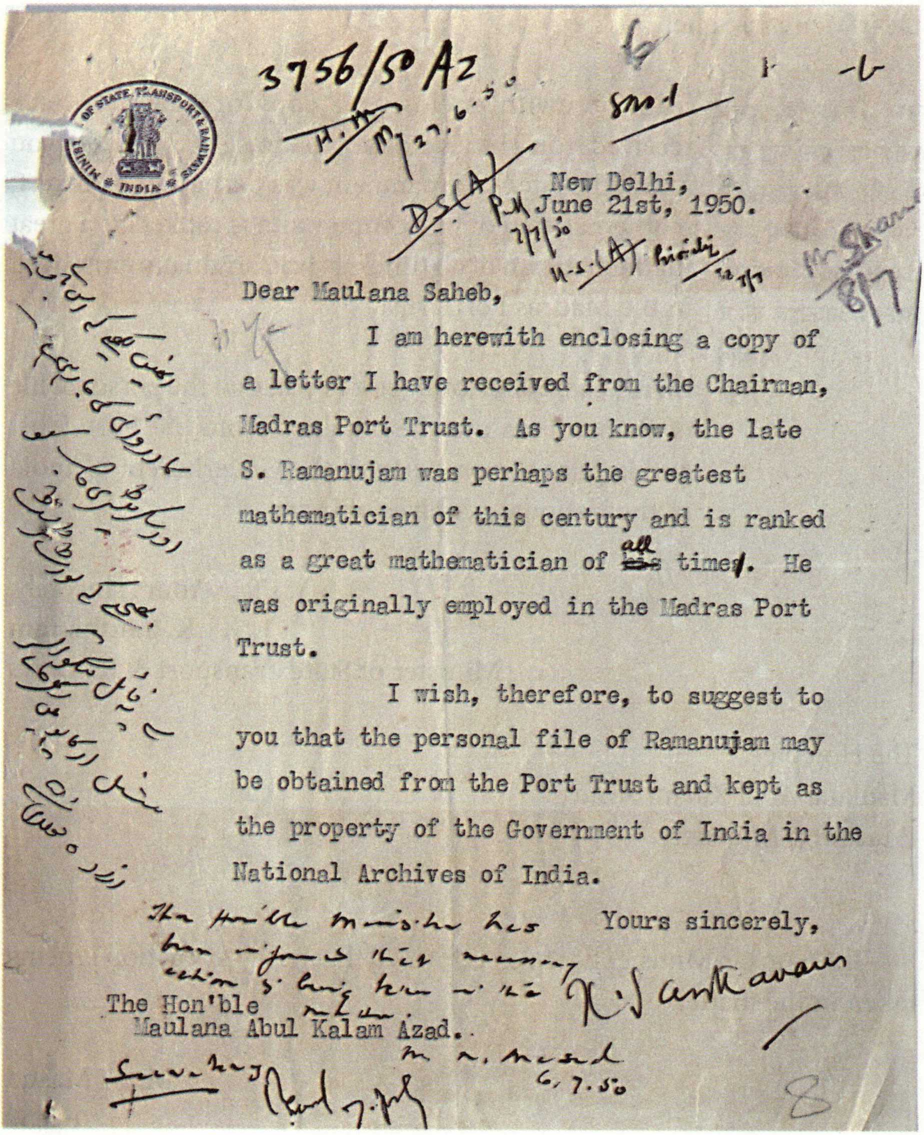

New Delhi,
June 21st, 1950.

Dear Maulana Saheb,

I am herewith enclosing a copy of a letter I have received from the Chairman, Madras Port Trust. As you know, the late S. Ramanujam was perhaps the greatest mathematician of this century and is ranked as a great mathematician of all times. He was originally employed in the Madras Port Trust.

I wish, therefore, to suggest to you that the personal file of Ramanujam may be obtained from the Port Trust and kept as the property of the Government of India in the National Archives of India.

Yours sincerely,

The Hon'ble
Maulana Abul Kalam Azad.

MINISTRY OF EDUCATION

File No. 50-66/ 50 A*

Notes

Subject: - Keeping of the personal file of late S. Ramanujan in the N.A.I.

……

S. No. 1

Inform the Hon'ble Shri K. Santhanam that necessary action is being taken and send the file to Secretary for obtaining the file from Madras Port Trust and keeping it in the N.A.I.

Sd
Maulana Azad
5.7.1950

The Hon'ble Minister has been informed that necessary action is being taken in the matter.

Sd
M.N.Masud
6.7.1950

We may request the Chairman, Madras Port Trust to arrange to send the personal file of the late S. Ramanuj an to the National Archives of India for being kept as the property of the Government of India.

Draft put up.

P.N. Kirpal
Under Secretary
10.7.50

S. No. 2 (Issued)
S. No. 3

---

* First initiative to transfer file from Madras Port Trust (Now Chennai Port Trust) to National Archives of India.

Paras 1 and 2. We may await further communication from the Madras Port Trust.

Para 3 – Director of Archives may in the first instance see and state if it would be possible to arrange for a photostat copy of the file for the Madras Port Trust.

PS to HM, may see paras 1 and 2 of the FR for information. Thereafter DA may see.

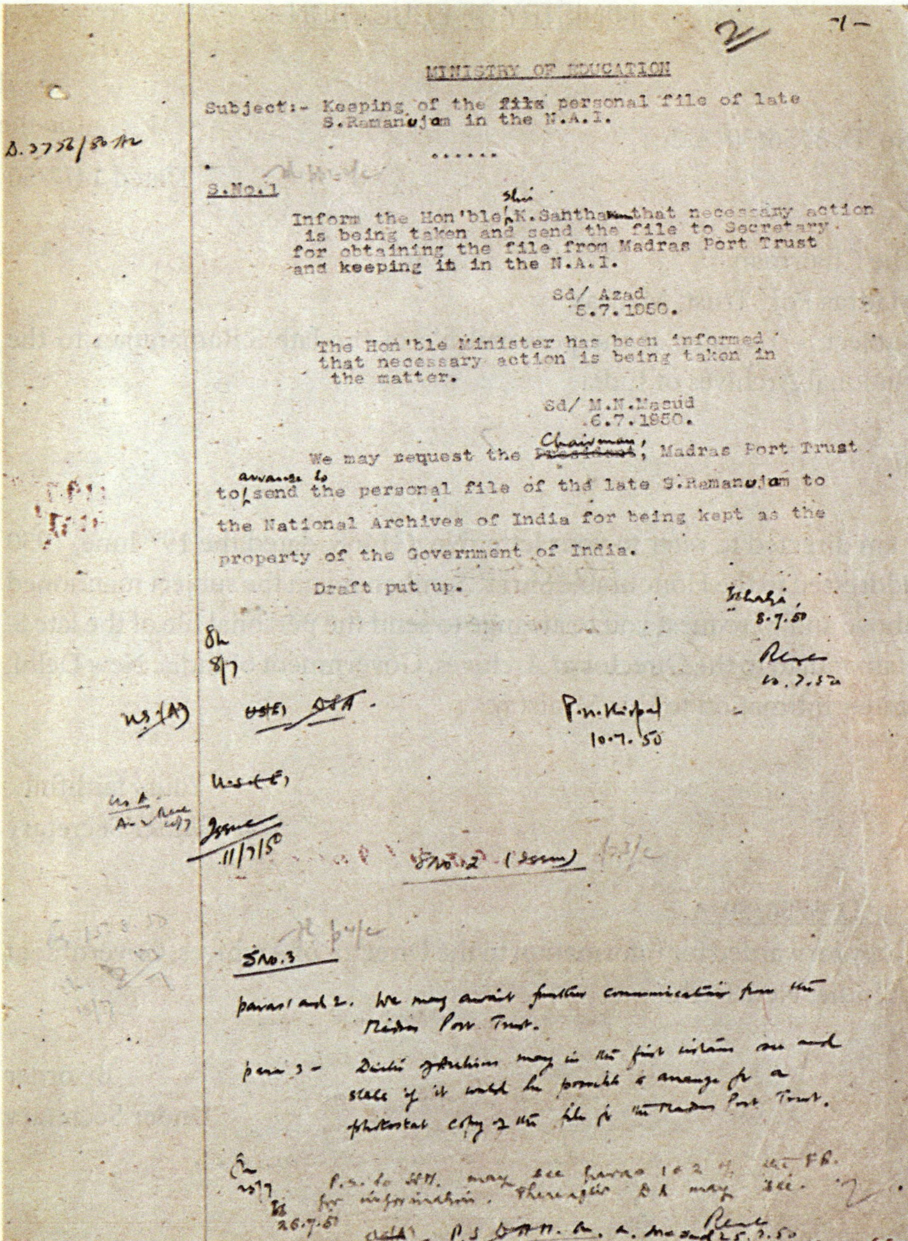

MINISTRY OF EDUCATION

Subject:- Keeping of the ~~fiis~~ personal file of late S.Ramanujam in the N.A.I.

......

S.No.1

Inform the Hon'ble Shri K.Santhanam that necessary action is being taken and send the file to Secretary for obtaining the file from Madras Port Trust and keeping it in the N.A.I.

Sd/ Azad
5.7.1950.

The Hon'ble Minister has been informed that necessary action is being taken in the matter.

Sd/ M.N.Masud
.6.7.1950.

We may request the ~~President~~ Chairman, Madras Port Trust to arrange to send the personal file of the late S.Ramanujam to the National Archives of India for being kept as the property of the Government of India.

Draft put up.

8.7.50

10.7.50

P.N. Kirpal
10.7.50

Issue
11/7/50

S.No.2 (Issue)

S.No.3

paras 1 and 2. We may await further communication from the Madras Port Trust.

para 3 - Director of Archives may in the first instance see and state if it would be possible to arrange for a photostat copy of the file for the Madras Port Trust.

P.S. to HM may see paras 1 & 2 of the F.R. for information. Thereafter D.A. may see.

26.7.50

P.S. to H.M. M.N. Masud 25.7.50

D.A. U.O. No. D 3750/50 Azad 27/7/50

DEPARTMENT OFFICE
MINISTRY OF EDUCATION

No. D. 3756/50-A.2

Dated 14/7/50

To,
The Chairman,
Madras Port Trust, Madras.
Subject: - Transfer of the personal file of the late S.Ramanujan to the National Archives of India.

....

Sir,

I am directed to refer to your letter No. G1468, dated the 19th June, 1950 addressed to the Honourable Shri K.Santhanam on the subject mentioned above and to request you to arrange to send the personal file of the late S. Ramanujan to the Director of Archives, Government of India, New Delhi, under intimation to this Ministry.

Yours faithfully,
Under Secretary

No .D. 3756/50-A.2
Copy forwarded for information to the Director of Archives, Government of India, New Delhi,

By order
Under Secretary

4070/50 A2

Transfer of documents to the National Archives of India

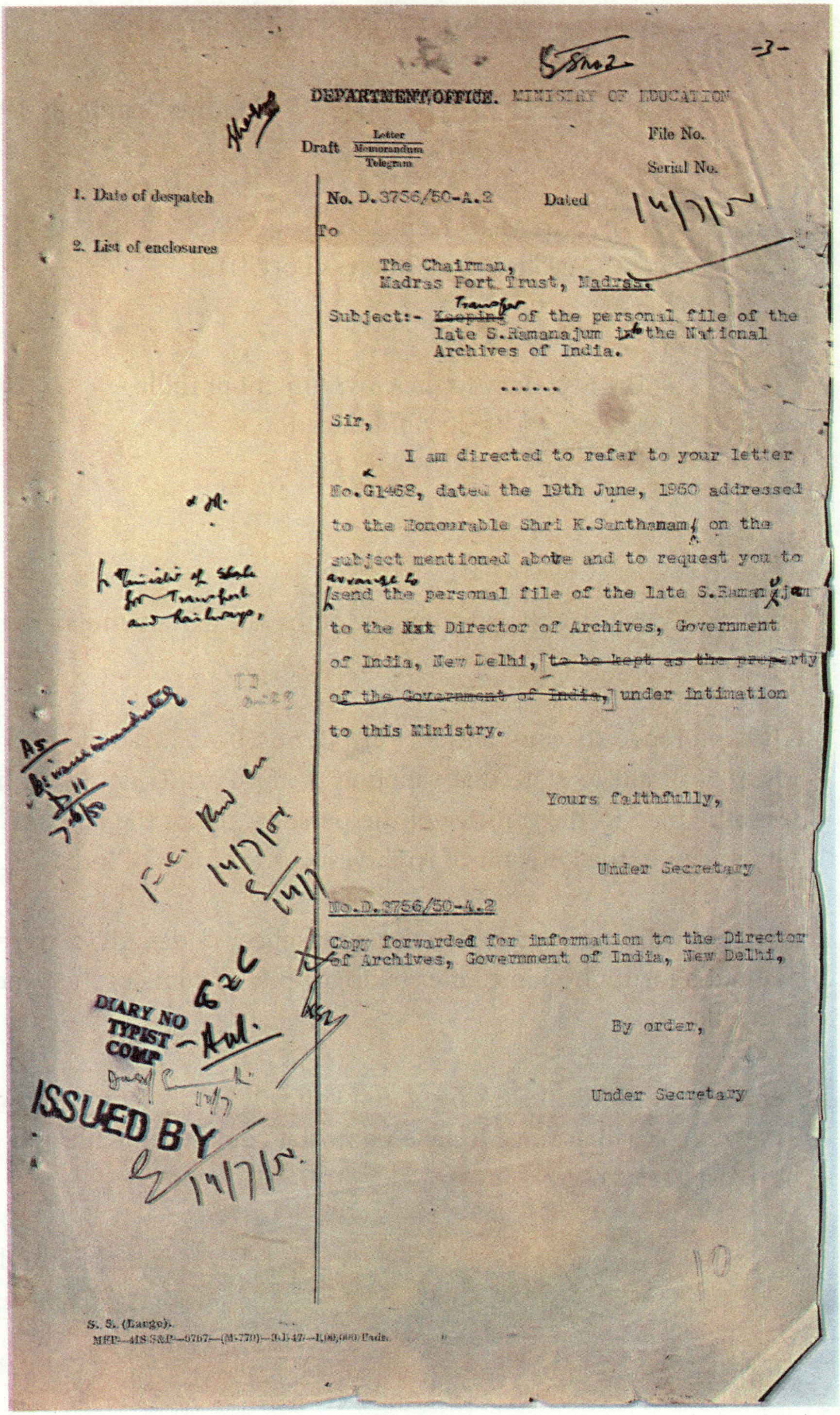

-3-

DEPARTMENT/OFFICE. MINISTRY OF EDUCATION

Draft Letter / Memorandum / Telegram

File No.

Serial No.

1. Date of despatch

2. List of enclosures

No. D.3756/50-A.2 Dated 14/7/50

To

The Chairman,
Madras Port Trust, Madras.

Subject:- ~~Keeping~~ Transfer of the personal file of the late S.Ramanajum ~~in~~ to the National Archives of India.

......

Sir,

I am directed to refer to your letter No.G1468, dated the 19th June, 1950 addressed to the Honourable Shri K.Santhanam, Minister of State for Transport and Railways, on the subject mentioned above and to request you to arrange to send the personal file of the late S.Ramanujam to the ~~Nat~~ Director of Archives, Government of India, New Delhi, ~~[to be kept as the property of the Government of India,]~~ under intimation to this Ministry.

Yours faithfully,

Under Secretary

No.D.3756/50-A.2

Copy forwarded for information to the Director of Archives, Government of India, New Delhi,

By order,

Under Secretary

DIARY NO
TYPIST
COMP

ISSUED BY
14/7/50.

S. S. (Large).
MFP—418 S&P—6767—(M-770)—9.1.47—1,00,000 Pads.

MADRAS PORT TRUST

Madras, 22nd July 1950

From

Shri M. S. Venkataraman, B. A.,
Ag.Chairman, Madras Port Trust.

To

The Secretary to the Government of India,
Ministry of Education,
NEW DELHI.

Dear Sir,

Subject: - Transfer of the personal file of the late S. Ramanujan to the National Archives of India.

With reference to your letter No.D. 3756/50- A.2 dated the 14th July 1950, I am to state that sanction of the Port Trust Board has been obtained to the transfer of the personal file of the late Shri S. Ramanujan to the Director of Archives, Government of India.

2. The file will be despatched to the latter officer under advice to you, in about a fortnight's time, after taking copies of some of the papers in the file.

3. In the meanwhile, I shall be glad if you will kindly let me know if Government will arrange to take photostat copies of the file and let the Trust have a copy.

Yours faithfully,
Ag. Chairman

4070/50 A.2

M. P. T. No. D. F. 14
4000—31-8-49.

MADRAS PORT TRUST

Madras, 22nd July 1950.

No. G, 2152

From

Sri M.S.Venkataraman, B.A.,
Ag.Chairman, Madras Port Trust.

Ministry of Education
Government of India
Dy. No. ...
24 ...
File No. ...

To

The Secretary to the Government of India,
Ministry of Education,
NEW DELHI.

Dear Sir,

Subject.- Transfer of the personal file of the late S.Ramanujam to the National Archives of India.

With reference to your letter No.D.3756/50-A.2 dated the 14th July 1950, I am to state that sanction of the Port Trust Board has been obtained to the transfer of the personal file of the late Sri S. Ramanujam to the Director of Archives, Government of India.

2. The file will be despatched to the latter officer, under advice to you, in about a fortnight's time, after taking copies of some of the papers in the file.

Enclosures.

3. In the meanwhile, I shall be glad if you will kindly let me know if Government will arrange to take photostat copies of the file and let the Trust have a copy.

Yours faithfully,

Ag.Chairman.

NAI

Seen. Thanks. There is no arrangement in the NAI for photostating. We can, however, microfilm the file and give a microfilm positive copy to the Madras Port Trust.

Director of Archives
Government of India
28/7/50

M. Of Education U/O

N.A.I. U/O 7. no 26/5/50. Rec. on. 29/7/50

Ministry of Education

We may now inform the Madras Port Trust as per Director of Archives note above. Draft put up.

M. S. Sharma
1.8.50

Serial no 4 (Issued)

Serial no. 5

Information. Director of Archives may also kindly see & furnish the Madras Port Trust with a microfilm positive copy of the file when it is received in the N.A.I.

M. S. Sharma
14.8.50

5109/50 A2

Serial No 7.

No. F. 26/5/50-Rec.
Government of India,
National Archives of India,
Queensway,
New Delhi, the 2nd September, 1950.

From

Purnendu Basu,
Director of Archives,
Government of India

To

The Chairman,
Madras Port Trust,
Madras.

Sir,

I have the honour to acknowledge with thanks the receipt the personal file of the late Mr. S. Ramanujam forwarded with your letter No. G-2711 dated the 22nd August, 1950. As desired in your letter No. G-2493 dated the 9th August, 1950, arrangements are being made to supply the Trust with a microfilm positive copy of this file shortly. I presume you will have no objection to our supplying extracts from the file to such members of the public as may be interested in them. This may kindly be confirmed.

Yours faithfully,

Sd/- S. Roy
for Director of Archives,
Government of India.

No. F.26/5/50-Rec. Dated the September, 1950.

Copy forwarded for information to the Ministry of Education in continuation of this office u/o note of even number dated the 23rd August, 1950.

S. Roy
for Director of Archives,
Government of India.

4528/ 50 A2

MADRAS PORT TRUST

Madras, 9th August 1950

From

Shri M. S. Venkataraman, B. A.,
Ag.Chairman, Madras Port Trust.
Serial no. 5

To

The Secretary to the Government of India,
Ministry of Education,
NEW DELHI.

Dear Sir,

Subject.- Transfer of the personal file of the late S. Ramanujan to the National Archives of India.

With reference to your letter No. D. 3756/ 50 .A.2 dated the 7th August 1950, I shall be glad if arrangements can be made to supply the Trust with a microfilm positive copy of the abovementioned file which will be despatched to the Director of Archives, Government of India, next week.

Yours faithfully,

Enclosures.

Ag.Chairman.
M. S. Venkataraman

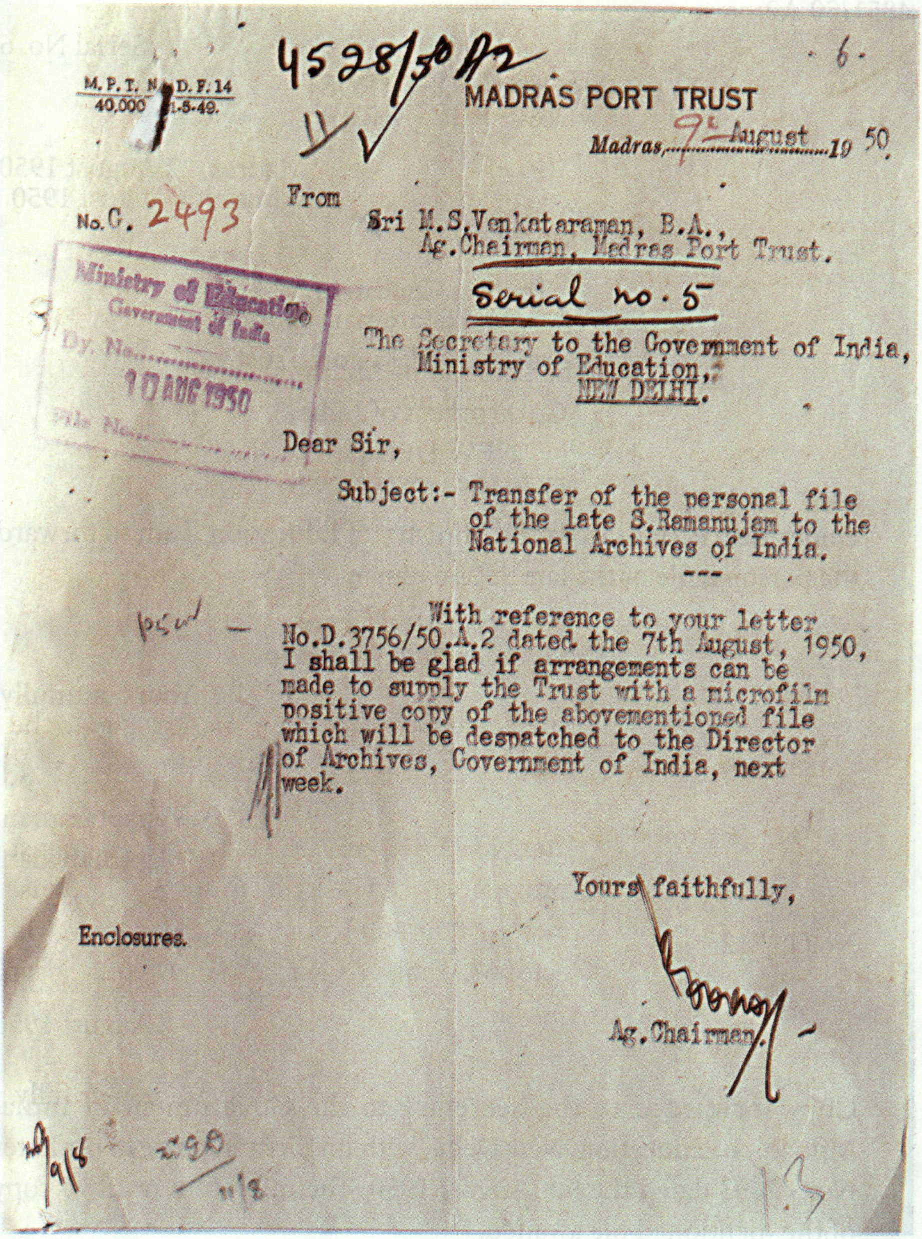

4528/50 A2

M.P.T. No. D.F.14
40,000 1-5-49.

MADRAS PORT TRUST

Madras, 9th August 1950.

No. G. 2493

Ministry of Education
Government of India
Dy. No. ....
10 AUG 1950
File No. ....

From

Sri M.S.Venkataraman, B.A.,
Ag.Chairman, Madras Port Trust.

Serial no. 5

The Secretary to the Government of India,
Ministry of Education,
NEW DELHI.

Dear Sir,

Subject:- Transfer of the personal file of the late S.Ramanujam to the National Archives of India.

With reference to your letter No.D.3756/50.A.2 dated the 7th August, 1950, I shall be glad if arrangements can be made to supply the Trust with a microfilm positive copy of the abovementioned file which will be despatched to the Director of Archives, Government of India, next week.

Yours faithfully,

Ag.Chairman.

Enclosures.

4851/50 A2.

Serial No. 6

MADRAS PORT TRUST

Madras, 22 August 1950

From

The Ag. Chairman,

To

The Director of Archives,
Government of India,
NEW DELHI,

Dear Sir,
Under Instructions from the Ministry of Education, I am to forward the personal file of the late S.Ramanujan.

Kindly acknowledge receipt.

Yours faithfully,

Sd.
M.S. Venkataraman,
Ag.Chairman.

No.G.2712

dated- 22nd
August 1950

Copy forwarded to the Secretary to the Government of India, Ministry of Education, New Delhi, with further reference to my letter No.G.2493 dated the 9th August,1950. The microfilm positive copy of the mentioned file awaited.

Enclosure

Ag. Chairman

5109/50A2

M. P. T. No. D. F. 14
40,000—31-5-49.

4851/50 A2.

Serial No. 6

MADRAS PORT TRUST

Madras, 22nd August 1950.

No. G. 2711

From

The Ag. Chairman.

To

The Director of Archives,
Government of India,
NEW DELHI.

Dear Sir,

Under instructions from the Ministry of Education, I am to forward the personal file of the late S. Ramanujan.

Kindly acknowledge receipt.

Yours faithfully,

Sd. M.S. Venkataraman,

Ag. Chairman.

Ministry of Education
Government of India
Dy. No.........
24 AUG 1950
File No.........

No.G.2712 dated 22nd August 1950.

Copy forwarded to the Secretary to the Government of India, Ministry of Education, New Delhi, with further reference to my letter No.G.2493 dated the 9th August, 1950. The microfilm positive copy of the above-mentioned file is awaited.

Enclosures.

Ag. Chairman.

National Archives of India

The instructions conveyed in the Ministry of Education note on the pre-page have been noted. The personal file under reference has not yet been received.

S. Roy
Director of Archives
Government of India

Ministry of Education U/O

N.A.I. U/O F. No. 26/5/50-Rec. , D/21.8.'50.

(Ministry of Education)

Information.Intimation concerning the receipt of the personal file of Mr. Ramanujan by the NAI may be awaited.

US (A)

24.8.50

Serial no 6.(p7/Cor)

For information.

The Director of Archives has already noted out instructions requesting the supply of microfilm positive copy of the late Ramanujan's file to the Madras Port Trust. He need not see again on this point, with reference to instruction in the FR.

US (A)

25.8.50

-3-

National Archives of India

The instructions conveyed in the Ministry of Education note on pre-page have been noted. The personal file under reference has not yet been received.

21.8.50.

21.8.50.

S. Roy
Director of Archives
Government of India

Ministry of Education u/o
N.A.I. u/o F.No.26/5/50-Rec., D/21.8.'50.

(Ministry of Education)

Information. Intimation concerning the receipt of the personal file of Dr. Ramanujan by the NAI may be awaited.

23.8.50

24.8.50

US(A)

Serial No 6.

For information.

25.8.50

The Dir. of Archives has already noted our instructions regarding the supply of microfilm positive copy of the late Ramanujan's file to the Madras Port Trust. We need not see again on this point, with ref. to our tel.

28.8.50

US(A)

25.8.50

Serial No 7

No. F. 26/5/50-Rec.
Government of India
National Archives of India, Queenway,
New Delhi, the 2nd September, 1950,

From,
Purnendu Basu,
Director of Archives,
Government of India

To,
The Chairman,
Madras Port Trust, Madras.

Sir,

I have the honour to acknowledge with thanks the receipt the personal file of the late Mr. S. Ramanujan forwarded with your letter No. G-2711 dated the 22nd August, 1950. As desired in your letter No. 0-2493 dated the 9th August, 1950, arrangements are being made to supply the Trust with a microfilm positive copy of this file shortly. I presume you will have no objection to our supplying extracts from the file to such members of the public as may be interested in them.
This kindly be confirmed.

Yours faithfully,
Sd.
S. Roy
for Director of Archives,
Government of India.

No. F.26/5/50-Rec.

Dated the
September, 1950,

Copy forwarded for information to the Ministry of Education in continuation of this office u/o note of even number dated the 23rd August, 1950.

S. Roy
for Director of Archives,
Government of India

5109/50 A2

Serial No 7

No.F. 26/5/50-Rec.
Government of India,
National Archives of India,
Queensway,
New Delhi, the 2nd September, 1950.

From

Purnendu Basu,
Director of Archives,
Government of India

To

The Chairman,
Madras Port Trust,
Madras.

Ministry of Education
Government of India
Dy. No.
5 SEP 1950
File No.

Sir,

I have the honour to acknowledge with thanks the receipt the personal file of the late Mr. S. Ramanujam forwarded with your letter No. G-2711 dated the 22nd August, 1950. As desired in your letter No. G-2493 dated the 9th August, 1950, arrangements are being made to supply the Trust with a microfilm positive copy of this file shortly. I presume you will have no objection to our supplying extracts from the file to such members of the public as may be interested in them. This may kindly be confirmed.

Yours faithfully,

Sd/- S. Roy
for Director of Archives,
Government of India.

No. F.26/5/50-Rec. Dated the September, 1950.

Copy forwarded for information to the Ministry of Education in continuation of this office u/o note of even number dated the 23rd August, 1950.

S. Roy
for Director of Archives,
Government of India.

TS.

No.F. 26/5/50-Rec.
Government of India,
National Archives of India,
New Delhi, the 11th November, 1950.

From,
Purnendu Basu,
Director of Archives,
Government of India.

To
The Chairman,
Madras Port Trust,
Madras.

Sir,
In continuation of the correspondence resting with your letter No.G-2959 dated the 5th September, 1950, I have great pleasure in advising you of the despatch by separate registered parcel of a positive microfilm copy of the personal file of the late Mr.S. Ramanujan for the purpose of maintaining your series of records unbroken.

The receipt may kindly be acknowledged.

Yours faithfully,
Sd.
S. Roy.
for Director of Archives,
Government of India

Transfer of documents to the National Archives of India

No.F.26/5/50-Rec.
Government of India,
National Archives of India,
New Delhi, the 11th November, 1950.

From

Purnendu Basu,
Director of Archives,
Government of India.

To

The Chairman,
Madras Port Trust,
Madras.

Sir,

In continuation of the correspondence resting with your letter No.G-2959 dated the 5th September, 1950, I have great pleasure in advising you of the despatch by separate registered parcel of a positive microfilm copy of the personal file of the late Mr.S.Ramanujam for the purpose of maintaining your series of records unbroken.

The receipt may kindly be acknowledged.

Yours faithfully,

Sd/- S.Roy.

for Director of Archives,
Government of India.

P.T.O.

No, P.26/5/50-Rec.
'Government of India,
National Archives of India,
New Delhi

the 13th November, 1950.

Copy forwarded for information to the Ministry of Education in continuation of this office endorsement even number dated the 2nd September, 1950. The Madras Port Trust have accorded permission for the supply from the personal file of excerpts to such members of the public as may be interested in them.

S. Roy
for Director of Archives
Government of India

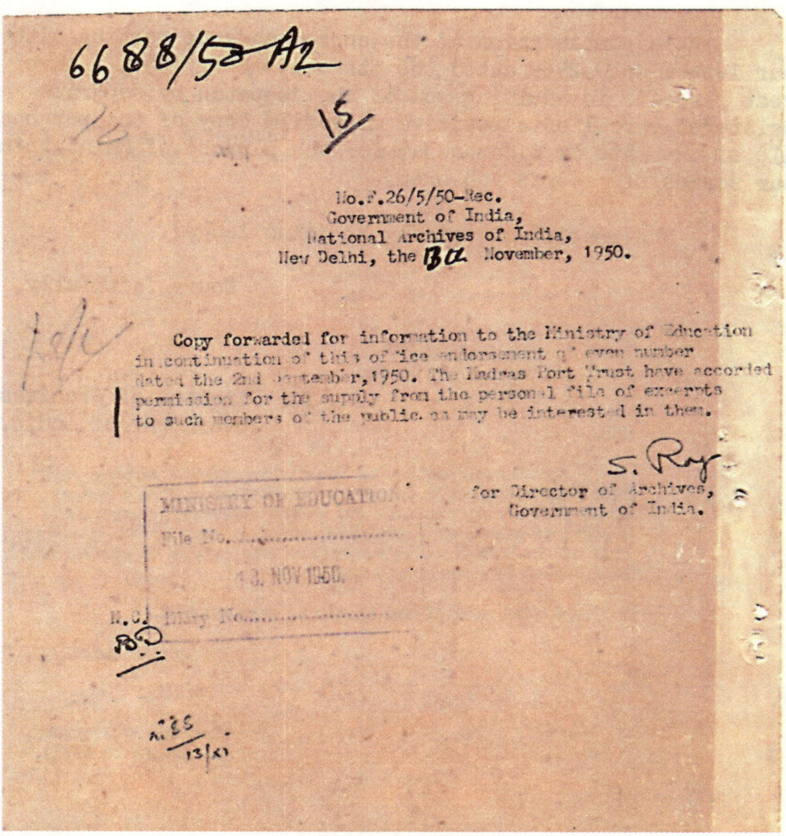

6688/50 A2

No.F.26/5/50-Rec.
Government of India,
National Archives of India,
New Delhi, the 13th November, 1950.

Copy forwarded for information to the Ministry of Education in continuation of this office endorsement of even number dated the 2nd September, 1950. The Madras Port Trust have accorded permission for the supply from the personal file of excerpts to such members of the public as may be interested in them.

S. Roy
for Director of Archives,
Government of India.

MINISTRY OF EDUCATION
File No.
13 NOV 1950.
Diary No.

Early Years

Srinivasa Ramanujan was born on December 22, 1887[1] in the quaint town of Erode, Mysore State, British India (now a part of Tamil Nadu, India) at 6.00 p.m. as mentioned in his horoscope. Ramanujan's journey unfolds against the backdrop of the traditional society of South India.

Hailing from a Tamil Brahmin Iyengar family, Ramanujan spent a major part of his life from 1888 to 1914 in Kumbakonam, his hometown. Situated between the Cauvery River and one of its tributaries, this town embodied the essence of staunch South Indian traditions. Within his family, the Goddess Namagiri, consort of the lion-God Narasimha, held a special place, with her shrine at Namakkal located some hundred miles from Kumbakonam. Ramanujan grew up in a spiritual and devout household with the Goddess Namagiri exerting tremendous influence over him. Coming from such an intricate world of heritage and identity, Srinivasa Ramanujan secured a place in the corridors of history, marking the beginning of an extraordinary mathematical journey.

The house on Sarangapani Sannidhi Street in Kumbakonam, now transformed into a museum, stands as a testament to Ramanujan's humble beginnings. His father, Srinivasa Iyengar, worked as a clerk in a local cloth shop, following in the footsteps of his own father, Kupuswamy. Komalatammal, Ramanujan's mother, adorned the role of a devout housewife who found solace in singing temple hymns and contributed to the family income by singing devotional songs at a nearby temple. In a time when the family income was Meager, her earnings held significant value. Komalatammal was the daughter of Narayana Iyengar, a well-known figure in Erode serving as an amin, an official in the district court. A strong and intense personality, Ramanujan's mother exerted a great influence over her son, throughout his life.

1. Horoscope of Srinivasa Ramanujan, Ramanujan Museum and Math Education Centre, Chennai.

In 1889, Ramanujan faced the threat of smallpox, a peril that could have truncated his budding brilliance. The scars of this childhood illness would accompany Srinivasa Ramanujan throughout his life. Fortunately, he survived and grew up as a cherished only child, having lost an infant brother and sister. It was only much later that two brothers, Lakshmi Narasimhan and Tirunarayanan, joined the family - the former born in 1898 when Ramanujan was ten, and the latter when he was seventeen.

Enrolled in school on October 1st, 1892, during the traditional school opening day, Vijayadasami, he began his education with ancient Vedic chants in the local school.

Over the next two years, Ramanujan moved between schools in his paternal and maternal hometowns, facing changes in language of instruction and location. Despite disputes and family movements, he continued his education. Notably, he attended a school in Kanchipuram, where the language shifted to Telugu briefly. After several shifts, he ended up in Kangayan Primary School in Kumbakonam.

The young scholar faced upheavals, returning to his maternal grandparents in Madras, and resisting school attendance. The family even enlisted a local constable to coerce him back to class once. By mid-1895, he found himself back in Kumbakonam. During his time at Kangayan Primary School, he started studying English. He excelled in his primary examinations and at the age of ten, he even scored first rank in the district. In January 1898 he joined Town High School where he met his first guru Krishnaswami Ayar.

Throughout his school years, Ramanujan showcased his mathematical prowess. Mastering S. L. Loney's Trigonometry by the age of thirteen, Ramanujan's mathematical understanding extended to solving cubic equations and grasping trigonometric functions in more advanced contexts. His fascination with transcendental numbers like π and e and his exposure to George Shoobridge Carr's compilation of mathematical results fuelled his independent exploration. Carr's book, A Synopsis of Elementary Results in Pure and Applied Mathematics, became a source of inspiration for Ramanujan, and he began treating each theorem as a unique research endeavour. This book, a compilation of some 5000 equations, theorems, formulas, geometric diagrams and other mathematical facts, captivated Ramanujan and sustained/ supported his love affair with mathematics.

In 1904, immediately following his encounter and fascination with Carr's book, Ramanujan completed his High School education and enrolled at Kumbakonam's Government College with a scholarship earned for his outstanding high school performance. Pursuing the F.A. program, equivalent to an associate degree in today's terms but carrying more significance in the Indian educational context, he found a mentor in math Professor P. V. Seshu Ayyar. Despite occasional encouragement, Ramanujan's intellectual prowess received limited attention, and he faced many challenges.

During his school days, Ramanujan had performed quite well in all his subjects. However, he struggled through Government College since he gradually started to become more and more involved and absorbed in mathematics only, neglecting the other subjects that he was supposed to be studying. In those days the course of studies in F. A. comprised many subjects. Ramanujan not only had Mathematics, but also had to study Physiology, Roman and Greek history, and English, along with an Indian language. He failed in English composition, a subject in which he had never been deficient earlier. All this finally led to the withdrawal of his scholarship.

Losing the scholarship issue was not just a prestige issue for Ramanujan, he needed it desperately. Everyone knew he had lost the scholarship, and his parents didn't have sufficient money. Ramanujan didn't want to divert his attention from mathematics. He tried hard to weather the situation, but was unsuccessful. After enduring the situation for a few months, he reached a breaking point. In August 1905, at the age of seventeen, Ramanujan ran away from home, seeking refuge in Visakhapatnam and later Rajahmundry.

An year later, at eighteen, Ramanujan made another attempt at college, this time at Pachaiyappa's College in Madras. Impressed by his mathematical prowess, his new math teacher introduced him to the Principal, who granted him a partial scholarship. N. Ramanujachariar, the mathematics teacher, and P. Singaravelu Mudaliar, the senior mathematics professor at the college, took an active interest in him. However, Ramanujan faced further setbacks, failing the F.A. examination in December 1906 and again in the following year. While he fared quite well in mathematics, the other subjects troubled him, especially Physiology. By 1908, he found himself without a job, languishing at his home in Kumbakonam, without any aim all direction. His parents put up with him for some time patiently, but gradually they began to fret in despair.

On July, 1909 the marriage of Ramanujan and Janki was solemnized. Some time after the marriage, Ramanujan fell sick. However, in 1910 he was treated with the help of doctor who volunteered to perform the surgery at no cost.[1]

After this he started his search for a job to earn a livelihood and took up a temporary job in Madras. From early 1911, he started receiving Rs. 25 per month from Ramchandra Rao to continue work in the field of Mathematics.[2]

1. Govil Narendra Kumar and Sharma Bhudev; Mathematics Wizard, Srinivas Ramanujan: Some Glimpses is to his life and work; Prabhat Prakashan, New Delhi, 2021, pp 40-41
2. Ibid 47

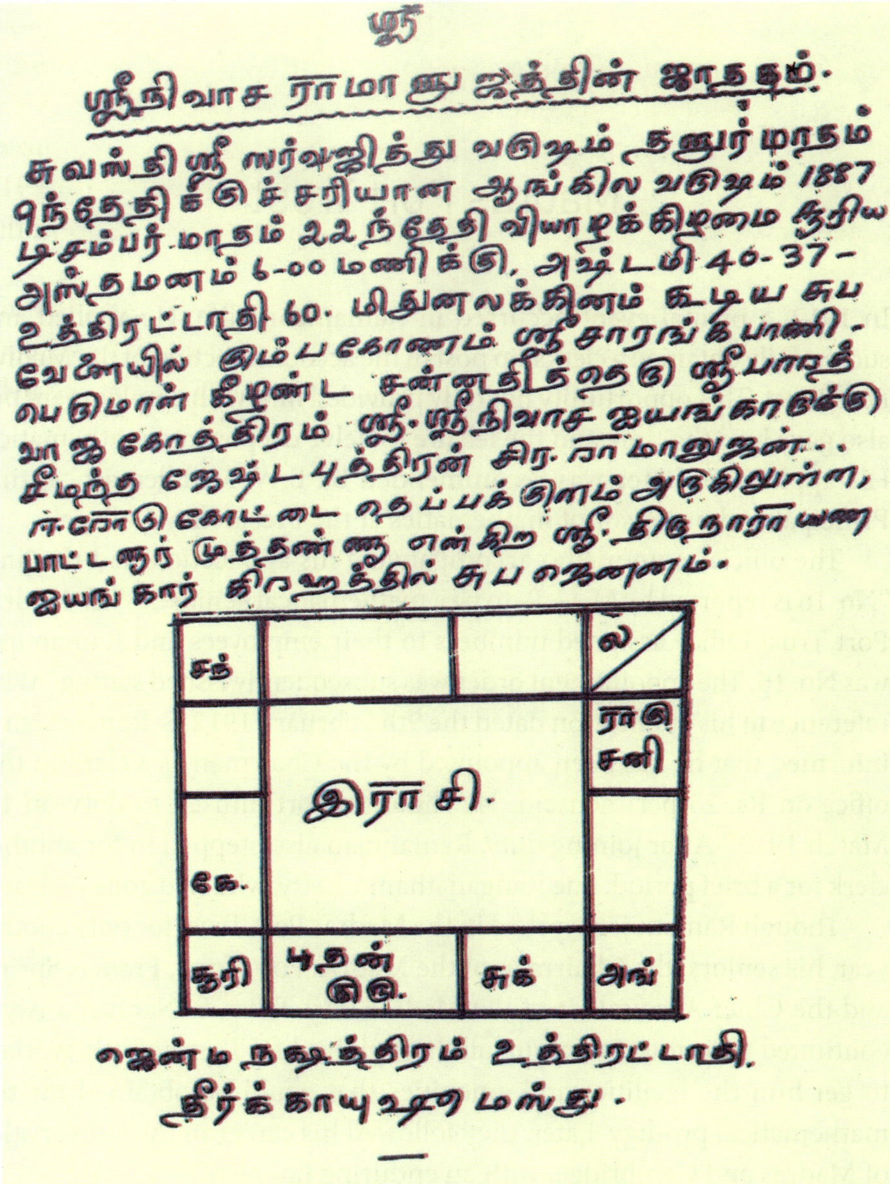

Horoscope of Srinivasa Ramanujan.
கணித மேதை இராமானுஜனின் ஜாதகம்.

* S. Ramanujan Kundli (Horoscope)

Madras Port Trust

In 1912, a pivotal event occurred in Ramanujan's life. He applied and successfully obtained a clerkship post in the accounts section of the Madras Port Trust. This opportunity not only provided him with employment but also gave him the time and the leisure to delve deeper into mathematics. His application letter was recommended by E.W. Middlemast, Acting Principal and professor of mathematics at the Presidency College[1].

The official note/memo accompanying his application had the line, "No. 16 is reported by M. G. R. to be a mathematical genius..." The Madras Port Trust Office assigned numbers to their employees and Ramanujan was No. 16. The appointment order was subsequently issued stating "With reference to his application dated the 9th February 1912, S. Ramanujan is informed that he has been appointed by the Chairman as a clerk in this office on Rs. 25 per mensem. He should report himself to duty on 1st March 1912." After joining duty, Ramanujan also stepped in for another clerk for a brief period, one Ranganatham Chetty, who had gone on leave.

Though Ramanujan worked in the Madras Port Trust for only about a year, his seniors, the Chairman of the Madras Port Trust, Francis Spring and the Chief Accountant of the Madras Port Trust, S. Narayana Aiyar continued their interest in him all through his life. They actively worked to get him the facilities and amenities that could be obtained for the mathematical prodigy. Later, they followed his career in the Universities of Madras and Cambridge, with an enduring interest.

Madras Port Trust was a landmark in Ramanujan's life. This was the place where Ramanujan had started his mathematical journey and where he got a lot of support from his colleagues. The significance of Madras Port Trust in Ramanujan's life cannot be understated. His colleagues were instrumental in his early development as a mathematician. They provided him with both moral and intellectual support, creating a

1. Letter of E.W. Middlemast Principal Presidency College, NAI, New Delhi.

conducive environment for his work. The recognition he received from this supportive network was invaluable in his journey towards becoming a mathematical luminary.

The story of Madras Port Trust's involvement with Ramanujan extends beyond his lifetime. After Ramanujan's untimely death in 1920, the institution took steps to support his bereaved family, acknowledging the significant contributions Ramanujan had made during his time there. In 1981, over six decades after Ramanujan's death, the Port Trust made a notable gesture towards Ramanujan's widow, Smt. Janaki. She was awarded a pension of Rs. 300 per month. While this amount might seem modest and little and the timing somewhat belated, the gesture was symbolic of the institution's respect for Ramanujan's legacy and its commitment to assisting his family[1].

This posthumous recognition, though delayed, reflects the adage "better late than never." It acknowledges the enduring impact of Ramanujan's work and the institution's role in supporting a remarkable mathematician. The pension provided to Smt. Janaki was a token of appreciation for her late husband's contributions and a form of support for her after his passing. This posthumous gesture of providing a pension to his widow underscores the lasting impact of Ramanujan's work and the institution's commitment to honoring his legacy. While the support came later than ideal, it symbolizes recognition of Ramanujan's remarkable contributions in the field of mathematics.

In the minutes of the meeting held on July 25th, 1981, at the Madras Port Trust, several key points were discussed regarding the commemoration of the late mathematician Shri Ramanujan. One of the primary proposals was to construct a statue of Ramanujan within the port's premises to honour his legacy and contributions[2].

Additionally, the Administration was exploring several other initiatives to ensure that Ramanujan's memory would be preserved and celebrated. They were considering the establishment of a dedicated institute named in his honour which would serve as a lasting tribute to his work and would potentially provide a platform for future scholars to engage in mathematical research and study. Another option being discussed was

1. File No. IR 4/20275/8115, Madras Port Trust Chennai.
2. Ibid.

the creation of a fund established in Ramanujan's name. This fund would be used to grant scholarships to deserving students, thereby supporting education in the field of mathematics and ensuring that Ramanujan's influence would continue to benefit future generations. The fund could also be used to offer financial assistance to members of Ramanujan's family, providing them with some level of support and recognition for their connection to the esteemed mathematician.

Madras Port Trust's role in Ramanujan's life is a testament to how institutions can play a pivotal role in the development of extraordinary individuals and their legacies. It serves as an example of how support, whether in the form of intellectual encouragement or financial assistance, can profoundly impact individuals and their families, both during their lifetimes and beyond.

S. Ramanujan's application to Madras Port Trust Office

Triplicane
9th February 1911

From

S. Ramanujan
7 Summer House
Triplicane

To

The Chief Accountant
Port Trust
Madras

Sir,

I understand there is a clerkship vacant in your office, and I beg to apply for the same. I have passed the Matriculation Examination and studied up to the F. A. but was prevented from pursuing my studies further owing to several untoward circumstances. I have, however, been devoting all my time to Mathematics and developing the subject. I can say I am quite confident I can do justice to my work if I am appointed to the post. I therefore beg to request that you be good enough to confer the appointment on me.

I beg to remain,

Sir,
Your most obedient Servant
S. Ramanujan

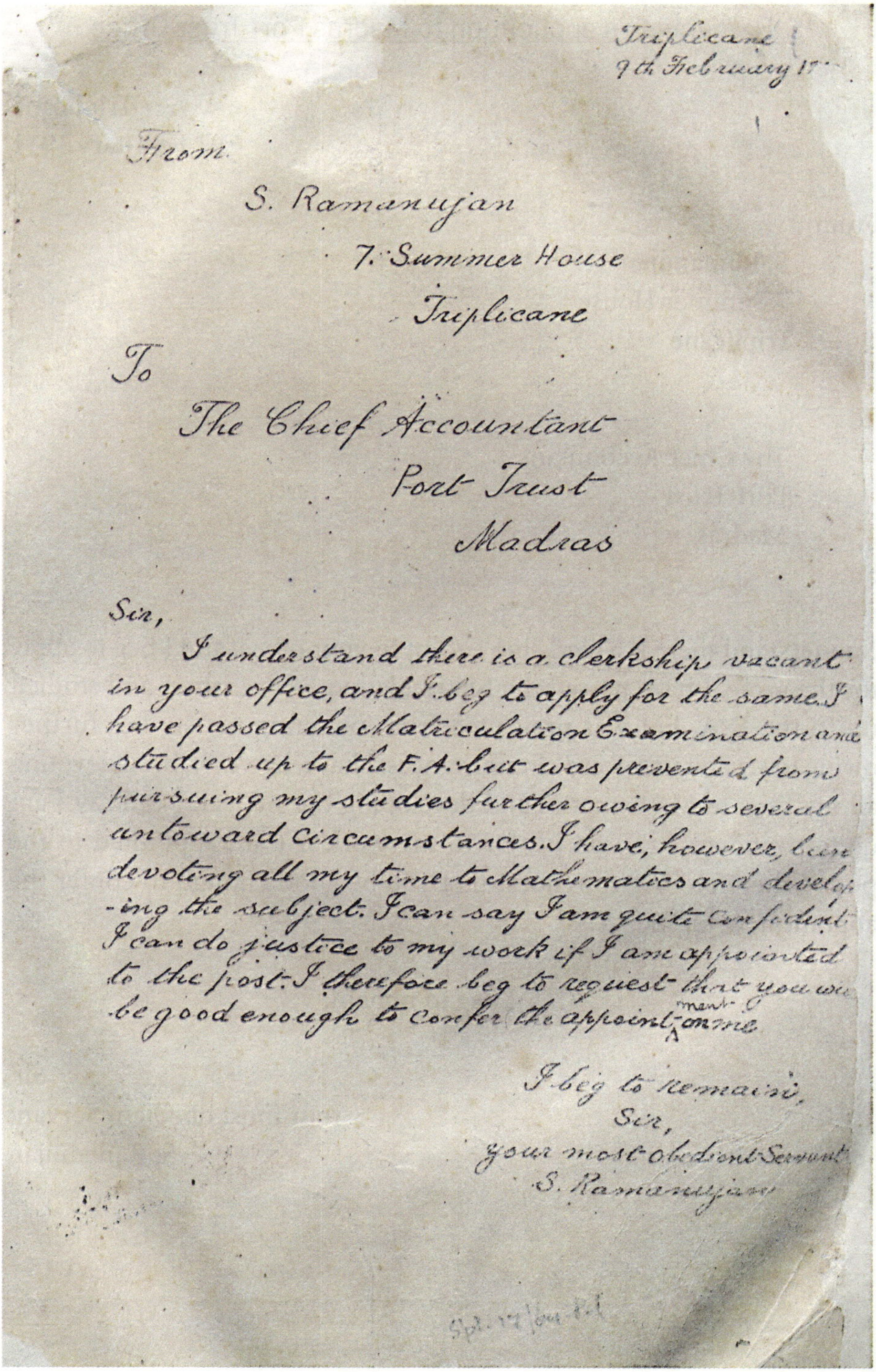

Triplicane
9th February 1[illegible]

From

S. Ramanujan
7. Summer House
Triplicane

To

The Chief Accountant
Port Trust
Madras

Sir,

I understand there is a clerkship vacant in your office, and I beg to apply for the same. I have passed the Matriculation Examination and studied up to the F.A. but was prevented from pursuing my studies further owing to several untoward circumstances. I have, however, been devoting all my time to Mathematics and developing the subject. I can say I am quite confident I can do justice to my work if I am appointed to the post. I therefore beg to request that you will be good enough to confer the appointment on me.

I beg to remain,
Sir,
your most obedient Servant
S. Ramanujan

Recommendation Letter

I can strongly recommend the applicant. He is a young man of quite exceptional capacity in Mathematics, and especially in work relating to numbers. He has a natural aptitude for computation and is very quick at figure work. Though he has had no experience of statistical work I am confident that he can pick up the details in a very short time.

Sd
E. W. Middlemast
Ag. Principal and
Professor of Mathematics
The Presidency College

Madras
21-9-1911

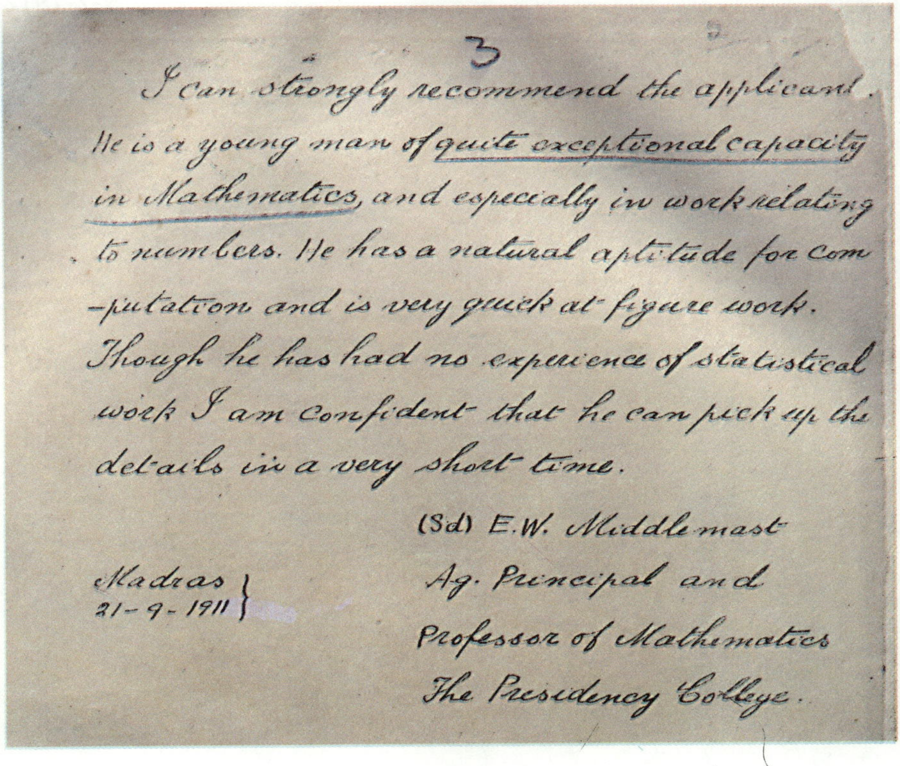
3

I can strongly recommend the applicant. He is a young man of quite exceptional capacity in Mathematics, and especially in work relating to numbers. He has a natural aptitude for computation and is very quick at figure work. Though he has had no experience of statistical work I am confident that he can pick up the details in a very short time.

(Sd) E.W. Middlemast
Ag. Principal and
Professor of Mathematics
The Presidency College.

Madras
21-9-1911

16. S. Ramanjam a new man, a matriculate, to be appointed to the Accounts Section in III class 4th grade.

About the men to be newly entertained No.7., an F.A., T. M. says, possesses a good knowledge of English. No. 16 is reported by M. G. R. to be a mathematical genius. Mr. Middlemast says of him to be "exceptionally intelligent in Mathematics".

Sanctioned.

F. J. E. S.
9-2-1912.

5 3

16. S. Ramanjam a new man, a matriculate, to be appointed to the Accounts Section in III class 4th grade.

About the man to be newly entertained No.7., an F.A., F.M. says, possesses a good knowledge of English. No.16 is reported by M.G.R. to be a mathematical genius. Mr.Middlemast says of him to be "exceptionally intelligent in Mathematics:

Sanctioned.

Intd.F.J.E.S.
9-2-12.

OFFICE OF THE CHAIRMAN, MADRAS PORT TRUST

Madras, Feb. 1912

From

The CHIEF ACCOUNTANT,
Madras Port Trust.

To

M. R. Ry. S. Ramanujan
9 Summer House,
Triplicane.

(Memo)

With reference to his application dated the 9th February 1912, S. Ramanujan is informed that he has been appointed by the Chairman as a clerk in this office on Rs. 25 per mensem. He should report himself to duty on 1st March 1912.

Chief Accountant

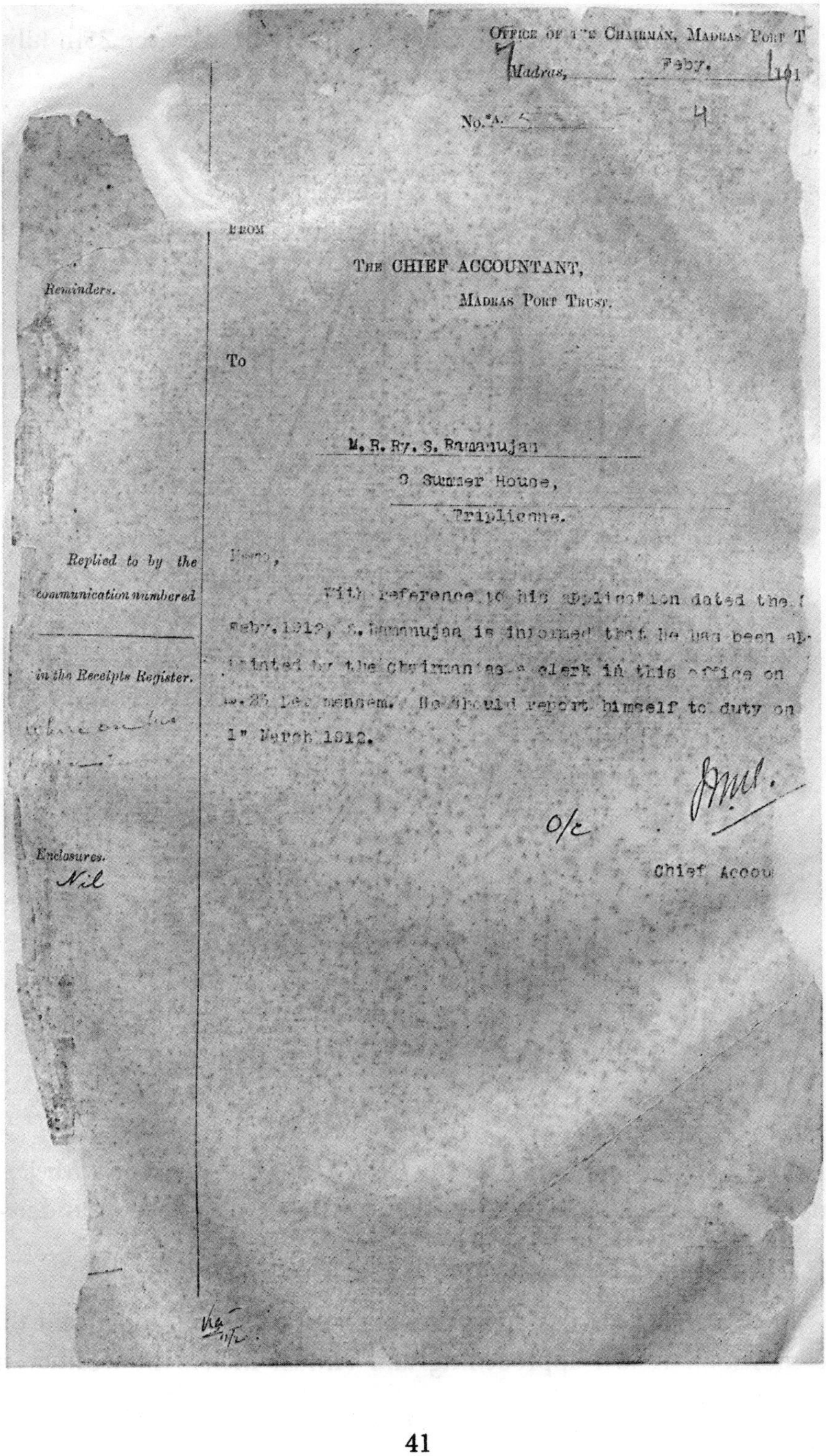

Office of the Chairman, Madras Port T

Madras, 7 Feby. 191

No. A. 4

From

The CHIEF ACCOUNTANT,

Madras Port Trust.

To

M. R. Ry. S. Ramanujan

8 Summer House,

Triplicane.

Reminders.

Replied to by the communication numbered

in the Receipts Register.

Memo,

With reference to his application dated the [illegible] Feby. 1912, S. Ramanujan is informed that he has been appointed by the Chairman as a clerk in this office on Rs. 25 per mensem. He should report himself to duty on 1st March 1912.

O/c

Chief Accou

Enclosures.
Nil

Minutes of meeting held in board room on saturday the 25th July, 1981 at 9.15 A.M.

Madras Port Trust

Shri V. Selvaraj, IA.S.	: :	Chairman
Shri P. R. Narasimhan	: :	Deputy Chairman
Shri P. K. Kandaswamy	: :	Chief Engineer
Shri N. Chandrasekaran	: :	Financial Adviser and Chief Accounts Officer.
Capt. G. A. Mande	: :	Deputy Part Conservator
Shri G. Chandrasekaran	: :	Traffic Manager
Shri A. Padmanabhan	: :	Sr. Dy. Secretary
Shri V. D. John	: :	Suptdg. Engr. (O. H.)
Shri M. Chandraswkaran	: :	Suptdg. Engr.
Shri G. Pajaram	: :	Dredging Supt.
Shri Albert Samuel	: :	Engg. Supdt.
Shri M. G. Bavanarayanam	: :	A. A. (S. G.) to C. E.
ShriPN. Nagaraja Rao.	: :	A. A. (F)
Shri K. A.Venkatesan	: :	A. S. V.
Shri C.T. Dorairaj	: :	A. A. to D. P. C.
Si M.Vedagiri	: :	A. A. to C. M. O.

Madras Dock Labour Board:

Shri S.K.Kanthimathinathan	: :	Deputy Chairman

Madras Port Trust Employees Union :

Sh S. C. C. Anthoni Pil-1	: :	President
Shri M. A-Anthony	: :	Vice-President

and eleven others.

The demands contained in the letter from the President, M. P .T. Employees' Union, dated the 20th July, 1981 were discussed as under:-

1. Payment of Centenary Bonus:

Initiating the discussion on the above subject Shri Pillai said that the monsoon is fast approaching and amidst inclement weather no major programme of Centenary Celebrations could be effectively arranged in Winter Session. He added that apart from the above, the undue delay in the announcement of the payment of Centenary bonus to the employees has caused dis-contentment among them. A discontented labour force is a liability to the administration and with a view to bring about a harmonious relationship between the employer and employees, Shri Pillai desired to know the line of thinking of the administration on the above subject and the quantum of amount that could be paid as Centenary bonus to the employees.

In reply, Chairman said that the question of payment of centenary bonus to the emloyees is under the active consideration of that administration. He said that arrangements are being made to celebrate the centenary functions in the first week of December 1981. There are several claims made with regard to grant of centenary award of gift and that these are under examination. Shri Pillai would be requested to come for a discussion with the administration on this subject. Based on the outcome of the discussion, further action would be taken.

2. Presentation of a watch to all the serving employees of the Trust Requested.

Shri Pillai said that in commemoration of the Centenary Year and making the future generations remember the passing of this milestone in the progress of Madras Port, he requested that a good quality H.M.T. day-dates, watch be presented to all the employees of the Trust. He said that the presentation of watch to the employees retiring from the Trust's Service could be dispensed with and in lieu the confirmed employees could be given the above watch. If his request is accepted by the administration would result in employees using the watch during their service period in the Trust instead of getting a watch after retirement when time does not mean anything to him.

The Chairman appreciated the spirit behind the argument and said that at present watches are being given every month to the retiring employees as a memento by the administration. This is within the budget amount. If all the employees, are to be given a watch now itself it would cost the Trust Rs.33,00,000 roughly, which the Trust is not in a position to commit at present.

3. Encouragement to the Family Planning Scheme among the Trust employees Requested:

Shri Pillai suggested that the administration with a view to encourage 'family planning' among its employees should announce a scheme under which an employee or his spouse undergoing vasectomy or cabectomy operation would be allowed a special pay equivalent to two increments in addition to the current incentives. Continuing Shri Pillai said that some of the Public Sector Undertakings are now offering lucrative incentives to its employees to popularise the concept of small family norms. He quoted that the great nation like China is now aiming at to achieve a zero growth and that our country should not lag behind in this exercise. However, Shri Pillai said that the incentive should not only cover the future cases, but should also made applicable to the past cases.

The Chairman said that he fully agreed with the views of the President of the Union in regard to small family norms. However, there are some practical difficulties in verifying the fact that whether or not, an individual underwent the vesectory/tubectomy operation to become eligible for the incentive. The administration of its own cannot admit an individuals version and extend him the necessary incentive, on the other it has to make quite sure whether the statement by the individual about the fact of vesectory/tubectomy operation by the Trust's Hospital. This exercise would definitely consume more time and hence this is not practicable. Chairman said that he has got an open mind on this issue and requested Shri Pillai to come for a discussion on this subject sometime later because there are other agencies Corporation of Madras and they are also to be roped into the programme scheme to be evolved by the Trust.

4. Reimbursement of the cost of text books irrespective of the pay limit Requested

Shri Pillai said that the reimbursement of the cost of text books to the children of the employees is now restricted to those who are in receipt of basic pay upto Rs.645/- and this reimbursement is subject to a maximum of Rs.75/- per annum. He requested that this concession should be extended to all employees of the Trust irrespective of the pay limit and that the maximum amount may also be increased from Rs. 75/- to Rs.150/- per annum in view of the increased cost of textbooks, etc.

Shri Pillai also said that the expenditure on this account, when compared to Bombay and Calcutta is very negligible in the case of Madras Port and hence there is a strong case for the administration to consider their request favourably.

The Chairman said that this request would be looked into in detail and a decision taken.

5. Erection of a statue of late Shri Ramanujam an eminent mathematician within the port premises:

Shri Pillai recalled the letter he wrote to the administration sometime back and requested that if the statue of late Shri Ramanujam is erected now, it would be cherished by one and all as a fittest tribute paid during the centenary year to one of the greatest sons of India who worked in the initial stage at the Port of Madras.

C.P.T. said that the erection of a statue would be considered by the administration in all its aspects and the Union would be intimated of the action taken in due course. Apart from this, the Administration is thinking loudly whether an Institute could be established to be named after late Shri Ramanujan or to create a fund to enable scholarships being granted out its proceeds or else to extend pecuniary help to the Members of his family.

6. Family Security Scheme- Inclusion of one more category into the beneficiary list - Requested:

Shri Pillai said that at present there is no 'pay protection' to such of the workers who have been sent for periodical medical check-up and get invalidated based on the medical classification. Those workers have to bear the burden of drop in emoluments. He requested that such workers be provided with financial assistance to cover the drop in emoluments from out of the family Security Scheme, for which purpose, an increased contribution from such of the employees who are subjected to periodical medical check-up may be collected besides the administration also contributing a matching grant. He said that an exercise has been made by him and the amount involved is very negligible. FA & CAO has stated that if such a facility/concession is provided, it may lead to a situation in which such of the employees who are subject to periodical medical check-up would volunteer to opt for medical disqualification by bringing in undue pressures on the doctors. Shri. Pillai said that his Union would not encourage such acts on the part of the employees and that he requested that this would be examined purely from an humanitarian angle. After some discussion, the Chairman said that the administration would look into this demand.

7. Promotional opportunities - Requested:

Shri Pillai said that due to progressive computerisation and mechanisation and rationalisation based on the O&M studies, the volume of employment of personnel would shrink relatively whereas there is bound to be increase in the traffic and efficiency. In this background of the matter, Shri Pillai requested the following:

(a) Early action be taken in regard to the filling up of the 98 posts of S. H. in the Traffic Department, from the date the promotions were allowed in the Accounts Department.

(b) In the Stores Department some clerks take action quickly and diligently and place orders on the firms well within the validity period. By such acts on the part of the clerks, the administration benefited to a great extent leading to savings in lakhs of rupees. Such areas should be located and to man those areas, posts carrying supervisory responsibilities should be created and filled without reference to the ratio.

(c) The nine functions which the D. C. Ms are doing as per the terms of settlement are purely clerical in nature. Hence they may be classified as a clerical cadre and a separate channel be formed exclusively for DCMs as in the case of clerical cadre. Therefore, the DCM should be redesignated as Section Clerk (L. D.), (U. D.), (S. H.), (H.C.) or Traffic Section Asst. Grade-I, Grade-II, Gr-III and Gr. IV, etc. and I brought within the Scheme of Grouped posts and allowed automatic promotion as is done in the case of clerical categories.

(d) A new post of Tally Supervisors should be created carrying the scale of pay/Rs. 575-953 /- and one-fourth of the Tally Clerks be promoted to this newly created category and the services of the promotees utilised for the purpose of 'relieving-cum-supervisory works. He mentioned in this connection that there is no effective supervision of the Tally works and the errors crept in the tally work go undetected.

(e) Shri Pillai said that Peons and Attenders should be enthused by the administration to get themselves better qualified by offering incentives like immediate promotion to higher clerical grades. Apart from the 30 per cent of the vacancies now being allotted for the Peons/Attenders in the category of L.D.C., a substantial quota be allotted in the vacancies that may arise in the categories of DCM/ Works Clerks/Timekeepers to be filled with Peons/Attenders.

(f) Shri Pillai said that consequent on the promotion given to some of the S.G. and Gr.I Stenographers to the post of P.A., the resultant vacancies have not been filled. This has affected adversely the promotional opportunities of the stenographers in the lower rung. Sr.Dy. Secretary said that there were resultant vacancies in the category of Steno. Gr.I, and Selection Grade since the posts have been upgraded to that of P.A. posts. Shri Pillai did not agree with the principle of upgradation as the same is not in the interest of the employees holding posts in the lower rung. He, therefore, suggested that the posts against which the Stenographers have been promoted as P.As be deemed as 'created posts' and the resultant vacancies be filled.

Minutes of meeting held in Board Room on Saturday the 25th July, 1981 at 9.15 A.M.

PRESENT

Madras Port Trust:

Shri V.Selvaraj, I.A.S. .. Chairman
Shri P.R.Narasimhan .. Deputy Chairman
Shri P.K.Kandaswamy .. Chief Engineer
Shri N.Chandrasekaran .. Financial Adviser and Chief Accounts Officer.

Capt. G.A.Mande .. Deputy Port Conservator
Shri G.Chandrasekaran .. Traffic Manager
Shri A.Padmanabhan .. Sr.Dy. Secretary
Shri V.D.John .. Suptdg.Engr. (O.H.)
Shri M.Chandraswkaran .. Suptdg. Engr.
Shri G.Rajaram .. Dredging Supdt.
Shri Albert Samuel .. Engg. Supdt.
Shri M.G.Bavanarayanan .. A.A. (S.G.) to C.E.
Shri P.N.Nagaraja Rao .. A.A. (F)
Shri K.A.Venkatesan .. A.S.V.
Shri C.T. Dorairaj .. A.A. to D.P.C.
Shri M.Vedagiri .. A.A. to C.M.O.

Madras Dock Labour Board:

Shri S.K.Kanthimathinathan .. Deputy Chairman

Madras Port Trust Employees' Union:

Shri S.C.C.Anthoni Pillai .. President
Shri M.A.Anthony .. Vice-President
and eleven others.

- - - -

The demands contained in the letter from the President, M.P.T. Employees' Union, dated the 20th July, 1981 were discussed as under:-

1. **Payment of Centenary Bonus:**

Initiating the discussion on the above subject Shri Pillai said that the monsoon is fast approaching and amidst inclement weather no major programme of Centenary Celebrations could be effectively arranged in Winter Session. He added that apart from the above, the undue delay in the announcement of the payment of Centenary bonus to the employees has caused discontentment among them. A discontented labour force is a liability to the administration and with a view to bring about a harmonious relationship between the employer and employees, Shri Pillai desired to know the line of thinking of the administration on the above subject and the quantum of amount that could be paid as Centenary bonus to the employees.

46

In reply, Chairman said that the question of payment of centenary bonus to the employees is under the active consideration of the administration. He said that arrangements are being made to celebrate the centenary functions in the first week of December 1981. There are several claims made with regard to grant of centenary award or gift and that these are under examination. Shri Pillai would be requested to come for a discussion with the administration on this subject. Based on the outcome of the discussion, further action would be taken.

2. Presentation of a watch to all the serving employees of the Trust - Requested.

Shri. Pillai said that in commemoration of the Centenary Year and making the future generations remember the passing of this milestone in the progress of Madras Port, he requested that a good quality H.M.T. day-date watch be presented to all the employees of the Trust. He said that the presentation of watch to the employees retiring from the Trust's Service could be dispensed with and in lieu the confirmed employees could be given the above watch. If his request is accepted by the administ- it would result in employees using the watch during their service period in the Trust instead of getting a watch after retirement when time does not mean anything to him.

The Chairman appreciated the spirit behind the argument and said that at present watches are being given every month to the retiring employees as a memento by the administration. This is within the budget amount. If all the employees, are to be given a watch now itself it would cost the Trust Rs.33,00,000 roughly, which the Trust is not in a position to commit at present.

3. Encouragement to the Family Planning Scheme among the Trust employees - Requested:

Shri Pillai suggested that the administration with a view to encourage 'family planning ' among its employees should announce a scheme under which an employee or his spouse undergoing vesectomy or tubectomy operation would be allowed a special pay equivalent to two increments in addition to the current incentives. Continuing Shri Pillai said that some of the Public Sector Undertakings are now offering lucrative incentives to its employees to popularise the concept of small family norm. He quoted that the great nation like China is now aiming at to achieve a zero growth and that our country should not lag behind in this exercise. However, Shri Pillai said that the incentive should not only cover the future cases, but should also made applicable to the past cases

-3-

-3-

The Chairman said that he fully agreed with the views of the President of the Union in regard to small family norms. However, there are some practical difficulties in verifying the fact that whether or not an individual underwent the vesectory/tubectomy operation to become eligible for the incentive. The administration of its own cannot admit an individual's version and extend him the necessary incentive; on the other it has to make quite sure whether the statement made by the individual about the fact of vesectory/tubectomy operation by the Trust's Hospital. This exercise would definitely consume more time and hence this is not practicable. Chairman said that he has got an open mind on this issue and requested Shri Pillai to come for a discussion on this subject sometime later because there are other agencies involved in this task, such as, State Government, Corporation of Madras and they are also to be roped into the programme scheme to be evolved by the Trust.

4. Reimbursement of the cost of text books irrespective of the pay limit - Requested:

Shri Pillai said that the reimbursement of the cost of text books to the children of the employees is now restricted to those who are in receipt of basic pay upto Rs.645/- and this reimbursement is subject to a maximum of Rs.75/- per annum. He requested that this concession should be extended to all employees of the Trust irrespective of the pay limit and that the maximum amount may also be increased from Rs.75/- to Rs.150/- per annum in view of the increased cost of textbooks,etc.

Shri Pillai also said that the expenditure on this account, when compared to Bombay and Calcutta is very negligible in the case of Madras Port and hence there is a strong case for the administration to consider their request favourably.

The Chairman said that this request would be looked into in detail and a decision taken.

5. Erection of a statue of late Shri Ramanujam an eminent mathematician within the port premises:

Shri Pillai recalled the letter he wrote to the administration sometime back and requested that if the statue of late Shri Ramanujam is erected now, it would be cherished by one and all as a fittest tribute paid during the centenary year to one of the greatest sons of India who worked in the initial stage at the Port of Madras.

C.P.T. said that the erection of a statue would be considered by the administration in all its aspects and the Union would be intimated of the action taken in due course. Apart from this, the Administration is thinking loudly whether an Institute could be

-4-

-4-

established to be named after late Shri Ramanujam or to create a fund to enable scholarships being granted out of its proceeds or else to extend pecuniary help to the Members of his family.'

6. Family Security Scheme - Inclusion of one more category into the beneficiary list - Requested:

Shri Pillai said that at present there is no 'pay protection' to such of the workers who have been sent for periodical medical check-up and got invalidated based on the medical classification. Those workers have to bear the burden of drop in emoluments. He requested that such workers be provided with financial assistance to cover the drop in emoluments from out of the Family Security Scheme, for which purpose, an increased contribution from such of the employees who are subjected to periodical medical check-up may be collected besides the administration also contributing a matching grant. He said that an exercise has been made by him and the amount involved is very negligible. FA & CAO has stated that if such a facility/concession is provided, it may lead to a situation in which such of the employees who are subject to periodical medical check-up would volunteer to opt for medical disqualifica by bringing in undue pressures on the doctors. Shri Pillai said that his Union would not encourage such acts on the part of the employees and that he requested that this would be examined purely from an humanitarian angle. After some discussion, th Chairman said that the administration would look into this demand.

7. Promotional opportunities - Requested:

Shri Pillai said that due to progressive computerisation and mechanisation and rationalisation based on the O&M studies, the volume of employment of personnel would shrink relatively whereas there is bound to be increase in the traffic and efficiency. In this background of the matter, Shri Pillai requested the following:

(a) Early action be taken in regard to the filling up of the 98 posts of S.H. in the Traffic Department, from the date the promotions were allowed in the Accounts Department.

(b) In the Stores Department some clerks take action quickly and diligently and place orders on the firms well within the validity period. By such acts on the part of the clerks, the administration benefited to a great extent leading to savings in lakhs of rupees. Such areas should be located and to man those areas, posts carrying supervisory responsibilities should be created and filled without reference to the ratio.

-5-

-5-

(c) The nine functions which the D.C.Ms are doing as per the terms of settlement are purely clerical in nature. Hence they may be classified as a clerical cadre and a separate channel be formed exclusively for DCMs as in the case of clerical cadre. Therefore, the DCM should be redesignated as Section Clerk (L.D.), (U.D.), (S.H.), (H.C.) or Traffic Section Asst.Grade - I Grade-II, Gr-III and Gr.IV, etc. and brought within the Scheme of Grouped Posts and allowed automatic promotion as is done in the case of clerical categories.

(d) A new post of Tally Supervisors should be created carrying the scale of pay/Rs.575-953 /of and one-fourth of the Tally Clerks be promoted to this newly created category and the services of the promotees utilised for the purpose of 'relieving-cum-supervisory works. He mentioned in this connection that there is no effective supervision of the Tally works and the errors crept in the tally work go undetected.

(e) Shri Pillai said that Peons and Attenders should be enthused by the administration to get themselves better qualified by offering incentives like immediate promotion to higher clerical grades. Apart from the 30 per cent of the vacancies now being allotted for the Peons/Attenders in the category of L.D.C., a substantial quota be allotted in the vacancies that may arise in the categories of DCM/Works Clerks/Timekeepers to be filled with Peons/Attenders.

(f) Shri Pillai said that consequent on the promotion given to some of the S.G. and Gr.I Stenographers to the post of P.A., the resultant vacancies have not been filled. This has affected adversely the promotional opportunities of the stenographers in the lower rung. Sr.Dy.Secretary said that there were resultant vacancies in the category of Steno. Gr.I and Selection Grade since the posts have been upgraded to that of P.A. posts. Shri Pillai did not agree with the principle of upgradation as the same is not in the interest of the employees holding posts in the lower rung. He, therefore, suggested that the posts against which the Stenographers have been promoted as P.As be deemed as 'created posts' and the resultant vacancies be filled.

A letter to Government seeking sanction to the above modified proposal has been sought for in Chairman's D.O. letter No. IR4/20275/81/8 dated 1.12.81.

3. After discussion with C.P.T. 1.12.81, it has been decided that the widow of late Sri Srinivasa Ramanujan, the World renowned mathematician would be granted a monthly ex-gratia payment at the rate of Rs.300/- p.m. from 1 Dec. 1981 till she is alive and that the sanction of the Board/Government would be sought for this separately.

4. Besides the above, a decision was taken on 1.12.81 to make an ex-gratia payment of Rs. 200/- to each of the employees of the following 3 canteens in the Port Trust, subject to the condition that in the case of daily rated casuals working in these canteens, if any, the payment would be restricted to Rs.100/- per heads-

I) M.P.T. Industrial Employees Co-operative Canteen

II) M.P.T. Administrative Offices Canteen.

III) M.P.T. Staff Canteen.

The expenditure in this regard would be subsidised by the Port Trust in full, subject to ratification by the Board.

5. A note furnishing guidelines to be observed by the departments in making payment of the Centenary Gift to the employees of the Port Trust including those retired, died while in service, discharged from service on medical grounds and normal discharge, dismissal, etc., is placed below.

Submitted for-approval.

By. C. A. O. A.S. IV.
Secretary.
C.P.T.

:: 20 ::

A letter to Government seeking sanction to the above modified proposal has been sought for in Chairman's D.O. letter No.IR4/20275/81/S dated 1.12.81.

3. After discussion with C.P.T. on 1.12.81, it has been decided that the widow of late Sri Srinivasa Ramanujan, the World renowned mathematician would be granted a monthly ex-gratia payment at the rate of Rs.300/- p.m. from 1st Dec. 1981 till she is alive and that the sanction of the Board/Government would be sought for this separately.

4. Besides the above, a decision was taken on 1.12.81 to make an ex-gratia payment of Rs.200/- to each of the employees of the following 3 canteens in the Port Trust, subject to the condition that in the case of daily rated casuals working in these canteens, if any, the payment would be restricted to Rs.100/- per head:-

i) M.P.T. Industrial Employees Co-operative Canteen
ii) M.P.T. Administrative Offices Canteen
iii) M.P.T. Staff Canteen.

The expenditure in this regard would be subsidised by the Port Trust in full, subject to ratification by the Board.

5. A note furnishing guidelines to be observed by the departments in making payment of the Centenary Gift to the employees of the Port Trust including those retired, died while in service, discharged from service on medical grounds and normal discharge, dismissal, etc., is placed below.

Submitted for approval.

Dy.C.A.O. A.S. IV.

SECRETARY.

C.P.T.

Reso. No. 245.

245 Read (i) the Board Resolution No. 191 dated 28th November, 1981 and (ii) the note by the Chairman dated 20th January, 1982 reporting that in anticipation of the sanction of the Board and the Government, he had approved of the payment of a monthly ex-gratia payment of Rs.300/- with effect from 1st December, 1981, to the widow of Shri Srinivasa Ramanujan, till she is alive, in the circumstances explained in the note and seeking ratification of the above action.

GRA /20275/81/S

Resolved, after discussion to ratify the above action and to seek the sanction of the Government in this regard.

: 5 :

lights, cyclone filter and breather cap, driver's overhead guard, load back rest, side shifter attachment, special transmission tool kit (without hydraulic jack) and standard tool kit (without hydraulic jack) at a total approximate cost of Rs.48,51,200.64 inclusive of Excise Duty, Special Excise Duty and Central Sales Tax, ex-works Vikhroli, Bombay, as per Tender No.G/RV/FLT/24/6070 dated 18th August, 1981 and subsequent letters dated 10th October, 1981, 15th October, 1981 and 7th January, 1982 and minutes of Tender Committee meeting dated 12th October, 1981 and (ii) to enter into an agreement with the firm.

BR/2915/82/S & CH/N1/4779/81/EME II

Reso. No. 244 — 244 Read the note by the Chairman dated the 22nd January, 1982 recommending in the circumstances explained in the note, to remit the sum Rs.9,50,479.12 due from M/s. Shri Rama Vilas Service Limited in respect of the storage of two Overdimensional packages each weighing about 108 M/T and 97 M/T ex. s.s. GOLDEN FELS arrived on the 12th May, 1980, in the transit area at South Quay-1.

BR/2928/82/S & C1/14807/80/T

Resolved, after discussion, to approve of the above recommendation.

Reso. No. 245 — 245 Read (i) the Board Resolution No. 191 dated 28th November, 1981 and (ii) the note by the Chairman dated 20th January, 1982 reporting that in anticipation of the sanction of the Board and the Government, he had approved of the payment of a monthly ex-gratia payment of Rs.300/- with effect from 1st December, 1981, to the widow of Shri Srinivasa Ramanujan, till she is alive, in the circumstances explained in the note and seeking ratification of the above action.

GRA/20275/81/S

Resolved, after discussion, to ratify the above action and to seek the sanction of the Government in this regard.

Reso. No. 246 — 246 Read (i) Board's Resolution No.260, dated the 30th January, 1980 and (ii) the note by the Chairman dated the 20th January, 1982 recommending the renewal of stevedoring licences issued in favour of the following, for the calendar years 1982 and 1983:-

(652/82/S / 22785/81/T)

1. M/s. United Stevedores
2. Shri A. Arumugam Chettiar
3. M/s. Krishna & Company
4. M/s. Binny Limited
5. M/s. K.P.V. Shaik Mohamed Rowther & Company Private Limited

/6/

ITEM NO.12 ON THE AGENDA.

Port Centenary Celebrations - Grant of Centenary Gifts.

Attention of the Trustees is invited to my note dated 26th November, 1981, wherein it was proposed Inter-alio to grant to the widow of Shri Srinivasa Ramanujan, the eminent world renowned mathematician, who was once in the employment of the Trust, a monthly ex-gratia payment of Rs.300/- with effect from 1st January, 1981, till she is alive.

2. The Board at its meeting held on 28th November, 1981, had approved of the following proposals:-

a) to grant Special Centenary gift to the Trust's employees subject to the conditions laid down in the Board Resolution No.191 dated 28.11.1981.

b) to create a Special Centenary Commemoration Fund, and

c) to examine the suggestion to constitute a fund with monthly contribution from the employees and a matching contribution from the Administration for compensating the loss in wages that may be suffered by an employee in high medical classification when he is reverted or offered alternative employment.

The proposal for payment of monthly ex-gratia ef Rs.300/-to the widow of Shri Srinivasa Ramanujan was not discussed and decision taken. However, to mark the occasion of the concluding celebrations of the Centenary, I have in anticipation of the sanction of the Board and Government approved the payment of a monthly ex-gratia payment of Rs.300/- with effect from 1.12.1981 to the widow of Shri Srinivasa Ramanujan till she is alive. Advance payments for the months of December 1981 and January 1982 have already been made. The Board may kindly approve by according sanction for the payment of a monthly sum of Rs. 300/- from 1.12.1981 to the widow of Shri Srinivasa Ramanujan, till she is alive.

3. On Board's approval, the sanction of amount for this monthly ex-gratia payment to the widow of Shri Srinivasa Ramanujan will be obtained.

Circulated.

Chairman, Madras Part
20-1-1981

ITEM No. 12 ON THE AGENDA.

Port Centenary Celebrations - Grant of Centenary Gifts.

....

Attention of the Trustees is invited to my note dated 26th November, 1981, wherein it was proposed inter-alia to grant to the widow of Shri Srinivasa Ramanujan, the eminent world renowned mathematician, who was once in the employment of the Trust, a monthly ex-gratia payment of Rs.300/- with effect from 1st January, 1981, till she is alive.

2. The Board at its meeting held on 28th November, 1981, had approved of the following proposals:-

a) to grant Special Centenary gift to the Trust's employees subject to the conditions laid down in the Board Resolution No.191 dated 28.11.1981.

b) to create a Special Centenary Commemoration Fund, and

c) to examine the suggestion to constitute a fund with monthly contribution from the employees and a matching contribution from the Administration for compensating the loss in wages that may be suffered by an employee in high medical classification when he is reverted or offered alternative employment.

The proposal for payment of monthly ex-gratia of Rs.300/- to the widow of Shri Srinivasa Ramanujan was not discussed and decision taken. However, to mark the occasion of the concluding celebrations of the Centenary, I have in anticipation of the sanction of the Board and Government approved the payment of a monthly ex-gratia payment of

/2/

:: 2 ::

Rs.300/- with effect from 1.12.1981 to the widow of Shri Srinivasa Ramanujan till she is alive. Advance payment for the months of December 1981 and January 1982 have already been made. The Board may kindly approve by according sanction for the payment of a monthly sum of Rs.300/- from 1.12.1981 to the widow of Shri Srinivasa Ramanujan, till she is alive.

3. On Board's approval, the sanction of amount for this monthly ex-gratia payment to the widow of Shri Srinivasa Ramanujan will be obtained.

Circulated.

Chairman, Madr
20-1-19

pgs/20.1

D.0. No. IR4/20275/81/S Dated the 7th May 82.

Dear Shri Ambrose,

Sub: Fort Centenary Celebretions, Grant of Centenary gift to the Part Trust employees.

Creation of Centenary fund and grant of Ex-gratia payment to the widow of late Sri Srinivasa Ramanujan, an eminent world renowned mathematician Sanction Requested.

Please refer to the correspondence on the above subject regarding Shri V. Salvaraj D.O letter of even No. dated 2nd April 1982.

I shall be grateful if you will kindly convey the sanction of the government to the following proposals urgently:-

1) Creation of a Special Centenary Commemoration Fund with a contribution of Rs. 25 lakhs by the Trust on the model of the fund created by the Bombay Port Trust. The maintence of the fund will be vested with a comittee of officers and the labour trustees and this committee will evolve the objectives etc., for administering the fund.

2) Grant of monthly ex-gratia payment of Rs. 300/- to the widow of Srinivasa Ramanujan, the eminent world renowned mathematician who was once an employee of the Trust, with effect from December, 1981 till she is alive.

3) To constitute a fund with a monthly contribution from the employees and a matching contribution from the administration for the purpose of compensating the loss in wages that may be suffered by an employee in a high medical classification when he is reverted or offered alternative employment on medical grounds.

with kind regards,

Yours sincerely,

(V-SELVARAJ)

Shrt S.P. Ambrose, I.A.S.
Additional Secretary,
Mintatry of Shipping and Transport,
(Transport wing).
Transport-Bhavan,
1. Parliament street,
New Delhi-110001

Dated the 7th May 82.

D.O.No.IRA/20275/81/S

Dear Shri Ambrose,

Sub: Port Centenary Celebrations –
Grant of Centenary Gift to the
Port Trust employee –
Creation of Centenary fund and
grant of Ex-gratia payment to the
widow of late Sri Srinivasa Ramanujam,
an eminent world renowned mathematician –
Sanction – Requested.

Please refer to the correspondence on the above subject resting with Shri Joshi's D.O. letter of even No. dated the 22nd April, 1932.

I shall be grateful if you will kindly convey the sanction of the Government to the following proposals urgently:-

1) Creation of a special Centenary Commemoration Fund with a contribution of Rs.25 lakhs by the Trust on the model of the fund created by the Bombay Port Trust. The maintenance of the fund will be vested with a committee of officers and the labour trustees and this committee will evolve the objectives etc., for administering the fund.

2) Grant of monthly ex-gratia payment of Rs.300/- to the widow of Sri Srinivasa Ramanujam, the eminent world renowned Mathematician who was once an employee of the Trust, with effect from December, 1981 till she is alive.

3) To constitute a fund with a monthly contribution from the employees and a matching contribution from the administration for the purpose of compensating the loss in wages that may be suffered by an employee in a high medical classification/he is /when reverted or offered alternative employment on medical grounds.

With kind regards,

Yours sincerely,

(V SELVARAJ)

Shri S.P. Ambrose, I.A.S.,
Additional Secretary,
Ministry of Shipping and Transport,
(Transport Wing),
Transport Bhavan,
1, Parliament Street,
New Delhi-110 001.

Ramanujan's Growing Influence

Ramanujan was gradually becoming well known to professors in various colleges in Madras, and they were keen to help him to further his studies and to foster his genius and brilliance. The first step was taken by C.L.T. Griffith, a Civil Engineering professor at Madras Engineering College. A graduate of University College, London, he wrote to his former mathematics professor, M.J.M. Hill, enclosing some of Ramanujan's work[1]. Hill replied back, and his two letters conveyed his viewpoints and recommendations regarding Ramanujan's mathematical abilities.

Griffith had also written to Francis Spring, after Ramanujan had obtained the job at the Port Trust. Other important personalities such as Sir Gilbert Walker, Head of the Indian Meteorological Department and a former Senior Wrangler, were also approached.

Francis Spring wrote to A. G. Bourne, Madras's Director of Public Instruction, who advised Spring to send Ramanujan to see one or both of the two Madras mathematicians that he had mentioned in his letter. Following up on this, two weeks later, Ramanujan went to see J. F. Graham, Accountant-General, Madras.

Ramanujan sent letters to three well-known Cambridge mathematicians, Professor H.F. Baker, Professor E.W. Hobson, and Professor G.H. Hardy, the Cayley Lecturer in Mathematics and a Fellow of Trinity College. Professor G. H. Hardy's reply was favourable and encouraging. Several letters were exchanged between them, finally leading to Ramanujan going to England. Infact, the story of the collaboration between G. H. Hardy and Srinivasa Ramanujan has attained near-legendary status.

When Hardy received Ramanujan's letter, he called his close aide and fellow mathematician, J.E. Littlewood. They had started collaborating a few years back, and were submitting joint papers at the London Mathematical Society; their first paper was published in 1911. Both of them pored

1. Letter from C.L.T. Griffith to FJ Spring dated November 12, 1912, NAI, New Delhi.

through the letter and were amazed at what they were looking at. Both of them immediately recognised Ramanujan's potential and calibre in the field of mathematics.

On 8th February, 1913, Hardy sent a letter back to Ramanujan starting the letter with "Dear Sir, I was exceedingly interested by your letter and by the theorems that you state..." His letter was very encouraging and appreciative. Littlewood sent 'Further Notes' along with the letter sent by G. H. Hardy as a sort of appendix. Another letter was sent by Hardy to Ramanujan, on 26th March 1913, in which he wrote, "...and I have considered further some of your results."[1]

1. Letter from G.H. Hardy to S. Ramanujan dated 8th Feb, 1913, NAI New Delhi.

College of Engineering
Madras,
12.11.1912

Dear Sir Francis,

You have in your office as an accountant on Rs. 25, a young man named S. Ramanujan. who is a most remarkable mathematician. He may be a very poor accountant, but I hope you will see that he is kept happily employed until something can be done to make use of his extraordinary gifts. I am writing to one of the leading Math. professors at home about him & sending copies of some of Ramanujan's papers & results. Our Math.professor here says that very few people could follow or criticise the work. It is of course far beyond my scope, but I happen to know who is at work in the same time at home, & I hope to get instructions as to what this fellow ought to do.

If there is any real genius in him, he will have to be provided with money for books & with leisure, but until I hear from home, I don't feel sure that it is worthwhile spending much time or money on him.

Yours Sincerely,
C. L. T. Griffith
(Civil Engineering Professor,
Madras Engineering College)

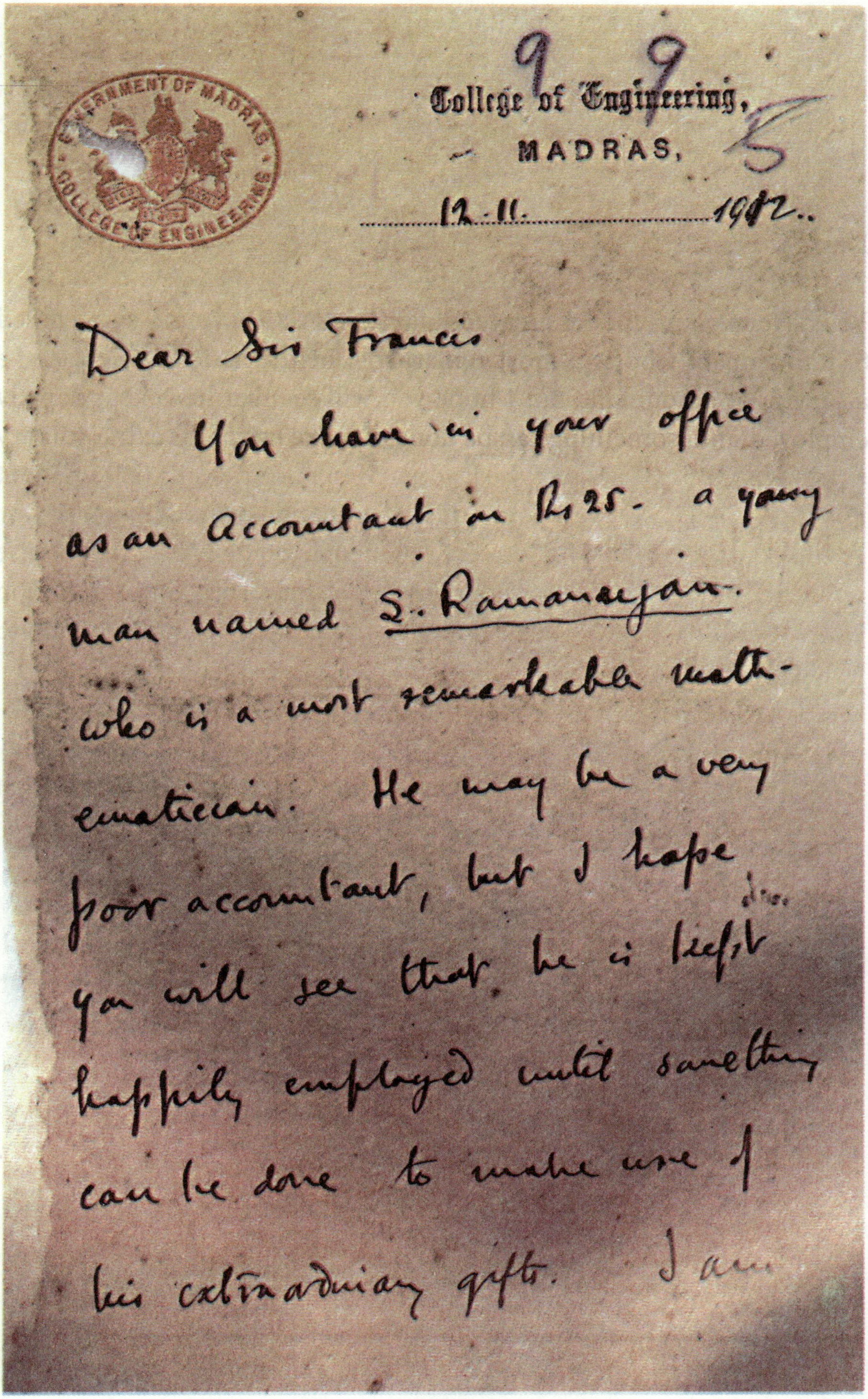

College of Engineering,
MADRAS,
12.11. 1912..

Dear Sir Francis

You have in your office as an Accountant on Rs 25- a young man named S. Ramanujan who is a most remarkable mathematician. He may be a very poor accountant, but I hope you will see that he is kept happily employed until something can be done to make use of his extraordinary gifts. I am

60

writing to one of the leading
Math. professors at home about
him & sending copies of some
of Ramanujan's papers & results.
Our Math. professor here says that
very few people could follow or
criticise the work. It is of course
far beyond my scope, but I happen
to know who is at work in the same
line at home, & I ~~am~~ hope to
get instructions as to what this

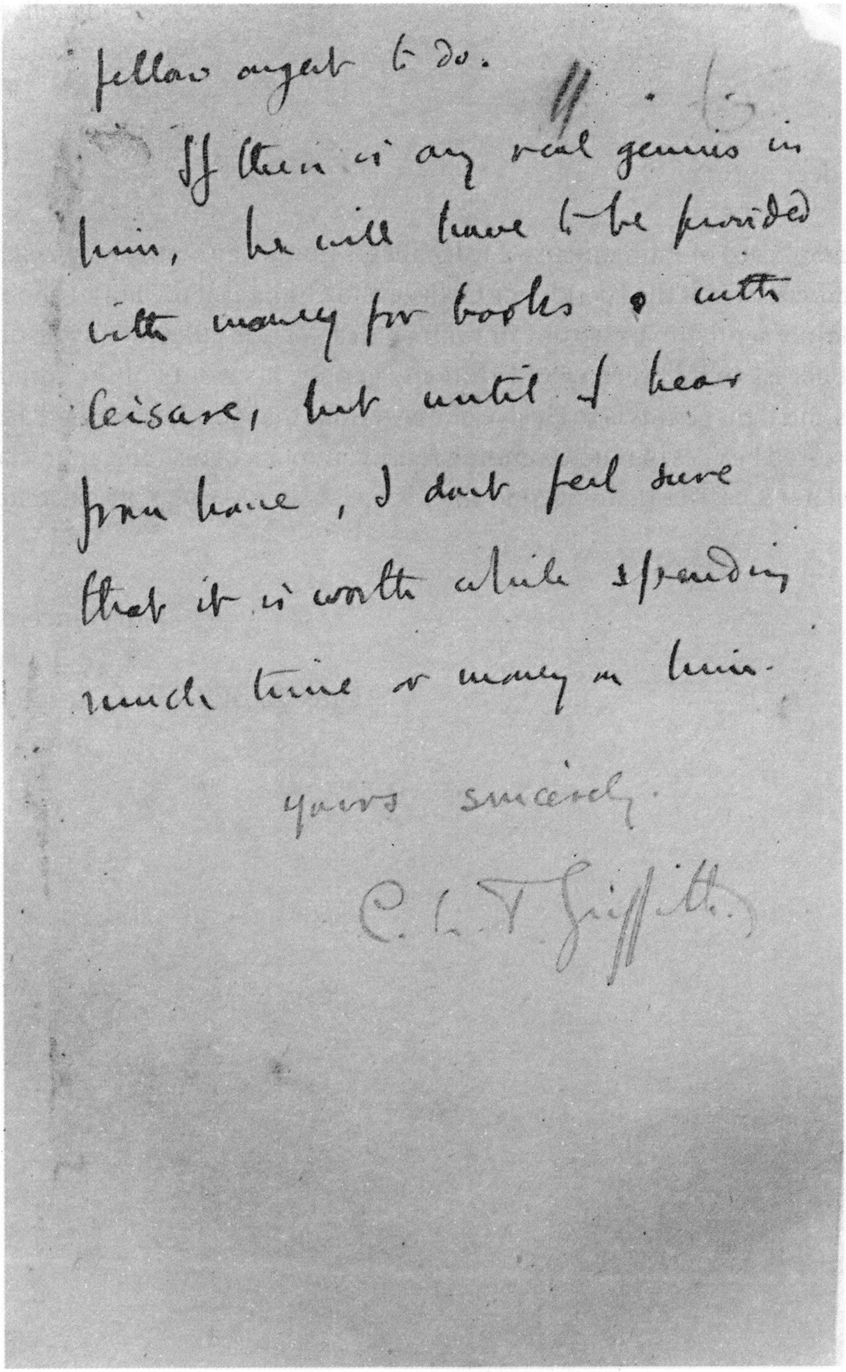

fellow ought to do.

If there is any real genius in him, he will have to be provided with money for books & with leisure, but until I hear from home, I don't feel sure that it is worth while spending much time or money on him.

Yours sincerely.

C. L. T. Griffith.

The Old College,
Nungambakam,
14th Nov. 1912

My dear Spring,

I never heard of Ramanujan – Littlehailes is now away on the west coast - Middlemast is at the Presidency College and Graham at the Fort. I should certainly send him to see one or both of these - I don't like the suggestion that access to a library would ruin any genius, it savours of the middle ages and if his genius is so elusive or mysterious that good mathematicians possessed besides of much common sense cannot recognise and appreciate it even if it carries them beyond their scope, I should doubt its existence.

Yours Sincerely,
A. G. Bourne
(Director of Public Instruction,
Madras)

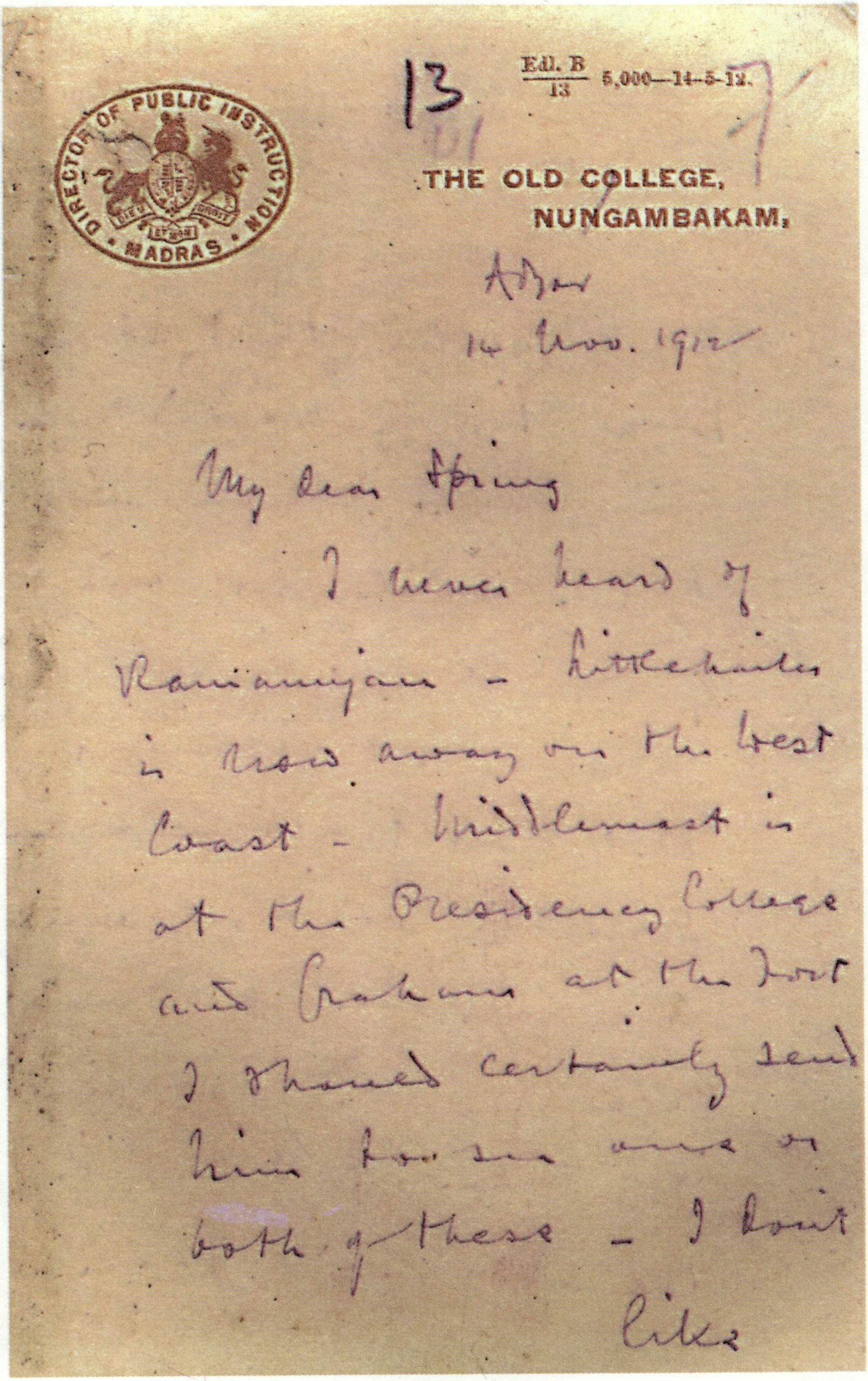

13

Edl. B / 13 5,000—14-5-12.

DIRECTOR OF PUBLIC INSTRUCTION • MADRAS •

THE OLD COLLEGE,
NUNGAMBAKAM,

Adyar
14 Nov. 1912

My dear Spring

I never heard of Ramanujan — Littlehailes is now away on the West Coast — Middlemast is at the Presidency College and Graham at the Fort

I should certainly send him to see one or both of these — I don't like

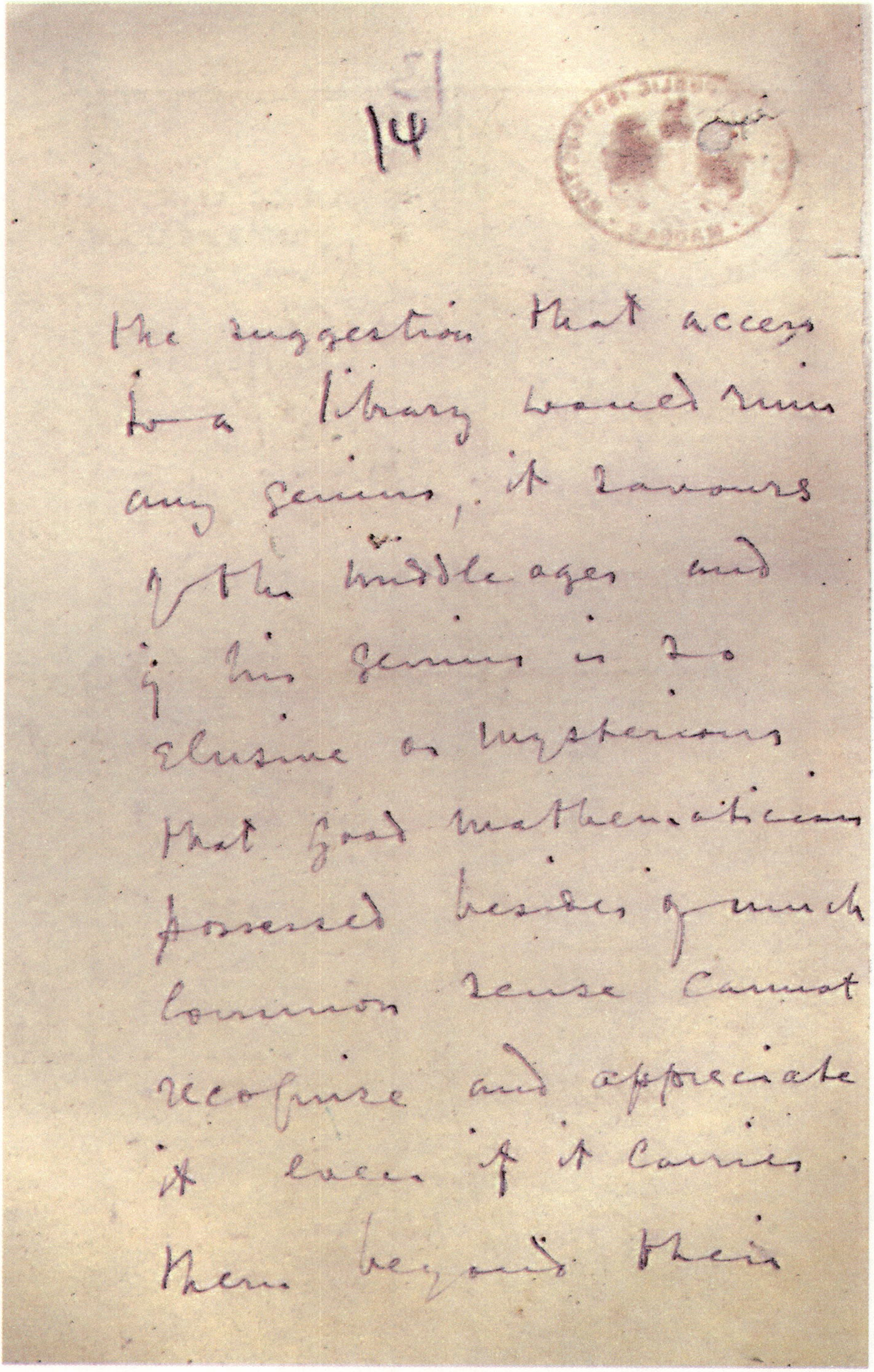
14

the suggestion that access to a library would ruin any genius, it savours of the middle ages and if his genius is so elusive or mysterious that good mathematicians possessed besides of much common sense cannot recognise and appreciate it even if it carries them beyond their

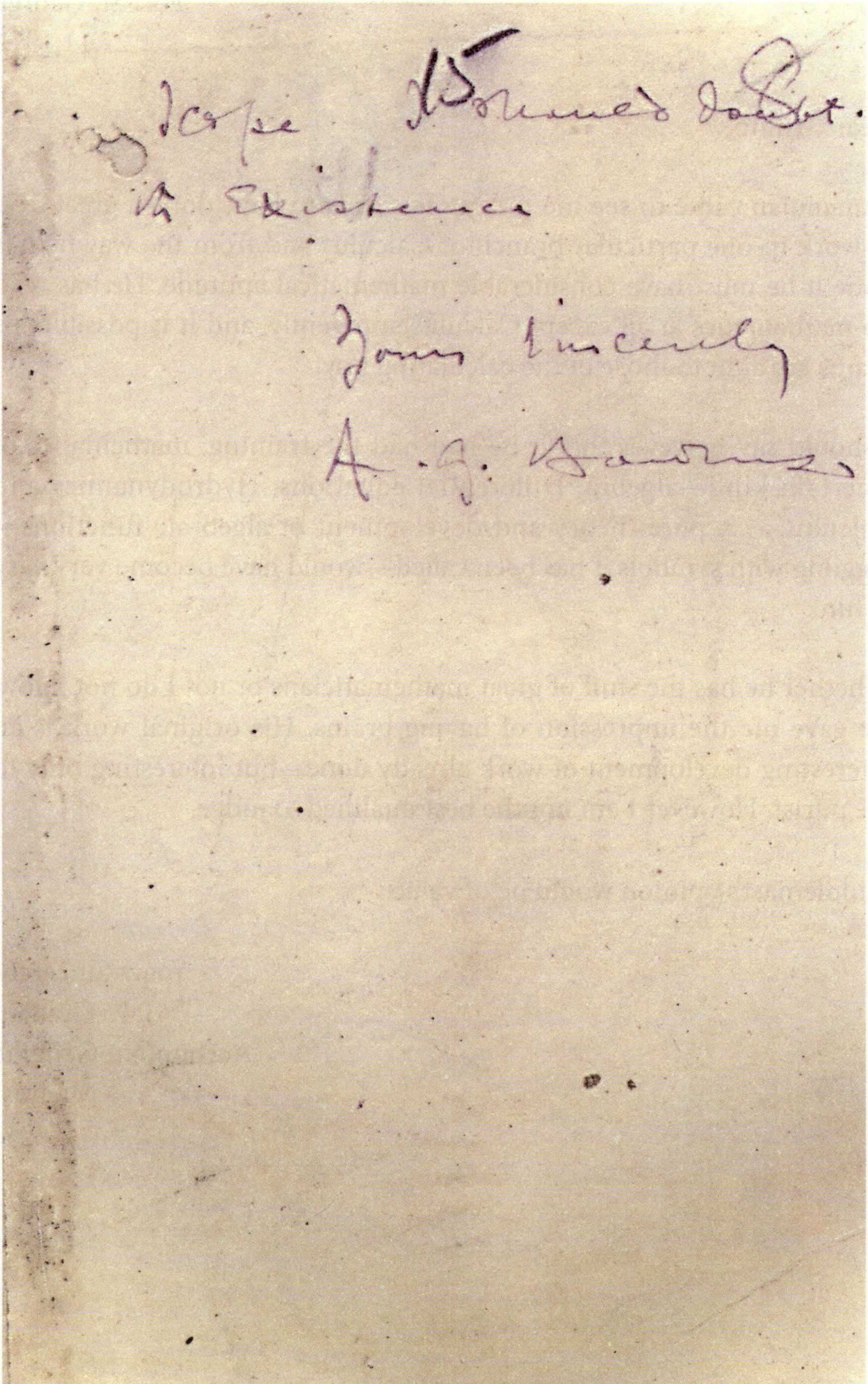

the Existence

Yours sincerely

Fort St. George
27.11.1912

Dear Griffith,

Ramanujan came to see me today. He seems to have done a great deal of work in one particular branch of Calculus and from the way he has done it he must have considerable mathematical aptitude. He has read no mathematics at all except Calculus apparently, and it is possible his brains are akin to those of the calculating boy!

I should say however that if he had had the training, mathematics of a certain kind—algebra, Differential equations, Hydrodynamics and Calculus—i.e. pure theory and development of algebraic functions—juggling with symbols it has been called—would have become very easy to him.

Whether he has the stuff of great mathematicians or not I do not know. He gave me the impression of having brains. His original work is an interesting development of work already done—but interesting only to the purist. However I am not the best qualified to judge.

Middlemast's opinion would be of value.

Yours Sincerely,
J. F. Graham
(Accountant General,
Madras)

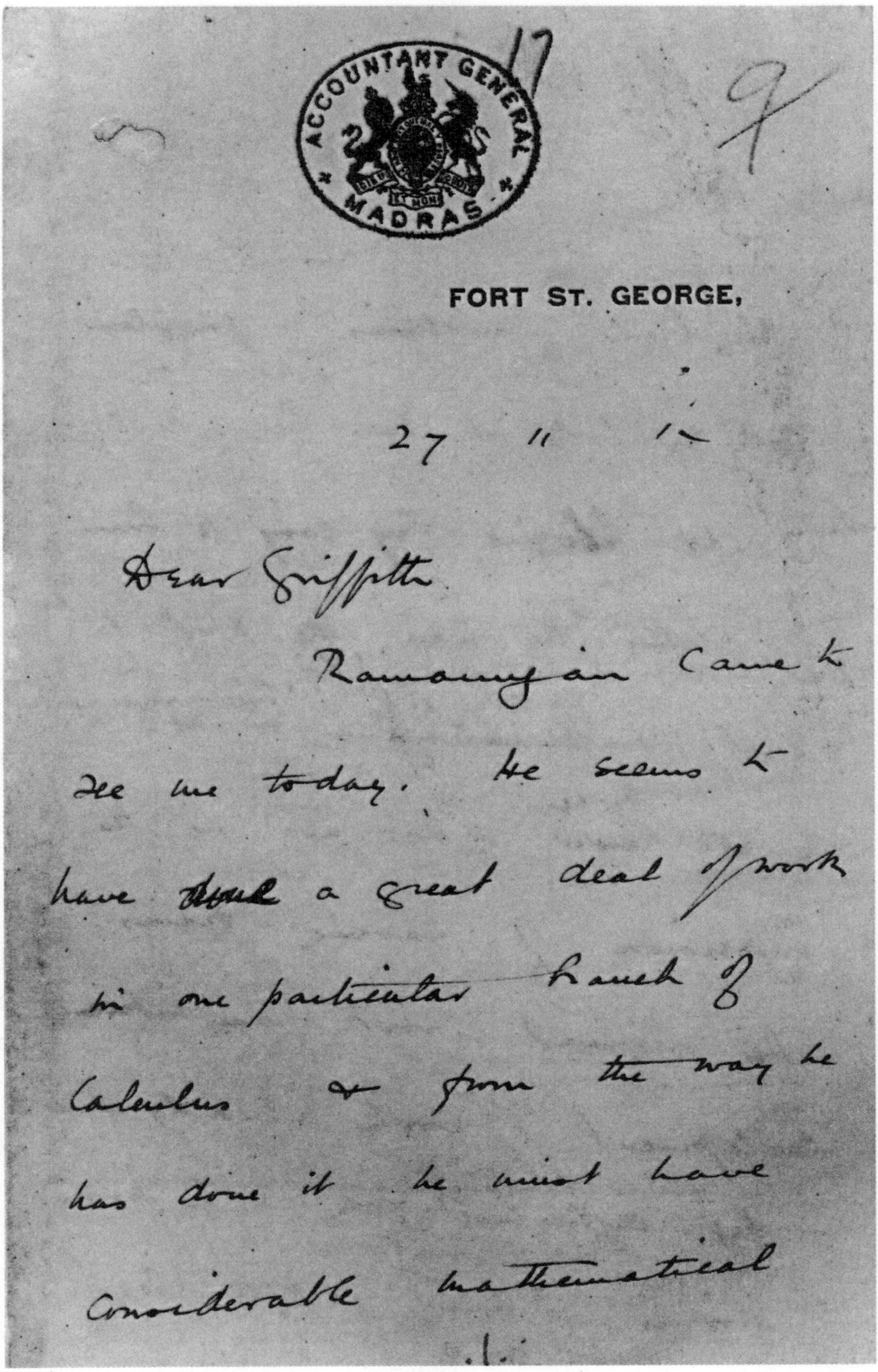

ACCOUNTANT GENERAL MADRAS

FORT ST. GEORGE,

27 11 12

Dear Griffith

Ramanujan came to see me today. He seems to have ~~done~~ a great deal of work in one particular branch of Calculus & from the way he has done it he must have considerable mathematical

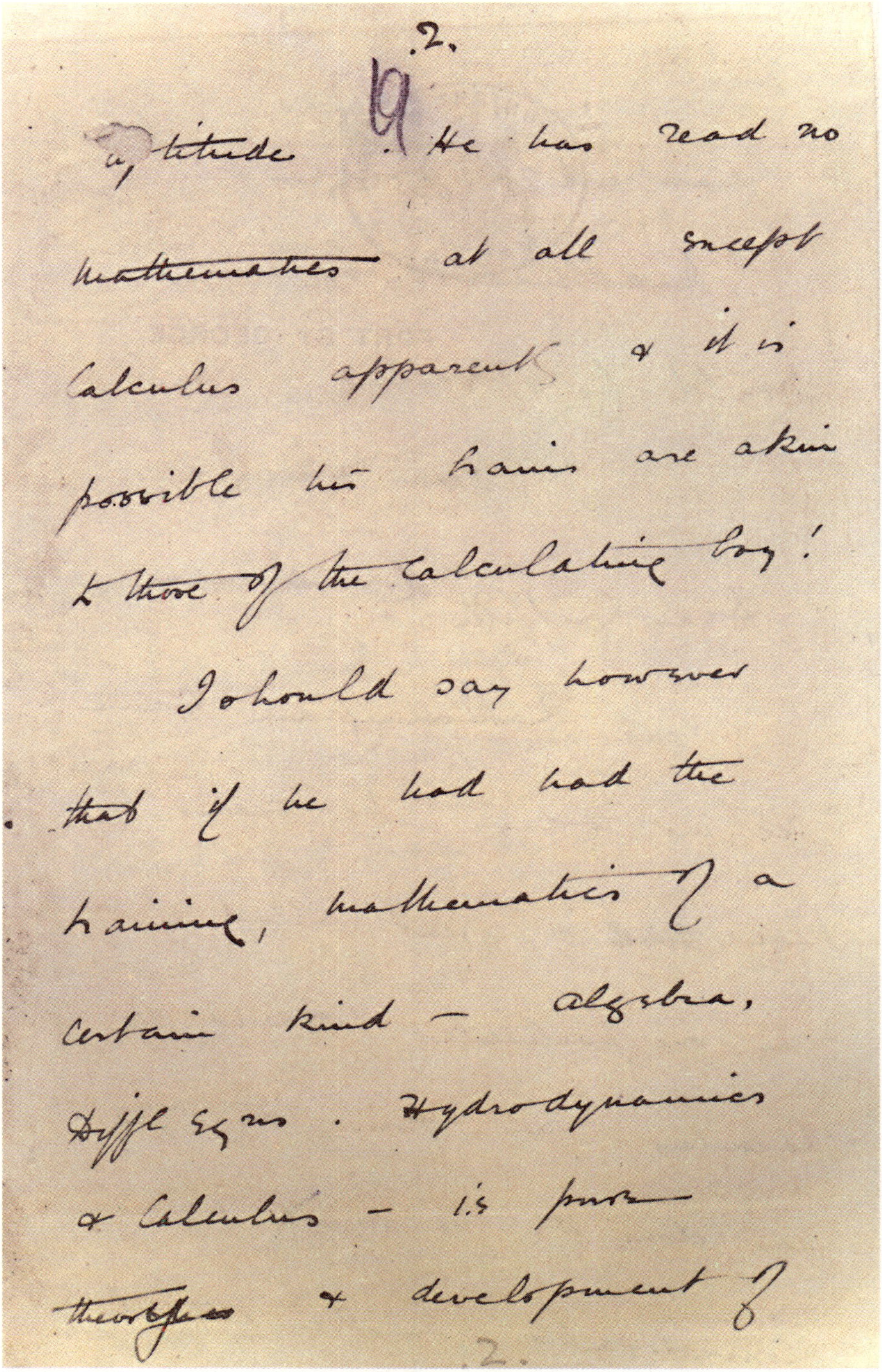

2.

19

aptitude. He has read no
mathematics at all except
Calculus apparently & it is
possible his brains are akin
to those of the calculating boy!

I should say however
that if he had had the
training, mathematics of a
certain kind — algebra,
Diffl Eqns. Hydrodynamics
& Calculus — i.e. pure
theory & development of

2.

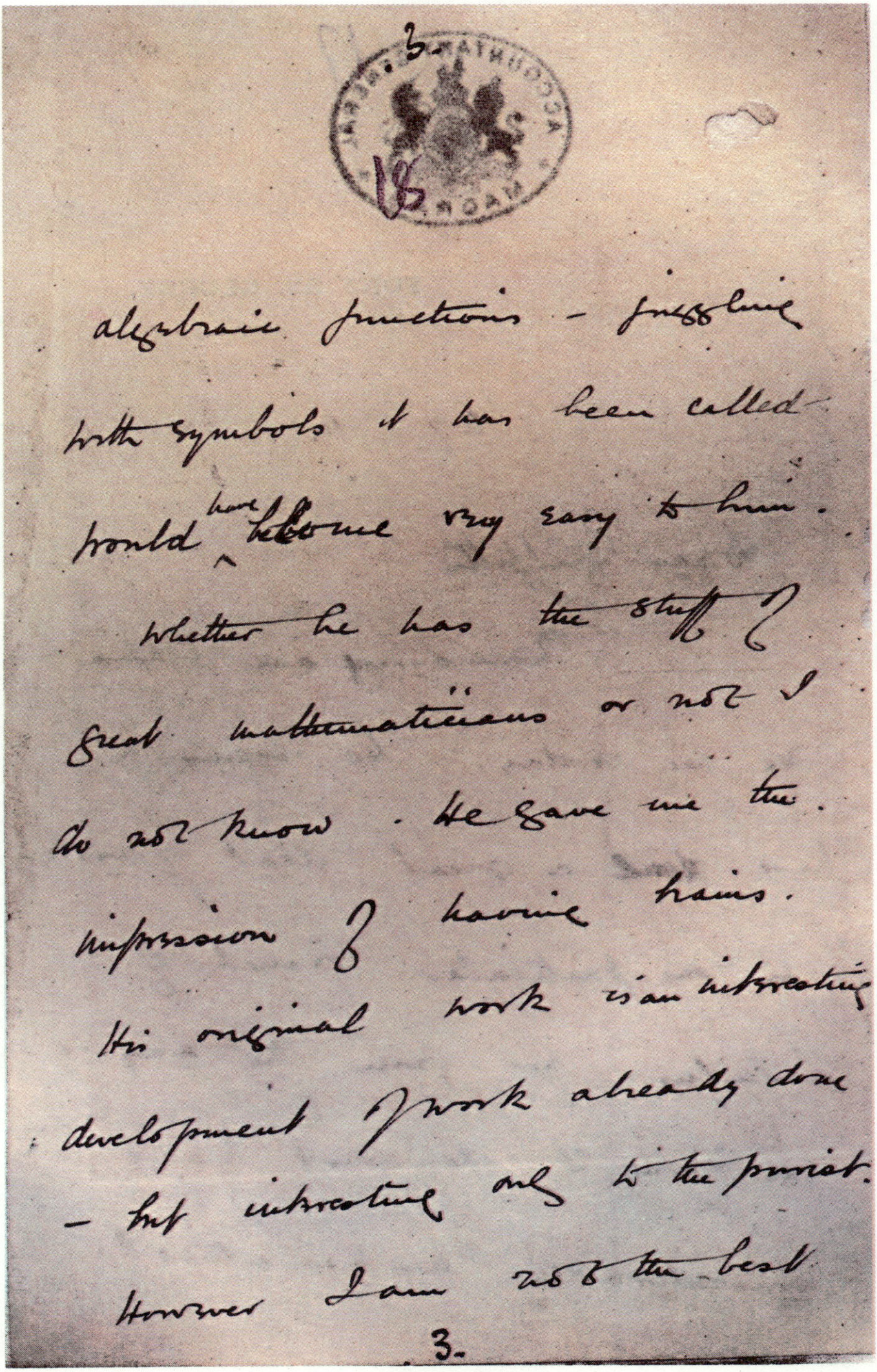

3.

algebraic functions — juggling
with symbols it has been called
would ^have ~~become~~ very easy to him.
Whether he has the stuff of
great mathematicians or not I
do not know. He gave me the
impression of having brains.
His original work is an interesting
development of work already done
— but interesting only to the purist.
However I am not the best

3.

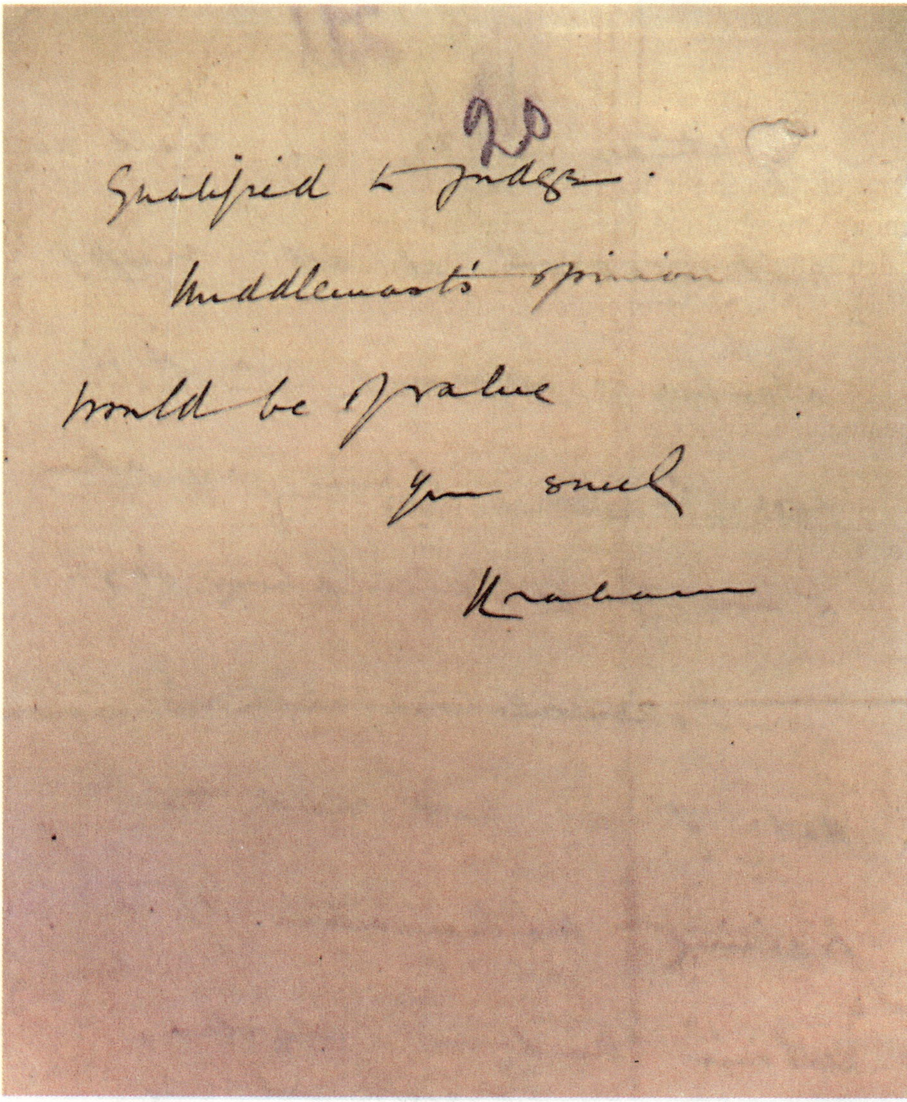

qualified to judge.
Middlemast's opinion
would be of value.
Yours sincerely

College of Engineering
28. 11. 1912

Dear Sir Francis,

I enclose the letter re Ramanujan, which Graham has been kind enough to send me. He says the man has brains, but may be of the calculating boy type: but like the other mathematicians here modestly disclaims the power of criticizing R.'s work.

R. seems to have seen Mr. Middlemast already & he, also, appears to be unable to criticize.

I think I was right in writing to Prof. Hill in London & we must wait for his opinions which I hope to get during January.

Yours Sincerely,
C.L.T. Griffith

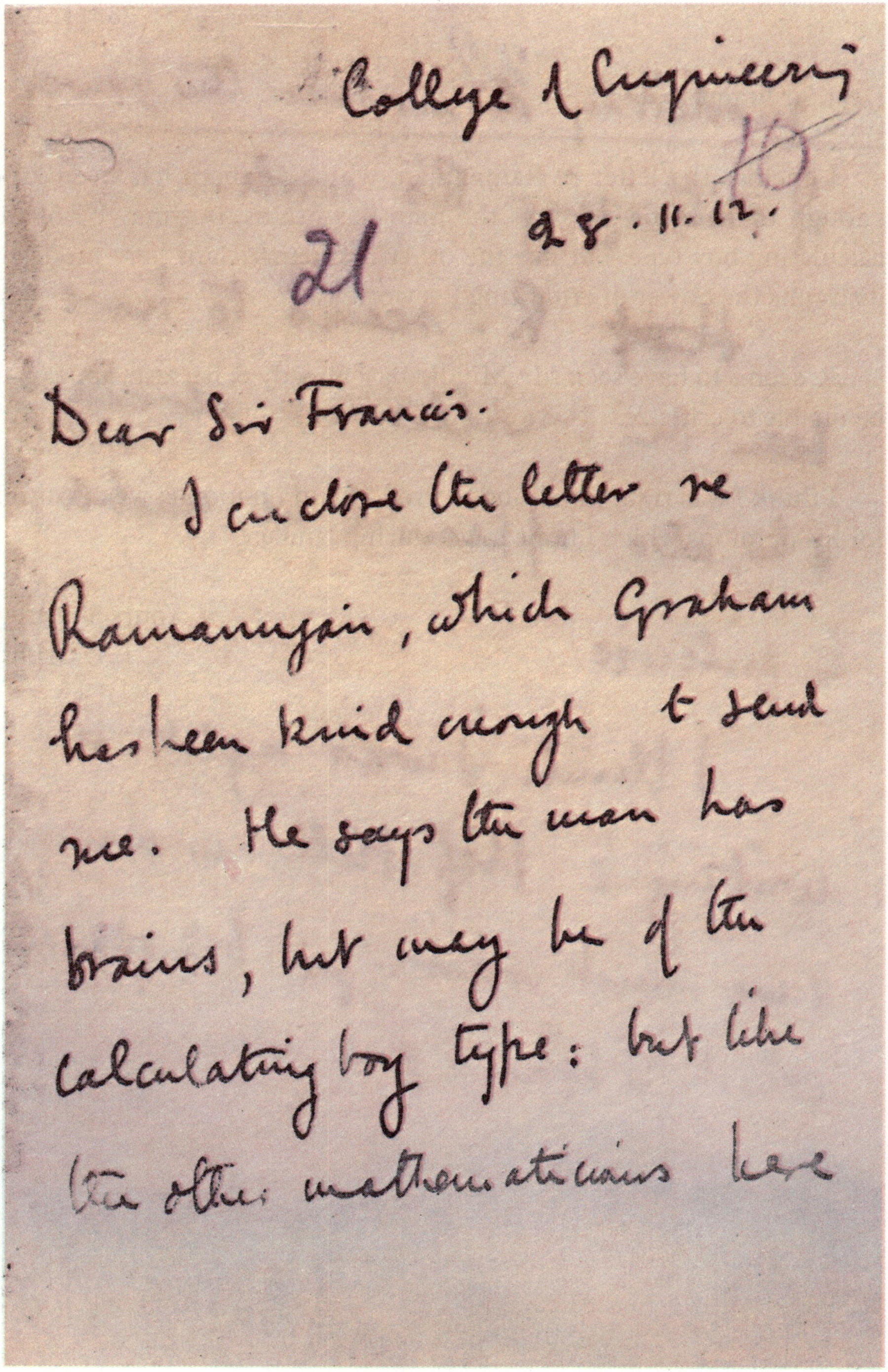

College of Engineering

10

21

28.11.12.

Dear Sir Francis.

I enclose the letter re Ramanujan, which Graham has been kind enough to send me. He says the man has brains, but may be of the calculating boy type: but like the other mathematicians here

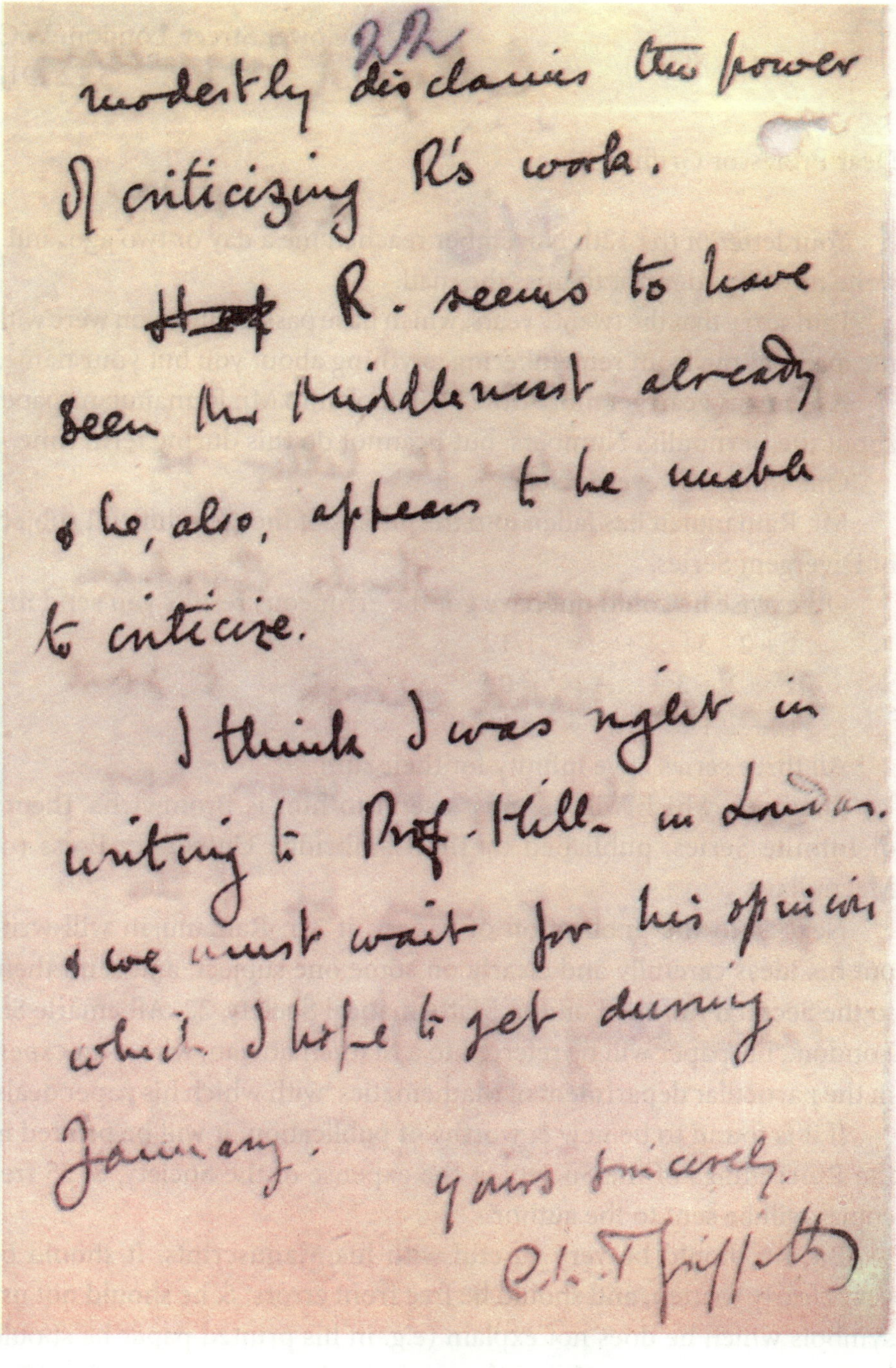

modestly disclaims the power of criticizing R's work.

R. seems to have seen the Middlemist already & he, also, appears to be unable to criticize.

I think I was right in writing to Prof. Hill in London & we must wait for his opinion which I hope to get during January.

Yours sincerely

C. T. Griffith

University of London, University College

Gower Street, London, W.C.
3.12.1912

Dear Professor Griffith,

Your letter of the 12th November reached me a day or two ago, and I write now in order not to miss the mail.

I am sorry that the twenty years, which have passed since you were with me, prevent me from remembering anything about you but your name.

As soon as I can get more time I will look into Mr. Ramanujan's paper about the Bernoulli's Numbers, but I cannot do this during term time.

One thing however is clear.

Mr. Ramanujan has fallen into the pitfalls of the very difficult subject of Divergent Series.

Otherwise he could not have got the erroneous results you send me

$1 + 2 + 3 + \ldots + \infty. = - 1/12$

$1^2 + 2^2 + 3^2 + \ldots. + \infty^2 = 0$

$1^3 + 2^3 + 3^3 + \ldots. + \infty^3 = 1/240$

All three series have infinity for their sum.

The book which will be most useful to him is Bromwich's Theory of Infinite Series, published by the Cambridge University Press (or Macmillan).

Next as to the publication of papers, if Mr. Ramanujan will write out his ideas carefully and clearly on some one subject, and send them to the Secretary of the London Mathematical Society, 22, Albemarle St., London., his paper will be referred to a Mathematician, who is an expert in the particular department of Mathematics, with which his paper deals.

If it is found to be new & worthy of publication, it will be printed in the Proceedings of the Society at the expense of the Society, & 25 free copies will be sent to the author.

But he should be very careful with his Manuscripts. It should be very clearly written, and should be free from errors; & he should not use symbols which he does not explain (e.g. in his printed paper he should have explained on page 1 that the symbols c1, c2, c3 ...mean; & § 12 to which he refers on p. 5 does not apparently exist). He passes from § 11 to §13. What you say about him personally is very interesting, and I hope something may come of his work.

I will write later when I have had more time to look into his paper.

I remain,

With Kind regards,
Yours Sincerely,
M. J. M. Hill

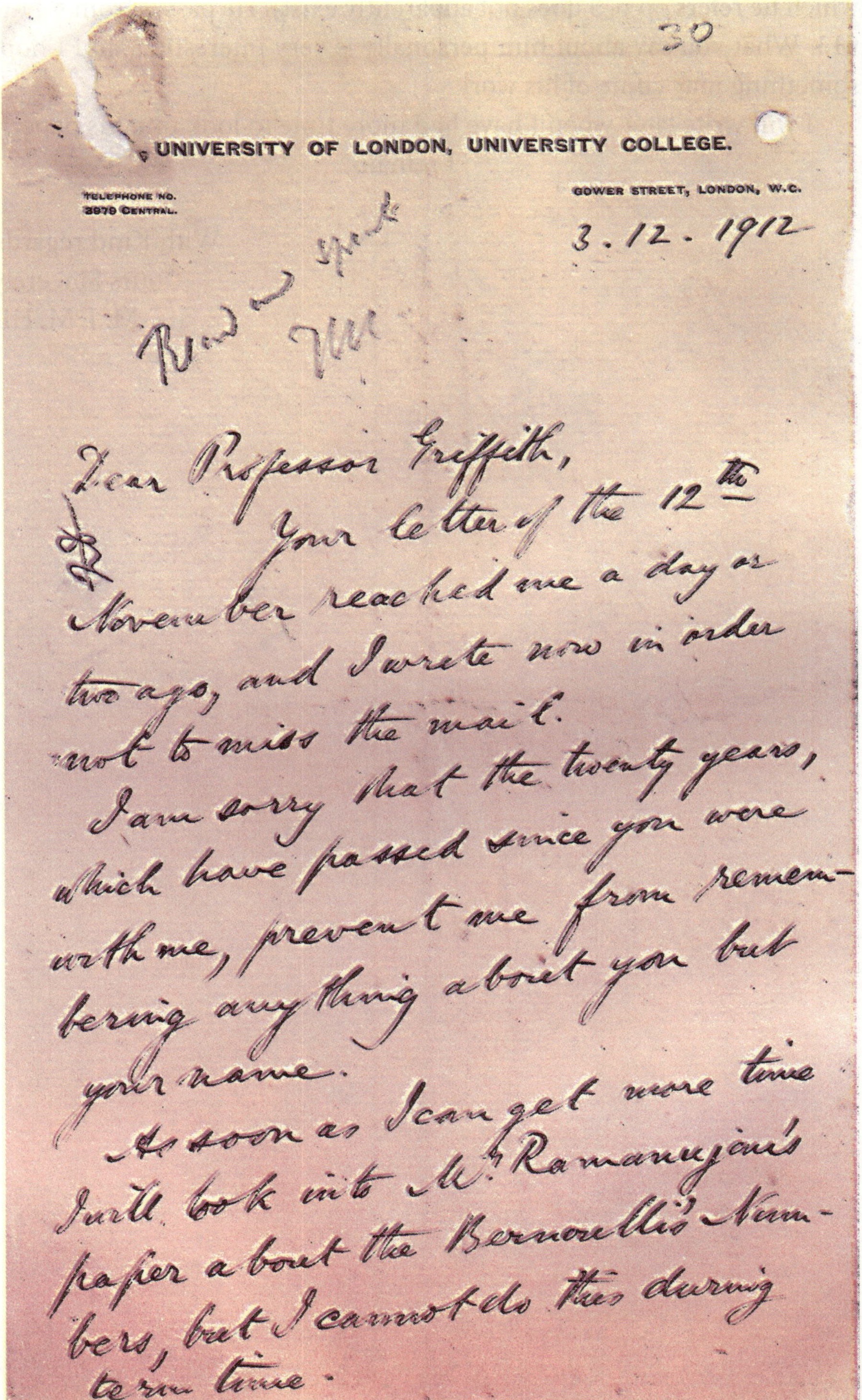

30

UNIVERSITY OF LONDON, UNIVERSITY COLLEGE.

TELEPHONE NO.
2879 CENTRAL.

GOWER STREET, LONDON, W.C.

3. 12. 1912

Dear Professor Griffith,
Your letter of the 12th
November reached me a day or
two ago, and I write now in order
not to miss the mail.
I am sorry that the twenty years,
which have passed since you were
with me, prevent me from remem-
bering anything about you but
your name.
As soon as I can get more time
I will look into Mr Ramanujan's
paper about the Bernoulli's Num-
bers, but I cannot do this during
term time.

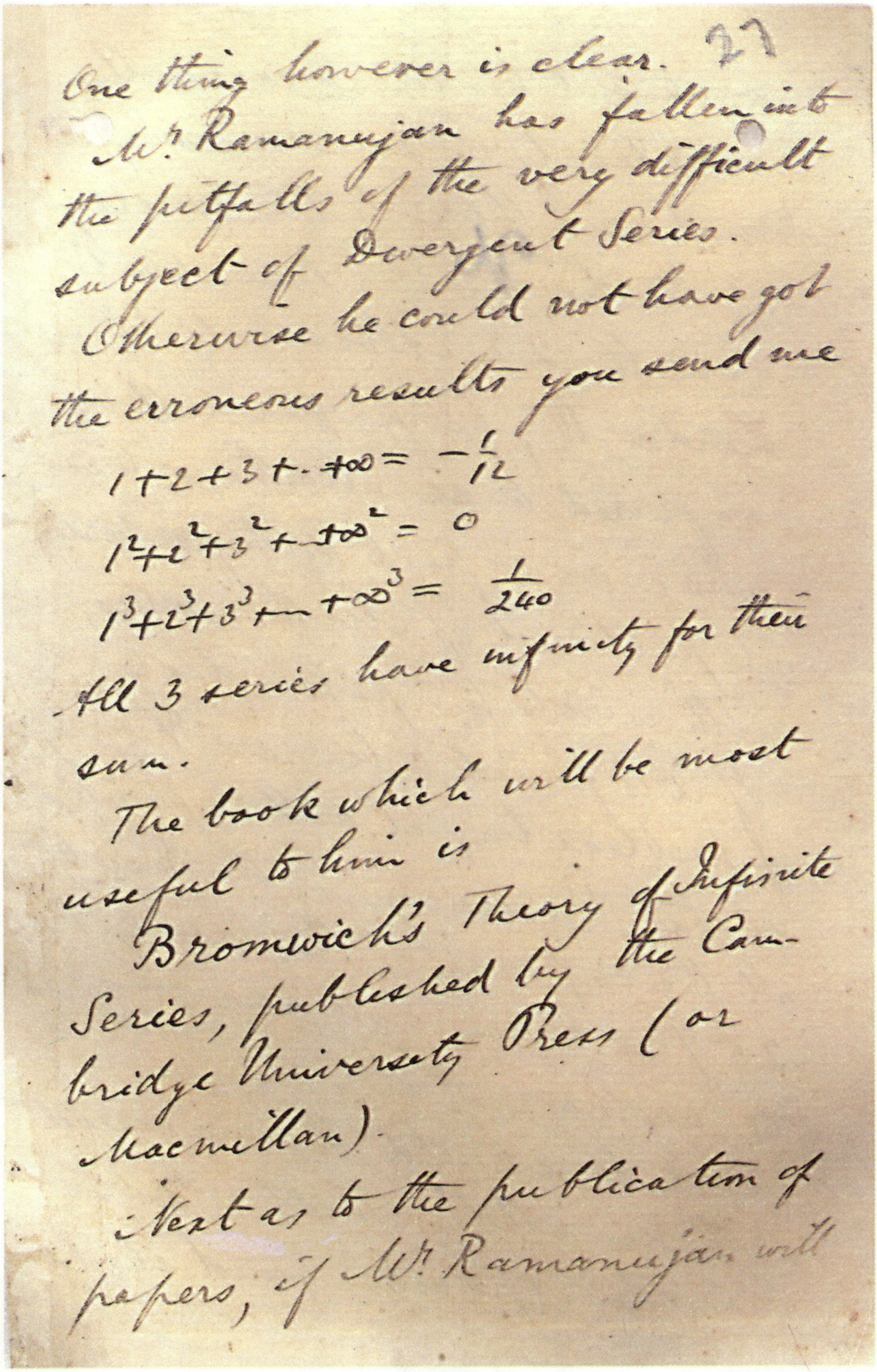

27

One thing however is clear.
Mr. Ramanujan has fallen into the pitfalls of the very difficult subject of Divergent Series. Otherwise he could not have got the erroneous results you send me

$$1+2+3+\ldots+\infty = -\frac{1}{12}$$

$$1^2+2^2+3^2+\ldots+\infty^2 = 0$$

$$1^3+2^3+3^3+\ldots+\infty^3 = \frac{1}{240}$$

All 3 series have infinity for their sum.

The book which will be most useful to him is Bromwich's Theory of Infinite Series, published by the Cambridge University Press (or Macmillan).

Next as to the publication of Mr. Ramanujan's papers, if Mr. Ramanujan will

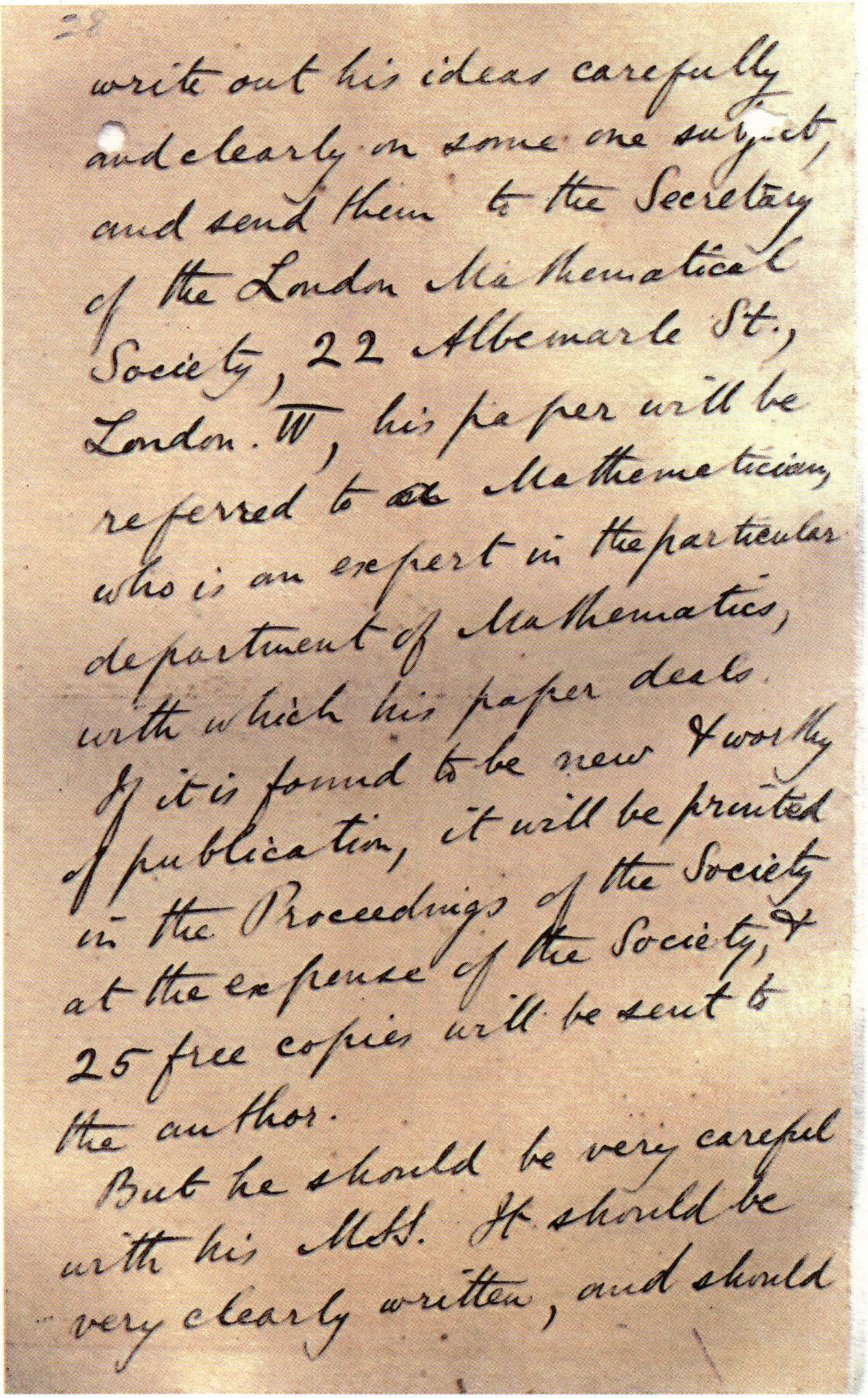

28

write out his ideas carefully
and clearly on some one subject,
and send them to the Secretary
of the London Mathematical
Society, 22 Albemarle St.,
London. W, his paper will be
referred to a Mathematician
who is an expert in the particular
department of Mathematics,
with which his paper deals.
If it is found to be new & worthy
of publication, it will be printed
in the Proceedings of the Society
at the expense of the Society, &
25 free copies will be sent to
the author.

But he should be very careful
with his MSS. It should be
very clearly written, and should

be free from errors; & he should not use symbols which he does not explain (e.g. in his printed paper he should have explained on page 1 what the symbols $c_1, c_2, c_3 \cdots$ mean; & § 12 to which he refers on p. 5 does not apparently exist). He passes from §11 to §13.

What you say about him personally is very interesting, and I hope something may come of his work.

I will write later when I have had more time to look into his paper.

I remain,
With kind regards,
Yours sincerely,
M. J. M. Hill

University of London, University College.

Gower Street, London, W. C.
7. 12. 1912

Dear Mr. Griffith,

I have been going through Mr. Ramanujan's paper to-day.

If you will look at formulae (14), (15), & (16) on pp 5-6 you will see that he refers in the footnote for their proofs to § 12 below.

He has omitted to mark §12, but I think it begins on p. 9 near the foot with the words

"Results (14) to (17), (20) & (21) can be got from the following result" –

This result he numbers (28). [It is not proved anywhere in the paper, and therefore a reference should have been given to the place from which it has been taken].

It does not however give him what he wants, for he says at the top of p. 10

"If we can prove the L. H. S. of (28) can be expanded in ascending powers of 1/x with integral coefficients, then (20) & (21) are at once deduced as follows" : -

But he gives as proof that he can effect the desired expansion. The same kind of thing occurs with regard to formula (16) in the first three lines of p. 11 and on the last four lines of the section which ends just above the commencement of §13 on p. 11, "From the above theorem.... of (16) is at once got."

He has in fact observed certain properties of the earlier Bernoulli numbers and assumed them to be true of them all without proof.

For these reasons I feel sure that the London Mathematical Society would not have accepted the paper for their Proceedings.

Mr. Ramanujan is evidently a man with a taste for Mathematics, and with some ability, but he has got on the wrong lines. He does not understand the precautions which have to be taken in dealing with divergent series, otherwise he could not have obtained the erroneous results you send me, viz: -

$1 + 2 + 3 + \ldots + \infty. = -1/12$

$1^2 + 2^2 + 3^2 + \ldots. + \infty^2 = 0$

$1^3 + 2^3 + 3^3 + \ldots. + \infty^3 = 1/240$

The sums of n terms of these series are ½ n (n+1), 1/3 n(n+1/2)(n+1), $[1/2n(n+1)]^2$ and they all tend to ∞ as n tends to ∞. I do not think you can do better for him than get him a copy of the book I recommended, Bromwich's Theory of Infinite Series, published by Macmillan & Co, who have branches in Calcutta and Bombay. Price 15'/£ net.

Chapter XI of this book on Non-Convergent and Asymptotic Series, will show him the difficulties to be studied in handling divergent series; and in other parts of the book, he will learn how to handle integrals with infinite limits in such a manner that they do not lead to paradoxical results.

When I was a student in Cambridge 1876-9, these things were not properly understood, and the modern theory has only recently been established on a firm basis.

Many illustrious mathematicians of earlier days stumbled over these difficulties, so it is not surprising that Mr. Ramanujan, working by himself, has obtained erroneous results. I hope he will not be discouraged.

If this book could be obtained for him, and he would work at it from the beginning, it would be much better for him than for those who are interested in him to spend money on printing his papers at the present time.

At the same time if he will write out what he has written on the exact values of the Elliptic Functions to which you refer in your letter, and which he mentioned when you showed him the British Association Report for 1911, I will go into the matter.

And I hope that after Mr. Ramanujan has read Mr. Bromwich's book he will be able to write something which will stand the test of modern criticism.

With Kind regards, I remain,

Yours Sincerely,
M. J. M. Hill
(Professor of Mathematics
University College, London.)

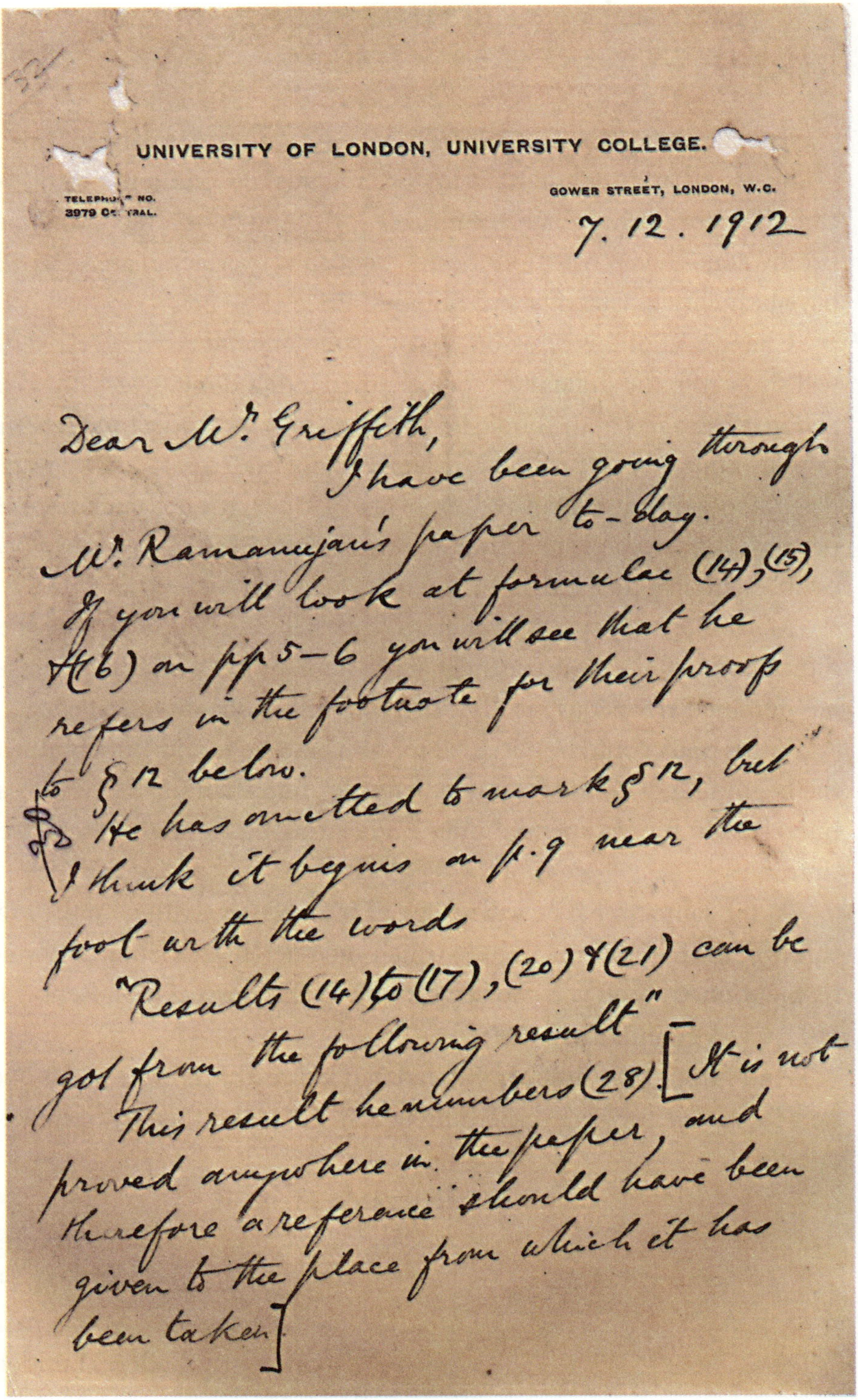

UNIVERSITY OF LONDON, UNIVERSITY COLLEGE.

TELEPHONE NO. 3979 CENTRAL.

GOWER STREET, LONDON, W.C.

7. 12. 1912

Dear Mr Griffith,

I have been going through Mr Ramanujan's paper to-day. If you will look at formulae (14), (15), & (6) on pp 5–6 you will see that he refers in the footnote for their proof to § 12 below.

He has omitted to mark § 12, but I think it begins on p. 9 near the foot with the words

"Results (14) to (17), (20) & (21) can be got from the following result"

This result he numbers (28). [It is not proved anywhere in the paper, and therefore a reference should have been given to the place from which it has been taken]

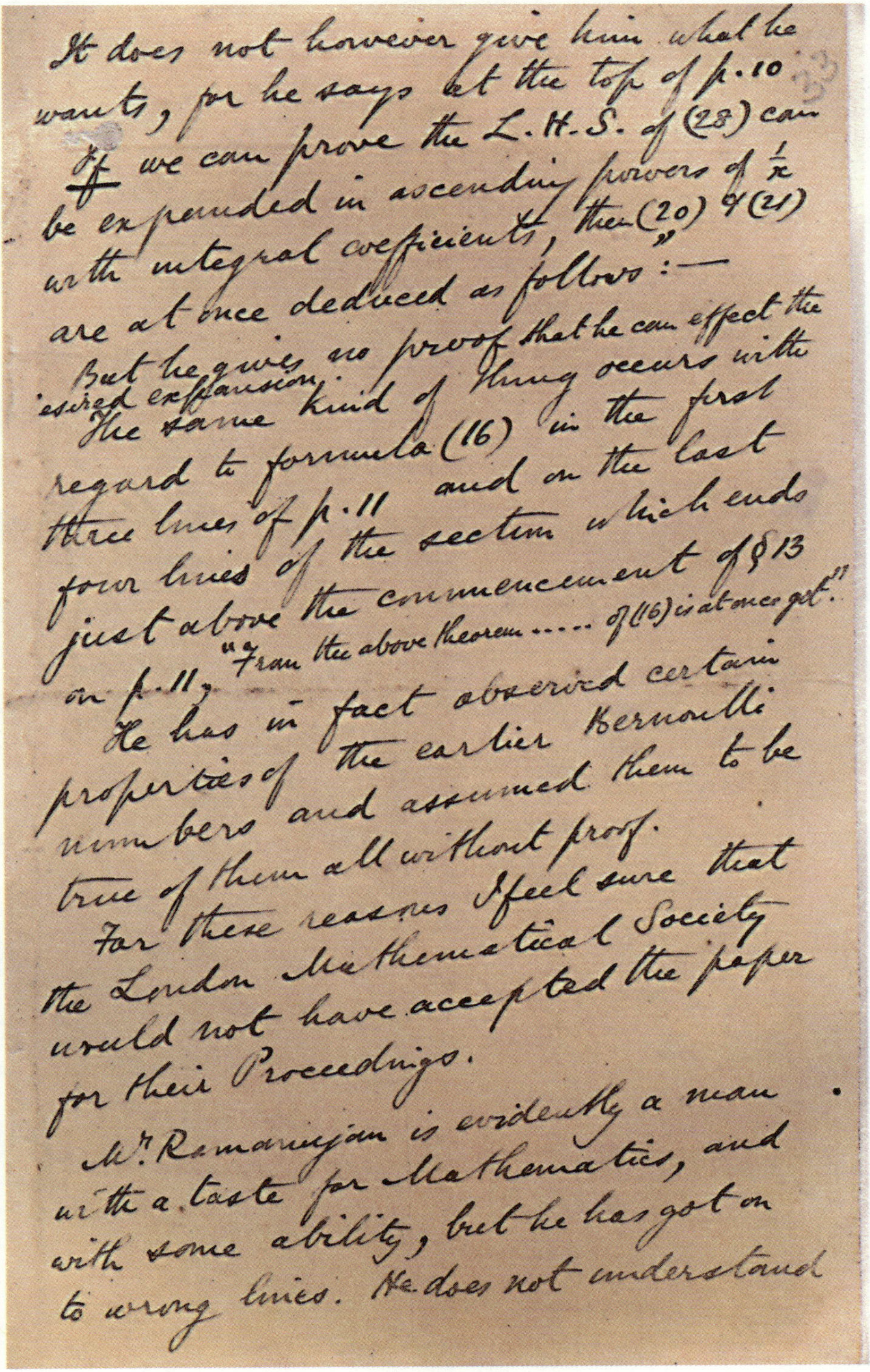

It does not however give him what he wants, for he says at the top of p. 10 "If we can prove the L.H.S. of (28) can be expanded in ascending powers of $\frac{1}{x}$ with integral coefficients, then (20) & (21) are at once deduced as follows:—"

But he gives no proof that he can effect the desired expansion.

The same kind of thing occurs with regard to formula (16) in the first three lines of p. 11 and on the last four lines of the section which ends just above the commencement of §13 on p. 11, "From the above theorem ..... of (16) is at once got."

He has in fact observed certain properties of the earlier Bernoulli numbers and assumed them to be true of them all without proof.

For these reasons I feel sure that the London Mathematical Society would not have accepted the paper for their Proceedings.

Mr. Ramanujan is evidently a man with a taste for Mathematics, and with some ability, but he has got on to wrong lines. He does not understand

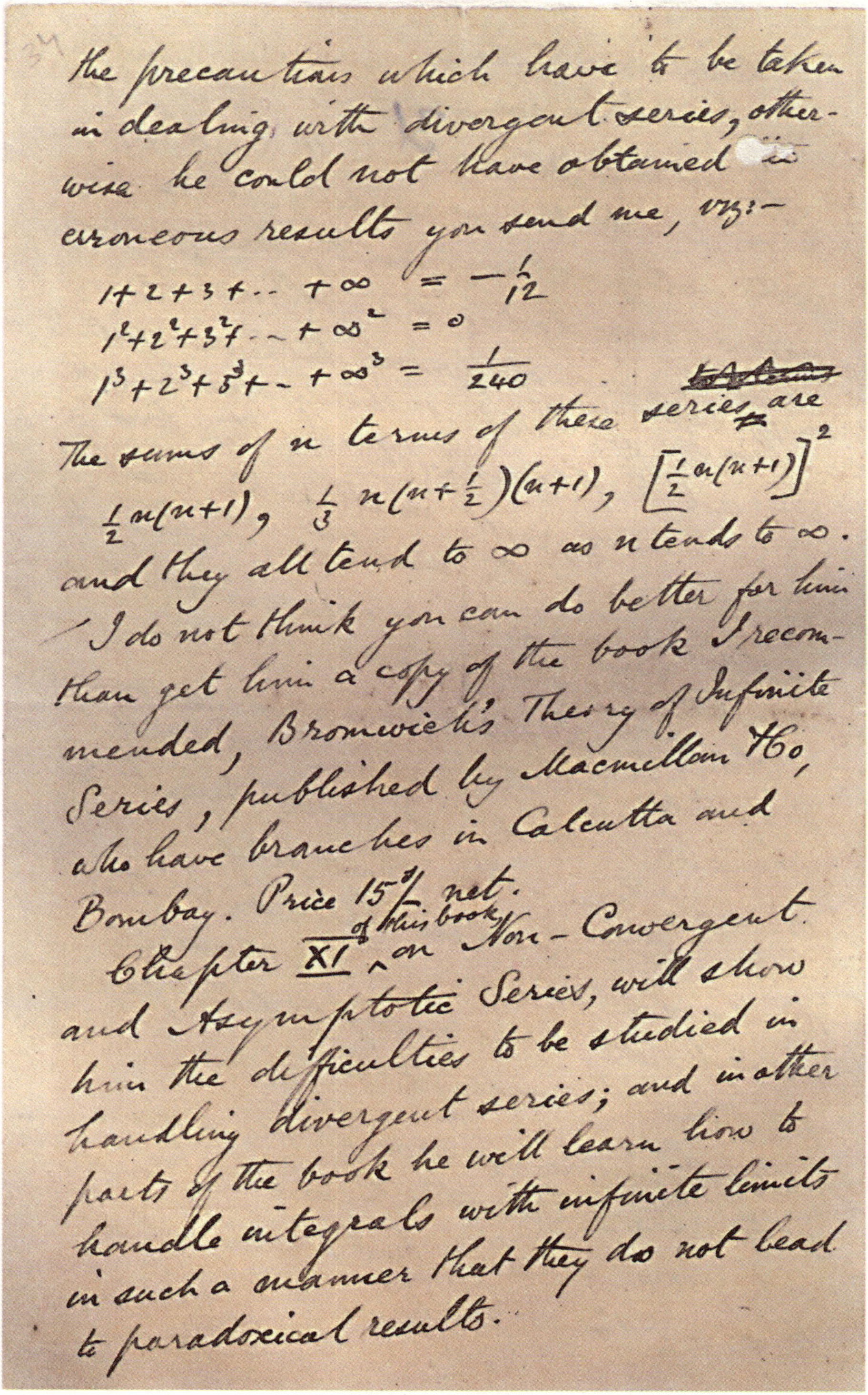

the precautions which have to be taken in dealing with divergent series, otherwise he could not have obtained the erroneous results you send me, viz:—

$$1+2+3+\dots+\infty = -\frac{1}{12}$$

$$1^2+2^2+3^2+\dots+\infty^2 = 0$$

$$1^3+2^3+3^3+\dots+\infty^3 = \frac{1}{240}.$$

The sums of n terms of these series are

$$\tfrac{1}{2}n(n+1), \quad \tfrac{1}{3}n(n+\tfrac{1}{2})(n+1), \quad \left[\tfrac{1}{2}n(n+1)\right]^2$$

and they all tend to ∞ as n tends to ∞.

I do not think you can do better for him than get him a copy of the book I recommended, Bromwich's Theory of Infinite Series, published by Macmillan & Co, who have branches in Calcutta and Bombay. Price 15/- net.

Chapter XI of this book, on Non-Convergent and Asymptotic Series, will show him the difficulties to be studied in handling divergent series; and in other parts of the book he will learn how to handle integrals with infinite limits in such a manner that they do not lead to paradoxical results.

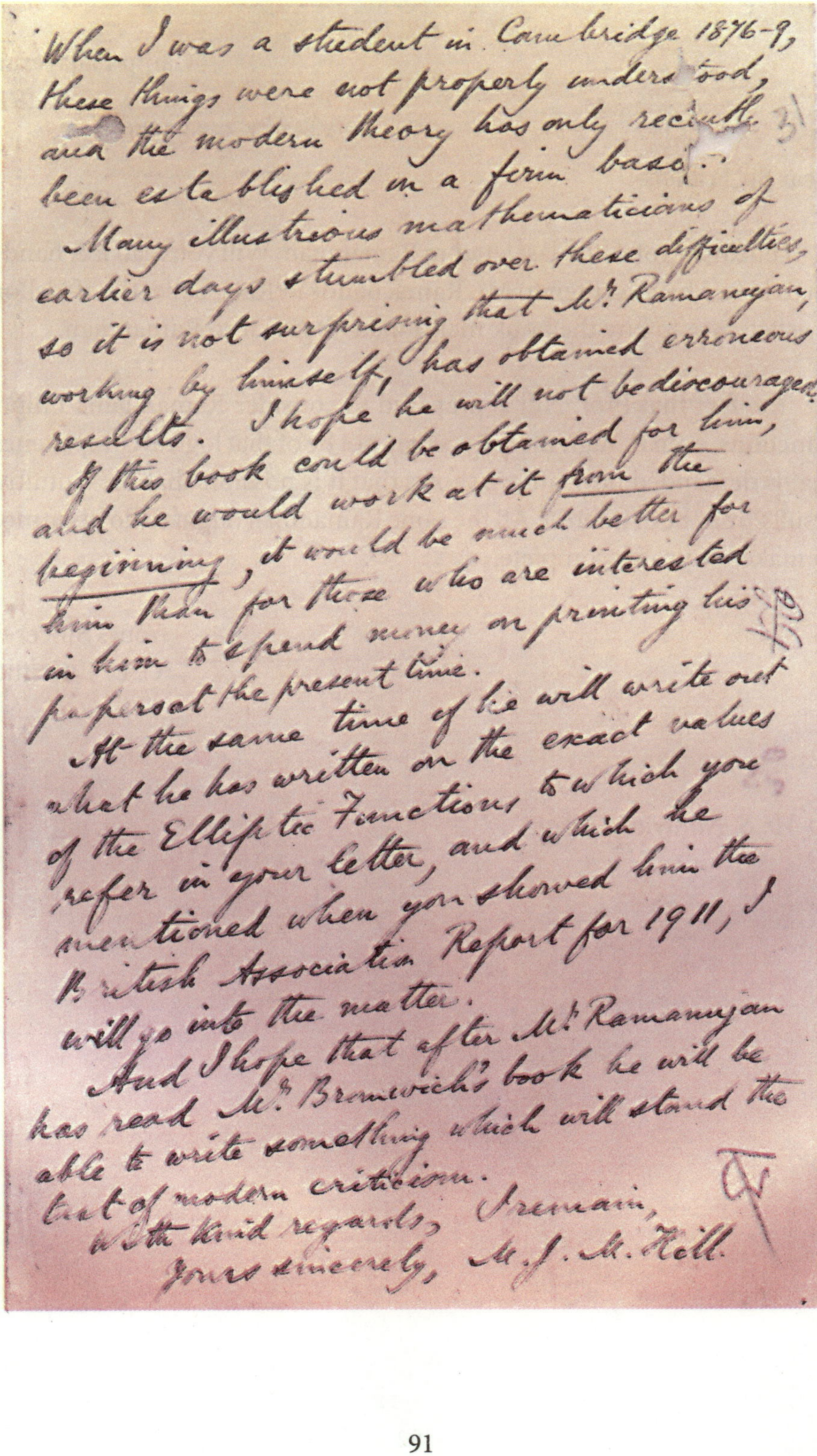

When I was a student in Cambridge 1876-9, these things were not properly understood, and the modern theory has only recently been established on a firm basis.

Many illustrious mathematicians of earlier days stumbled over these difficulties, so it is not surprising that Mr Ramanujan, working by himself, has obtained erroneous results. I hope he will not be discouraged.

If this book could be obtained for him, and he would work at it from the beginning, it would be much better for him than for those who are interested in him to spend money on printing his papers at the present time.

At the same time if he will write out what he has written on the exact values of the Elliptic Functions, to which you refer in your letter, and which he mentioned when you showed him the British Association Report for 1911, I will go into the matter.

And I hope that after Mr Ramanujan has read Mr Bromwich's book he will be able to write something which will stand the test of modern criticism.

With kind regards, I remain,

Yours sincerely, M. J. M. Hill.

Camp Pallaverain
5. 1. 1913

Dear Sir Francis.

I enclose Prof. Hills' last letter re Ramanujan. Will you read it & hand it on to him. I have written to Mr. Ramachandran Rao, Collector of Nellore & asked him to buy the book mentioned, & give it to Ramanujan.

The fact that Prof. Hill is prepared to consider Ramanujan's Elliptic Functions, even though the proofs may not be of that logical completeness that is demanded now-a-days shows that it is possible that the "intuitive results" may be of interest. All the same Ramanujan ought to do his utmost to make his proofs complete.

Yours Sincerely
C. L. T. Griffith

To Mr. S. Narayana Aiyar

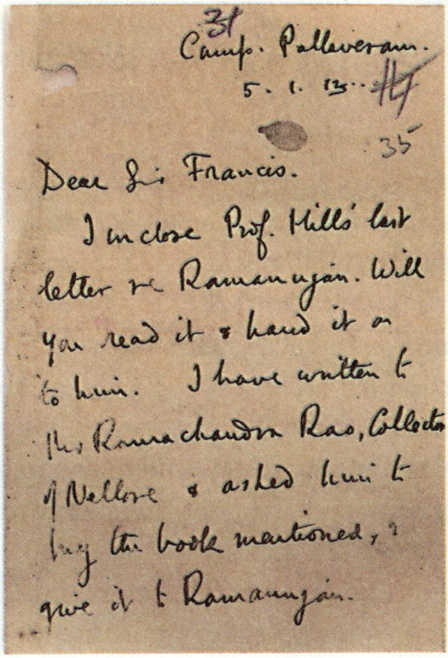

Camp. Pallaveram.
5. 1. 13.

Dear Sir Francis.

I enclose Prof. Hill's last letter re Ramanujan. Will you read it & hand it on to him. I have written to Mr Ramachandra Rao, Collector of Nellore & asked him to buy the books mentioned, & give it to Ramanujan.

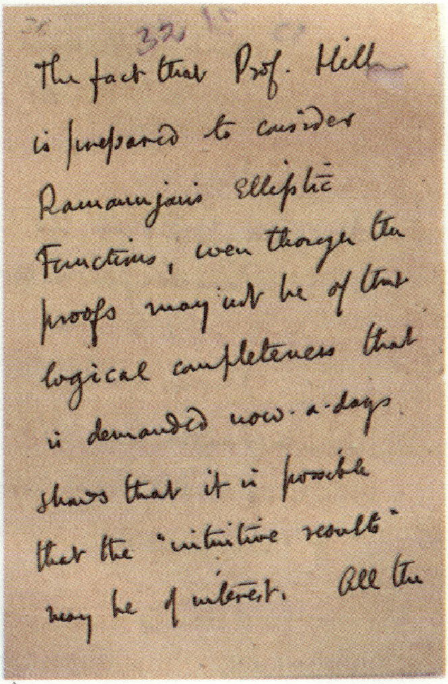

The fact that Prof. Hill is prepared to consider Ramanujan's Elliptic Functions, even though the proofs may not be of that logical completeness that is demanded now-a-days shows that it is possible that the "intuitive results" may be of interest. All the

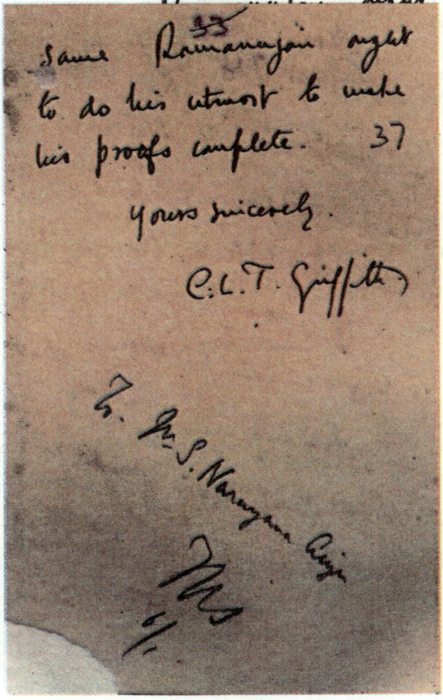

same Ramanujan ought to do his utmost to make his proofs complete.

Yours sincerely.

C.L.T. Griffith.

To Mr S. Narayana Aiyar

Z

G. H. Hardy to S. Ramanujan

Trinity College
Cambridge
8 February 1913

Dear Sir,

I was exceedingly interested by your letter and by the theorems which you state. You will however understand that, before I can judge properly of the value of what you have done, it is essential that I should see proofs of some of your assertions.

Your results seem to me to fall into roughly 3 classes:

(1) there are a number of results which are already known, or are easily deducible from known theorems;

(2) there are results which, so far as I know, are new and interesting, but interesting rather from their curiosity and apparent difficulty than their importance;

(3) there are results which appear to be new and important, but in which almost everything depends on the precise rigour of the methods of proof which you have used.

As instances of thesc 3 classes I may mention

(1) (a) the formula

$$\frac{\log 1}{\sqrt{1}} - \frac{\log 3}{\sqrt{3}} + \cdots$$
$$= \left(\frac{\pi}{4} - \frac{\gamma}{2} - \frac{1}{2}\log 2\pi\right)\left(\frac{1}{\sqrt{1}} - \frac{1}{\sqrt{3}} + \cdots\right)$$

(easily deducible from a known theorem about $1^{-3}-3^{-3}+5^{-3}+\ldots$, which is to be found, e.g. in Bromwich's Infinite Series),

(b) if $\alpha\beta = \pi$

$$\sqrt{\alpha}\int_0^\infty \frac{e^{-x^2}}{\cosh \alpha x}dx = \text{ etc.}$$

(this I proved myself in a paper in the Quarterly Journal of Math.),

(c) some at any rate of your theorems about B_n, in your printed paper,

(d) $1^2 \log 1 + 2^2 \log 2 + \ldots + x^2 \log x = \text{etc.}$

(a special case of the 'Euler-Maclaurin formula', given e.g. in Bromwich),

(e) I think your expression of $\int_0^a e^{-x^2} dx$ as a continued fraction,

(f) I think a number of your special results on series

(e.g. $\frac{1^{13}}{e^{2\pi}-1}+\cdots=\frac{1}{24}$.

I fancy this is not hard to prove by Cauchy's Theory of Residues).

I need not say that, if what you say about your lack of training is to be taken literally, the fact that you should have rediscovered such interesting results is all to your credit. But you must be prepared for a certain amount of disappointment of this kind.

There are also of course known theories of divergent series, fractional orders of differentiation and integration, and so on. I should be extremely interested to compare your theories with these.

In this class also come some of your theorems about numbers. Thus the formula you give for the sum of all the divisors of all numbers < n is known; and so is your formula $K\int_0^x \frac{dx}{\sqrt{\log x}} + \text{etc.}$ for the number of numbers of the form $p^2 + q^2$.

But I want particularly to see your proofs of your assertions here. You will understand that, in this theory, everything depends on rigorous exactitude of proof.

I should add that theorems of this character are not only interesting, but very difficult and important. If you have made sound and independent proofs of them, it would be, in my opinion, a very remarkable achievement. They are much more noteworthy theorems than those on p. 3.

(3) In this class I should put (assuming the proofs to be rigorous) some of your theorems about prime numbers–e.g. the expression you say you have for the number of primes <x, which is so nearly exact.

It is of course possible that some of the results I have classed under (2) are really important, as examples of general methods. You always state your results in such particular forms that it is difficult to be sure about this.

I hope very much that you will send me as quickly as possible at any rate a few of your proofs, and follow this more at your leisure by a more detailed account of your work on primes and divergent series. It seems to me quite likely that you have done a good deal of work worth publication; and, if you can produce satisfactory demonstrations, I should be very glad to do what I can to secure it.

I have said nothing about some of your results-notably those about elliptic functions. I have not got them to refer to, as I handed them to another mathematician more expert than I in this special subject.

Hoping to hear from you again as soon as possible.

I am

Yours very truly,

G.H. Hardy

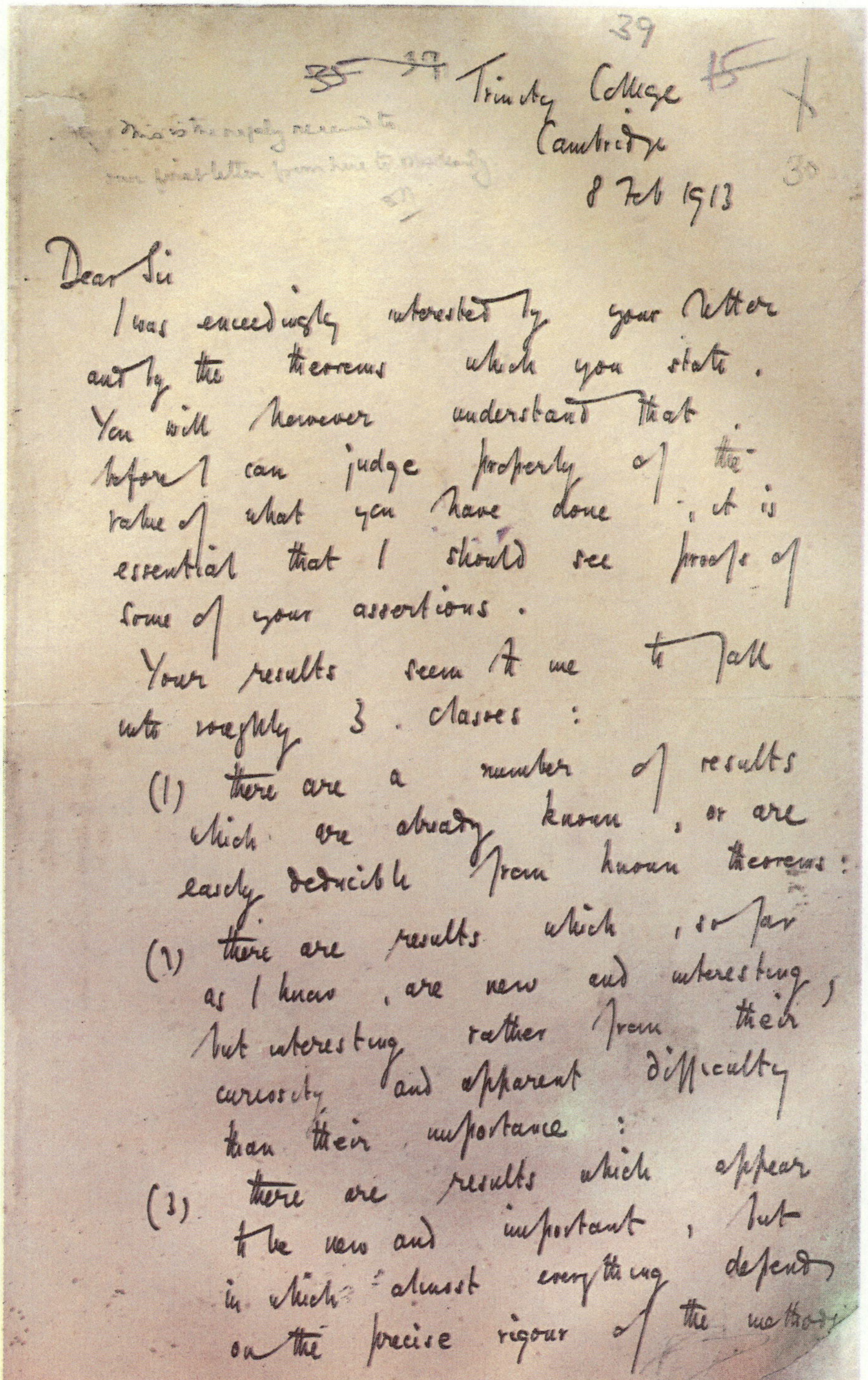

Trinity College
Cambridge
8 Feb 1913

Dear Sir

I was exceedingly interested by your letter and by the theorems which you state. You will however understand that, before I can judge properly of the value of what you have done, it is essential that I should see proofs of some of your assertions.

Your results seem to me to fall into roughly 3 classes:

(1) there are a number of results which are already known, or are easily deducible from known theorems;

(2) there are results which, so far as I know, are new and interesting, but interesting rather from their curiosity and apparent difficulty than their importance;

(3) there are results which appear to be new and important, but in which almost everything depends on the precise rigour of the methods

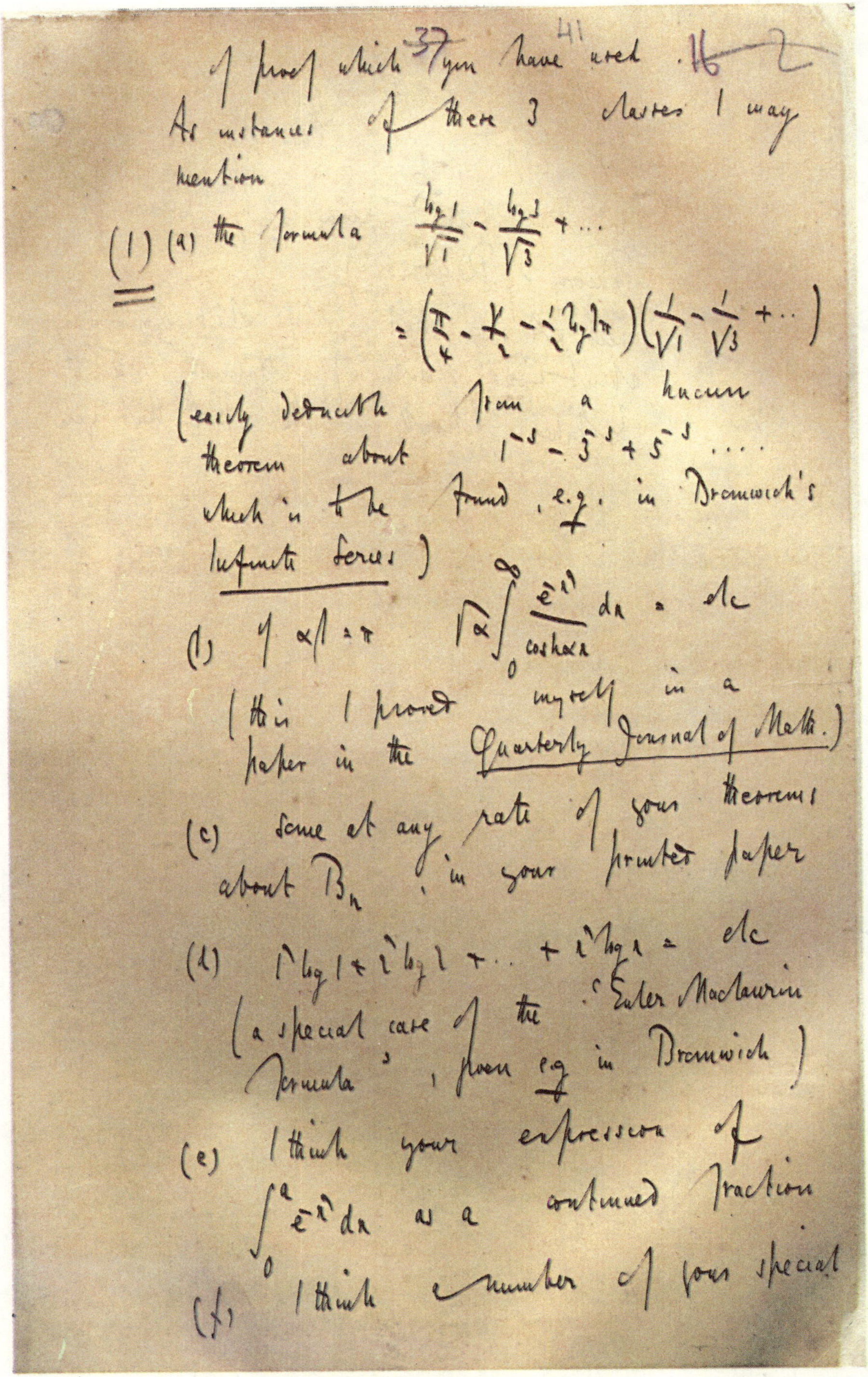

of proof which you have used.

As instances of these 3 classes I may mention

(1) (a) the formula $\frac{\log 1}{\sqrt{1}} - \frac{\log 3}{\sqrt{3}} + \dots$

$$= \left(\frac{\pi}{4} - \frac{\gamma}{2} - \frac{1}{2}\log 2\pi\right)\left(\frac{1}{\sqrt{1}} - \frac{1}{\sqrt{3}} + \dots\right)$$

(easily deducible from a known theorem about $1^{-s} - 3^{-s} + 5^{-s} \dots$ which is to be found, e.g. in Bromwich's Infinite Series)

(b) If $\alpha\beta = \pi$ $\sqrt{\alpha}\int_0^\infty \frac{e^{-x^2}}{\cosh \alpha x}dx =$ etc

(This I proved myself in a paper in the Quarterly Journal of Math.)

(c) some at any rate of your theorems about B_n in your printed paper

(d) $1^2 \log 1 + 2^2 \log 2 + \dots + n^2 \log n =$ etc (a special case of the 'Euler Maclaurin sum formula', proved e.g. in Bromwich)

(e) I think your expression of $\int_0^a e^{-x^2}dx$ as a continued fraction.

(f) I think a number of your special

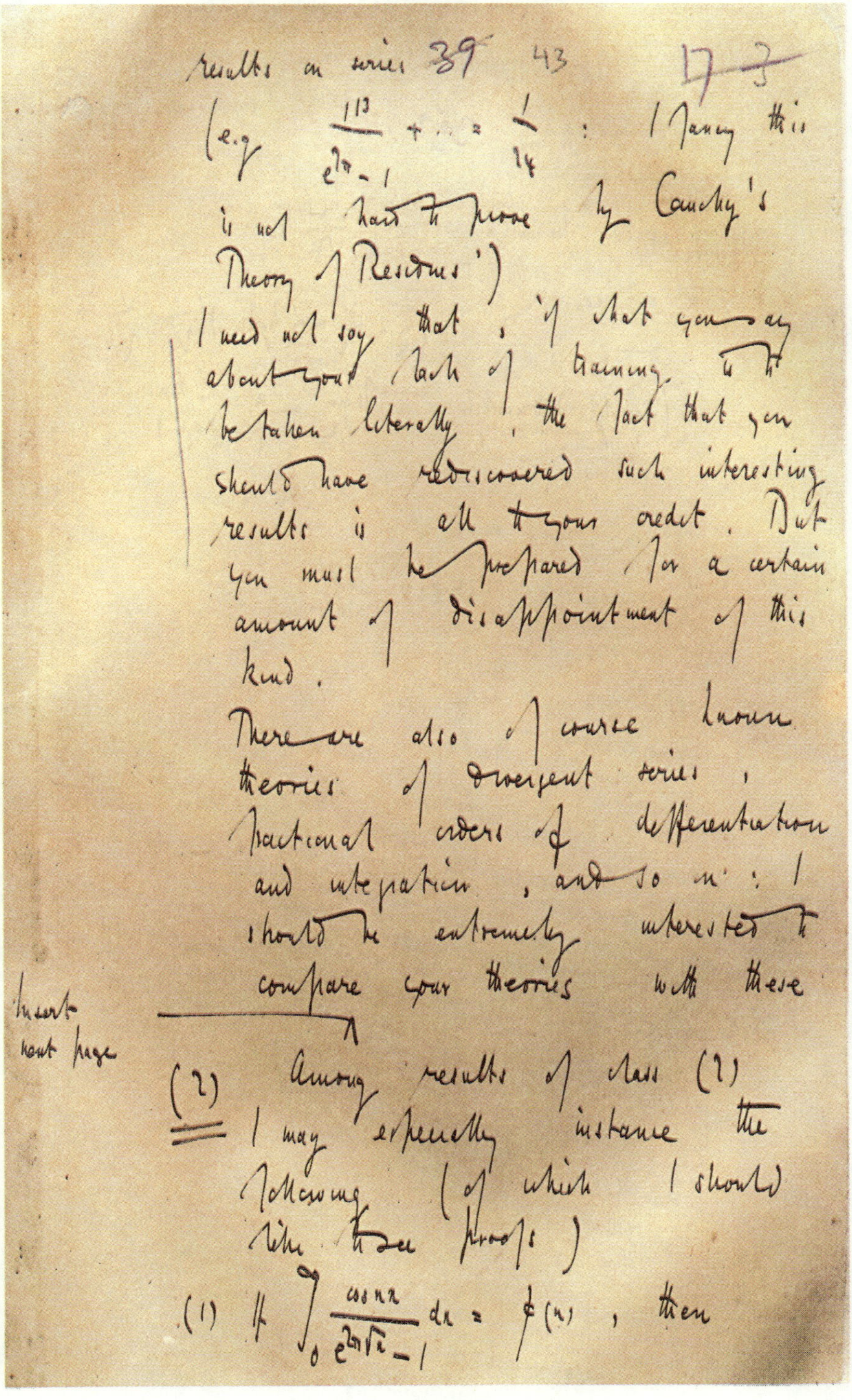

results on series ~~39~~ 43 17 ~~3~~

(e.g. $\frac{1^{13}}{e^{2\pi}-1}+\dots=\frac{1}{24}$: I fancy this is not hard to prove by Cauchy's Theory of Residues')

I need not say that, if what you say about your lack of training is to be taken literally, the fact that you should have rediscovered such interesting results is all to your credit. But you must be prepared for a certain amount of disappointment of this kind.

There are also of course known theories of divergent series, fractional orders of differentiation and integration, and so on: I should be extremely interested to compare your theories with these

Insert next page

(2) Among results of class (2) I may especially instance the following (of which I should like to see proofs)

(1) If $\int_0 \frac{\cos nx}{e^{2\pi\sqrt{x}}-1}dx = \phi(n)$, then

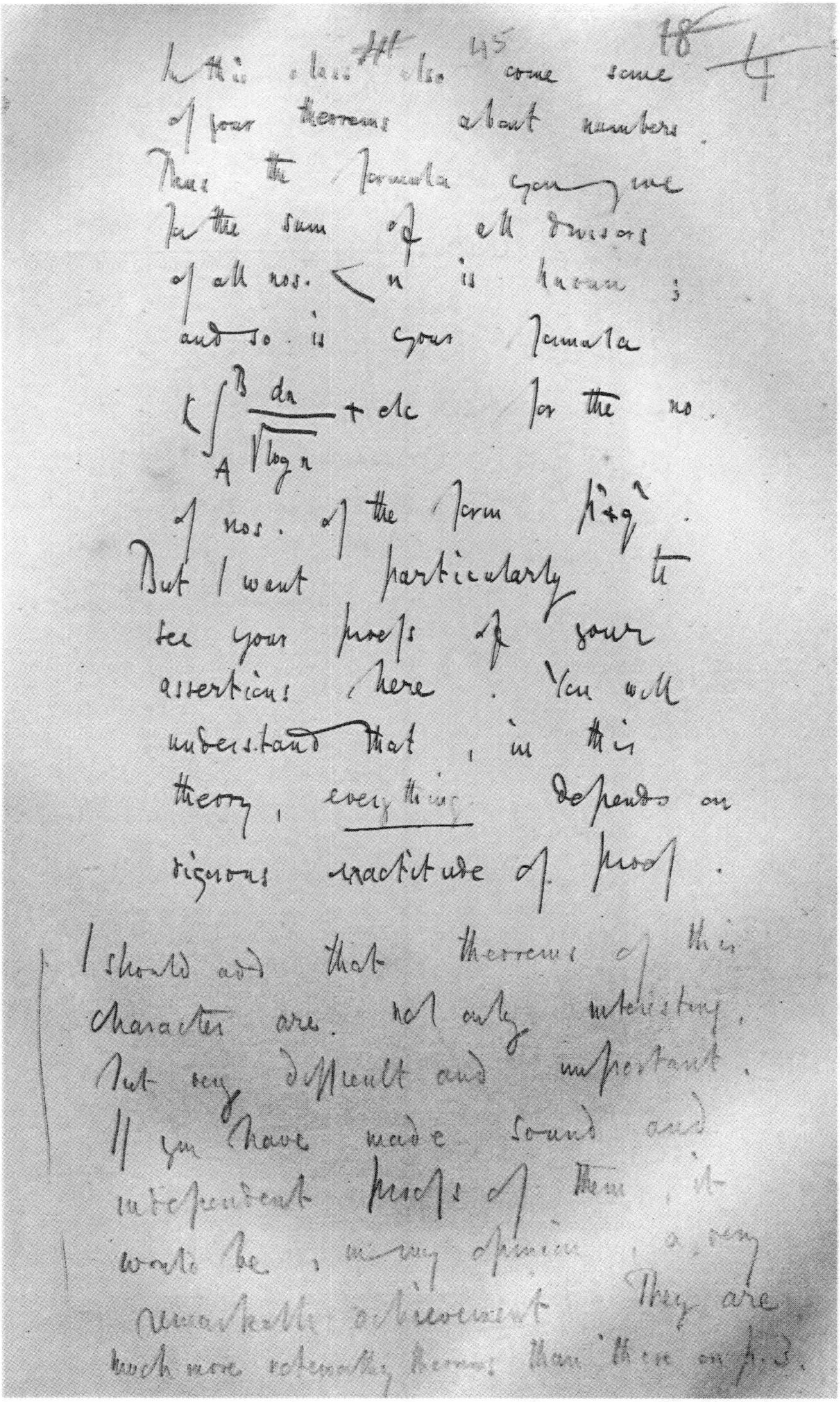

45 4

In this class also come some of your theorems about numbers. Thus the formula you give for the sum of all divisors of all nos. < n is known; and so is your formula

$$k\int_A^B \frac{dx}{\sqrt{\log x}} + \text{etc}$$

for the no. of nos. of the form p^2+q^2. But I want particularly to see your proofs of your assertions here. You will understand that, in this theory, everything depends on rigorous exactitude of proof.

I should add that theorems of this character are not only interesting, but very difficult and important. If you have made sound and independent proofs of them, it would be, in my opinion, a very remarkable achievement. They are much more noteworthy theorems than those on p. 3.

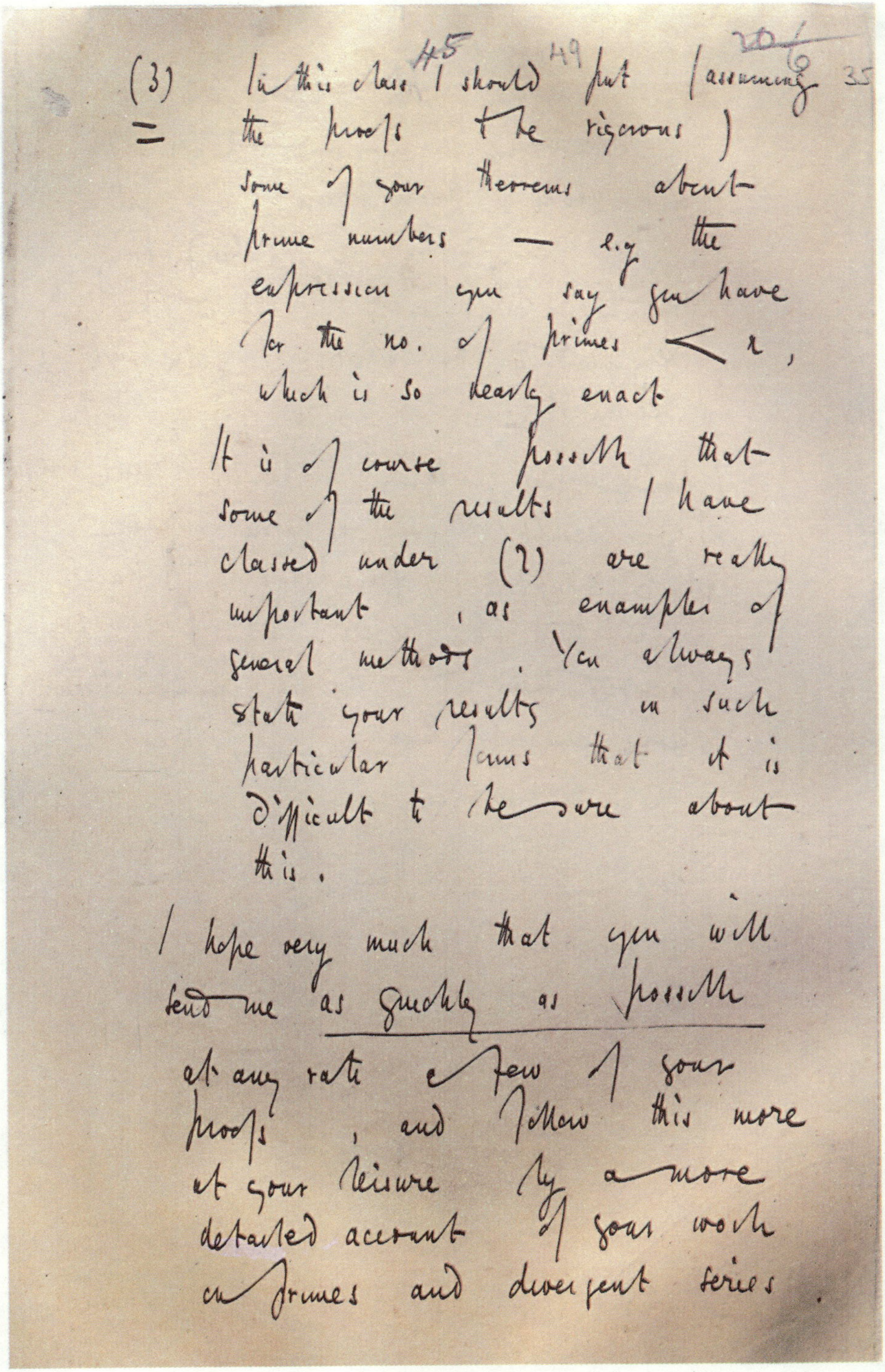

(3) In this class I should put (assuming the proofs to be rigorous) some of your theorems about prime numbers — e.g. the expression you say you have for the no. of primes $< x$, which is so nearly exact.

It is of course possible that some of the results I have classed under (2) are really important, as examples of general methods. You always state your results in such particular forms that it is difficult to be sure about this.

I hope very much that you will send me as quickly as possible at any rate a few of your proofs, and follow this more at your leisure by a more detailed account of your work on primes and divergent series.

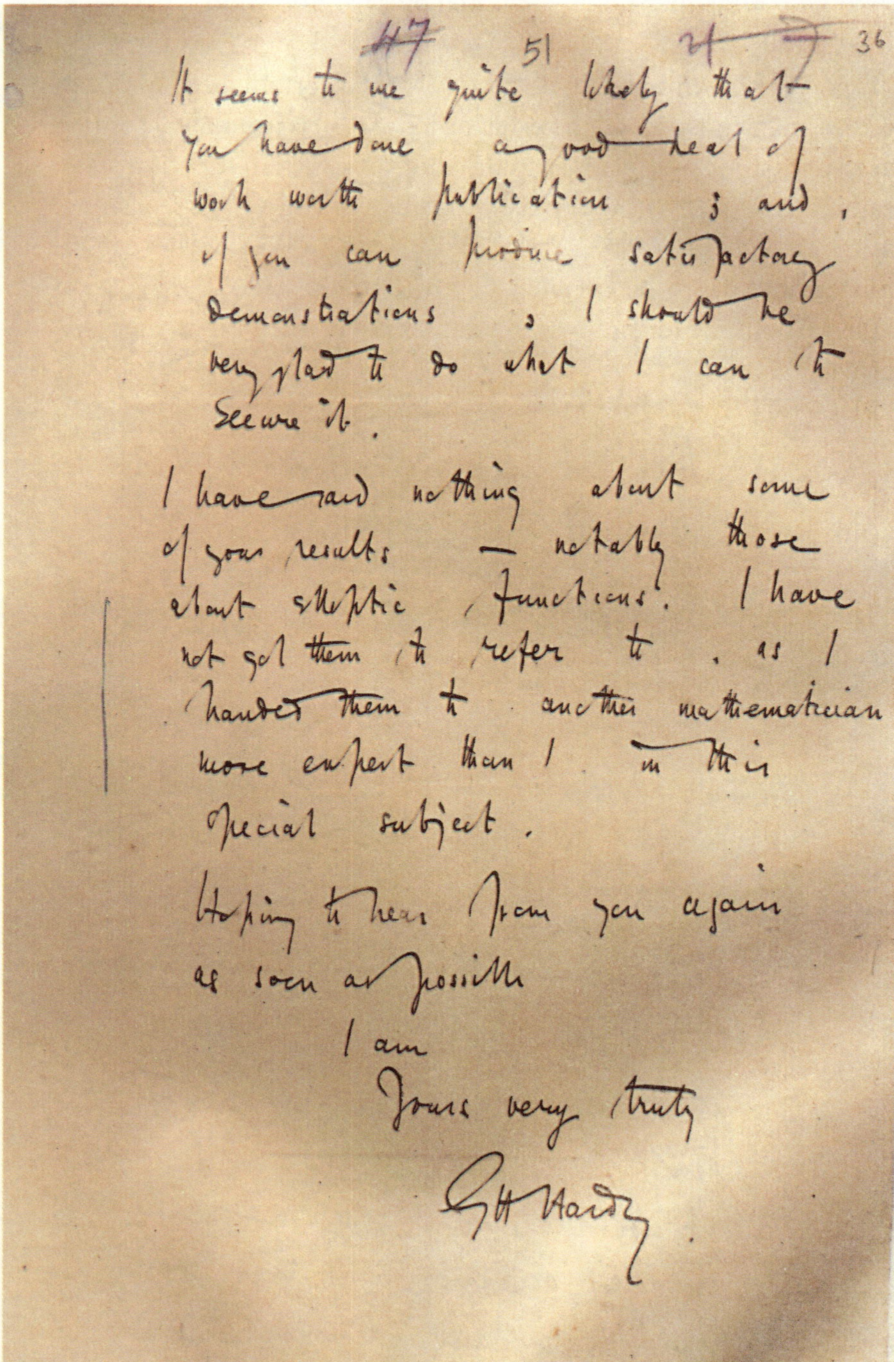

It seems to me quite likely that you have done a good deal of work worth publication; and, if you can produce satisfactory demonstrations, I should be very glad to do what I can to secure it.

I have said nothing about some of your results — notably those about elliptic functions. I have not got them to refer to, as I handed them to another mathematician more expert than I in this special subject.

Hoping to hear from you again as soon as possible

I am

Yours very truly

G H Hardy.

Further notes suggested by Mr Littlewood

1. $p(x)$ is known to be $O\left(e^{-\alpha\sqrt{\log x}}\right)$ for a certain α, and not to be $O(x^{\frac{1}{2}-\delta})$ for any positive δ. The exact order of $p(x)$ is intimately connected with a very famous problem as to the roots of a certain function : if these are all real, $p(x) = O(x^{\frac{1}{2}-\delta})$ for every positive δ. The converse also holds, and an independent rigorous proof of $p(x) = O(x^{\frac{1}{2}-\delta})$ would be of extreme importance.

Please send the formula for the number of primes and as much proof as possible quickly.

PDG

2. Do you mean to have strictly proved that (no. of primes 4x-1)-(no. of primes 4x+1)→ ∞?

This would be more than is known. It is known the excess is sometimes large. In the formula

$$f(x) = K\int_A^B \frac{dx}{\sqrt{\log x}} + \theta(x),$$

what is the order of f The best known result is

$$f(x) \sim \frac{Kx}{\sqrt{\log x}},$$

where

$$K = \frac{1}{\sqrt{(1-\frac{1}{3^2})(1-\frac{1}{7^2})(1-\frac{1}{(11)^2})\cdots}}.$$

Does this agree with your formula?

3. In your formula for Σ (number of divisors of n) do you mean that the error is < the last term you retain. If so it should be important. But to get the leading terms is comparatively easy.

Of course in all these questions everything depends on absolute rigour.

G.H.H

~~49~~ 53 ~~22~~ 8

Further notes suggested by Mr Littlewood

1. $\rho(x)$ is known to be $O(e^{-\alpha\sqrt{\log x}})$ for a certain α; and not to be $O(x^{\frac{1}{2}-\delta})$ for any $+\ \delta$.
The exact order of $\rho(x)$ is intimately connected with a very famous problem as to the roots of a certain function: if these are all real, $\rho(x) = O(x^{\frac{1}{2}+\delta})$ for every $+\ \delta$.
The converse also holds, and an independent rigorous proof of $\rho(x) = O(x^{\frac{1}{2}+\delta})$ would be of extreme importance.

Please send the formula for the no. of primes & as much proof as possible quickly.

2. Do you mean to have strictly proved that

$$(\text{no of primes } 4n-1) - (\text{no of primes } 4n+1) \to \infty\ ?$$

This would be more than is known.
It is known the excess is sometimes large.

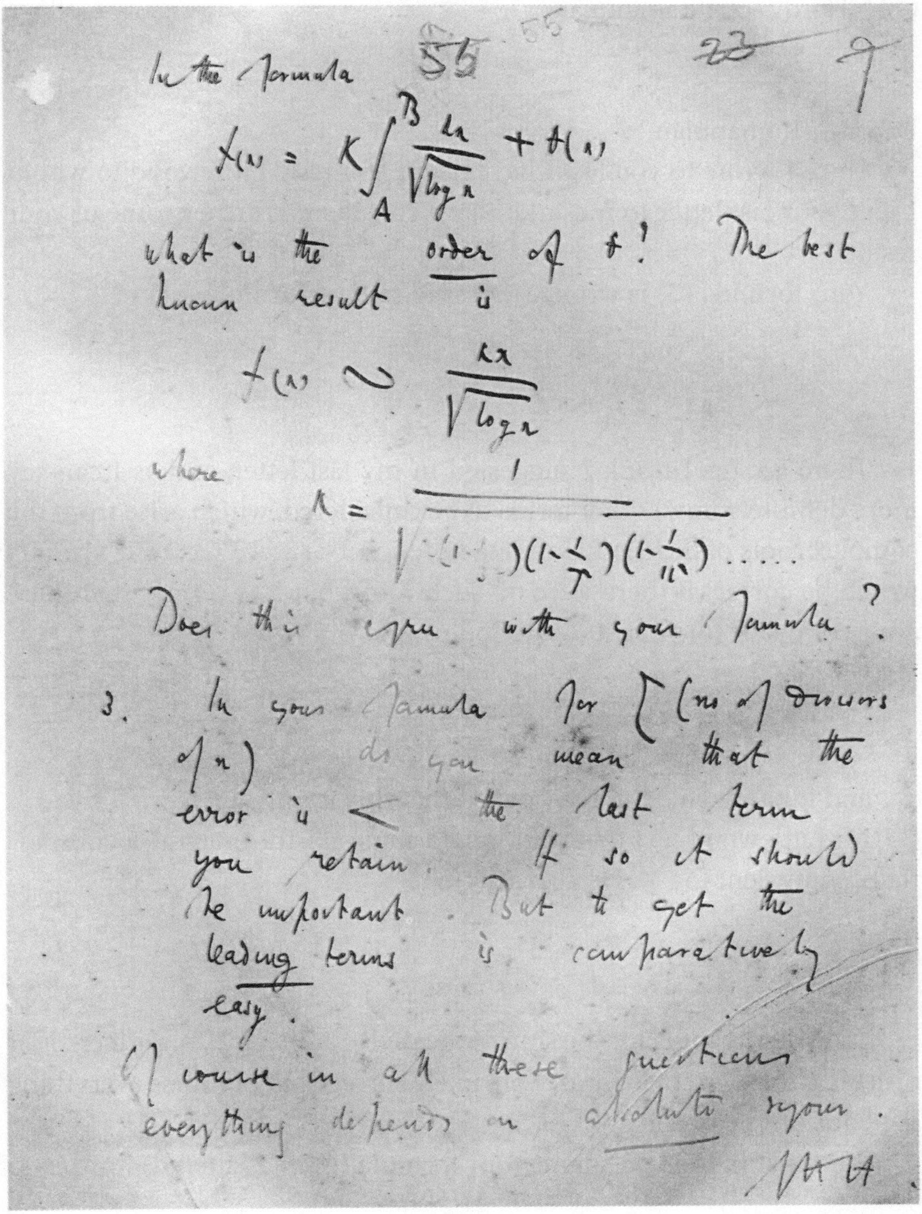

In the formula

$$f(x) = K\int_A^B \frac{dx}{\sqrt{\log x}} + \theta(x)$$

what is the order of θ? The best known result is

$$f(x) \sim \frac{kx}{\sqrt{\log x}}$$

where

$$k = \frac{1}{\sqrt{(1-\frac{1}{3})(1-\frac{1}{7})(1-\frac{1}{11})\cdots}}$$

Does this agree with your formula?

3. In your formula for Σ(no of divisors of n) do you mean that the error is < the last term you retain. If so it should be important. But to get the leading terms is comparatively easy.

Of course in all these questions everything depends on absolute rigour.

GHH

G.H. Hardy to S. Ramanujan

Trinity College
Cambridge
26 March 1913

Dear Mr Ramanujan,

Since I wrote to you last I have heard from Mr Littlewood to whom I sent your last letter to me, and I have considered further some of your results.

Your formula (3) is wrong (that is to say the formula

$$\int_{\mu}^{n} \frac{dx}{\log x} - \frac{1}{2}\int_{\mu}^{\sqrt{n}} \frac{dx}{\log x} - \frac{1}{3}\ldots\ldots)$$

There are (as I think I suggested in my last letter, and as I can say more definitely now) other terms to be considered, which arise from the complex roots of the Riemann Zeta function $1^{-5}+2^{-5}+3^{-5}$.... Your formula would be correct if there were no such roots; but it is certain that there are. From your formula it would follow that

$$\pi(n) - \int^{n} \frac{dx}{\log x} + \frac{1}{2}\int^{\sqrt{n}} \frac{dx}{\log x} = O\frac{\sqrt{n}}{\log n}$$

and it has been definitely proved that this is untrue.

Mr Littlewood says that your first formula (1)-the integral-is substantially equivalent to (3). He also says that

$$\theta(n) = O\sqrt{\frac{n}{\log n}}$$

and your formula for the sum of the divisors of 1, 2,..., n, with error of order less than that of logn, are very likely correct; but of course everything depends on the proofs.

We are still doubtful about your formula (even as altered) for the

coefficient of x^n in $\frac{1}{1-2x+2x^4-\cdots}$.

The theory of divergent series leads, as a rule, to correct results. The important exceptions to this general rule lie in the theory of prime numbers, the most difficult of all branches of pure mathematics. If, as stems to me probable, it has led you here with mistakes, my view that what you have done is very remarkable would not in any way be shaken; the results you gave concerning continued fractions and elliptic functions are enough in themselves to show it (assuming, as I am quite willing to do, that they are correct).

Mr Littlewood suggested to me also that your unwillingness to give proofs was probably due to apprehensions as to the use I might make of your results. Let me put the matter quite plainly to you. You have in your possession now 3 long letters of mine, in which I speak quite plainly about what you have proved or claim to be able to prove. I have shown your letters to Mr Littlewood, Dr Barnes, Mr Berry, and other mathematicians. Surely it is obvious that, if I were to attempt to make any illegitimate use of your results, nothing would be easier for you than to expose me. You will, I am sure, excuse my stating the case with such bluntness: I should not do so if I were not genuinely anxious to see what can be done to give you a better chance of making the best use of your obvious mathematical gifts.

What I should like above all is a definite proof of some of your results concerning continued fractions of the type

$$\frac{x}{1}+\frac{x^2}{1}+\frac{x^3}{1}+\cdots;$$

and I am quite sure that the wisest thing you can do, in your own interests, is to let me have one as soon as possible.

I am
Yours very sincerely
G.H. Hardy.

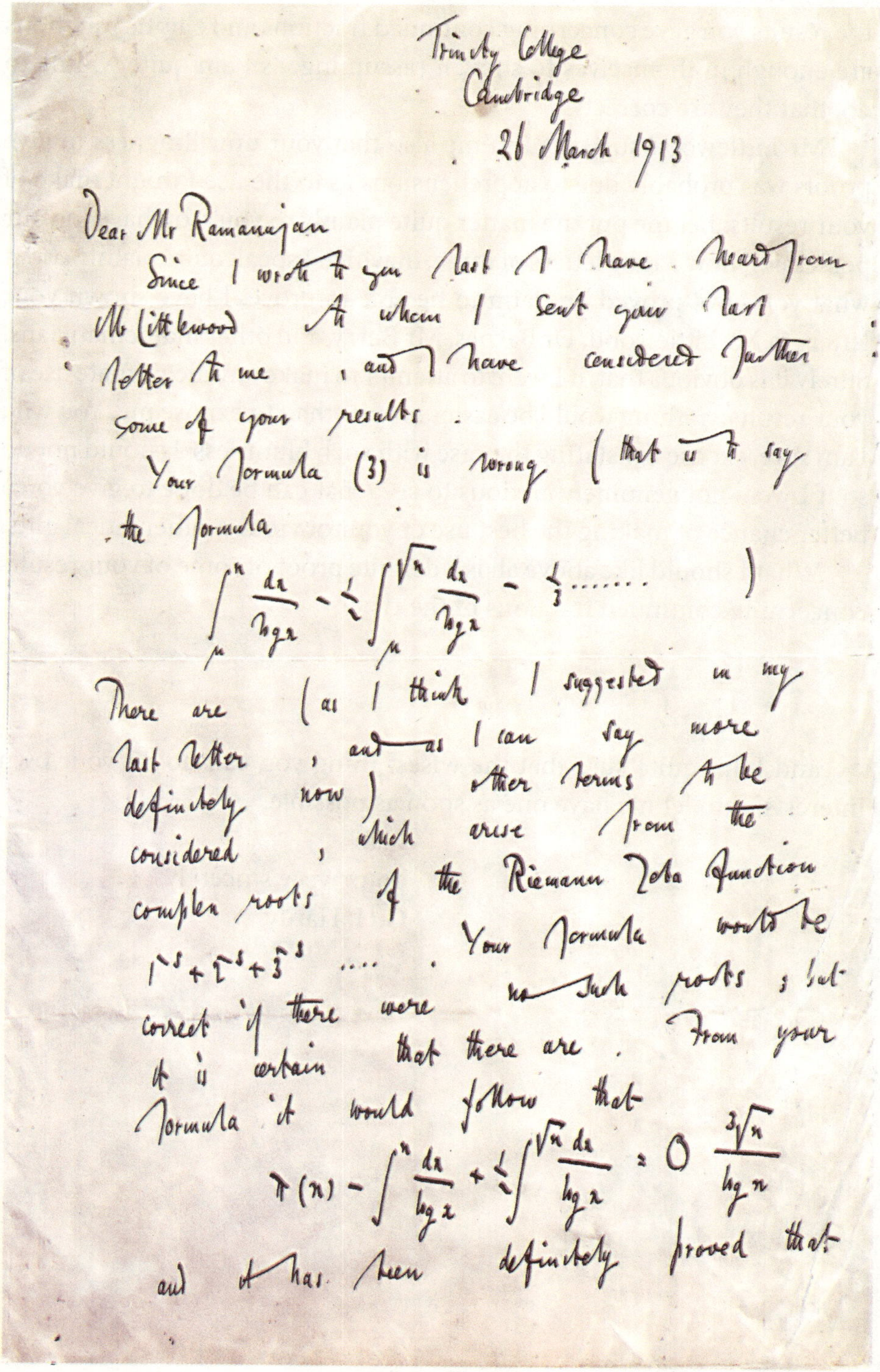

Trinity College
Cambridge
26 March 1913

Dear Mr Ramanujan

Since I wrote to you last I have heard from Mr Littlewood to whom I sent your last letter to me, and I have considered further some of your results.

Your formula (3) is wrong (that is to say the formula

$$\int_\mu^n \frac{dx}{\log x} - \frac{1}{2}\int_\mu^{\sqrt{n}} \frac{dx}{\log x} - \frac{1}{3}\ldots\ldots)$$

There are (as I think I suggested in my last letter, and as I can say more definitely now) other terms to be considered, which arise from the complex roots of the Riemann Zeta function $1^{-s}+2^{-s}+3^{-s}\ldots$. Your formula would be correct if there were no such roots; but it is certain that there are. From your formula it would follow that

$$\pi(n) - \int^n \frac{dx}{\log x} + \frac{1}{2}\int^{\sqrt{n}} \frac{dx}{\log x} = O\,\frac{\sqrt[3]{n}}{\log n}$$

and it has been definitely proved that

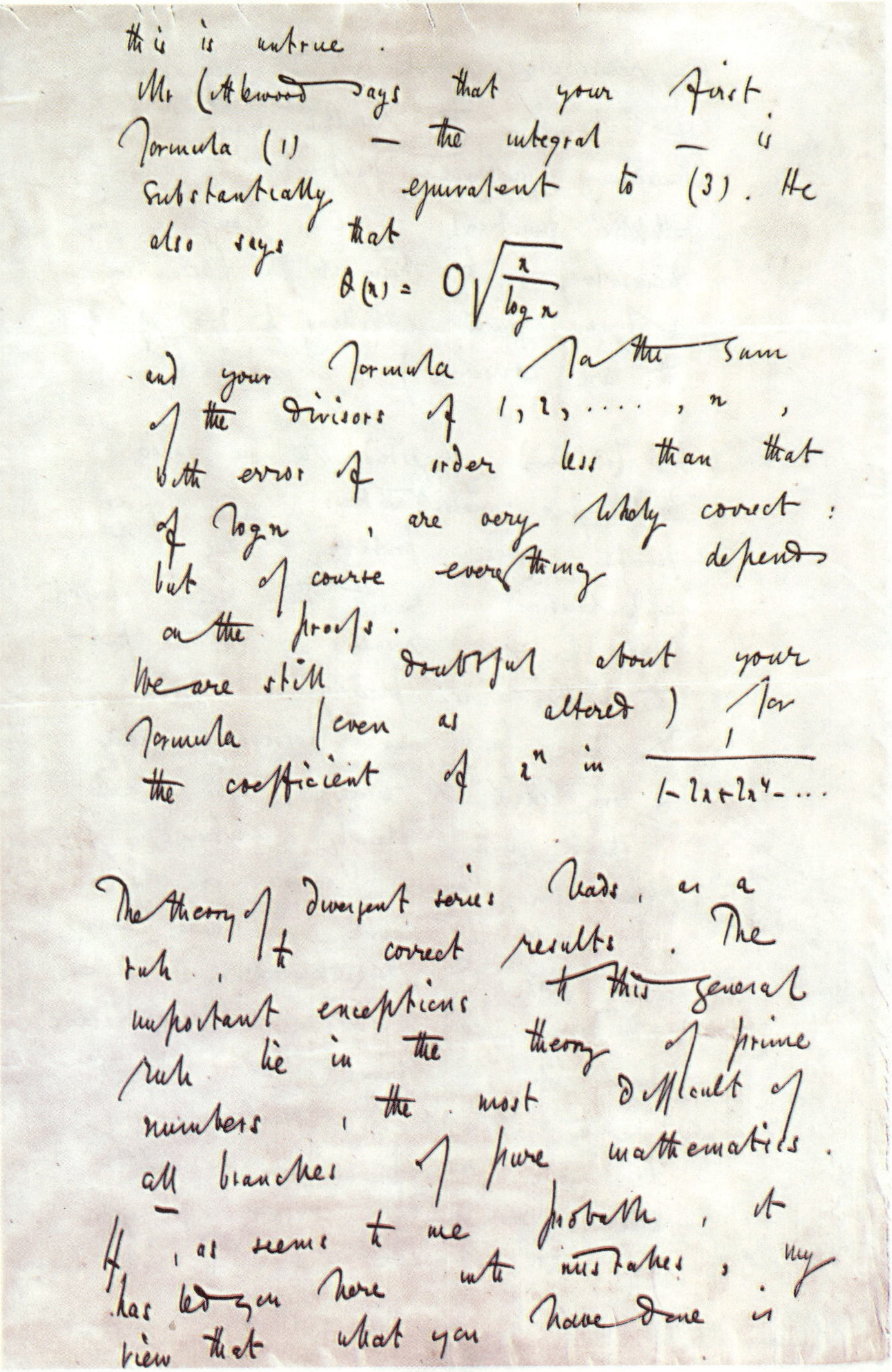

this is untrue.
Mr Littlewood says that your first formula (1) — the integral — is substantially equivalent to (3). He also says that

$$\theta(x) = O\sqrt{\frac{x}{\log x}}$$

and your formula for the sum of the divisors of $1, 2, \ldots, n$, with error of order less than that of $\log n$, are very likely correct: but of course everything depends on the proofs.
We are still doubtful about your formula (even as altered) for the coefficient of x^n in $\dfrac{1}{1-2x+2x^4-\ldots}$

The theory of divergent series leads, as a rule, to correct results. The important exceptions to this general rule lie in the theory of prime numbers, the most difficult of all branches of pure mathematics.
If, as seems to me probable, it has led you here into mistakes, my view that what you have done is

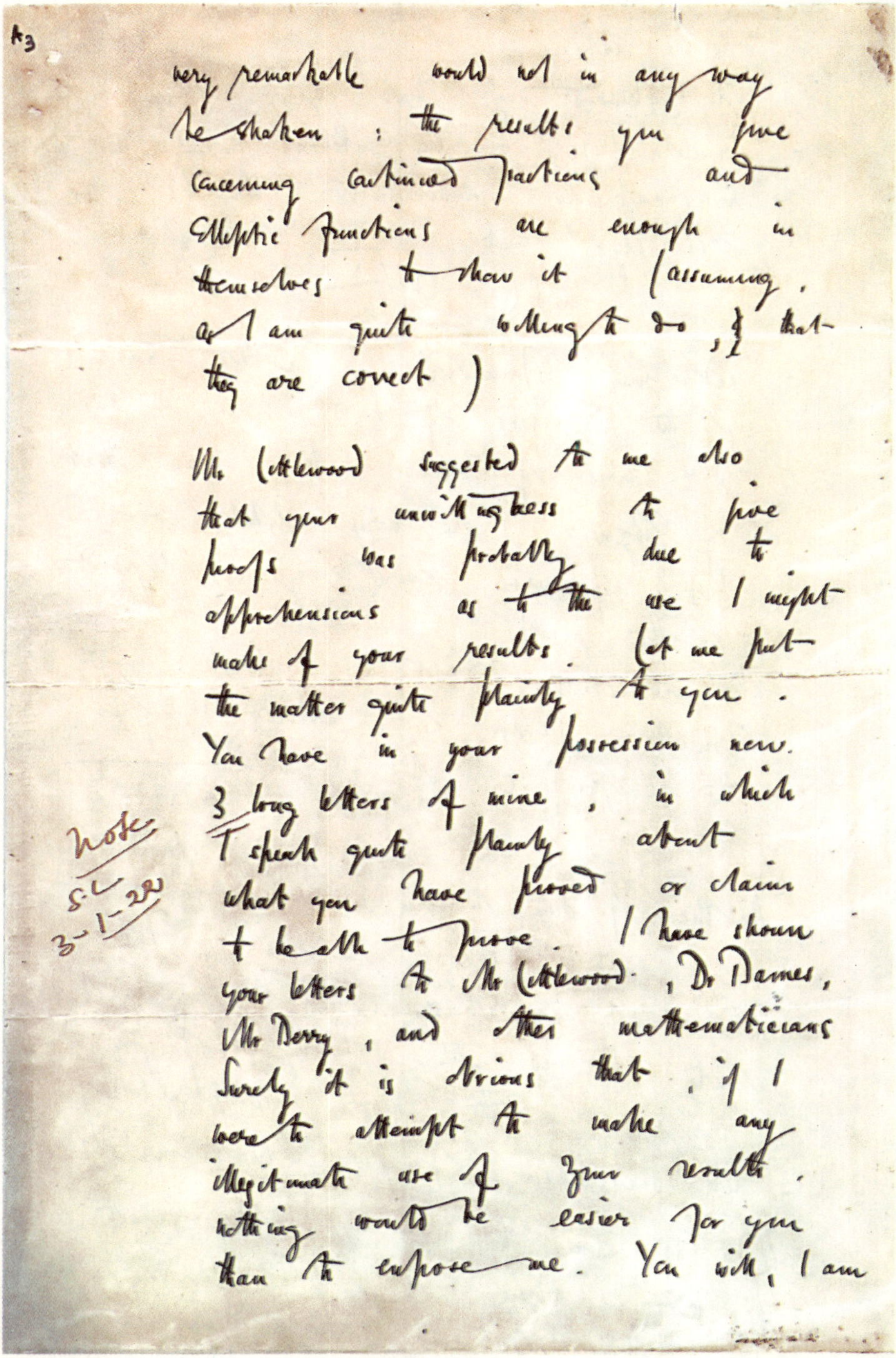

A3

very remarkable would not in any way be shaken: the results you give concerning continued fractions and elliptic functions are enough in themselves to show it (assuming, as I am quite willing to do, that they are correct)

Mr Littlewood suggested to me also that your unwillingness to give proofs was probably due to apprehensions as to the use I might make of your results. Let me put the matter quite plainly to you. You have in your possession now 3 long letters of mine, in which I speak quite plainly about what you have proved or claim to be able to prove. I have shown your letters to Mr Littlewood, Dr Barnes, Mr Berry, and other mathematicians. Surely it is obvious that, if I were to attempt to make any illegitimate use of your results, nothing would be easier for you than to expose me. You will, I am

Note S.L. 3-1-22

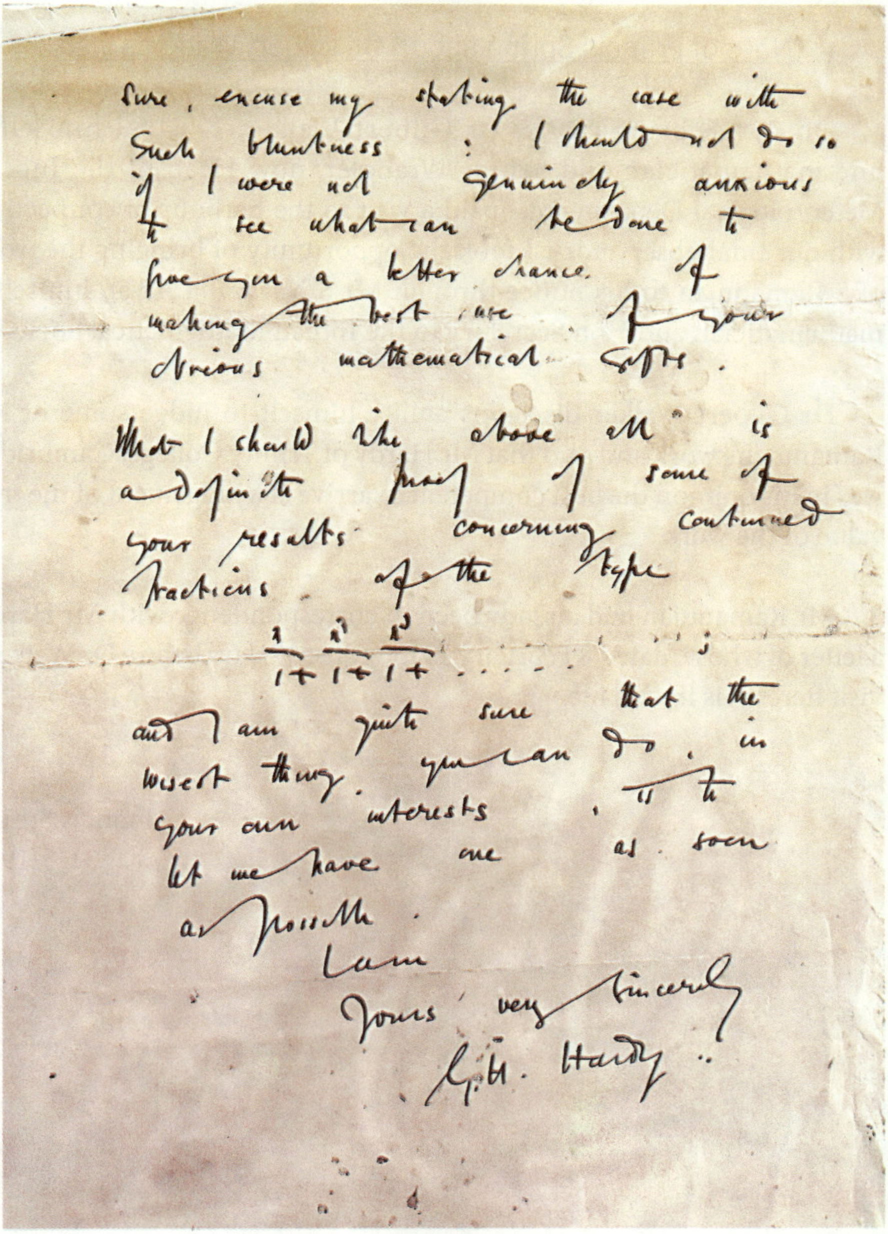

sure, excuse my stating the case with such bluntness: I should not do so if I were not genuinely anxious to see what can be done to give you a better chance of making the best use of your obvious mathematical gifts.

What I should like above all is a definite proof of some of your results concerning continued fractions of the type

$$\frac{x}{1+}\,\frac{x^2}{1+}\,\frac{x^3}{1+}\cdots\cdots ;$$

and I am quite sure that the wisest thing you can do, in your own interests, is to let me have one as soon as possible.

I am

Yours very sincerely

G. H. Hardy.

(Note of Francis Spring about) Dr. Gilbert Walker's visit

On 25th February 1913 Dr Gilbert Walker, F. R. S., himself a fine mathematician and Senior Wrangler, now Head of the Indian Meteorological Department,- paid a visit to the harbour in connection with our tidal observatory. I took the opportunity of bringing the work of S Ramanujan to his notice through Mr S Narayana Aiyar, himself a mathematician and Hon Secretary to the Indian Mathematical Society.

Dr Gilbert Walker disclaims ability himself to judge some of Mr Ramanujan's work and said that Mr Hardy of Trinity College, Cambridge was in his opinion the best competent to arrive at a judgement of the true value of the work.

Mr Ramanujan had already been in correspondence with Mr Hardy, a letter of whose, dated 8 February 1913 — just 17 days before Dr Walker's visit here — is in this file.

Francis Spring
31/3/1913

* A note by Mr Francis Spring about Dr. Gilbert Walker's visit to the Madras Port Trust.

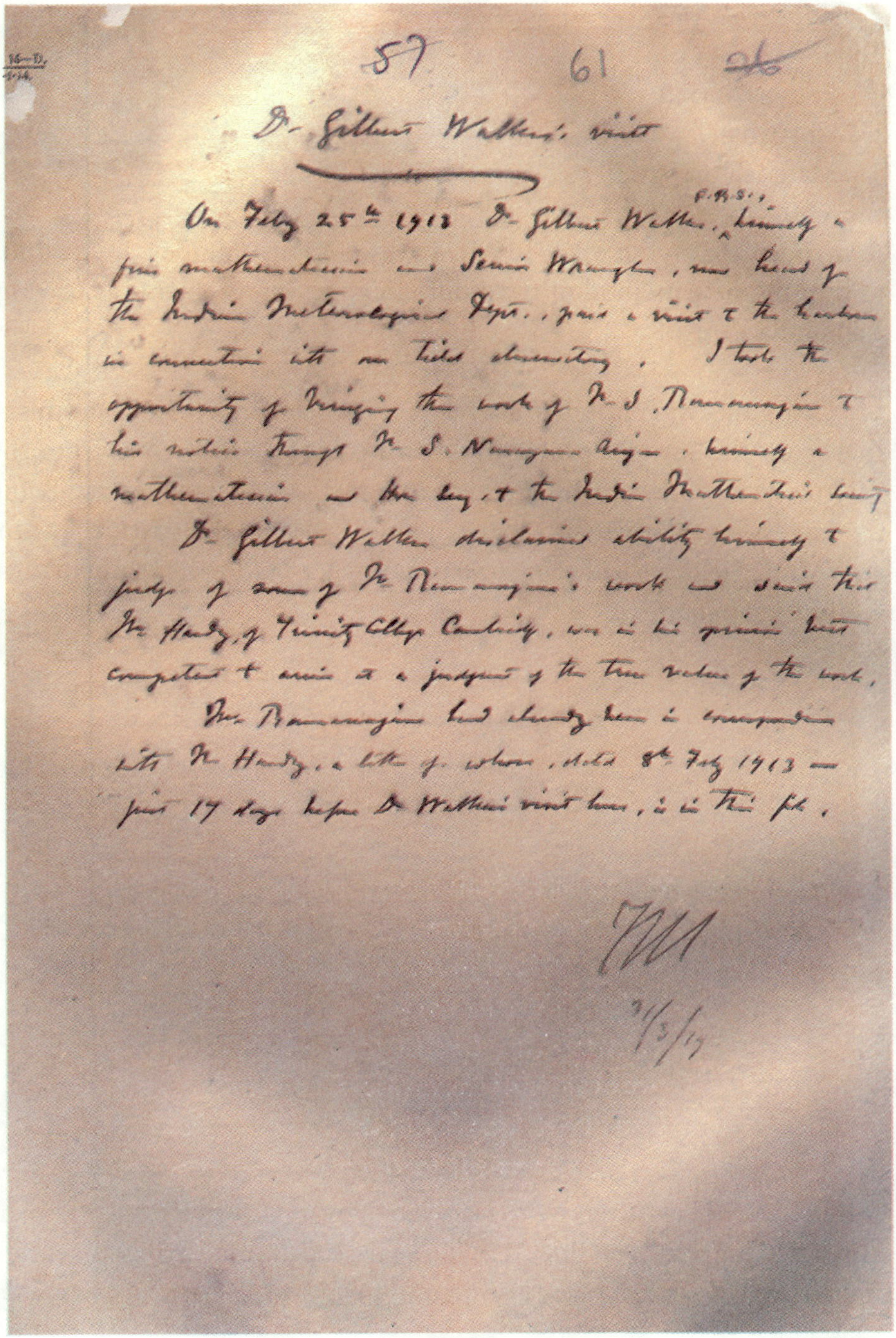

Dr. Gilbert Walker's visit

On Feby 25th 1913 Dr. Gilbert Walker, F.R.S., himself a fine mathematician and Senior Wrangler, now head of the Indian Meteorological Dept., paid a visit to the harbour in connection with our tidal observatory. I took the opportunity of bringing the work of Mr. S. Ramanujan to his notice through Mr. S. Narayana Aiyar, himself a mathematician and Hon. Secy. to the Indian Mathematical Society.

Dr. Gilbert Walker disclaimed ability himself to judge of some of Mr. Ramanujan's work and said that Mr. Hardy, of Trinity College Cambridge, was in his opinion best competent to arrive at a judgment of the true value of the work.

Mr. Ramanujan had already been in correspondence with Mr. Hardy, a letter of whom, dated 8th Feby 1913 — just 17 days before Dr. Walker's visit here, is in this file.

31/3/13

To,

Francis Spring
Chairman
Madras Port Trust

Ramanujan & myself went to Mr. Littlehailes last Sunday. I explained to him the new method of procedure in attacking problems as used by Ramanujan.

Mr. Littlehailes was pleased to see many of Ramanujan's results & promised that from the 1st of December, when he expects to be free from the Metrological work, he would regularly study Ramanujan's results. Being the Professor of Mathematics in the premier college of this presidency I am sure Mr. Littlehailes will bring into prominence before the Mathematical world Ramanujan's researches.

S. Narayana Aiyar
C.A.C.
31st October 1913

I am glad to learn all this.
Francis Spring
C. P. T.

* This letter was written by S. Narayana Aiyar, C. A. C. to Mr. Francis Spring, Chairman of Port Trust regarding Ramanujan's research. Interestingly Francis Spring also wrote "I am glad to learn all this."

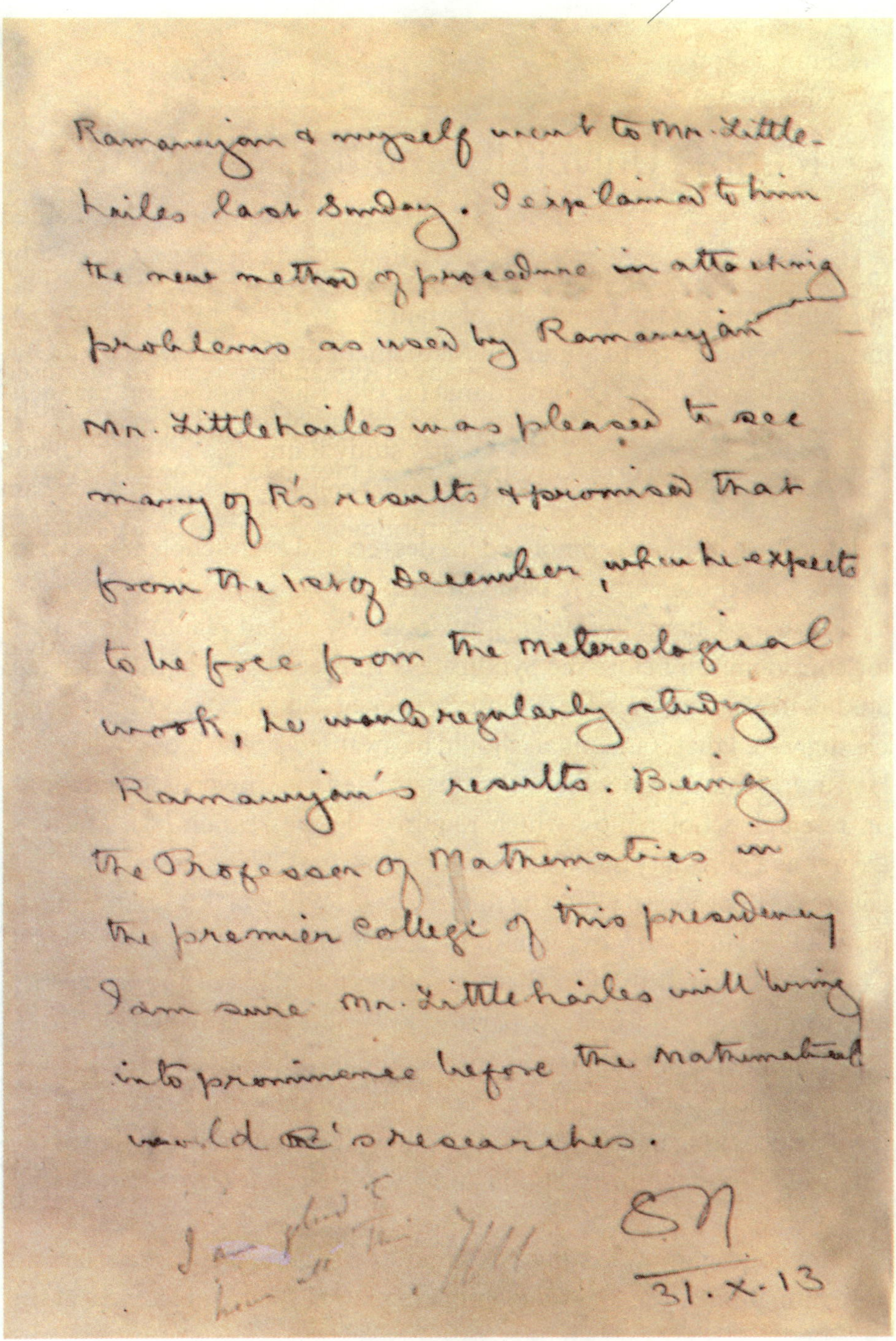

Ramanujan & myself went to Mr. Little-
hailes last Sunday. I explained to him
the new method of procedure in attacking
problems as used by Ramanujan.
Mr. Littlehailes was pleased to see
many of R's results & promised that
from the 1st of December, when he expects
to be free from the metereological
work, he would regularly study
Ramanujan's results. Being
the Professor of Mathematics in
the premier College of this presidency
I am sure Mr. Littlehailes will bring
into prominence before the mathematical
world R's researches.

S N

31.X.13

Madras University and the Syndicate

In March 1913, B. Hanumanta Rao, the Chairman of the Board of Studies of Mathematics at the University of Madras, invited Narayana Aiyar to a meeting of the Board of Studies in Mathematics to discuss what could be done for Ramanujan[1]. The Board met on 19th March and recommended to the Syndicate, the University's governing body, that Ramanujan receive a research scholarship of seventy-five rupees a month for the next two years. But when the Syndicate met again in April, Ramanujan's case received a setback since he hadn't completed his degree, and such scholarships were reserved for those with a Master's degree.

The Vice-Chancellor, P. R. Sundaram Ayyar, had placed the matter for consideration before the Syndicate with the support of the Board of Studies in Mathematics. He personally backed it as an extraordinary case. He suggested that Ramanujan should be awarded a research scholarship. However, some members of the Syndicate cited the University regulations on research scholarships, which required the possession of a Master's Degree as a necessary qualification. For some time, it looked as if the Vice-Chancellor's proposal would be turned down. While in this predicament, Justice P R Sundaram Ayyar, also the Chief Justice of the Madras High Court, highlighted the fact that one of the functions of the University was to promote research, as per the Preamble to the University Act. And Ramanujan was a phenomenal candidate who possessed immense potential and capability. If the University did not grant him research rights, it would be failing in its duty. The University then obtained consent of the Chancellor to make an exception and give a special research scholarship to Ramanujan.

The good news was soon conveyed to Ramanujan. The scholarship gave him ample time to engage in mathematics, to attend lectures at the

1. Letter from B.Hanumanta Rao to Narayana Aiyar dated March 13, 1913, NAI New Delhi.

University, and to use its library. He joined the University of Madras as a Research Scholar on 1st May 1913 on a stipend of Rs 75 per month. He was asked to submit a quarterly report about his work. Ramanujan sent three quarterly reports before leaving for Cambridge early in 1914.

After he became a Research scholar, Ramanujan was granted two years' leave on loss of pay from the Madras Port Trust from 1st May 1913 onwards. A postcard from Arthur Davies, the Secretary of the Madras Students Arriving Committee, Principal and Senior Professor at the Madras Law College, was sent to S. Narayana Aiyar on 7th June 1913, about Ramanujan's scholarship.

Tiruva Aeswarnpet
13th March 1913

My dear Mr. Narayana Aiyar

I am calling a meeting of the Board of Studies in Mathematics in the Senate House at 5.30 p.m on Wednesday the 19th instant for the purpose of considering what we can do for S. Ramanujan. Will you kindly come over and assist us? You have seen some of his results & can help us to understand them better than the author himself.

Yours Sincerely
B. Hanumanta Rao

*A letter from Bhimasena Hanumanta Rao, the Chairman of the Board of Studies of Mathematics at the University of Madras and Deputy Accountant-General, Madras to S. Narayana Aiyar, C.A.C. regarding Ramanujan's scholarship at the Madras University.

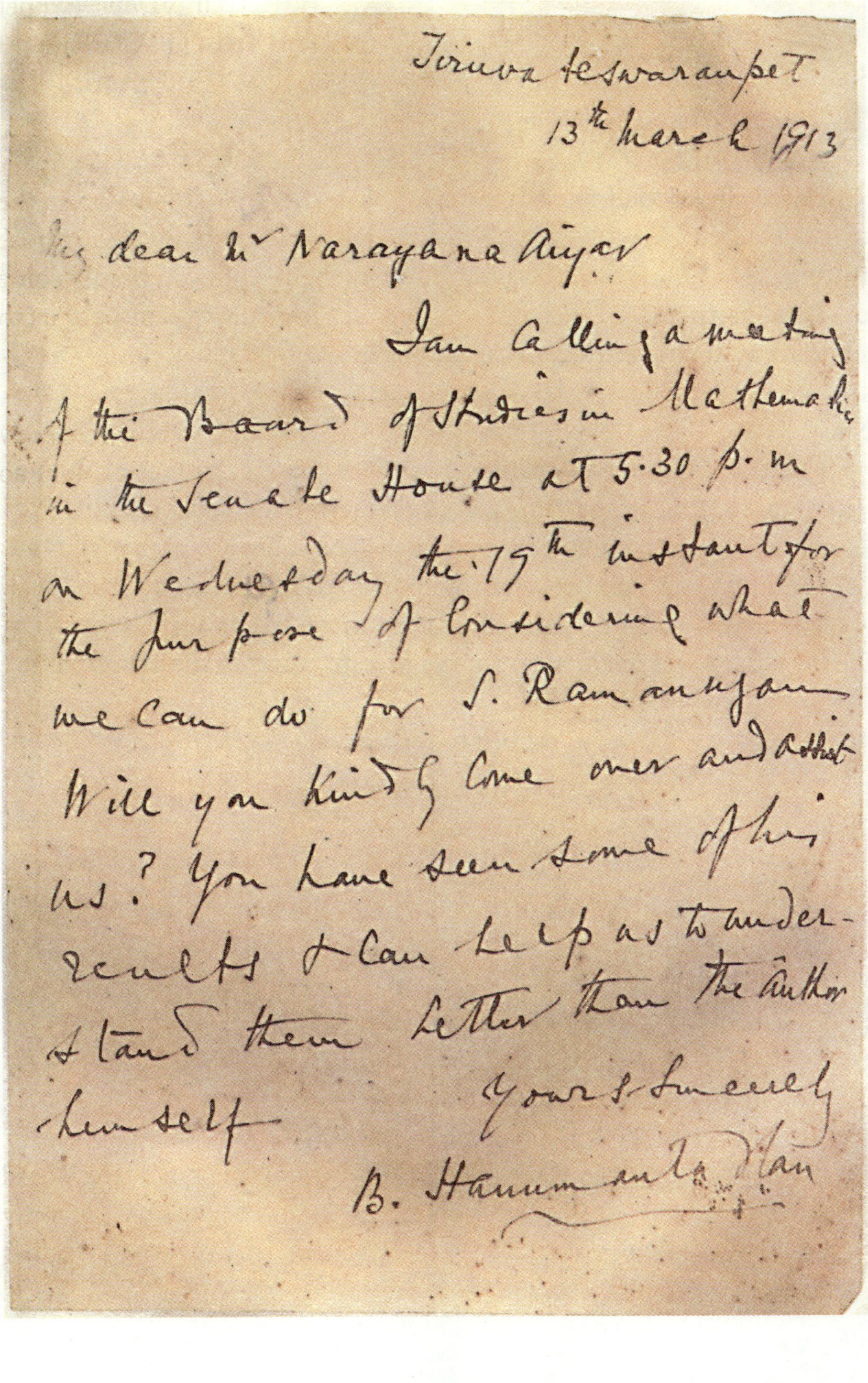

Tiruvateswarampet
13th March 1913

My dear Mr Narayana Aiyar

I am calling a meeting of the Board of Studies in Mathematics in the Senate House at 5.30 p.m on Wednesday the 19th instant for the purpose of considering what we can do for S. Ramanujan. Will you kindly come over and assist us? You have seen some of his results & can help us to understand them better than the author himself.

Yours sincerely

B. Hanumantha Rau

Accounts Department,
Port Trust Office, Madras.
18th April 1913.

To

The Registrar,
University of Madras.

Through

The Chairman,
Madras Port Trust.

Sir,

I have the honour to acknowledge with thanks the receipt of your letter No. 1631 dated the 9th April 1913 offering me a scholarship of Rs. 75 per mensem tenable for two years. In reply I beg to inform you that I am willing to take up the scholarship from the 1st May and that I shall abide by the conditions detailed in your above letter. The Chairman of the Port Trust will relive me from my present work on the 1st proximo.

I beg to remain,

Sir,
Your Obedient Servant,
S. Ramanujan

No. G 50 dated 14th April 1913.

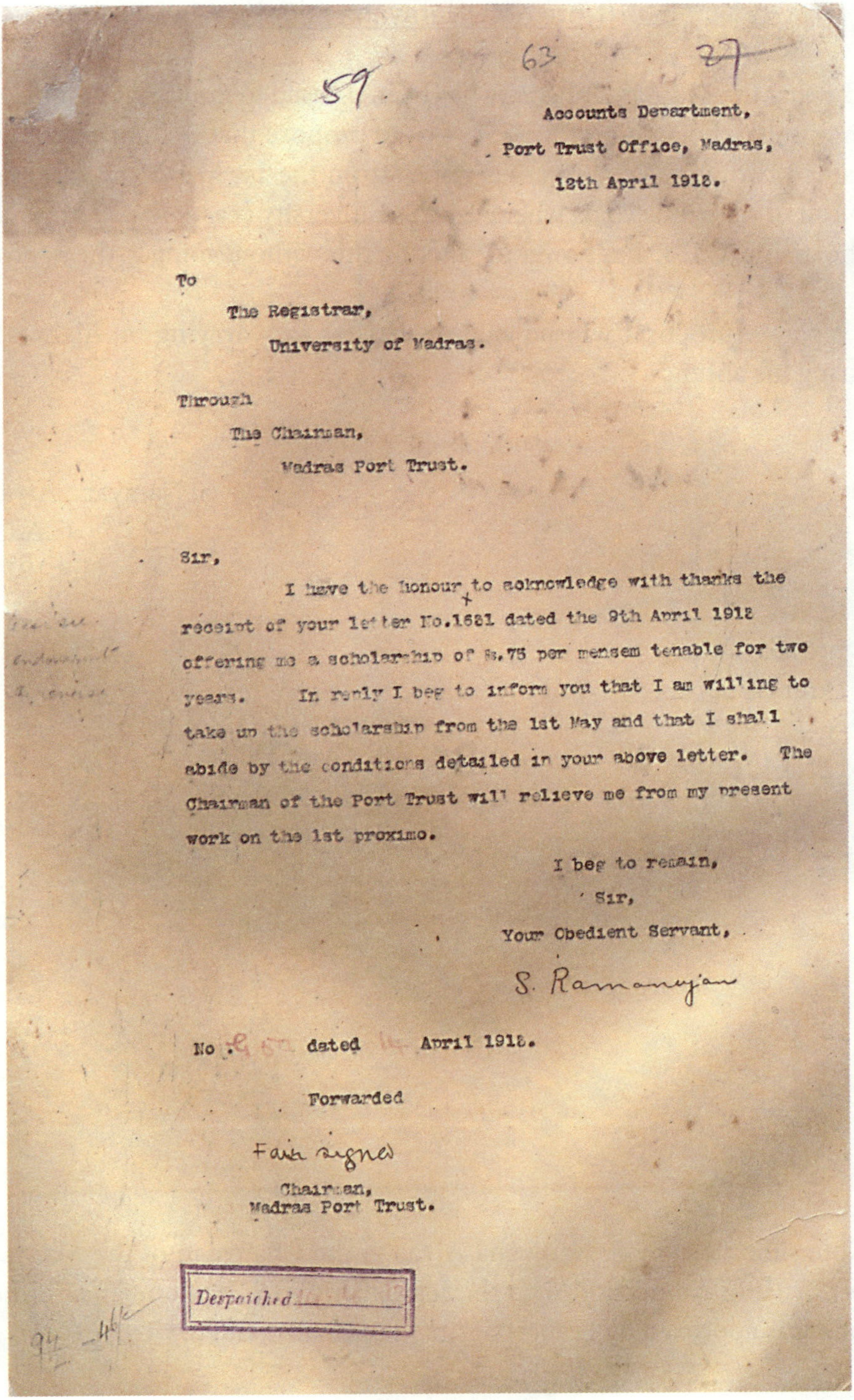

59 63 27

Accounts Department,
Port Trust Office, Madras,
12th April 1913.

To

The Registrar,
University of Madras.

Through

The Chairman,
Madras Port Trust.

Sir,

I have the honour to acknowledge with thanks the receipt of your letter No.1631 dated the 9th April 1913 offering me a scholarship of Rs.75 per mensem tenable for two years. In reply I beg to inform you that I am willing to take up the scholarship from the 1st May and that I shall abide by the conditions detailed in your above letter. The Chairman of the Port Trust will relieve me from my present work on the 1st proximo.

I beg to remain,
Sir,
Your Obedient Servant,
S. Ramanujan

No. 650 dated 14 April 1913.

Forwarded

Fair signed

Chairman,
Madras Port Trust.

Despatched

(Note of S. Narayana Aiyar)

Now that the Madras University has been pleased to grant S. Ramanujan a monthly scholarship of Rs. 75, I beg to propose that S. Ramanujan be granted two years' leave on loss of pay from the 1st May 1913 with the option of returning to us whenever the University ceases to pay him the scholarship. C.P. T. has power to sanction this without going to the Board.

A separate proposal will be submitted later for carrying on his work during his absence.

S. Narayana Aiyar
C.A.C.
11.4.1913

Approved
Francis Spring
C.P.T.
11.4.1913

*Note submitted by S. Narayana Aiyar to the Chairman of the Madras Port Trust in connection with the scholarship to S. Ramanujan and the same was approved by Francis Spring, the Chairman Port Trust.

64 65 28

Now that the Madras University has [illegible]eased to grant S. Ramanujan a monthly scholarship of Rs.75 I beg to propose that S. Ramanujan be granted two years' leave on loss of pay from the 1st May 1913 with the option of returning to us whenever the University ceases to pay him the scholarship. C.P.T. has power to sanction this without going to the Board.

A separate proposal will be submitted later for carrying on his work during his absence.

C.A.C.

11-4-13.

To

S. Narayana Aiyar
C.A.C.

I have to acknowledge with thanks your letter about the scholarship that has been awarded to Mr. S. Ramanujan. I am conveying the news to Mr. Walker at the Meteorological Office, and he will tell the gentlemen at Cambridge, who will watch his future career with the greatest interest.

Arthur Davies
7.6.1913

*A postcard written by Arthur Davies, Secretary of Madras Students Arriving Committee to Mr. S. Narayana Aiyar regarding Ramanujan's scholarship and his future in Cambridge University.

On H. M. S.

India Service Post Card.

(The address only to be written on this side: the address includes the signature and official designation of the sender.)

MADRAS 8.30 A.M. 9 JU.13

KODAIKANAL 7 JU.13 5 PM

69

M.R.Ry S. Narayana Ariyar Avl
Madras Port Trust
Madras

Arthur Davies, Secret
Madras & S. Mahr. Advisory Committee

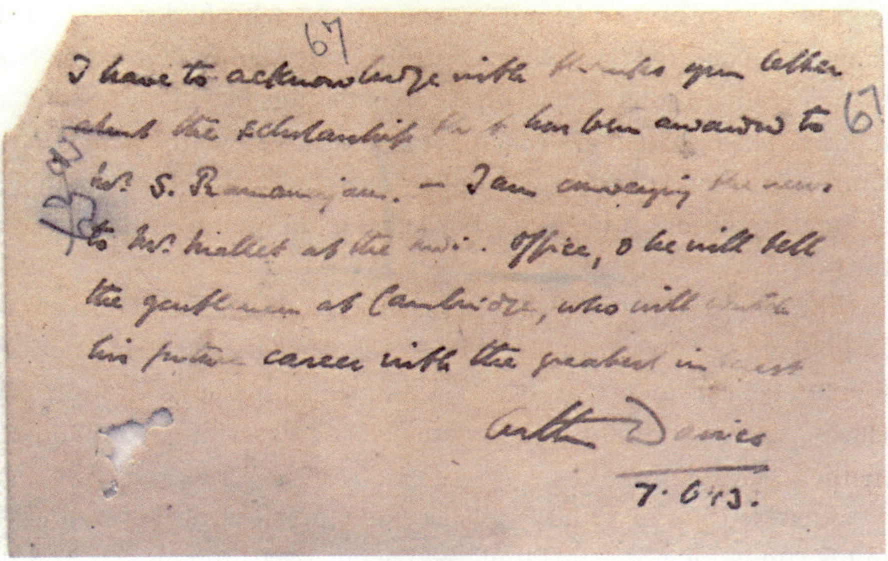

67

I have to acknowledge with thanks your letter about the scholarship that has been awarded to Mr S. Ramanujan. — I am conveying the news to Mr Mallet at the India Office, & he will tell the gentleman at Cambridge, who will watch his future career with the greatest interest.

Arthur Davies

7.6.13.

Journey to Cambridge University

Madras Port Trust Chairman Francis Spring wrote a letter on 5th February 1914 to Lord Pentland's Secretary, E. B. Cotterell[1]. Pentland was the Governor of Madras at that time. Spring had come to learn that the University was prepared to set aside ten thousand rupees, equivalent to more than six hundred pounds, for sending Ramanujan to England for two years. The decision was to be taken on the basis of approval from higher authorities and so arose the reason for his letter.

The previous year, it had been Pentland who had consented to Ramanujan's special research scholarship at the Madras University. Now he was ready to intercede again on Ramanujan's behalf. His Secretary replied, "His Excellency cordially sympathises with your desire that the University should provide Ramanujan with the means of continuing his researches at Cambridge, and will be glad to do what he can to assist in the proposal."

The scholarship was finally approved and Ramanujan set on a voyage to England. The Madras Mail, dated 15th May 1914, carried news of Ramanujan's residence at Trinity, Cambridge, his collaboration with Hardy, Littlewood and Neville, and Hardy describing Ramanujan's mathematical genius.

After settling in Trinity College, Ramanujan wrote several letters to his family members in Tamil and friends regarding his stay and the challenges he was facing, the current war situation, and his routine. In one of his letters from 17th December 1914, he wrote to C. N. Ganapathy Iyer discussing "Definite Integrals connected with Gauss sums". A Professor of Mathematics at Presidency College, he and Ramanujan used to meet regularly at the beach the evenings to discuss mathematics, while Ramaujan was working at the Madras Port Trust. A few of his

1. Letter from Francis Spring to E. B. Cotterell dated Feb 5, 1914, NAI, New Delhi.

letters from 1914-15, were written to his dear friend from his college days, Vinayaka Rao, discussing his life at Trinity and the challenges he encountered there.

In 1915, a lot of correspondence ensued related to Ramanujan's continuation of leave on loss of pay at the Madras Port Trust, and the extension of his scholarship. Regarding his scholarship, the discussion was focussed around whether the scholarship was to be renewed for one year or two years. Ramanujan himself was of the opinion that his scholarship be extended for two years, as he mentioned in his letter, dated 11th November 1915, "Unless I remain here for two years more I cannot do all I have to do."[1]

There are also transcripts of telephone and telegram messages between the Registrar of the University of Madras to the Chairman's Office, Madras Port Trust, asking for information regarding Ramanujan's father such as his father's name, whether Ramanujan's father was still alive, and whether he was a District Munsiff. Additional information was also sought about Ramanujan such as his date of birth, whether he was matriculate and whether he had applied for the F.A. or Intermediate Exam.[2]

In two letters written by Ramanujan, both dated 11th November, 1915, he talks about various things happening in his life: one of his math papers which had been read before the London Mathematical Society, last November, (wrongly printed as June), how he might be conferred with the Research Degree in March 1916, etc.[3]

There is also a note on Ramanujan by the Madras Port Trust; a biography that was put together by Narayana Aiyar and Francis Spring.[4]

A Certificate of a Candidate for Election was given to Ramanujan stating "being desirous of admission into the ROYAL SOCIETY OF LONDON" undersigned by many eminent mathematicians like G. H. Hardy, E. W. Hobson, F. J. Baker, J. E. Littlewood. It was read to the

1. Extract from a letter dated 11 Nov., 1915 from S. Ramanujan, Ramanujan Paper's Acc No. 78 pp 97, NAI, New Delhi
2. Ramanujan Paper's, Acc No. 78, pp 108, NAI, New Delhi
3. Letter from S. Ramanujan to S. Narayana Aiyar dated 11th No. 15
4. Ramanujan Paper's, Acc No. 78, NAI, New Delhi

society on 24th January 1918. An extract from the Madras Mail, dated March 7th, 1918, mentions Ramanujan's achievement in getting elected as a Fellow of the Royal Society.[1]

In a letter from Seshu Aiyar to Narayana Aiyar, dated 17th March 1918, the former discusses holding a congratulatory meeting on Ramanujan's election to the Fellowship of the Royal Society, and to have Francis Spring preside over this meeting. Francis Spring however declined to preside at the meeting, citing his lack of mathematical knowledge.[2]

A newspaper article dated 10.12.1918 mentions Ramanujan's election as a Fellow of the Trinity College, Cambridge.[3]

1. Ramanujan Paper's, Acc No. 78, NAI, New Delhi
2. Letter from P.V. Seshu Aiyar to Narayan Aiyar dated 17 March, 1918, NAI, New Delhi
3. Ramanujan Paper's, Acc No. 78, NAI, New Delhi

5th February 1914

My dear Cotterell,

If I understand right, His Excellency has the Educational Portfolio. So I am anxious to interest him in a matter which I presume will come before him within the next few days – a matter which under the circumstances is, I believe, very urgent. It relates to the affairs of a clerk of my office named S. Ramanujan who, as I think His Excellency has already heard from me, is pronounced by very high Mathematical authorities to be a Mathematician of a new and high, if not transcendental, order of genius.

A few months ago the Madras University gave S. Ramanujan a scholarship to enable him to fill certain gaps in his education which operated to prevent his conveying his conceptions to the outside world. Meanwhile during the last 8 or 9 months various Mathematicians in the first rank in Cambridge, Simla and Madras have had before them selections from his work and have pronounced upon them in terms of the very highest eulogy.

Just now, as probably His Excellency is sure, a Mr. Neville, who, I think, is a Senior Wrangler and a Fellow of Trinity, Cambridge, has been in Madras giving a series of lectures on certain phases of the Higher Mathematics to Honours students and others interested. Under a mandate from Cambridge he has interested himself greatly in Ramanujan and there is every reason to hope that he may be persuaded to go to Cambridge for a year or two so that under expert guidance not only may the fruits of his genius be given to the World but also, we may hope, his own fame, future usefulness and personal prosperity may be secured - matters probably quite impossible if he remained in a backwater like Madras for the rest of his life.

I now come to the point where His Excellency may perhaps be able to interfere with advantage. Last evening I learnt from Mr Littlehailes and others that the University Syndicate had decided, subject to sanction of Government, to set aside a sum of Rs. 10,000 in order to secure Ramanujan's visit to England for a couple of years. Messrs Littlehailes and Neville begged me to intercede with His Excellency with a view to the speedy confirmation of this notion of the University Syndicate. But I wish to make it quite clear that I write under no mandate from the Syndicate but merely as a private individual interested in my own employee, Ramanujan, as well as in Mathematics.

Mr. Arthur Davies will doubtless arrange for the voyage to England and that Ramanujan's orthodoxy may be maintained unimpaired. Mr. Neville assures me that he will meet him on his arrival in London and conduct him personally to Cambridge, and that when there he will interest himself personally in his welfare, generally and in all matters of Brahman orthodoxy, so that he may return to India without any loss of the esteem of his caste men.

I myself am very far from being Mathematician enough to express adequately what has been said to me by several who are fully qualified to express an opinion on the subject of the potential value to Science of the new line of thought in which Ramanujan's investigations lie. I am assured however by those who ought to know what I am talking about that they may conscionably be epoch-making and as such well worthy of financial support at the hands of the Madras University.

Needless to say Professor Hardy and other high Mathematicians may be trusted to give Ramanujan the fullest credit in the scientific world for his work. My reason for saying anything so obvious as this is that I am told that certain of his Indian friends have been suggesting to us that all that the Scientists of England desire is to steal his ideas - - obviously an utterly impossible suggestion with men of that class.

Yours sincerely,
Francis Spring

C.B. Cotterell Esq., B.A., I.C.S.,

* Cecil Barnard Cotterell was appointed Private Secretary to Lord Pentland in 1912. John Sinclair, or as he was commonly known, Lord Pentland, became Governor of Madras in 1912.

7F.75 335

5th February 4

My dear Cotterell,

If I understand right, His Excellency has the Educational portfolio. So I am anxious to interest him in a matter which I presume will come before him within the next few days — a matter which under the circumstan is, I believe, very urgent. It relates to the affairs of a clerk of my office named S. Ramanujan who, as I think His Excellency has already heard from me, is pronounced by very high Mathematical authorities to be a Mathematician of a new and high, if not transcendental, order of genius.

A few months ago the Madras University gave S. Ramanujan a scholarship to enable him to fill certai gaps in his education which operated to prevent his conveying his conceptions to the outside world. Meanwhil during the last 8 or 9 months various Mathematicians in the first rank in Cambridge, Simla and Madras have had before them selections from his work and have pronounced upon them in terms of the very highest eulogy.

Just

792

Just now, as probably His Excellency is aware, a Mr. Neville, who, I think, is a Senior Wrangler and a Fellow of Trinity, Cambridge, has been in Madras giving a series of lectures on certain phases of the Higher Mathematics to Honours students and others interested. Under a mandate from Cambridge he has interested himself greatly in Ramanujan and there is every reason to hope that he may be persuaded to go to Cambridge for a year or two so that under expert guidance not only may the fruits of his genius be given to the World but also, we may hope, his own fame, future usefulness and personal prosperity may be secured — matters probably quite impossible if he remained in a backwater like Madras for the rest of his life.

I now come to the point where His Excellency may perhaps be able to interfere with advantage. Last evening I learnt from Mr. Littlehailes and others that the University Syndicate had decided, subject to sanction of Government, to set aside a sum of Rs.10,000 in order to secure Ramanujan's visit to England for a couple of years. Messrs Littlehailes and Neville begged me to

intercede

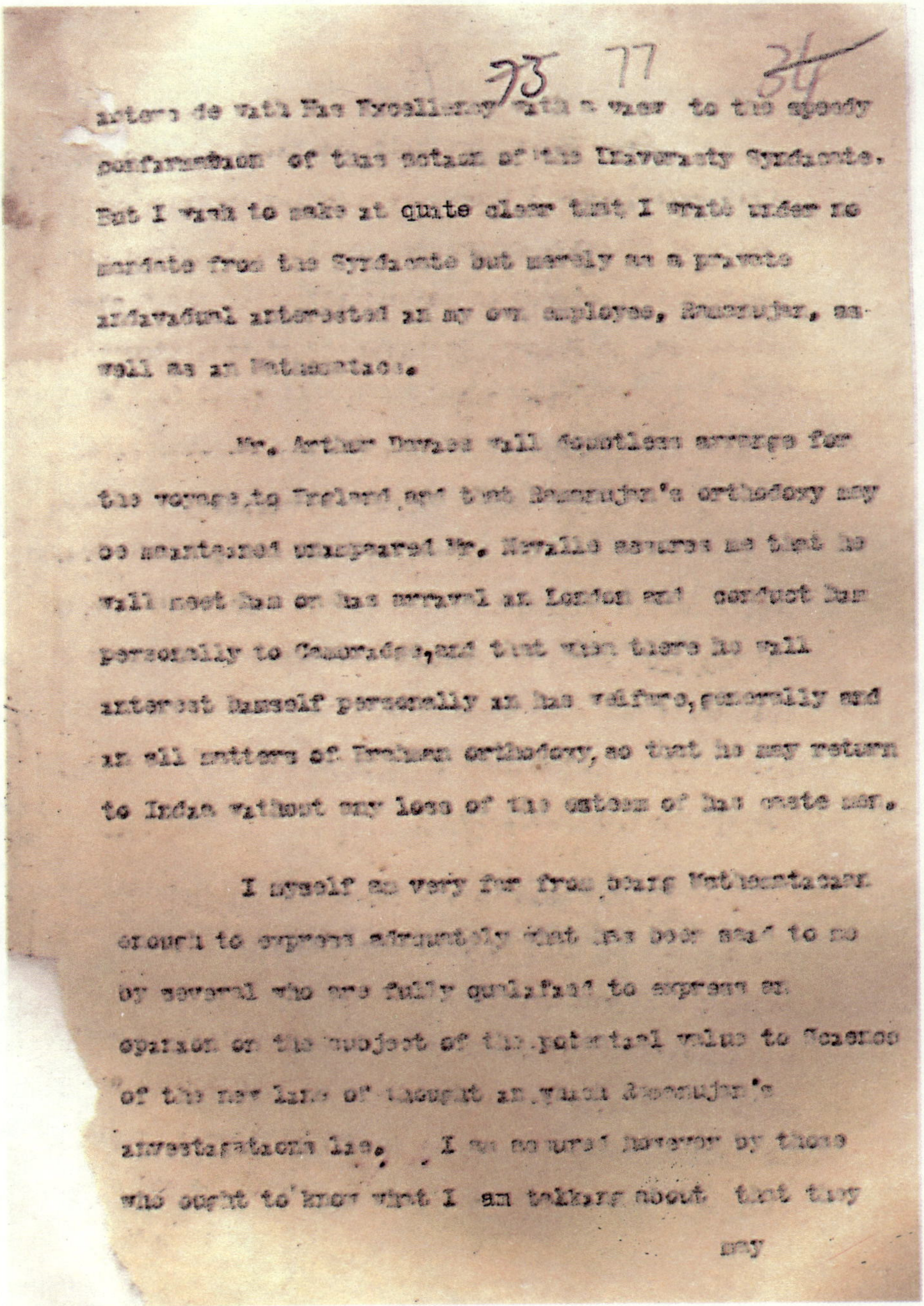

intercede with His Excellency with a view to the speedy confirmation of this action of the University Syndicate. But I wish to make it quite clear that I write under no mandate from the Syndicate but merely as a private individual interested in my own employee, Ramanujan, as well as in Mathematics.

Mr. Arthur Davies will doubtless arrange for the voyage to England and that Ramanujan's orthodoxy may be maintained unimpaired Mr. Neville assures me that he will meet him on his arrival in London and conduct him personally to Cambridge, and that when there he will interest himself personally in his welfare, generally and in all matters of Brahman orthodoxy, so that he may return to India without any loss of the esteem of his caste men.

I myself am very far from being Mathematician enough to express adequately what has been said to me by several who are fully qualified to express an opinion on the subject of the potential value to Science of the new line of thought in which Ramanujan's investigations lie. I am assured however by those who ought to know what I am talking about that they

may

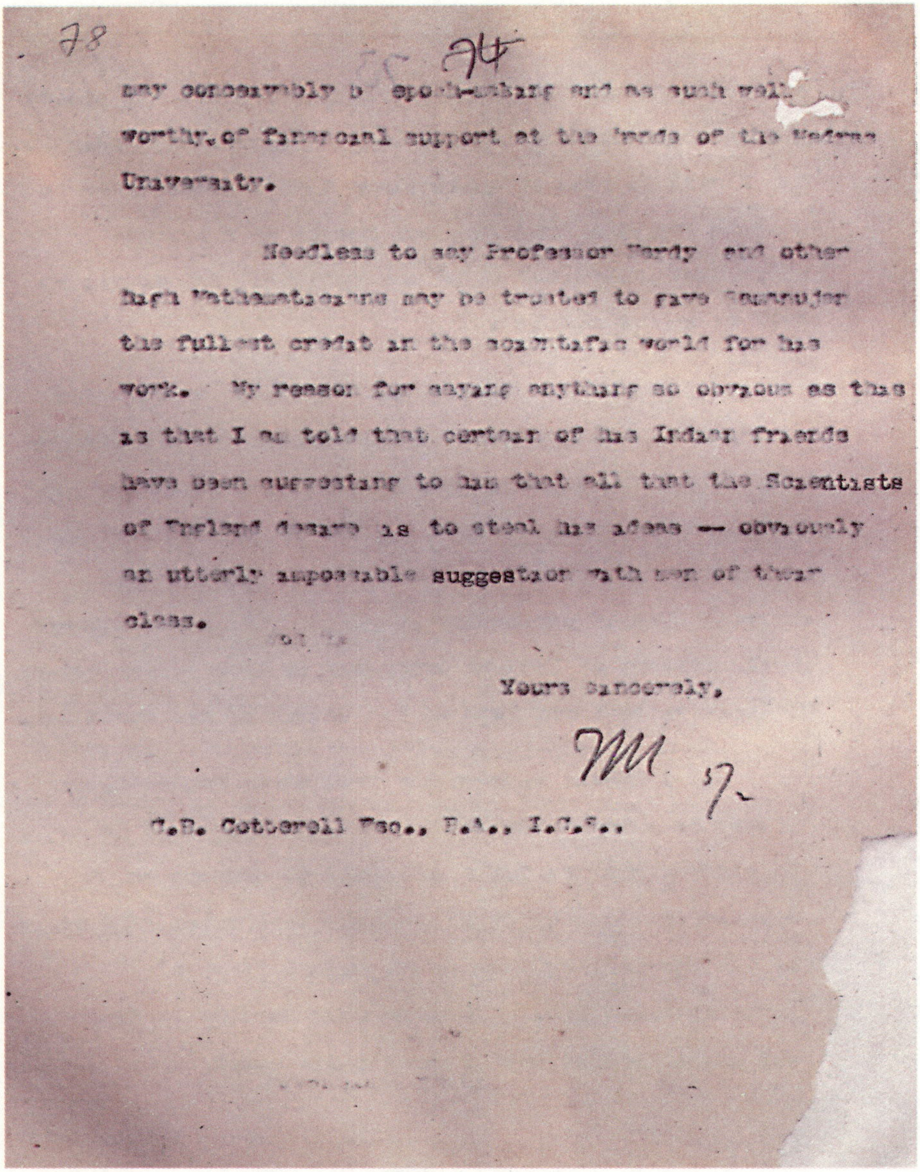

78

74

may conceivably be epoch-making and as such well worthy of financial support at the hands of the Madras University.

Needless to say Professor Hardy and other high Mathematicians may be trusted to give Ramanujan the fullest credit in the scientific world for his work. My reason for saying anything so obvious as this is that I am told that certain of his Indian friends have been suggesting to him that all that the Scientists of England desire is to steal his ideas — obviously an utterly impossible suggestion with men of their class.

Yours sincerely,

C.B. Cotterell Esq., M.A., I.C.S.,

GOVERNMENT HOUSE
MADRAS
5TH February 1914

Dear Sir Francis,

Your letter of 5th February.

His Excellency cordially sympathises with your desire that the University should provide Ramanujan with the means of continuing his researches, at Cambridge, and will be glad to do what he can to assist in the proposal.

Yours sincerely,
C. B. Cotterell

The Hon'ble Sir Francis spring, K.C.I.E;
Chairman, Madras Port Trust,
Madras.

~~25~~ 79 ~~35~~

GOVERNMENT HOUSE,
MADRAS.

5th February 1914

No. 89–1

Dear Sir Francis,

Your letter of 5th February.

His Excellency cordially sympathises with your desire that the University should provide Ramanujan with the means of continuing his researches, at Cambridge, and will be glad to do what he can to assist in the proposal.

Yours sincerely,

B. Clavus

The Hon'ble Sir Francis Spring, K.C.I.E.,
Chairman, Madras Port Trust,
Madras.

Extract from the "Madras Mail" dated the 15th May 1914.

Mr. S. Ramanujan, of Madras, whose work in the higher mathematics has excited the wonder of Cambridge, is now in residence at Trinity. He will read mainly with three fellows of the College – Mr. Hardy, Mr. Littlewood and Mr. Neville. They are going through masses of work he has already done, and are making some surprising discoveries in it. Mr. Hardy, Fellow of Trinity, says :- "The first I knew of him was about fifteen months ago. He wrote to me explaining who he was, and sent a large number of mathematical theorems which he had proved. There were a great many very remarkable results. His theorems were all in pure mathematics, particularly in the theory of numbers and the theory of elliptic functions. While many of them were quite new, others had been anticipated by writers of whom he had never heard, and of whose work he was quite innocent. That is the wonderful thing; he discovered for himself a great number of things which the leading mathematicians of the last hundred years, such as Cauchy and Jacobi, had added to the knowledge of schoolmen."

* This newspaper article is on Ramanujan who had gone and settled in Cambridge and had started working in collaboration with Hardy, Littlewood and Neville.

~~77~~ 81 ~~36~~

Extract from the "Madras Mail" dated the 15th May 1914.

Mr. S. Ramanujan, of Madras, whose work in the higher mathematics has excited the wonder of Cambridge, is now in residence at Trinity. He will read mainly with three fellows of the College -- Mr. Hardy, Mr. Littlewood and Mr. Neville. They are going through masses of work he has already done, and are making some surprising discoveries in it. Mr. Hardy, Fellow of Trinity, says :- "The first I knew of him was about fifteen months ago. He wrote to me explaining who he was, and sent a large number of mathematical theorems which he had proved. There were a great many very remarkable results. His theorems were all in pure mathematics, particularly in the theory of numbers and the theory of elliptic functions. While many of them were quite new, others had been anticipated by writers of whom he had never heard, and of whose work he was quite innocent. That is the wonderful thing; he discovered for himself a great number of things which the leading mathematicians of the last hundred years, such as Cauchy and Jacobi, had added to the knowledge of schoolmen."

Trinity College
11th June 1914

My dear Vinayaka Row,

Your kind letter to hand. Very glad to hear that Suryanarayanan has got the Scholarship. Please excuse me for the long delay in writing to you. It is because that I felt quite uncomfortable till now.

The voyage on the whole was very pleasant though I suffered from Sea sickness for two or three days in the Mediterranean. As soon as I arrived in England on the 14th April, Mr Neville was kind enough to come to the docks and take me to Cromwell road. After staying a few days at London I came to Cambridge on 18th evening. But as I came here m the middle of the year I couldn't find licensed lodging here and stayed in Mr Neville's house for ...

... weeks, and then came to the college.

Living in college is more costly than in lodging houses. Cambridge is a costly place, next comes.... I have no idea of the cost. I have to pay all the expenses every term unlike the lodging houses where the expenses are paid weekly. The college pays me £40 a year of which at present £20 is given to the college for my entrance and other fees.

I am staying in the college because there will be much inconvenience to the professors and myself if I stay outside the college. I would advise Suryanarayanan to try to live in lodging-houses and if he can fortunately live in an unlicensed lodging house, he will find it by far cheaper than other places.

As for the food I would have suffered much more had it not been for the good milk obtained here. For the first two months I felt why I had come here. Now I am alright. Suryanarayanan also will feel the same for two months from the time he comes let him not be discouraged it is only a matter of two months .... a vegetarian will be home ..... Let him select such lodgings where good vegetarian food was given previously to the Indian occupant. He can easily get information when he is coming in.

There is another Suryanarayan here who was a tutor in the Pachayappa's College. He says that he knew you all. He is living in a lodging where they prepare excellent vegetarian food. During voyage there will be no difficulty because most of them will be Indians and he may tell them whatever he wants. Let him be prepared to take meals in an English Restaurant in Madras, for it will be very awkward in the beginning if he remains taking food in his house to the last moment. It is also better for him to cook one or two things for himself after coming here, if he cannot find a good house and if he finds time. Let him be careful not to use fried things as they After coming here he ... cooks to fry things wants. For vegetarian ... eggs it will be in the beginning ... is no difficulty.

As for my studies, I am attending a few lectures and have begun to write articles and publish my results. I have two articles one on Definite Integrals and another on Elliptic functions. Another I am going to write soon on contd. fractions. My hearty congratulations to Suryanarayanan.

Yours affectionately
S. Ramanujan

* Letter from S. Ramanujan to Vinayaka Rao dated 11, 1514, Ramanujan Museum & Math Education Centre, Chennai.

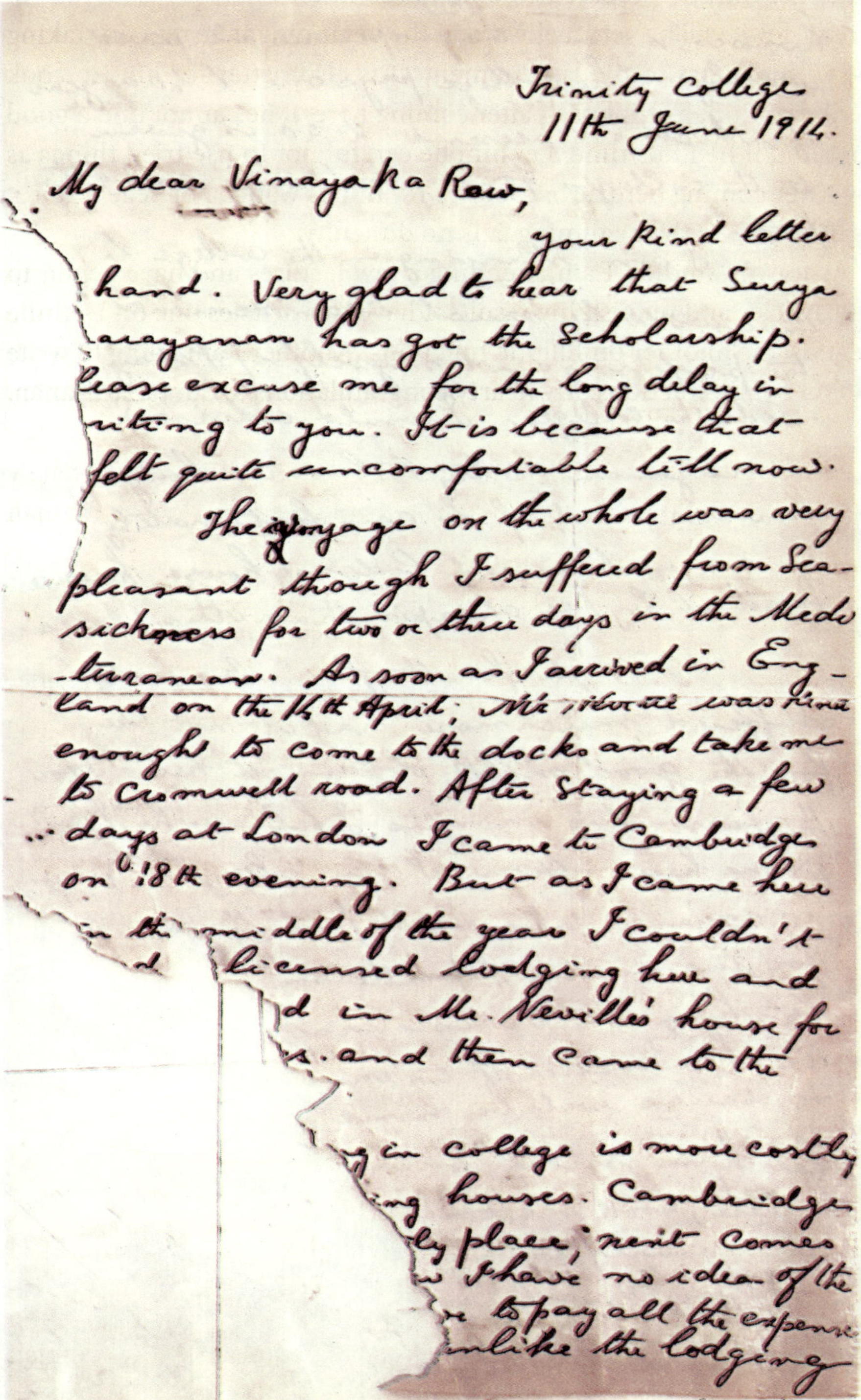

Trinity College
11th June 1914.

My dear Vinayaka Raw,

your kind letter
hand. Very glad to hear that Surya
arayanan has got the Scholarship.
lease excuse me for the long delay in
riting to you. It is because that
felt quite uncomfortable till now.

The voyage on the whole was very
pleasant though I suffered from Sea-
sickness for two or three days in the Medi
-terranean. As soon as I arrived in Eng-
land on the 14th April, Mr. Hoste was kind
enough to come to the docks and take me
to Cromwell road. After staying a few
days at London I came to Cambridge
on 18th evening. But as I came here
in the middle of the year I couldn't
d licensed lodging here and
d in Mr. Neville's house for
s. and then came to the

g in college is more costly
ng houses. Cambridge
ly place; next comes
w I have no idea of the
e to pay all the expense
unlike the lodging

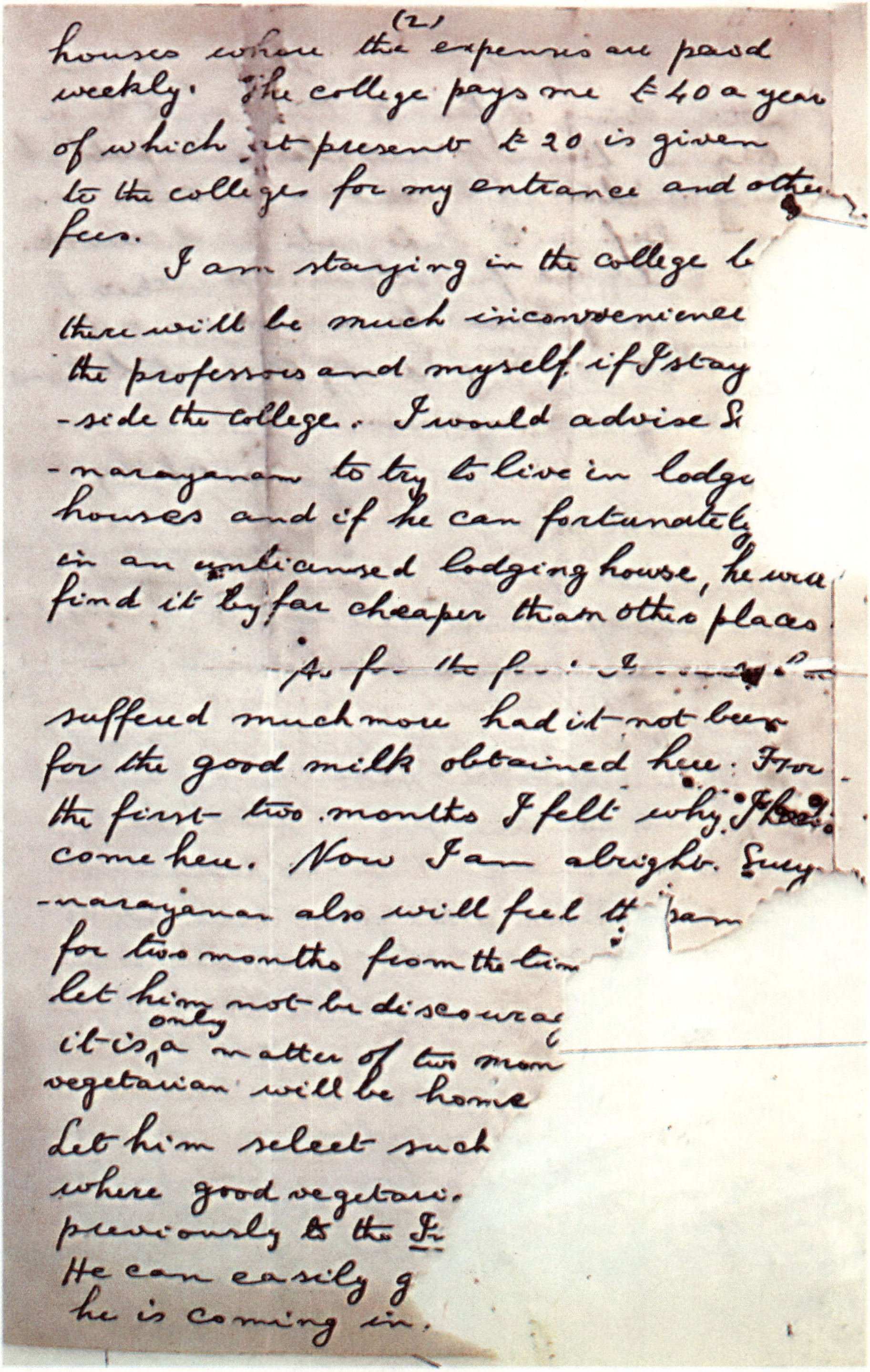

(2)
houses where the expenses are paid
weekly. The college pays me £40 a year
of which at present £20 is given
to the colleges for my entrance and other
fees.
I am staying in the college b
there will be much inconvenience
the professors and myself if I stay
-side the college. I would advise S
-narayanan to try to live in lodg
houses and if he can fortunately
in an unlicensed lodging house, he will
find it by far cheaper than other places
As for the f...
suffered much more had it not been
for the good milk obtained here. From
the first two months I felt why I had
come here. Now I am alright. Sury
-narayanan also will feel the same
for two months from the tim
let him not be discourag
it is only a matter of two mon
vegetarian will be home
Let him select such
where good vegetari
previously to the I
He can easily g
he is coming in.

(3)

There is another Suryanarayan here
who was a tutor in the Pachaiyappa's
college.. He says that he ~~knows~~ knew you all;
He is living in a lodging where they
prepare excellent vegetarian food.
During voyage there will be no-
-culty because most of them w
be Indians and he may tell the
whatever he wants. Let him be p
pared to take meals in ~~a non~~ an Engl
~~Brahmin hotels~~ Restaurant in Madras, for
it will be very awkward in the begin
-ning if he remains taking food in
his house to the last moment.
It is also better for him to cook one
or two things for himself after coming
here, if he cannot find a good house
and if he finds time.
Let him be careful not to t
things as they will put s
fat, and not to take
-dings as they may
After coming here he
cooks to fry things i
wants. For veget
eggs it will be s
in the beginning
is no difficulty.

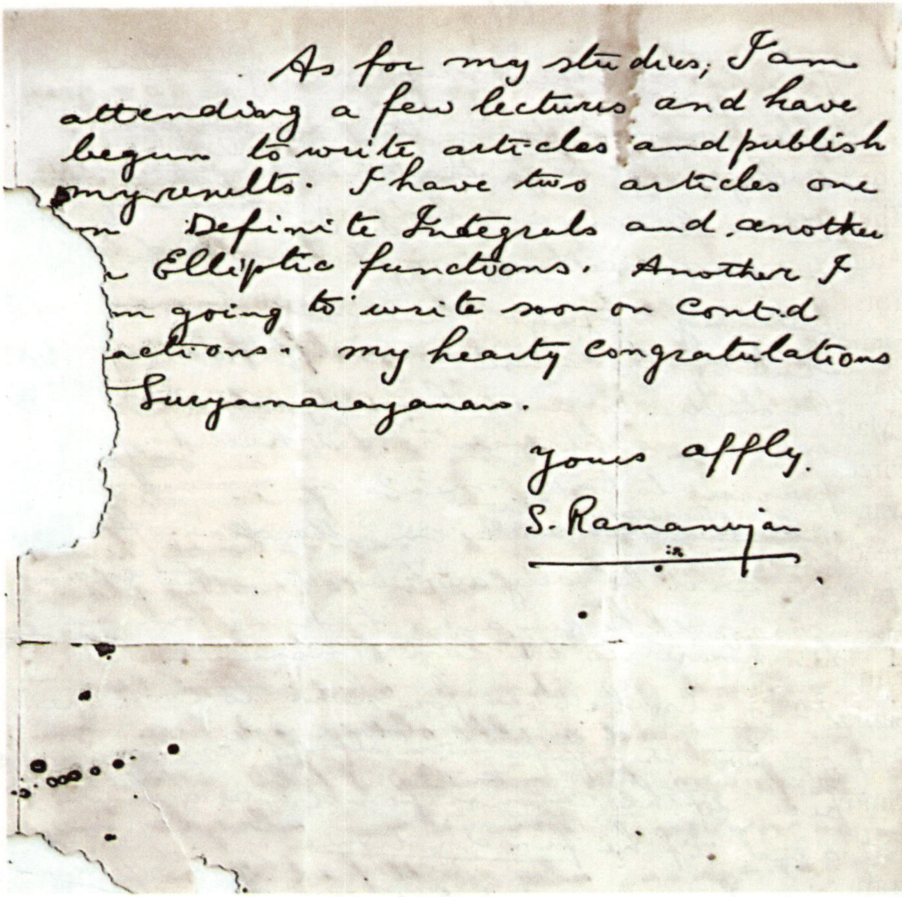

As for my studies; I am
attending a few lectures and have
begun to write arti-cles and publish
my results. I have two articles one
n Definite Integrals and another
n Elliptic functions. Another I
m going to write soon on Cont.d
actions. my hearty congratulations
Suryanarayanan.

Yours affly.
S. Ramanujan

Trinity College
11th September 1914

Salutations to the great Ramanuja! Ramanujan makes his countless prostrations to his mother and writes. Please write about your welfare. The letters you write reach me regularly. The three letters written on August 4, 10 and 11 reached me. 1 could not write letters for two weeks. You will henceforth be getting letters every week. There is no war in this country. War is going on only in the neighbouring country. That is to say, war is waged in a country that is as far as Rangoon is away from the city (Madras). Lakhs of persons have come here from our country to join the forces. Seven hundred Rajas have come here from our country to wage war. Ultimate victory will come only to the king of this country. You need not send any provisions. Ramachandra Rao's relative Ananda Rao, a youngster, has come to this country for study. He has not yet reached this place. He will come in October. Mr. Seshu Aiyar has told him to take with him numerous articles for being given to me. He and another youngster Sankara Rao have arrived in England.

When they reached the town of Port Said, the war commenced. Unknowingly they had sailed in the enemy ship. Their intention was to travel in an Austrian ship, get down at Austria and reach here by train. But while nearing the Island of Crete on the way to Austria after leaving Port Said, the crew of the English ship fired in the air to stop the ship and know its identity. Providentially, the ship stopped as it carried no guns. If the men of the ship had also fired, the ship would have been shot and sunk. The ship was captured and all the persons in the ship were taken prisoners and carried to Alexandria and the ship was seized. The people coming from our country and the Englishmen were put in another ship and sent here. These two youngsters reached after escaping this danger.

No war like this has raged before. The present war affects crores of people. It is not one or two crores. Germans set fire to many a city, slaughter and throw away all the people, the children, the women and the old. The small country Belgium is almost destroyed. Each town has buildings fifty to hundred times more valuable than those in Madras city.

In many towns, the people of the towns themselves blow off the supports of the bridges over rivers, leave them hanging in mid-air, spread gunpowder all over the streets, lay mines and cover them up and remain ready to flee. When enemies come, the bridges fall and half of them are carried off by the current of the river and when the rest enter the city, the dwellers themselves bum the city and flee. When streets arc ablaze, the enemies try to escape but the iron wires get round their legs and they perish, unable to run away.

War is waging at many places. Each place has an extent of 200 miles. This is on the land. Many ships are sunk by battles raging in mid oceans. These are of two kinds. One is to fire directly at a ship; the other is to go under water, knock at the enemy ship and sink it. Not only this. They fly in aeroplanes at great heights, bomb the cities and ruin them. As soon as enemy planes are sighted in the sky, the planes resting on the ground take off and fly at great speeds and dash against them resulting in destruction and death.

All that you sent got broken but reached me without falling off because of the supporting cloth. I get everything here. I get certain provisions from the city (Madras). You need not send anything.

Yours,
Ramanujan

* Letter from S. Ramanujan to his Mother Komalatammal dated Sept 11, 1914.

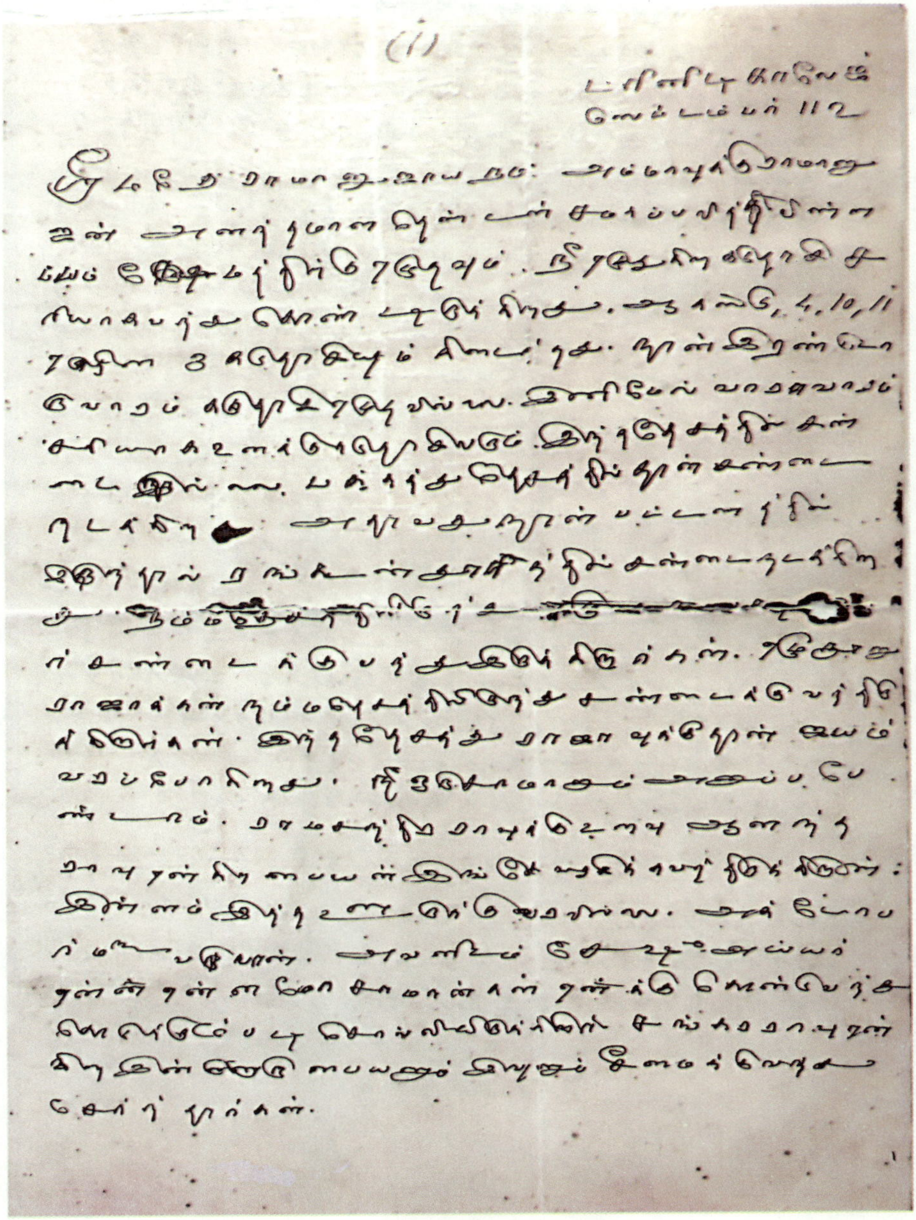
(1)

ட்ரினிடி காலேஜ்
செப்டம்பர் 11

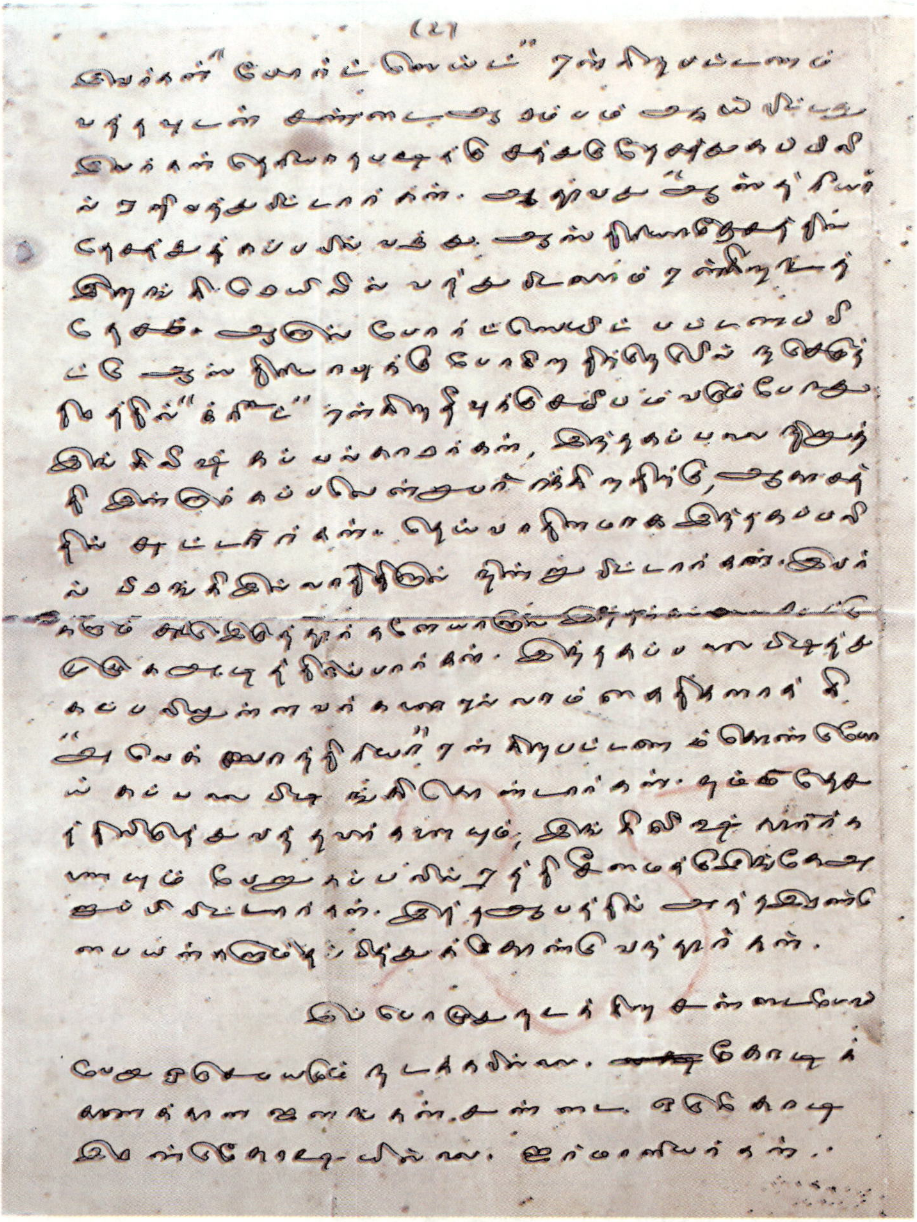

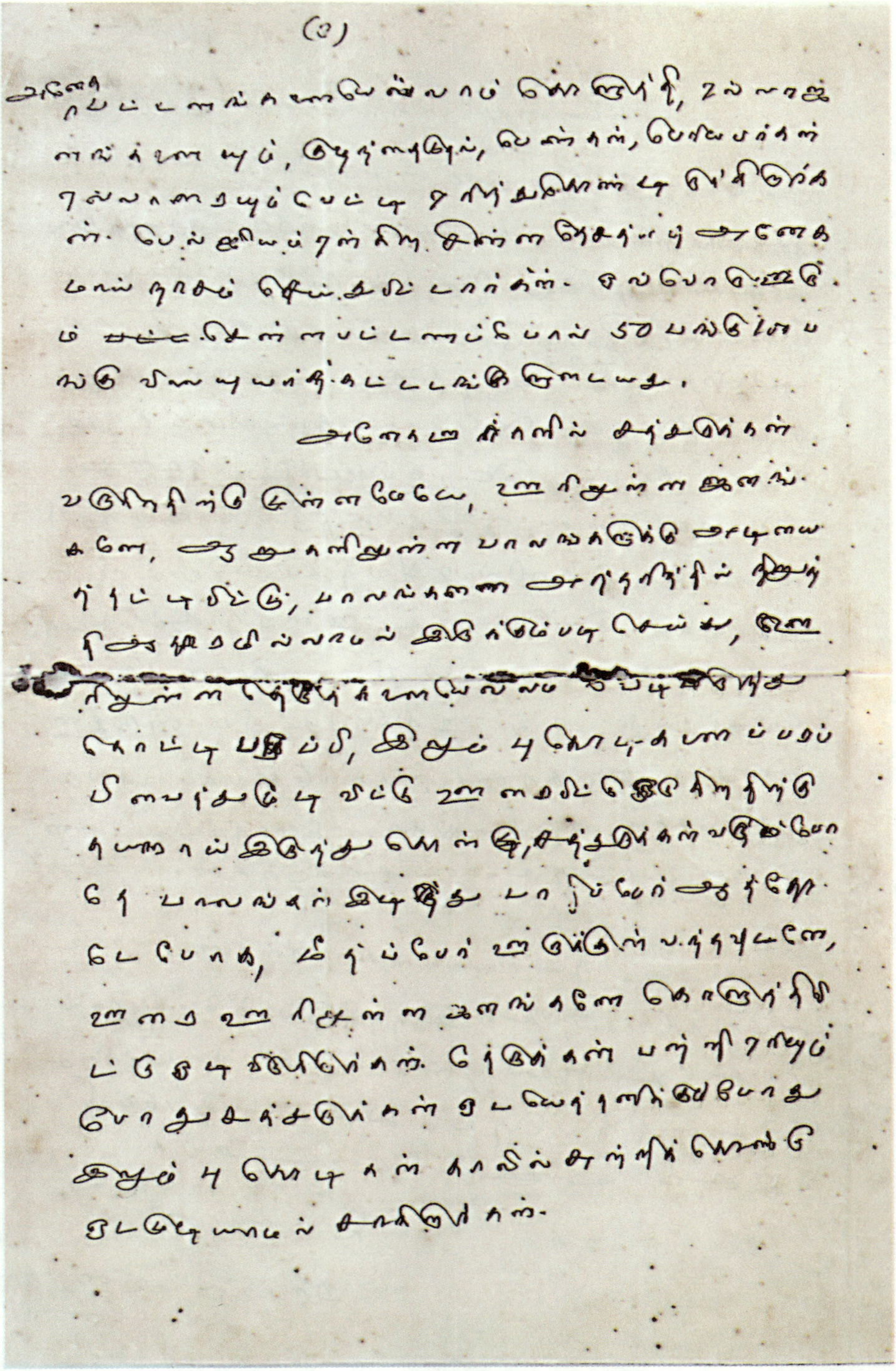

(6)

சண்டை அனேகயிடங்களில் நடக்கிறது.
ஒவ்வொரு இடத்திலும் 200 மைல் [illegible] பூமியில்
ஜனங்கள் சண்டை போடுகிறார்கள். இது பூமியி
ல் சண்டை, சமுத்திரத்தில் [illegible]
டு சண்டை போட்டு அனேக கப்பலை [illegible]
டிக்கிறார்கள். [illegible]
[illegible]
போய் கப்பலை [illegible]
இது மட்டுமல்ல. ஆகாசத்தில் [illegible]
ல் விமானங்களில் [illegible] ஆகாசத்திலி
ருந்து [illegible]
றார்கள். ஆகாசத்தில் விமானங்கள் [illegible]
[illegible]
[illegible] ஆகாசத்தில் [illegible]
ந்து போய், விமானங்களை [illegible], விமான
ங்கள் உடைந்து போய் சாகிறார்கள்.

[illegible]
நடந்து போய், [illegible]
[illegible]
[illegible]
[illegible]

[illegible]

ராமானுஜன்

Trinity College
17.11.14

Salutations to the great Ramanuja! Ramanujan makes his countless prostrations to his father and writes. Well and wish to hear the same from you. I got your letter. I have also received the letter written earlier by Tirunarayanan. I have all the pickles. I get tamarind etc. from Madras. You need not send anything. Except the kuzhuvidam (dried up precooked foodstuff made of flour) which you are sending now, do not send any other thing. My college was closed last week. It is to open in the middle of January.

I am getting on well. Keep the house in such a way that it is attractive to look at. Do not allow the gutter to run as usual. Pave the place with bricks and keep it well. I am getting on well. The students who have come from our place have joined the neighbouring college.

Yours,
Ramanujan

* Letter from S. Ramanujan to his father Srinivasa Aiyangar dated Nov 17, 1914, Ramanujan Museum and Math Education Centre Chennai.

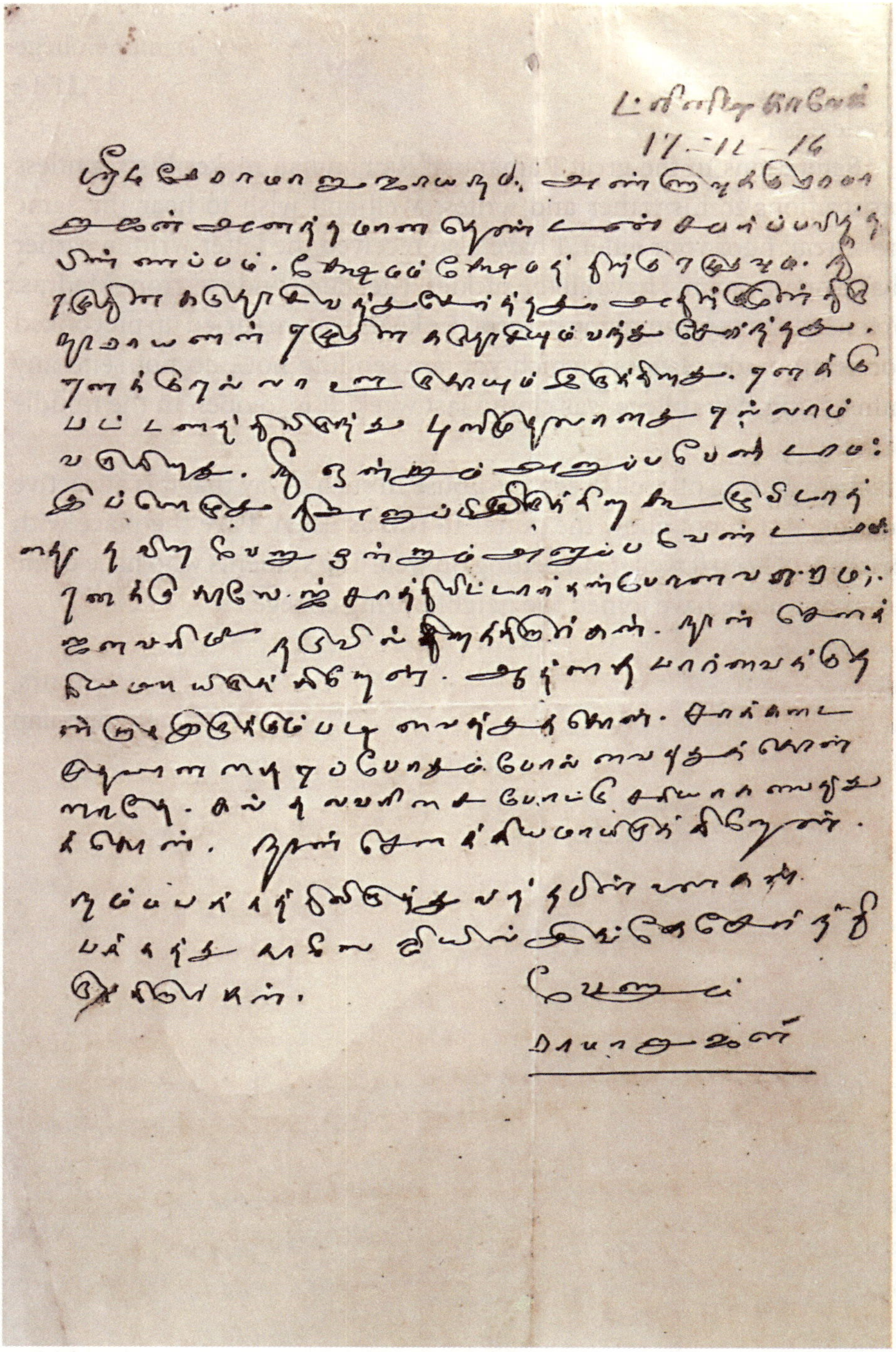

கேம்பிரிட்ஜ்
17-11-16

ராமானுஜன்

Trinity College
17th December 1914

My dear Sir,

Received your letter of 2/11. My thanks to your wife for all her well wishes. It is a great mystery to me how my pamphlets reached you without my letter. You did not mention of my previous letter also. Very glad to hear that Godavery and her child are doing well. I send you herewith a copy of the "Definite Integrals connected with Gauss sums". This has really no connection with Gauss's sums except that one will be reminded of Gauss's sums. I think that I am really fortunate in having made the friendship of such nice gentlemen as Messrs Hardy and Littlewood. They are the greatest of English pure mathematicians, and at the same time the most rigorous. Mr Neville also is a very nice gentleman and I am very sorry that our fields in Mathematics are very different and far away from each other and so have no chance of meeting him as often as with these. You must remember that the "Orders of Infinity' which I found in your room introduced me to Messrs Hardy and Littlewood. They are doing researches in the most difficult and advanced part of pure mathematics. They have proved many properties of the zeta function (Riemann's) which defied all attempts to prove them for these so many years. I shall tell you one of the recent researches of Mr Littlewood. If you see the last paragraph in "Mathew's Theory of Numbers" you will find the statement "Hence we conclude that Gauss's approximation was too great". Mr Littlewood has proved that this is wrong beyond a certain value, in fact beyond $10^{10^{10}}$! Gauss's approximation was too great only when $x < 10^{10^{10}}$. I shall tell you one of the researches of Mr Hardy (not recent) about irrational numbers. He has shown that, if you take any irrational number, say $\sqrt{2}$, cos 20°, π or e and write these as decimals, e.g., $\sqrt{2}$= 1.4142135... to a large number of decimal places, say a billion or trillion decimal places, then the ratio of the number of 0's, 1's, 2's, 3's, ... tends to 1 as the number of decimal places becomes larger. He has shown more than this. Let n_o, n_1, n_2, n_3, ... be the number of 0's, 1's, 2's, 3's, ... within n decimal places. Then

$\sqrt{n_0} - \sqrt{n_1}$ is finite when n becomes infinite,

$\sqrt{n_0} - \sqrt{n_2}$ ... ditto,

$\sqrt{n_0} - \sqrt{n_3}$ ... ditto,

and so on. These results are true in any scale of notation.

I am at present doing research in Arithmetical functions such as the number of divisors of N, the number of decompositions of N into two squares, etc. and functions connected with Arithmetical numbers. Here we get many sorts of functions that cannot be imagined at all. I shall show you an example. Suppose

$$F(x) = \frac{\cos\left(\sec\frac{1}{\sqrt{1-x}}\right)}{1^2} + \frac{\cos\left(\sec\frac{1}{\sqrt{1-2x}}\right) + \cos\left(\frac{1}{\sqrt{2-x}}\right)}{2^2} + \frac{\cos\left(\sec\frac{1}{\sqrt{1-3x}}\right) + \cos\left(\frac{1}{\sqrt{3-x}}\right)}{3^2} + \frac{\cos\left(\sec\frac{1}{\sqrt{2-3x}}\right) + \cos\left(\frac{1}{\sqrt{3-2x}}\right)}{4^2} + \cdots.$$

I write for the denominators the squares of the natural numbers 1^2, 2^2, 3^2, ... For the numerators first I take all rational numbers

$$1, \frac{1}{2}, \frac{1}{3}, \frac{2}{3}, \frac{1}{4}, \frac{2}{4}, \frac{3}{4}, \frac{1}{5}, \frac{2}{5}, \frac{3}{5}, \frac{4}{5},$$

and construct the numerators in order with these fractions. The series is absolutely convergent. But *F (x)* does not exist for any rational value, say 2/3, since one term will be of the form cos(sec ∞) which is not definite. But *F(x)* exists for all irrational values. There is another peculiarity. Suppose you approach any rational point, say 2/3, from the right side, then $\sqrt{2 - 3.x} = \sqrt{-0}$ and so

$$\cos\left(\sec\frac{1}{\sqrt{2-3x}}\right) \to \cos(\operatorname{sech}\infty) = 1.$$

But when you approach the same 2/3 from the left side, then $\sqrt{2\text{-}3x} = \sqrt{+0}$, and so

$$\cos\left(\sec\frac{1}{\sqrt{2-3x}}\right) = \cos(\sec\infty),$$

which is indeterminate. Hence *F(x)* exists as the limit from one side and not from the other side when you approach any rational point.

Mr Hardy read before the London Mathematical Society some of my re- sults in Arithmetical functions. It will be printed in 2 or 3 months and you will find many interesting results there. In this paper I entirely devote myself to the number of divisors of N and the functions connected with it.

I hope you and your family are doing well. I thank you very much for your encouragement to my people. My compliments to your wife.

Is Mr Patrachariar doing well? Where is he now, in Saidapet or in Madras?

Yours sincerely,
S. Ramanujan.

* Letter from S. Ramanujan to C. N. Ganpathy Iyer, Professor of Mathematics, Presidency College dated Dec 17, 1914, Ramanujan Museum and Math Education Centre, Chennai.

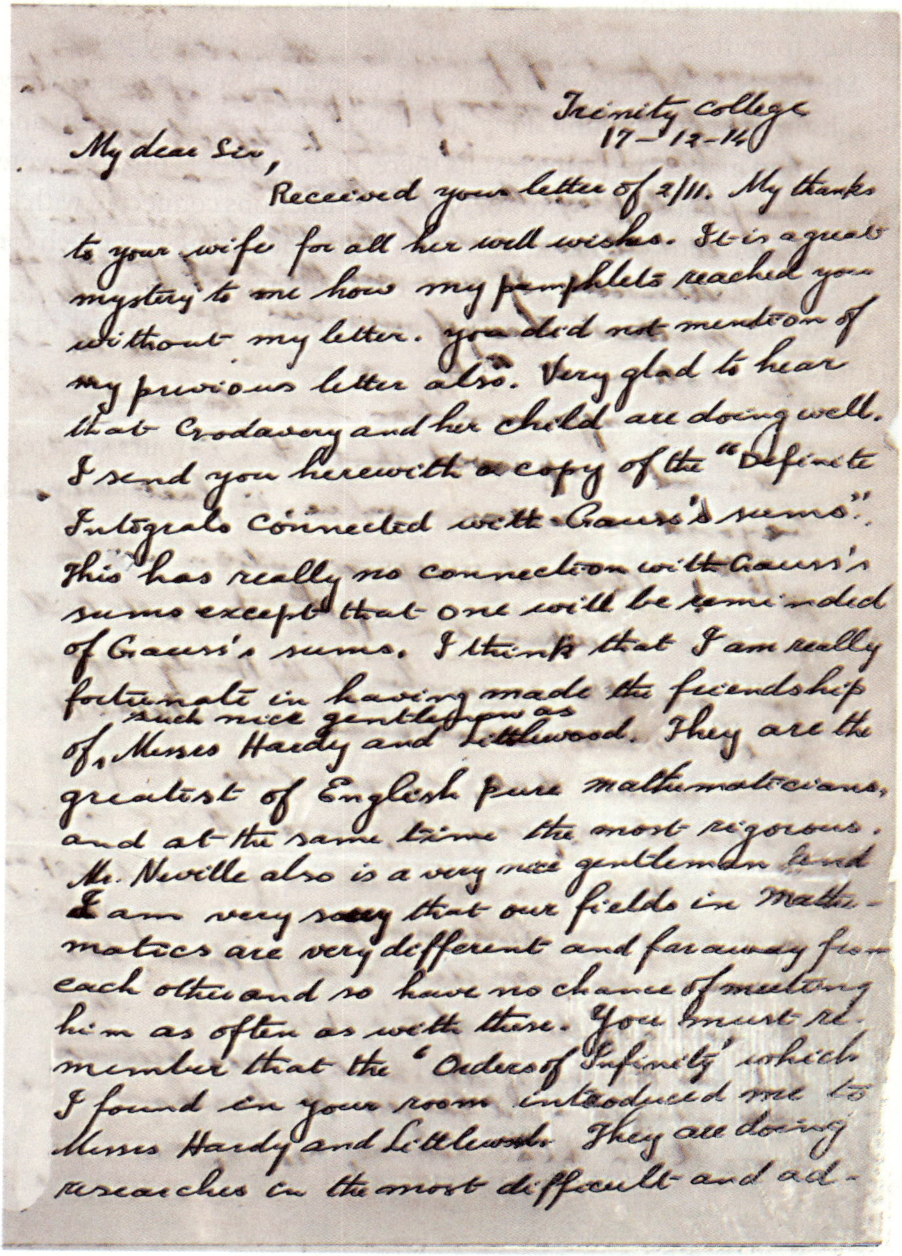

Trinity college
17-12-14

My dear Sir,

Received your letter of 2/11. My thanks to your wife for all her well wishes. It is a great mystery to me how my pamphlets reached you without my letter. you did not mention of my previous letter also. Very glad to hear that Godavary and her child are doing well. I send you herewith a copy of the "Definite Integrals connected with Gauss's sums". This has really no connection with Gauss's sums except that one will be reminded of Gauss's sums. I think that I am really fortunate in having made the friendship of such nice gentlemen as Messrs Hardy and Littlewood. They are the greatest of English pure mathematicians, and at the same time the most rigorous. Mr. Neville also is a very nice gentleman and I am very sorry that our fields in Mathematics are very different and far away from each other and so have no chance of meeting him as often as with these. You must remember that the 'Orders of Infinity' which I found in your room introduced me to Messrs Hardy and Littlewood. They are doing researches in the most difficult and ad-

vanced part of pure mathematics. They
have proved many properties of the zeta
function (Riemann's) which defied all at-
tempts to prove them for these so many years.
I shall tell you one of the recent researches of
Mr. Littlewood. If you see the last paragraph
in "Mathew's Theory of numbers" you will find
the statement "Hence we conclude that
Gauss's approximation was too great". Mr
Littlewood has proved that this is wrong
beyond a certain value, in fact beyond
$10^{10^{10}}$! Gauss's approximation was too
great only when $x < 10^{10^{10}}$. I shall tell
you one of the researches of Mr Hardy (not re-
cent), about irrational numbers. He
has shown that, if you take any ir-
rational no., say $\sqrt{2}$, $\cos 20^\circ$, π or e and
write these as decimals e.g. $\sqrt{2} = 1.4142135$—
to a large no. of decimal places, say a bil-
-lion or trillion decimal places, then
the ratio of the no. of 0's, 1's, 2's, 3's. tends
to 1 as the no. of decimal places becomes
~~or~~ larger and larger. He has shown
more than this. Let $n_0, n_1, n_2, n_3, \ldots$ be

the no. of 0's, 1's, 2's, 3's, ... there within n decimal places. Then

$\sqrt{n_0} - \sqrt{n_1}$ is finite when n becomes ∞

$\sqrt{n_0} - \sqrt{n_2}$ — — — — do ——

$\sqrt{n_0} - \sqrt{n_3}$ —————— do ——

and so on. These results are true in any scale of notation.

I am at present doing researches in Arithmetical functions such as, the no. of divisors of N, the no. of decompositions of N in to two squares, etc and functions connected with Arithmetical numbers. Here we get many sorts of functions that cannot be imagined at all. I shall show you an example.

Suppose

$$F(x) = \frac{\cos\left(\sec\frac{1}{\sqrt{1-x}}\right)}{1^2} + \frac{\cos\left(\sec\frac{1}{\sqrt{1-2x}}\right) + \cos\left(\sec\frac{1}{\sqrt{2-x}}\right)}{2^2}$$

$$+ \frac{\cos\left(\sec\frac{1}{\sqrt{1-3x}}\right) + \cos\left(\sec\frac{1}{\sqrt{3-x}}\right)}{3^2} +$$

$$\frac{\cos\left(\sec\frac{1}{\sqrt{2-3x}}\right) + \cos\left(\sec\frac{1}{\sqrt{3-2x}}\right)}{4^2}$$

I write for the denominators, the squares of the natural nos $1^2, 2^2, 3^2, \ldots$: For the numerators, first I take all rational nos. $1, \frac{1}{2}, \frac{1}{3}, \frac{2}{3}, \frac{1}{4}, \frac{2}{4}, \frac{3}{4}, \frac{1}{5}, \frac{2}{5}, \frac{3}{5}, \frac{4}{5}, \ldots$ and construct the numerators in order with these fractions. The series is absolutely convergent. But F(x) does not exist for any rational value, say $\frac{2}{3}$, since one term will be of the form $\cos(\sec\infty)$ which is not definite. But F(x) exists for all irrational values. There is another peculiarity. Suppose you approach any rational pt. say $\frac{2}{3}$ from the right side, then $\sqrt{2-3x} = \sqrt{-0}$; and so $\cos\left(\sec \frac{1}{\sqrt{2-3x}}\right) = \cos(\operatorname{sech}\infty) = 1$. But when you approach the same $\frac{2}{3}$ from the left side, then $\sqrt{2-3x} = \sqrt{+0}$; and so $\cos\left(\sec \frac{1}{\sqrt{2-3x}}\right) = \cos(\sec\infty)$ which is indeterminate. Hence F(x) exists as the limit from one side and not from the other side when you approach any rational point.

Mr. Hardy read before the London Math Society some of my results in Arithmetical functions. It will be printed in 2 or 3 months. You will find many interesting results there. In this paper I entirely devote myself to the no. of divisors of N and the functions connected with it.

I hope you and your family are doing well. I thank you very much for your encouragement to my people. My compliments to your wife.

Yours sincerely
S. Ramanujan.

Is Mr. Pattachariar doing well? Where is he now, in Saidapet or in Madras?

Trinity College
24th March 1915

My dear Vinayaka Row,

Received your letter of 18th Feb. I have received all your letters. It appears from your letter that you haven't received my letter. In that letter I wrote mainly about the war.

I was not well till the beginning of this term owing to the weather and consequently I couldn't publish anything for about 5 months. This term I have published 3 or 4 pamphlets and a long paper. Up to this time I have written on the following subjects

Definite Integrals, Modular Equations and approximations to π (Elliptic functions), Definite integrals (which come out in finite terms for the rational values of the parameter and not for the irrational values), Series connected with the Eulerian Constant, Sum of the square roots of the natural numbers (and some other allied sums), New expressions for the Riemann Zeta function, Some series having curious properties, and a very long paper on the Divisors of a number. All these are published in the 'Messenger of Mathematics', 'Quarterly Journal of Mathematics' and the 'London Mathematical Journal.

Except the first 3 papers all others are now being printed.

Suryanarayanan is not appearing for the I.C.S. as he has a very bad short-sight. He will not be selected even if he comes in the top of the list. He will enter the Educational Service. I am glad to inform you that he shines in public speeches in various societies and glorious tutorial reports in his college.

I hope you and your family are doing well and wish you success in the B.L. examination.

With Best Wishes
I am
Yours Sincerely
S. Ramanujan

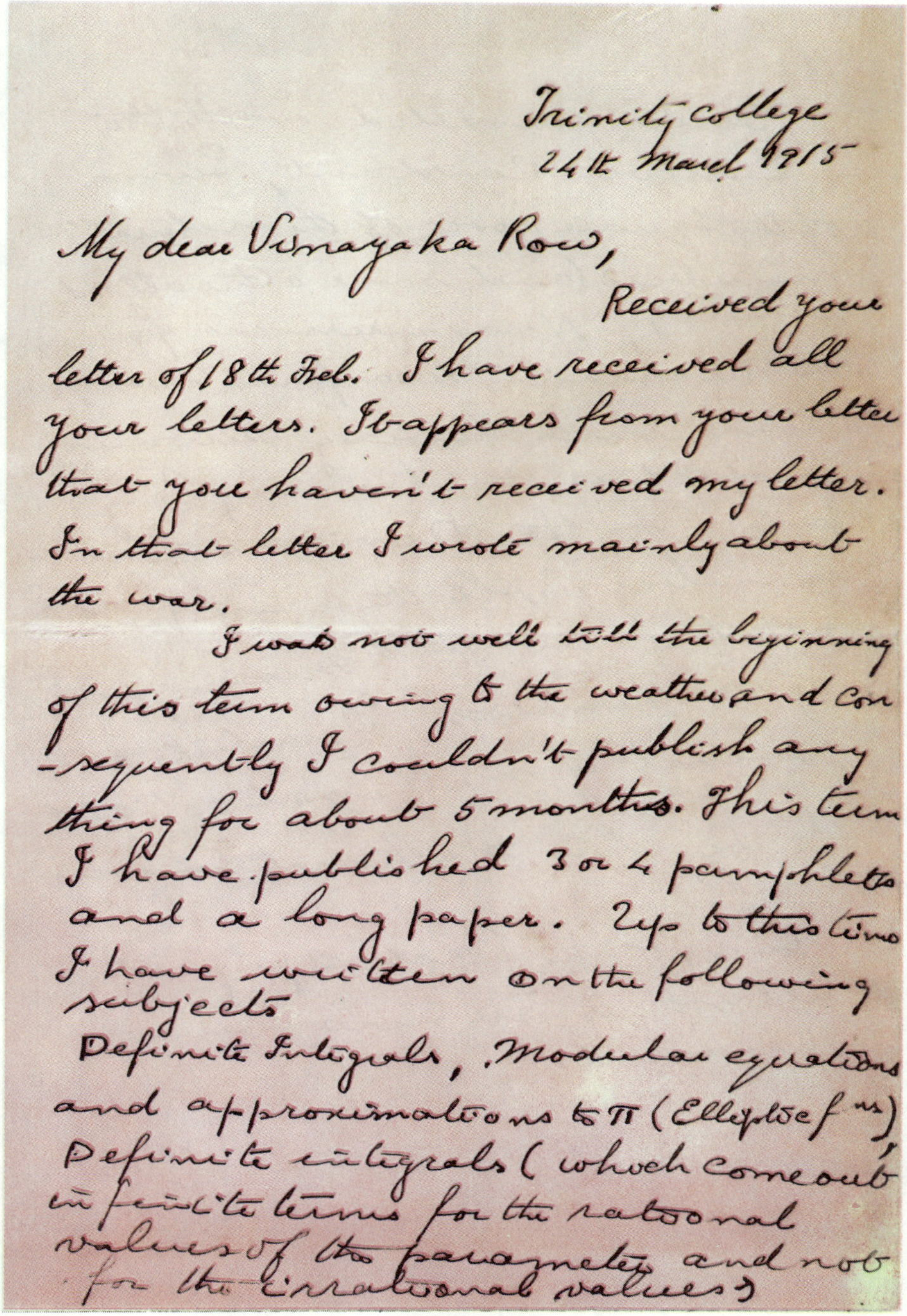

Trinity college
24th March 1915

My dear Vinayaka Row,

Received your letter of 18th Feb. I have received all your letters. It appears from your letter that you haven't received my letter. In that letter I wrote mainly about the war.

I was not well till the beginning of this term owing to the weather and consequently I couldn't publish anything for about 5 months. This term I have published 3 or 4 pamphlets and a long paper. Up to this time I have written on the following subjects

Definite Integrals, Modular equations and approximations to π (Elliptic fns)

Definite integrals (which come out in finite terms for the rational values of the parameter and not for the irrational values)

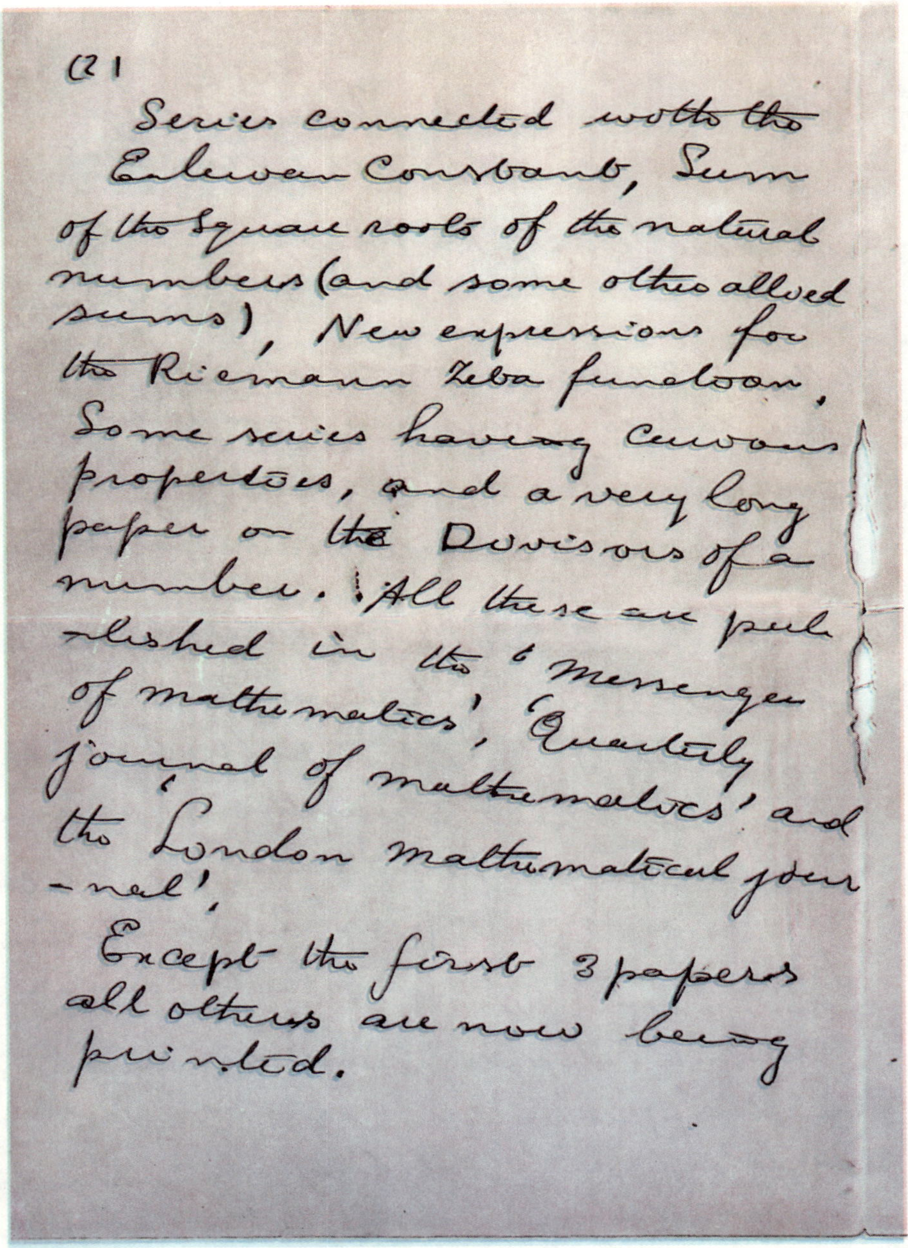

(2)

Series connected with the Eulerian Constant, Sum of the Square roots of the natural numbers (and some other allied sums), New expressions for the Riemann Zeta function, Some series having curious properties, and a very long paper on the Divisors of a number. All these are published in the 'Messenger of mathematics', 'Quarterly journal of mathematics' and the 'London mathematical journal'.

Except the first 3 papers all others are now being printed.

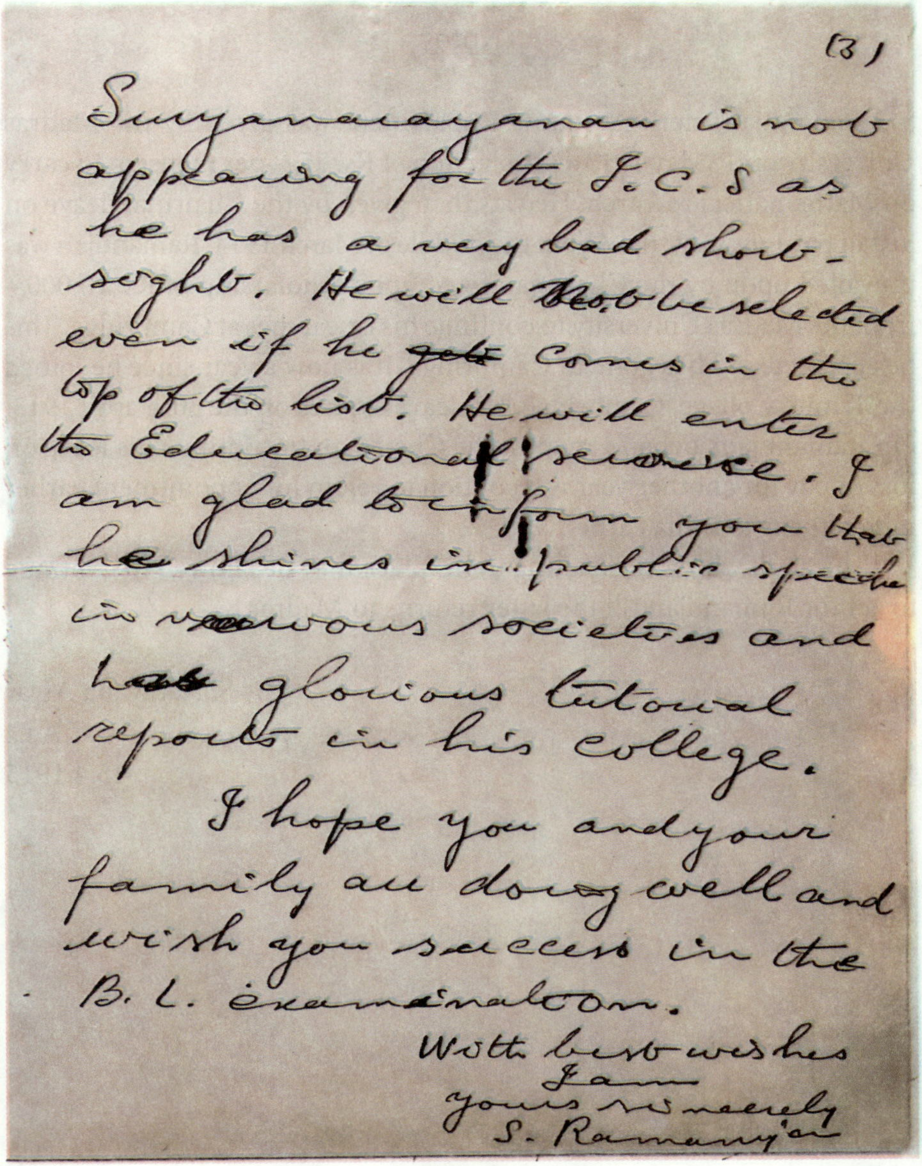

(3)

Suryanarayanan is not appearing for the I.C.S as he has a very bad short-sight. He will not be selected even if he comes in the top of the list. He will enter the Educational service. I am glad to inform you that he shines in public speeches in various societies and has glorious tutorial reports in his college.

I hope you and your family are doing well and wish you success in the B.L. examination.

With best wishes
I am
yours sincerely
S. Ramanujan

Madras Port Trust

Notes

S . Ramanujan, clerk Accounts Department was given by the Madras University on 1st May 1913 a scholarship of Rs. 75 /- per mensem to carry on Mathematical research. He was then given by the Chairman leave on loss of pay for two years. About the middle of March 1914, Ramanujan was prevailed upon by the Chairman to accept a scholarship of Rs. 10,000/- from the Madras University to continue his researches at Cambridge. This he accepted and has gone to Cambridge. It is now a year since he joined the Trinity College, Cambridge. His leave expires on the 30th april 1915. On Ramanujan's behalf I request the Chairman to continue his leave on loss of pay for another year with option to rejoin his appointment earlier if he returns to India earlier.

The clerk who is now acting in his place may be allowed to continue to act for Ramanujan till the latter returns to Madras.

S. Narayana Aiyar
C.A.C.
15.4.1915

M. P. T. No. 86—A.
4,000—14-5-12.

37

79

83

MADRAS PORT TRUST.

NOTES.

NOTE IN CONNECTION WITH LETTER.

No.________ IN RECEIPT REGISTER.

S. Ramanujam, clerk Accounts Department was given by the Madras University on 1st May 1913 a Scholarship of Rs 75/- per mensem to carry on Mathematical research. He was then given by the Chairman leave on loss of pay for two years. About the middle of March 1914 Ramanujam was prevailed upon by the Chairman to accept a Scholarship of Rs 10,000/- from the Madras University to continue his researches at Cambridge. This he accepted and has gone to Cambridge. It is now a year since he joined the Trinity College, Cambridge. His leave expires on the 30th April 1915. On Ramanujam's behalf I request the Chairman to continue his leave on loss of pay for another year with option to rejoin his appointment earlier if he returns to India earlier.

The clerk who is now acting in his place may be allowed to continue to act for Ramanujam till the latter returns to Madras.

C.A.C.

Sanctioned leave on loss of pay

15.

TRINITY COLLEGE
CAMBRIDGE

10th September 1915

My dear Vinayaka Row,

Received your letter ... Very glad to hear of the birth of a son to you. But I am sorry that you failed in the examination. Tenati Suryanarayan also was sorry when he heard of your failure in D.T.M. He sat for the I.C.S. exam last month. I shall let you know about the result when it is announced. I do not know any-thing about S.S. Suryanarayan for these four or five weeks. This being the long vacation most likely he may not be in Oxford at all.

Tenati Suryanarayan and I were exceedingly sorry to hear the sad death of Professor Singaravelu Mudaliyar at so early an age. We came to know of this unexpected sad news for the first time from your letter which reached here before the Indian Math. journal.

Do you want the general information about Cambridge or special information about all the colleges here? I shall write to you in my next letter the main reasons for the rapid progress in mathematics here unlike India...

Yours sincerely,
S. Ramanujan

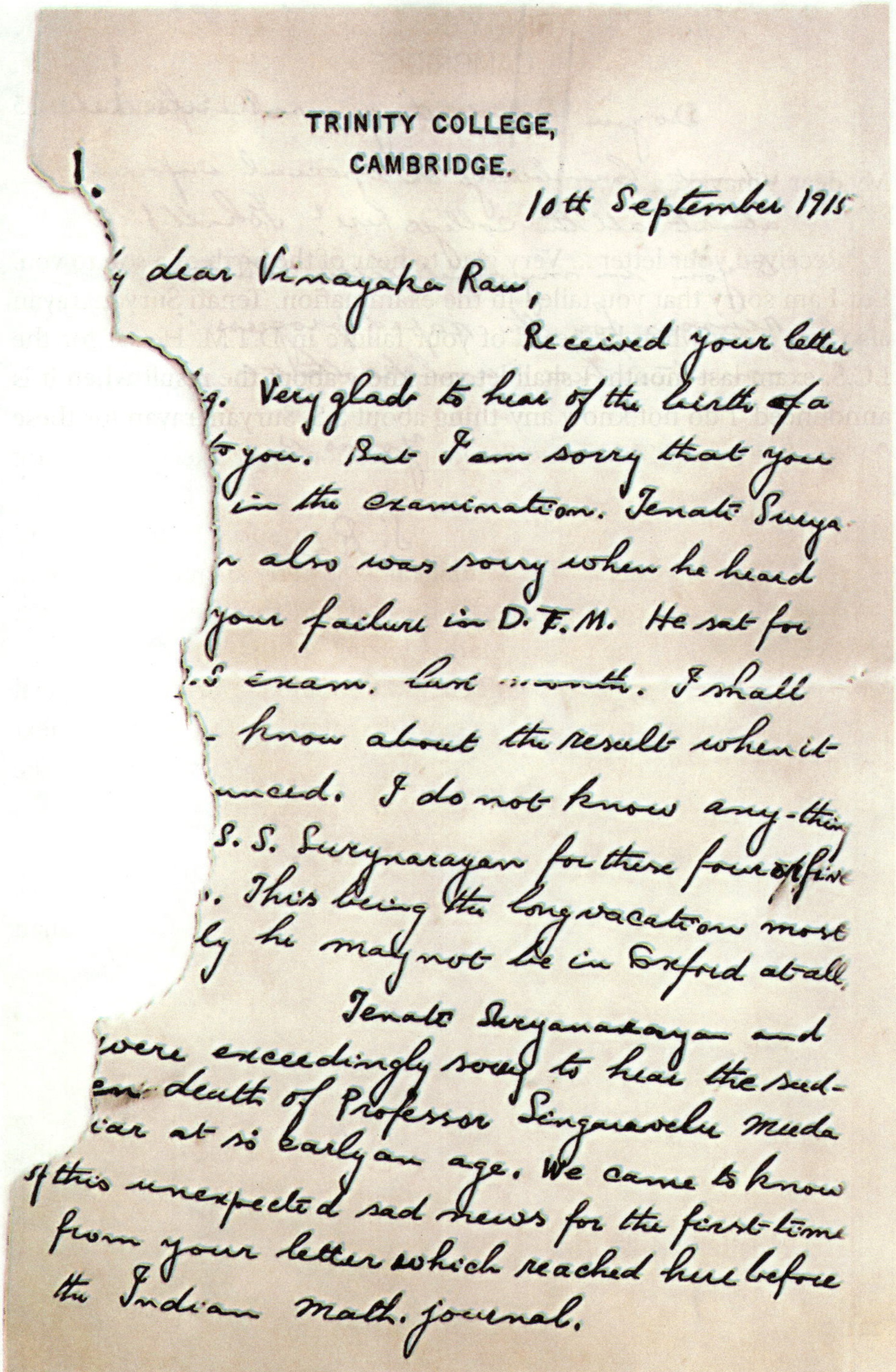

TRINITY COLLEGE,
CAMBRIDGE.

1.

10th September 1915

y dear Vinayaka Rau,

Received your letter
g. Very glad to hear of the birth of a
to you. But I am sorry that you
in the examination. Tenali Surya
r also was sorry when he heard
your failure in D.T.M. He sat for
.S exam. last month. I shall
know about the result when it
unced. I do not know any-thing
S. S. Surynarayan for these four of five
. This being the long vacation most
ly he may not be in Oxford at all.

Tenali Suryanarayana and
were exceedingly sorry to hear the sud-
en death of Professor Singaravelu Muda
iar at so early an age. We came to know
of this unexpected sad news for the first time
from your letter which reached here before
the Indian Math. journal.

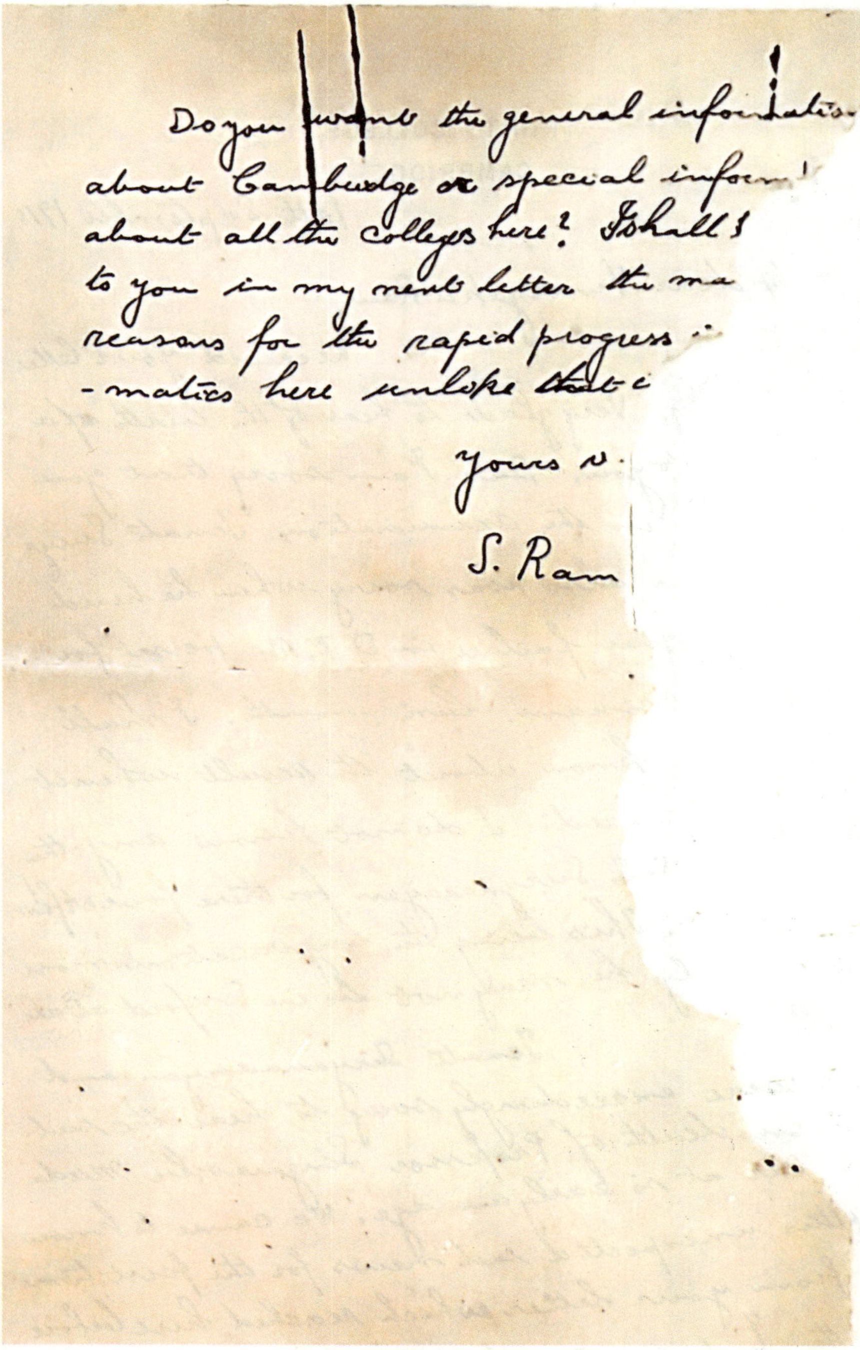

Do you want the general informatio-
about Cambridge or special inform'
about all the colleges here? I shall
to you in my next letter the ma
reasons for the rapid progress i
-matics here unlike that i

yours v

S. Ram

TRINITY COLLEGE-CAMBRIDGE

11th Nov. 1915

My dear Sir,

Your kind letter duly to hand. Very glad to hear of the kind remembrances of Sir Francis Spring. Had it not been for his special record mandate to the Government of Madras I would not have got the scholarship so easily and quickly from Madras University. He will be glad if he knows from you about my progress.

I am sending you one of my papers read before the London Math. Society in last November. It is wrongly printed in the paper that it was read in last June. The paper that was read in last June was about some of my results in my notebook. It will take some months for me to write that paper systematically and publish it.

As for your suggestion to publish more important and general results I have first to read French and German works and journals and to become very familiar with extremely rigorous proofs and then publish my results. Now I shall be going on to write something in my own way for 6 or 7 months to come. Unless I remain here for two years more, I cannot do all I have to do. If I just consider the enormous losses to this college owing to this terrible war I think I have no voice to ask the authorities of this college to do me anything if they cannot afford to retain me here of their own accord. There were about 700 students and even more than that sometimes before the war; but there are only about 150 this year. Perhaps there may be very few only next year if the war continues.

It appears that Madras University has asked this College about my work. I think the reports may reach Madras very soon after you receive this letter if they have not already reached there. If I could remain here for more than one year I should like to go over there for the coming long vacation so that I may not disappoint my people to whom I promised to return at the end of two years of my stay here.

I shall be very much obliged to you if you take so much trouble as to let Sir Francis Spring know all I have written to you. He will make all the necessary arrangements for my further stay here as well as for my voyage to India.

I am ever indebted to you and Sir Francis Spring for your zealous interest in my case from the very beginning of our acquaintance.

Yours Sincerely,
S. Ramanujan

P.S. - I am glad to tell you that I may be conferred upon the Research Degree next March.

* This letter was written by Ramanujan to S. Narayana Aiyar and gives details about what was happening in his life at this time. Expressing his gratitude and indebtedness to Francis Spring and Narayana Aiyar, he also sent Aiyar one of his papers.

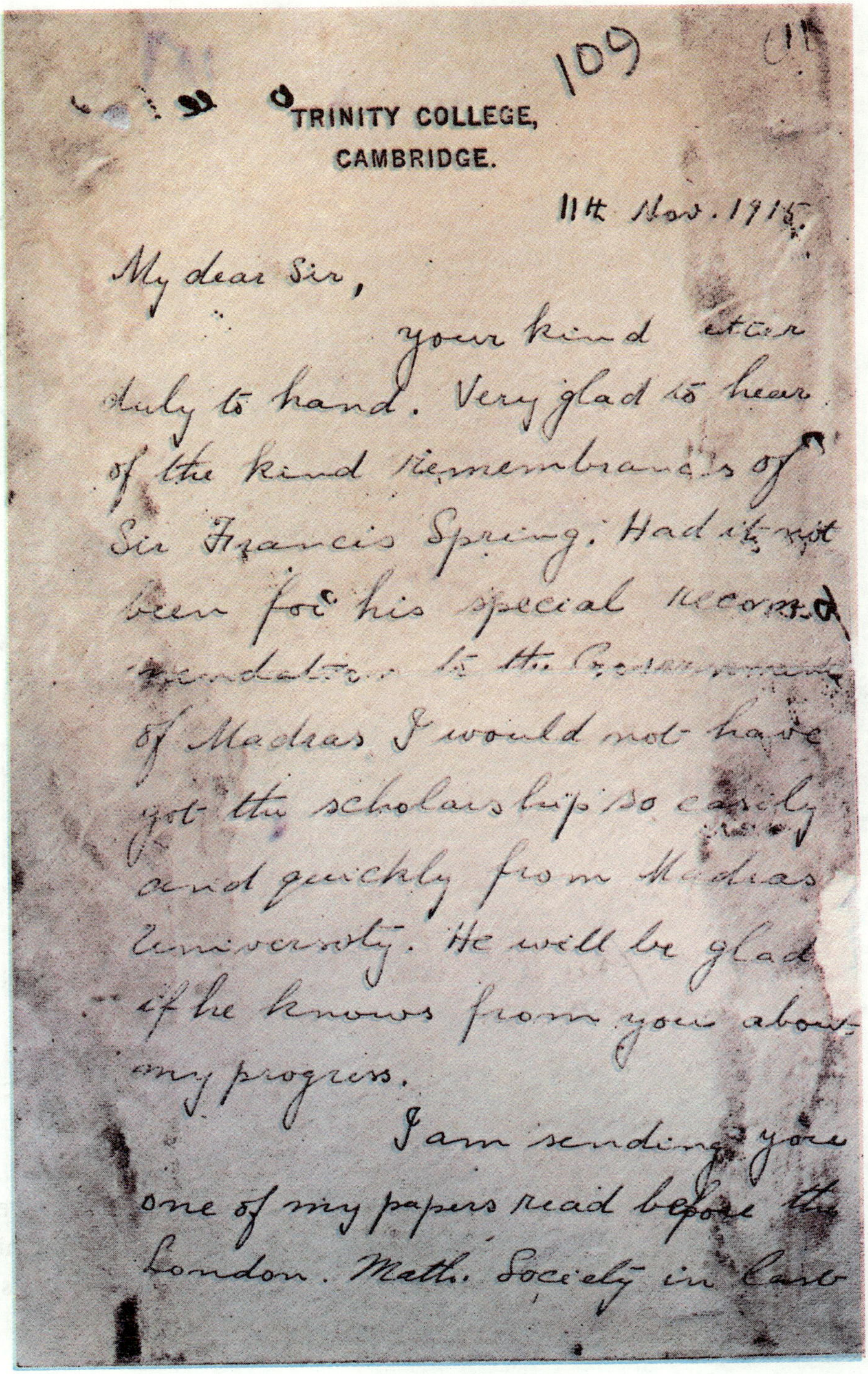

109

TRINITY COLLEGE,
CAMBRIDGE.

11th Nov. 1915.

My dear Sir,

your kind letter duly to hand. Very glad to hear of the kind remembrances of Sir Francis Spring. Had it not been for his special recommendation to the Government of Madras I would not have got the scholarship so easily and quickly from Madras University. He will be glad if he knows from you about my progress.

I am sending you one of my papers read before the London. Math. Society in last

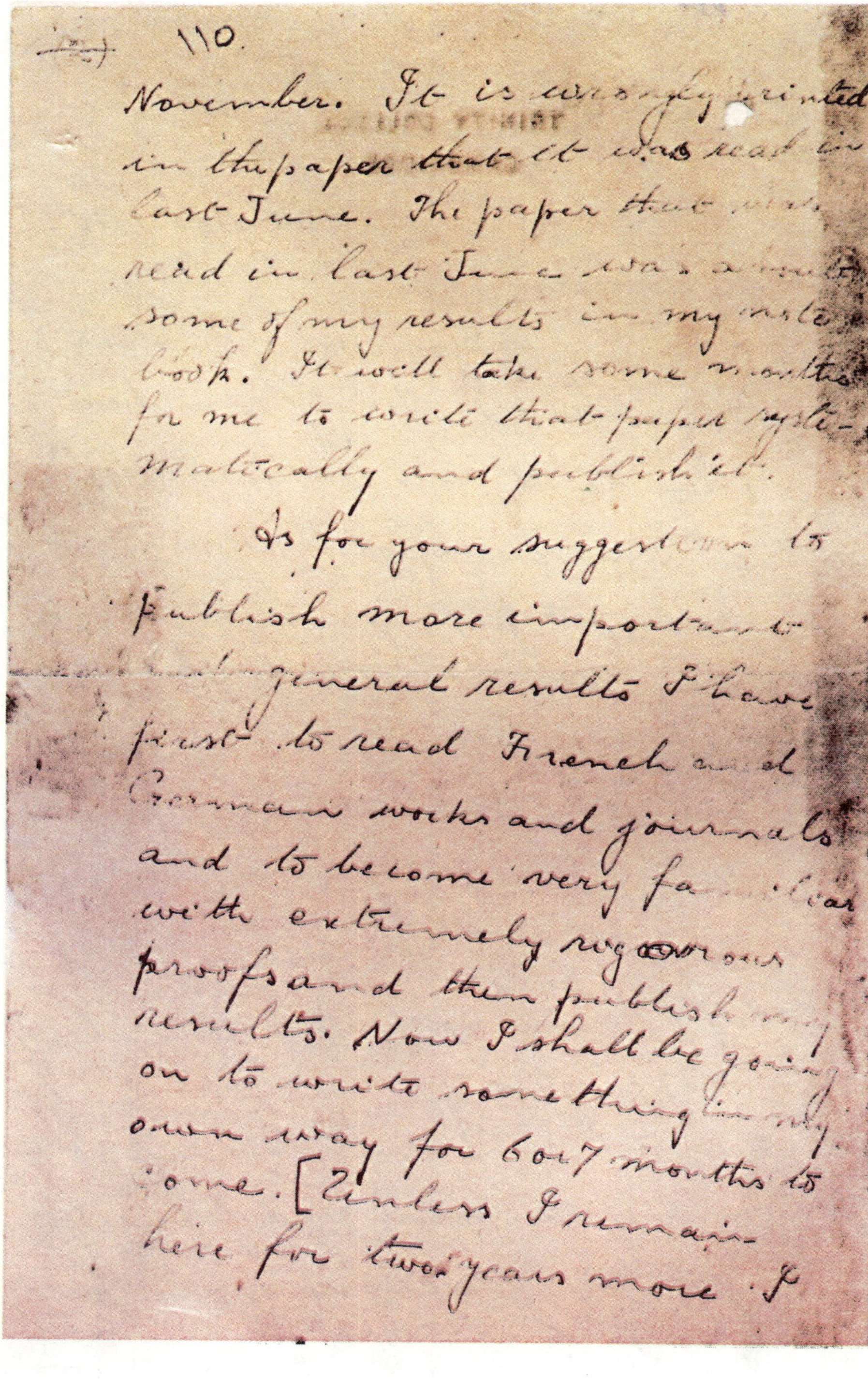

110.

November. It is wrongly printed in the paper that it was read in last June. The paper that was read in last June was a [illegible] some of my results in my note book. It will take some months for me to write that paper systematically and publish it.

As for your suggestion to publish more important and general results I have first to read French and German works and journals and to become very familiar with extremely rigorous proofs and then publish my results. Now I shall be going on to write something in my own way for 6 or 7 months to come. [Unless I remain here for two years more I

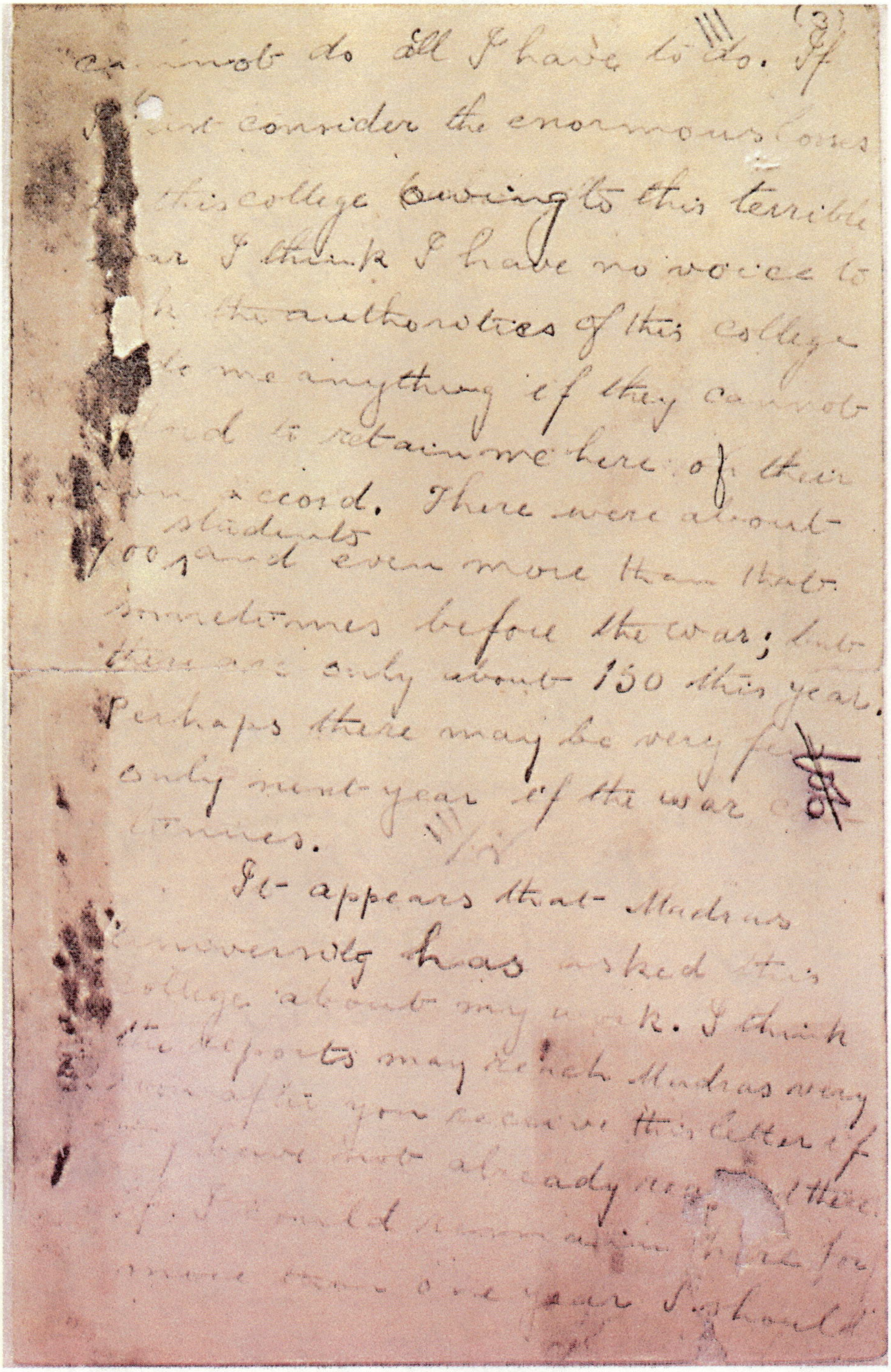

(3)

cannot do all I have to do. If I just consider the enormous losses to this college owing to this terrible war I think I have no voice to ask the authorities of this college to do me anything if they cannot afford to retain me here of their own accord. There were about 700 students and even more than that sometimes before the war; but there are only about 150 this year. Perhaps there may be very few only next year if the war continues.

It appears that Madras University has asked this college about my work. I think the reports may reach Madras very soon after you receive this letter if they have not already reached there. If I could remain here for more than one year I should

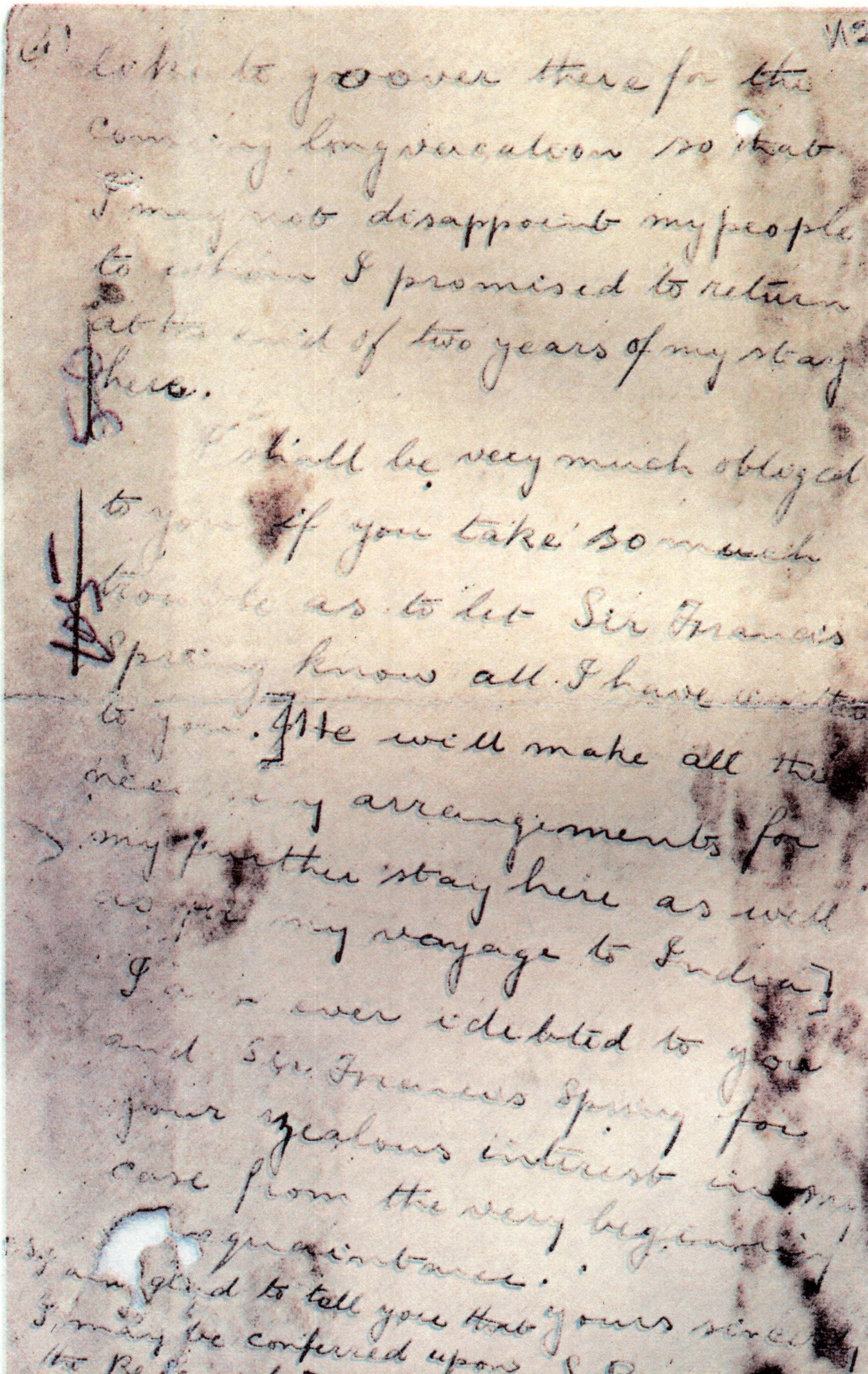
(3) like to go over there for the coming long vacation so that I may not disappoint my people to whom I promised to return at the end of two years of my stay there.

I shall be very much obliged to you if you take so much trouble as to let Sir Francis Spring know all I have written to you. [He will make all the necessary arrangements for my further stay here as well as for my voyage to India.]

I am ever indebted to you and Sir Francis Spring for your zealous interest in my case from the very beginning of my acquaintance.

I am glad to tell you that I may be conferred upon the Research Degree next March.

Yours sincerely

S. Ramanujan

TRINITY COLLEGE- CAMBRIDGE

11th Nov. 1915

My dear Sir,

I am glad to tell you that I may be conferred upon the Research Degree next March. I heard that Madras University was considering about my stay here but I do not know what they have decided. If I have to stay here for only one year more there is no use of my returning to Madras in the middle; but if I know for certain that I can remain here for more than one year and if circumstances favour me I am thinking of going over there for a short stay during the coming long vacation.

I am sending you a paper of mine read before the London. Math Society in last November. It is wrongly printed in the paper that it was read in last June when a different paper was read.

Hoping you and your family are doing well.

Yours Sincerely,
S. Ramanujan

* This letter was written by Ramanujan to Ramachandra Rao.

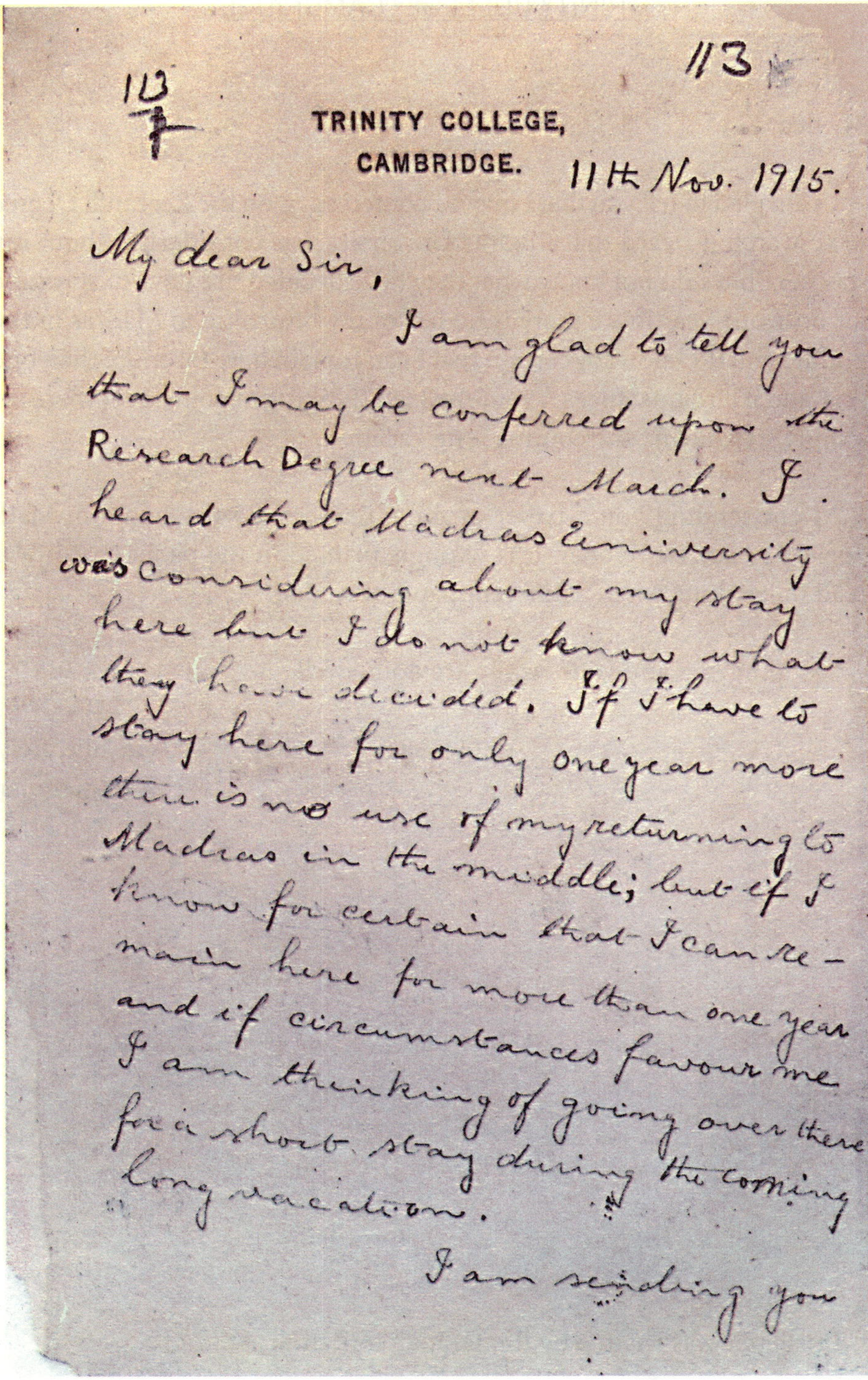

113

113/7

TRINITY COLLEGE,
CAMBRIDGE.

11th Nov. 1915.

My dear Sir,

I am glad to tell you that I may be conferred upon the Research Degree next March. I heard that Madras University was considering about my stay here but I do not know what they have decided. If I have to stay here for only one year more there is no use of my returning to Madras in the middle; but if I know for certain that I can remain here for more than one year and if circumstances favour me I am thinking of going over there for a short stay during the coming long vacation.

I am sending you

113A

a paper of mine read before the
London. math Society in last
November. It is wrongly printed
in the paper that it was read in
last June when a different
paper was read.

Hoping you and your
family are doing well.

Yours sincerely

S. Ramanujan.

Nellore
6th Dec 1915

Dear Sir,

The enclosed letter speaks for itself. I wrote to Ramanujan after I met you at Ooty at the Government House party & the enclosed is by way of reply.

I do not know exactly what he wants but it is probably a continuance of the University scholarship. I am not aware if the University means or can afford to do so. I can however say that Ramanujan has done a lot of work since he left –a fact which will be spoken to by Prof Hardy and I have seen in the crude some of his researches which if valid & published will revolutionise some of the departments of mathematical thought.

I have no doubt you will kindly help Ramanujan if possible.

Yours faithfully
Ramachandra Rao

* This letter was written by Ramachandra Rao to S. N. Aiyar.

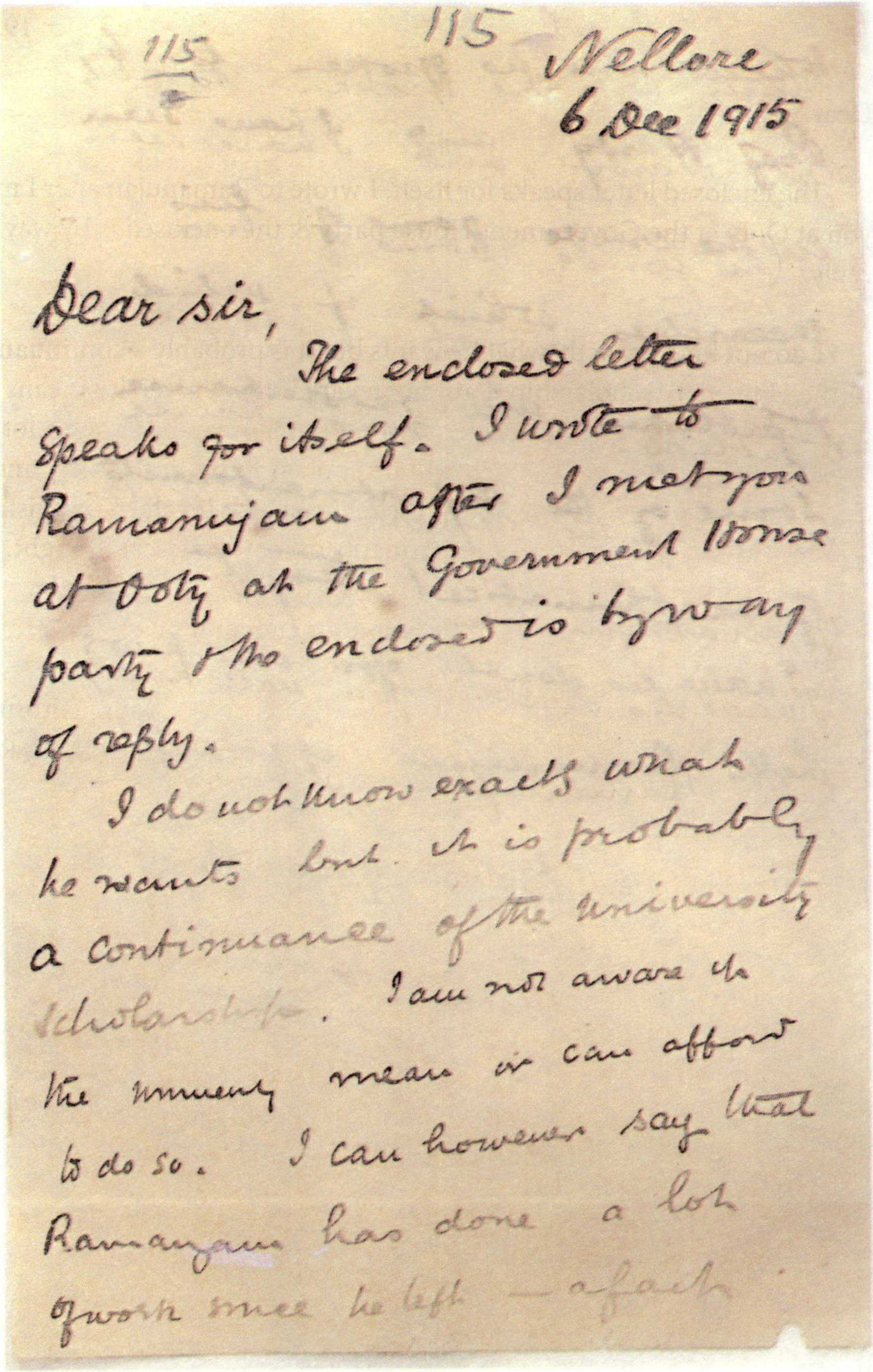

115

115

Nellore
6 Dec 1915

Dear sir,
The enclosed letter
speaks for itself. I wrote to
Ramanujam after I met you
at Ooty at the Government House
party & the enclosed is by way
of reply.
I do not know exactly what
he wants but it is probably
a continuance of the University
Scholarship. I am not aware the
University means or can afford
to do so. I can however say that
Ramanujam has done a lot
of work since he left — a fact

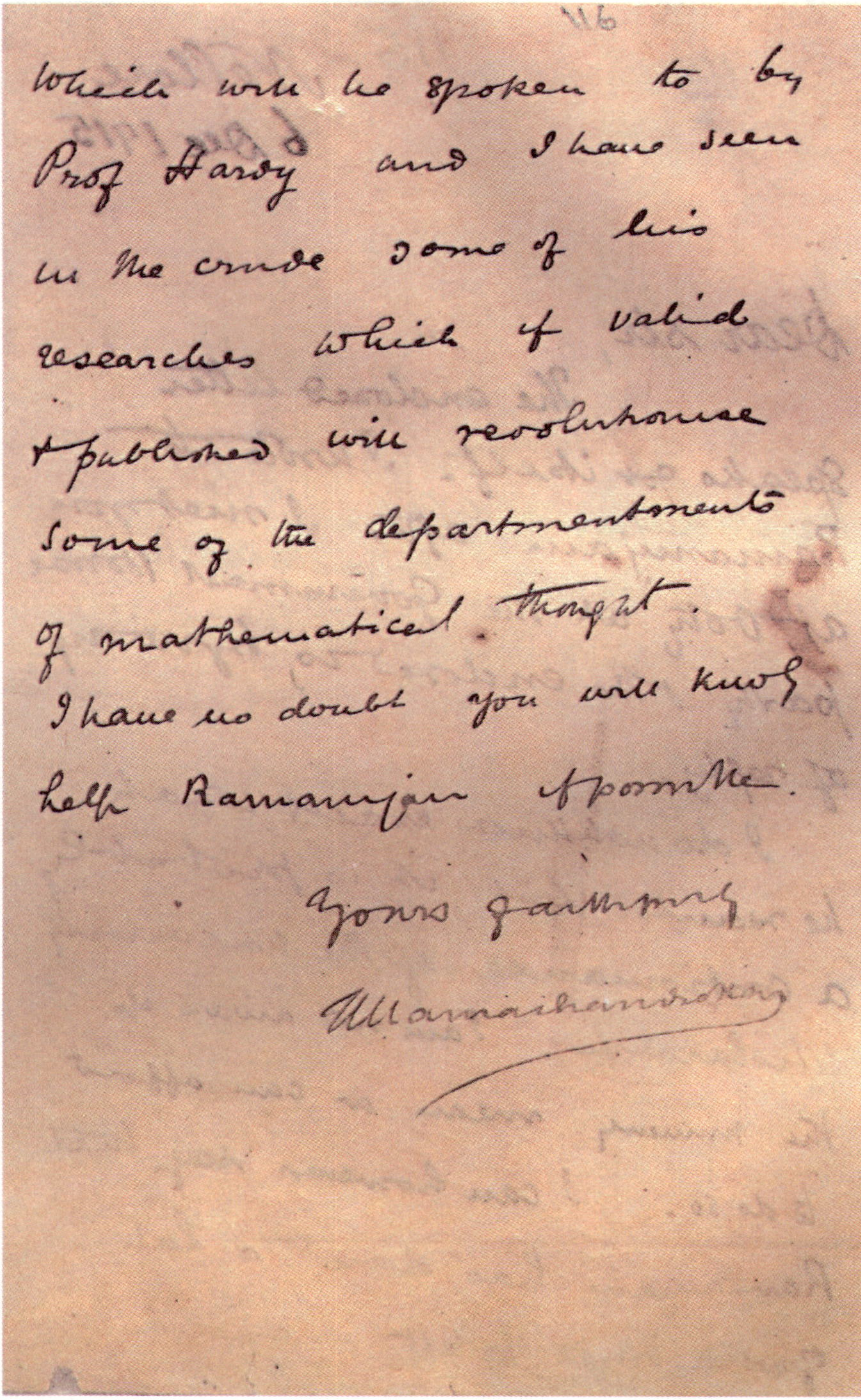

which will be spoken to by
Prof Hardy and I have seen
in the crude some of his
researches which if valid
& published will revolutionise
some of the departments
of mathematical thought.
I have no doubt you will kindly
help Ramanujan if possible.

Yours faithfully

[illegible]

Notes

I understand that the period of the scholarship given to Mr S.Ramanujan by the University of Madras has been extended by one year. This will carry him on to the end of March 1917. From private sources I learn that the University of Cambridge would like to keep him for another year more, i.e. to the end of March 1918.

2. Ramanujan himself has written to me that if the University of Madras should be pleased not to extend his scholarship beyond March 1917, he will be unable to keep his promise to his relations here that he would return in April 1917. For, if he comes to India during the long vacation of 1917, he will have to return after the vacation to England for the brief period of only nine months, which would not leave him time enough for the research work that he is minded to do there. Therefore, in that case, he would prefer not to come to India at all during the vacation of 1917. But if his term of scholarship be extended by two years more, i.e. up to March 1918, as is desired, I understand by mathematics Professors in Cambridge, this will enable him to come back to India during April 1916 and then return back to Cambridge for a further stay of a year and nine months.

3. May I therefore request you to use your influence with the University of Madras to have Ramanujan's term of scholarship extended by two years more instead of by one year, as has been done by the Syndicate in their meeting on the 7th December 1915.

4. As for Ramanujan's progress at Cambridge the attached extracts from letters will speak for themselves. I also understand that Prof.G.H.Hardy of Cambridge has written to the local University Registrar in highly eulogistic terms about the progress of his work there.

S. Narayana Aiyar
15.12.1915

The Honourable Sir Francis Spring, K.C.I.E

* Two typewritten copies of this letter above are to be found in the National Archives of India. Both are more or less the same with some minor changes, but one has several alterations/changes made to it, written by hand.

85 / 87 40

I understand that the period of scholarship given to Mr. S. Ramanujan by the University of Madras has been extended by one year. This will carry him on to March 1917. From private sources I learn that the University of Cambridge would like to have him for another year more, i.e. to March 1918.

2. Ramanujan himself has written to me that if the University of Madras is pleased to extend his scholarship only for one year more, i.e. up to March 1917, he will be unable to keep up his promise to his people here that he would return in April 1917. For, if during the long summer vacation in 1917 he comes to India, he shall have to return back after the vacation to England for a period of a short stay of only nine months. Therefore he would prefer not to come at all during the vacation to India. But if his term of scholarship be extended by two years more, i.e. up to March 1918, as is desired, I understand, by the Professors in Cambridge, this will enable him to come back to India during April 1916 and then return back to Cambridge for a further stay of a year and nine months.

3. May I therefore request you to use your influence with the University of Madras to have Ramanujan's term of scholarship extended to two years more instead of by one year, as has been done by the Syndicate in their meeting on the 7th December 1915.

4. As for Ramanujan's progress at Cambridge the attached extracts from letters will speak for themselves. I also understand that Prof. G. H. Hardy of Cambridge has written to the local University Registrar in highly eulogistic terms about Ramanujan's progress there.

S. Narayana Iyer
15-XII-1915

The Hon'ble Sir Francis Spring, K.C.I.E.

Madras Port Trust
15. 12.1915

The Registrar Madras University
Senate House, Madras

Dear Sir,

The accompanying papers refer to Mr. S. Ramanujan in whom I am interested if for no other reason than that he was discovered while working as a Clerk in my office. The papers have reached us from my office Manager Mr. S. Narayana Aiyar M.A., L.T., who, himself a good mathematician, was chiefly instrumental in bringing Mr. Ramanujan into notice.

In the interest of India's reputation as the birthplace of some good mathematicians of which Mr. Ramanujan is, I am assured, one of the most remarkable, I hope it may be possible for the University to ensure the uninterrupted continuation of his studies, but chiefly of his original research work at Cambridge, by promising him the enjoyment of his present scholarship up to the end of March 1918.

The Syndicate will, I have no doubt, give the matter their best consideration.

Yours Faithfully,
Francis J. E. Spring
C. P. T.

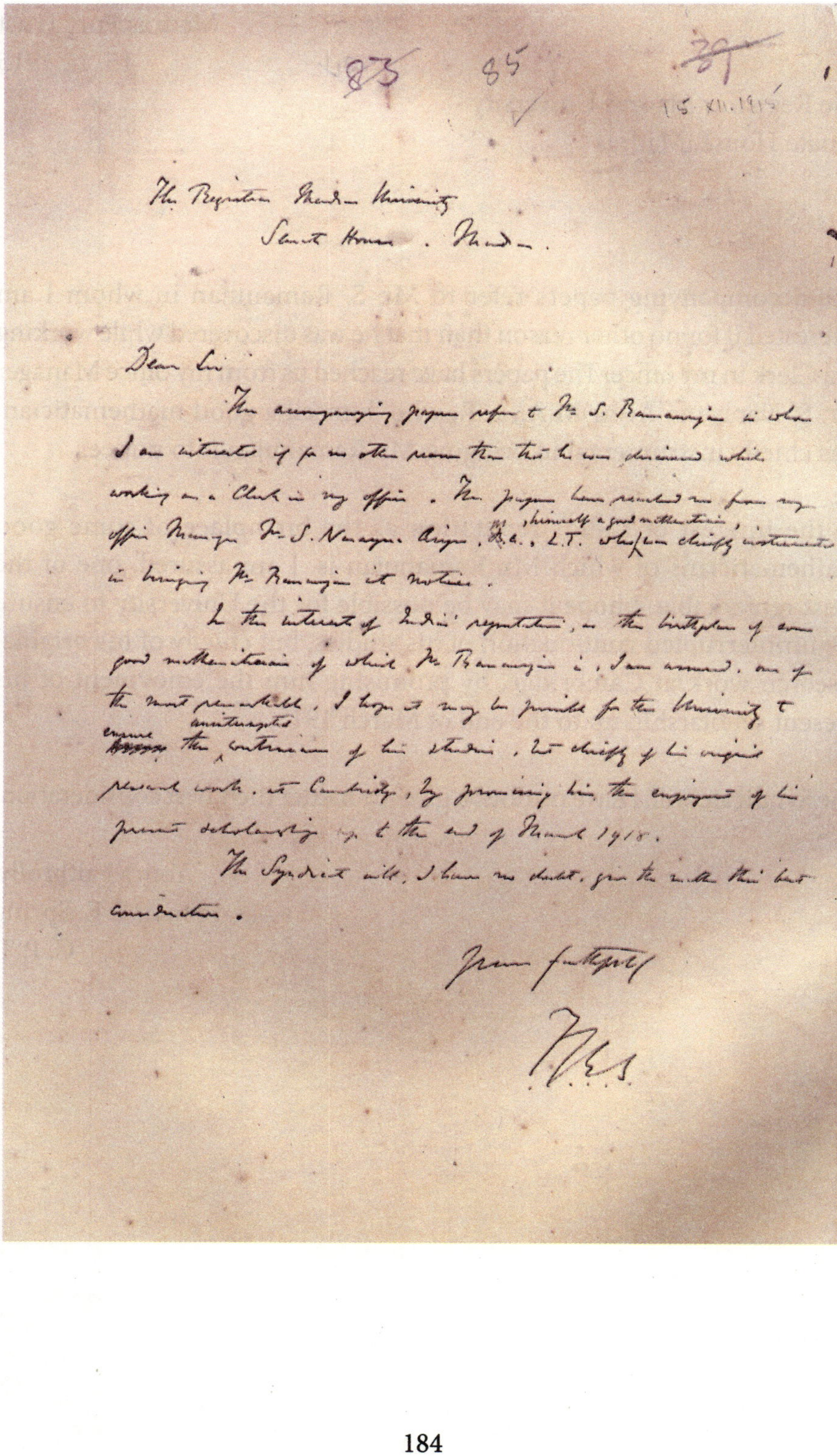

85

15.XII.1915

The Registrar Madras University
Senate House. Madras.

Dear Sir

The accompanying papers refer to Mr. S. Ramanujan in whom I am interested if for no other reason than that he was discovered while working as a Clerk in my office. The papers have reached me from my office Manager Mr. S. Narayana Aiyar, M.A., L.T. himself a good mathematician, who was chiefly instrumental in bringing Mr Ramanujan into notice.

In the interests of India's reputation, as the birthplace of some good mathematicians of which Mr Ramanujan is, I am assured, one of the most remarkable, I hope it may be possible for the University to ensure the uninterrupted continuance of his studies, but chiefly of his original research work, at Cambridge, by providing him the enjoyment of his present scholarship up to the end of March 1918.

The Syndicate will, I have no doubt, give the matter their best consideration.

Yours faithfully

F.F.S.

UNIVERSITY OF MADRAS

No. 7923

SENATE HOUSE, 16 DEC 1915

From
FRANCIS DEWSBURY, Esq., B.A., LLB.,
Registrar, University of Madras,

To
The Hon'ble Sir Francis Spring, K.C.I.E.

Sir,

In reply to your letter, dated December 15, 1915, I have the honour to state that the University of Madras has requested sanction for the allocation of funds for the extension of the scholarship to Mr. S. Ramanujam for another year, i.e. to the end of March, 1917. Your letter and enclosures will be placed before the Syndicate for orders. The Syndicate has been given to understand that it is quite possible that Mr. Ramanujam may become independent of a scholarship before the expiry of this extension. If this proves not to be the case a further extension can be considered at a later date. In the meantime it will be difficult for the Syndicate to consider the question of providing for a return of Mr. Ramanujam to India next year, in the absence of any representation on the point from him or from those connected with his work at Cambridge. Possibly Mr. Narayana Aiyar may be able to furnish the Syndicate with more detailed information on the matter.

I have the honour to be,

Sir,
Please Your most obedient servant,
Francis Dewsbury
Registrar

89 93

UNIVERSITY OF MADRAS

No. 7923

SENATE HOUSE, 16 DEC 1915

Enclosures.

FROM

FRANCIS DEWSBURY, Esq., B.A., LL.B.,
Registrar, University of Madras,

To

The Hon'ble Sir Francis Spring, K.C.I.E.

Sir,

In reply to your letter, dated December 15, 1915, I have the honour to state that the University of Madras has requested sanction for the allocation of funds for the extension of the scholarship to Mr. S. Ramanujam for another year, i.e. to the end of March, 1917. Your letter and enclosures will be placed before the Syndicate for orders. The Syndicate has been given to understand that it is quite possible that Mr. Ramanujam may become independent of a scholarship before the expiry of this extension. If this proves not to be the case a further extension can be considered at a later date. In the meantime it will be difficult for the Syndicate to consider the question of providing for a return of Mr. Ramanujam to India next year, in the absence of any representation on the point from him or from those connected with his work at Cambridge. Possibly Mr. Narayana Aiyar may be able to furnish the Syndicate with more detailed information on the matter.

I have the honour to be,
Sir,
Your most obedient servant,

Francis Dewsbury

Registrar.

Notes

With reference to the concluding portion of Letter No. 7923 dated the 16th December 1915 from the University Registrar, I attach an extract from Mr. S. Ramanujan's letter dated 11th November 1915.

If the question of providing for his return to India next year can be considered only after a formal representation from him I will write to him to put in a formal application through the University authorities there. But I doubt if there is enough time for this formal representation.

S. Narayana Aiyar
18.12.1915

He wants to arrive in Madras in April 1916 and to stay with his family during May and June, returning to England in July. If his scholarship is to end in March 1917 that leaves him only 8 or 9 months more for study at Cambridge. If he is to compete for the Fellowship mentioned by Mr. Hardy in Oct. 1916 and if he is successful then continuation to him of the Madras University scholarship will not be necessary.

The scholarship now granted to him (subject to sanction of fund) by the Madras University will come to an end in March 1917, so that there remains to him somemonths - that is between March and October 1917, assuming he gets the Fellowship - without any scholarship.

* Notes S. Narayana Aiyar and Francis Spring, regarding S. Ramanujan scholarship, Madras Port Trust Chennai.

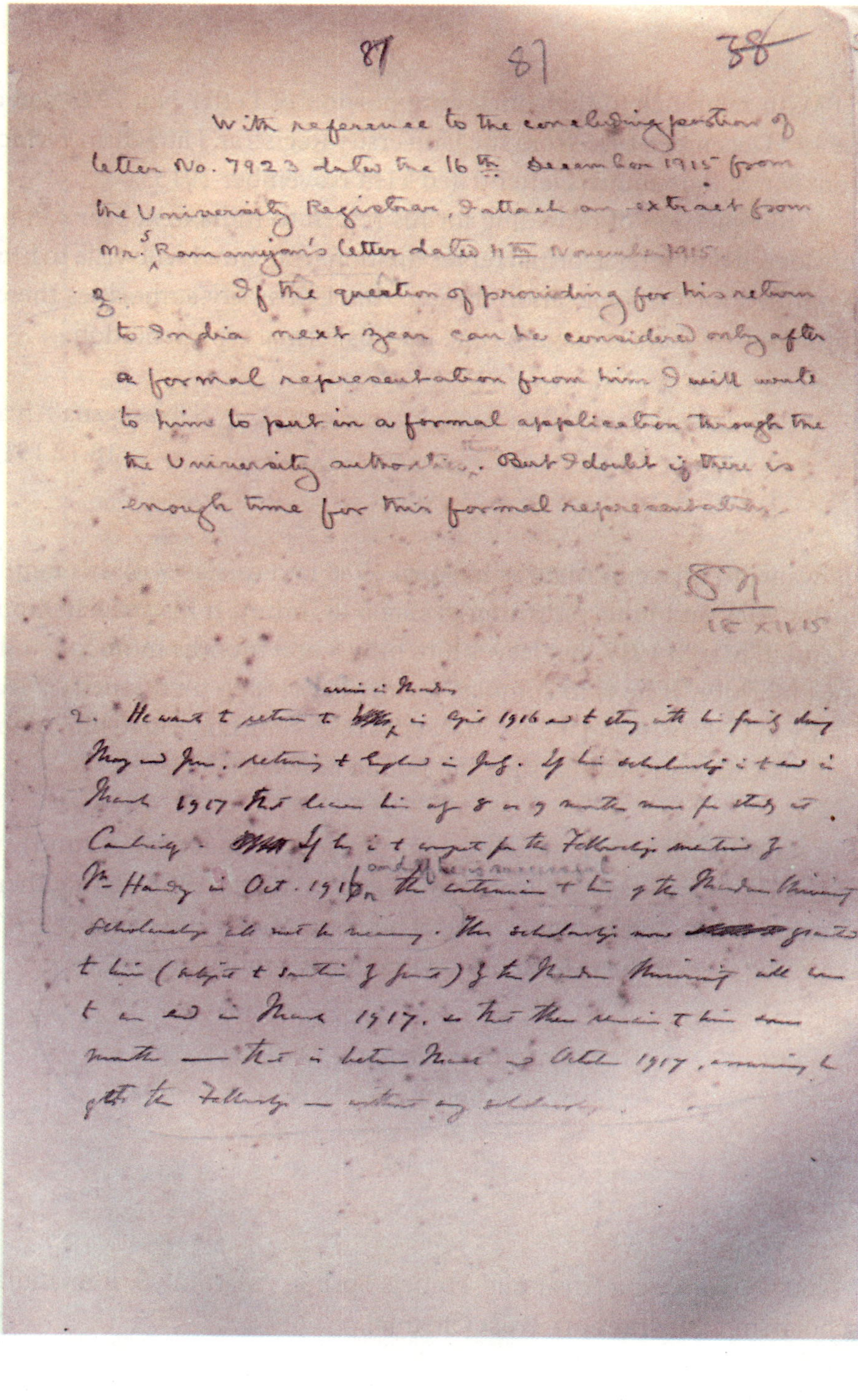

87 87 88

With reference to the concluding portion of letter No. 7923 dated the 16th December 1915 from the University Registrar, I attach an extract from Mr. S. Ramanujan's letter dated 11th November 1915.

2. If the question of providing for his return to India next year can be considered only after a formal representation from him I will write to him to put in a formal application through the the University authorities. But I doubt if there is enough time for this formal representation.

18 XII 15

2. He wants to return to [illegible] in April 1916 and to stay with his family during May and June, returning to England in July. If his scholarship is to end in March 1917 that leaves him only 8 or 9 months more for study at Cambridge. If he is to compete for the Fellowship mentioned by Mr Hardy in Oct. 1917 and if he is unsuccessful the extension & [illegible] of the Madras University Scholarship will not be necessary. The scholarship now granted to him (subject to sanction of Govt) by the Madras University will come to an end in March 1917, so that there remain to him seven months — that is between March and October 1917, assuming he gets the Fellowship — without any scholarship.

Notes

With reference to the concluding portion of letterNo. 7923 dated the 16th December 1915 from the University Registrar, I attach an extract from Mr. S. Ramanujan's letter dated 11th November 1915.

2. He wants to arrive in Madras in April 1916 and to stay with his family during May and June, returning to England in July. If his scholarship is to end in March 1917 that leaves him only 8 or 9 months more for study at Cambridge. If he is to compete for the Fellowship mentioned by Mr. Hardy in October 1916 and if he is successful the continuance to him of the Madras University scholarship will not be necessary.

3. If the question of providing for his return to India next year can be considered only after a formal representation from him I will write to him to put in a formal application through the University authorities there. But I doubt if there is enough time for this formal representation.

S. Narayana Aiyar
20-12-15

Forwarded to the Registrar of Madras University in reply tohis letter No.7923 dated the 16th Dec.1915

Francis J. E. Spring
20-12-15

With reference to the concluding portion of letter No. 7923 dated the 16th December 1915 from the University Registrar, I attach an extract from Mr. S.Ramanujan's letter dated 11th November 1915.

2. He wants to arrive in Madras in April 1916 and to stay with his family during May and June, returning to England in July. If his scholarship is to end in March 1917 that leaves him only 8 or 9 months more for study at Cambridge. If he is to compete for the Fellowship mentioned by Mr.Hardy in October 1916 and if he is successful the continuance to him of the Madras University scholarship will not be necessary.

3. If the question of providing for his return to India next year can be considered only after a formal representation from him I will write to him to put in a formal application through the University authorities there. But I doubt if there is enough time for this formal representation.

Intd. S.N.
20-12-15.

Forwarded to the Registrar of Madras University in reply to his letter No.7923 dated the 16th Decr.1915.

Intd. F.J.E.S.
20-12-15.

<u>University of Madras</u>

Senate House, 17 Jan 1916

From

FRANCIS DEWSBURY, ESQ, B.A; LL.B
Registrar, University of Madras,

To

The Hon'ble Sir Francis Spring, K.C.I.E

Sir,

With reference to recent correspondence on the matter of the Mathematical scholarship at Cambridge granted to Mr.S. Ramanujam, I have the honour to inform you that the Government has sanctioned the proposal of the Syndicate to extend this scholarship for one year. I am instructed to inform you that the Syndicate is not prepared to take any further action in the matter for the present.

I have the honour to be

Sir,
Your most obedient servant,
Francis Dewsbury
Registrar

95 99 65

UNIVERSITY OF MADRAS

No. 394

SENATE HOUSE, 17 JAN 1916

Enclosures.

FROM

FRANCIS DEWSBURY, ESQ., B.A., LL.B.,
Registrar, University of Madras,

To

The Hon'ble Sir Francis Spring, K.C.I.E.

Sir,

With reference to recent correspondence on the matter of the Mathematical scholarship at Cambridge granted to Mr. Ramanujam, I have the honour to inform you that the Government has sanctioned the proposal of the Syndicate to extend this scholarship for one year. I am instructed to inform you that the Syndicate is not prepared to take any further action in the matter for the present.

I have the honour to be,
Sir,
Your most obedient servant,

Francis Dewsbury

Registrar.

Mr. S. Narayana Aiyar

18/1

Madras Port Trust

Notes

S. Ramanujan, clerk Accounts Department, who is now in England on mathematical Research did not join his duty on the expiry of the two years' leave on loss of pay granted to him on the 1st May 1913. Then the C. P. T granted him an extension of another year from the 1st May 1915 which expired on the 30th april 1916. He has not yet joined our office. To save audit objections one of the two courses that are open to us regarding his appointment has to be adopted: -

1. (1)His services may be dispensed with,
2. Or (2) His leave on loss of pay may be extended for a further period of 2 years of CPT's option. (Under Act 198 of C.S.R).

It is submitted that course (2) may be adopted.

S. Narayana Aiyar
C.A.C
18.10.1916

I adopt course 2. Do the needful drafting of order.
Francis Spring
C.P.T.

No separate order seems necessary.
S. Narayana Aiyar
C.A.C.
18.11.1916

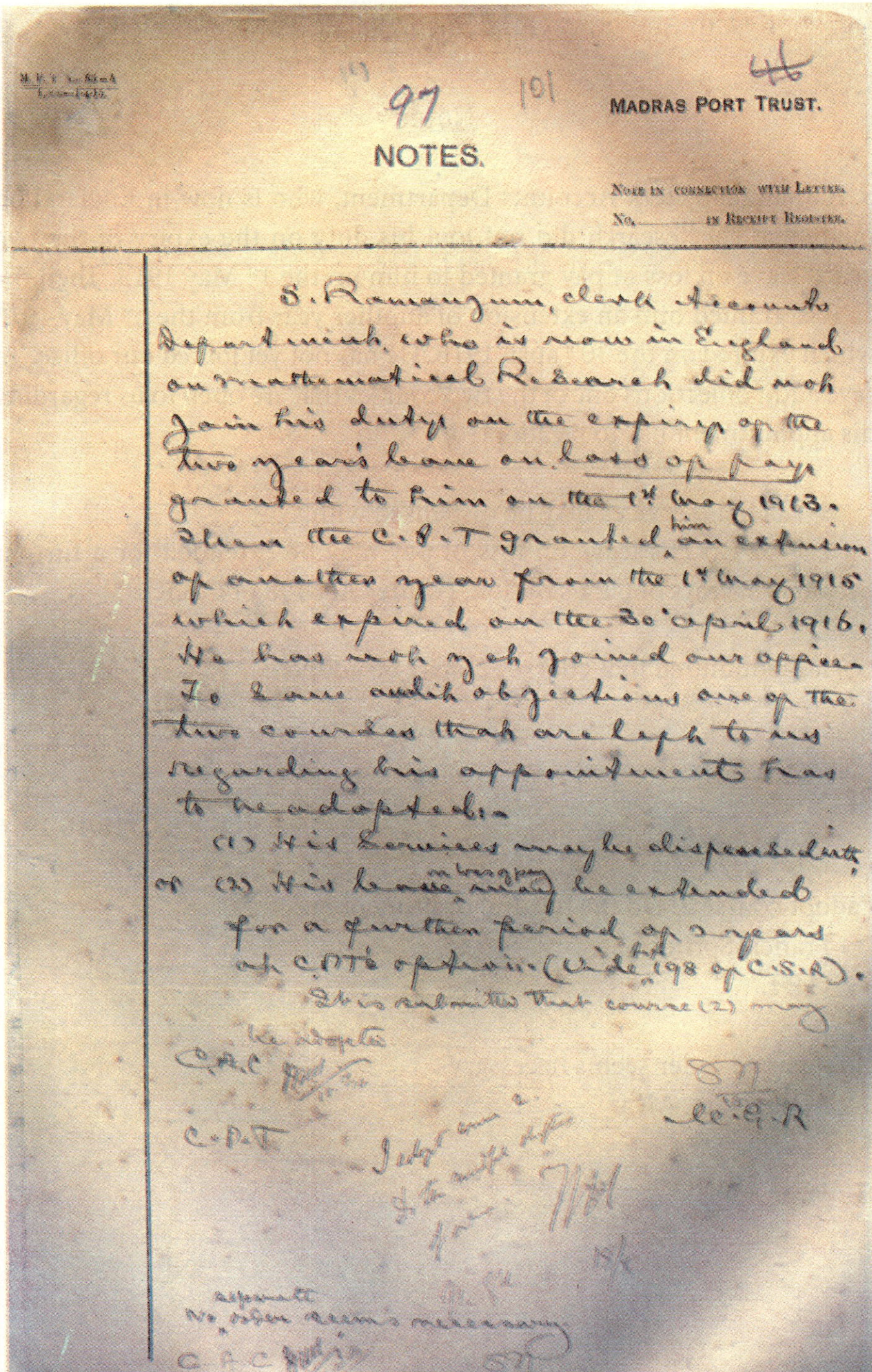

97 101

MADRAS PORT TRUST.

NOTES.

Note in connection with Letter No. ______ in Receipt Register.

S. Ramanujam, clerk Accounts Department, who is now in England on mathematical Research did not join his duty on the expiry of the two years leave on loss of pay granted to him on the 1st May 1913. Then the C.P.T granted him an extension of another year from the 1st May 1915 which expired on the 30th April 1916. He has not yet joined our office. To save audit objections one of the two courses that are left to us regarding his appointment has to be adopted:-

(1) His services may be dispensed with, or

(2) His leave on loss of pay may be extended for a further period of 2 years at C.P.T's option. (Vide Art 198 of C.S.R).

It is submitted that course (2) may be adopted.

C.A.C. [illegible]

S.N. [illegible] C.G.R

C.P.T.

I adopt course 2 [illegible]

No separate order seems necessary

C.A.C. [illegible]

Message from Registrar, University of Madras to Madras Port Trust

Date 14.5.1917
Time 13 HRS

From
Registrar of the University of Madras

To
Madras Port Trust

Message.

Kindly refer urgently to Mr. S. Ramanujan's register in your office, and let me know the date of his birth and the name of his father.

Please see your office No. G. 50 dated 14-4-1913. Mr. Ramanujan was a clerk in the accounts dept. of the Port Trust office and is now in England studying Mathematics in the University of Cambridge

C. B. Cotterell

Reply from S. Narayana Aiyar

We have no records in this office to show Ramanujan's date of birth nor the name of his father.

But I believe he was born in 1890 & his father's name is Srinivasa Aiyangar. His people are living at 17, Sarangapani Covil Sammadhi street Kumbakonam.

S. Narayana Aiyar
14.5.1917

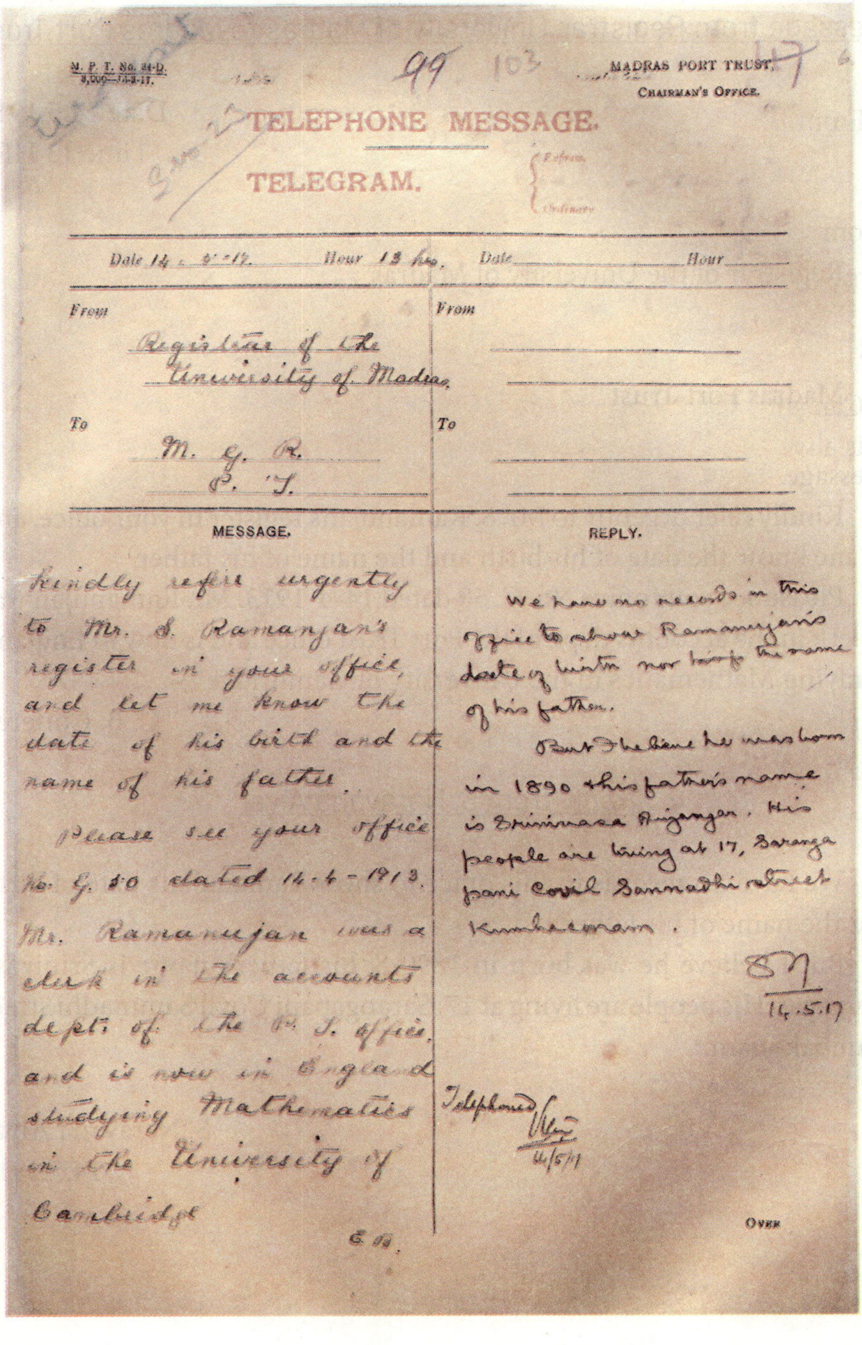

M. P. T. No. 34-D.
99 103 117
MADRAS PORT TRUST,
CHAIRMAN'S OFFICE.

TELEPHONE MESSAGE.

TELEGRAM.

Express / Ordinary

Date 14 . 5 . 17 Hour 13 hrs. Date Hour

From
Registrar of the University of Madras

To
M. G. R.
P. T.

MESSAGE.

Kindly refer urgently to Mr. S. Ramanujan's register in your office, and let me know the date of his birth and the name of his father.

Please see your office No. G. 50 dated 14-4-1913.

Mr. Ramanujan was a clerk in the accounts dept. of the P. T. office and is now in England studying Mathematics in the University of Cambridge

E. B.

REPLY.

We have no records in this office to show Ramanujan's date of birth nor [illegible] the name of his father.

But I believe he was born in 1890 & his father's name is Srinivasa Aiyangar. His people are living at 17, Saranga pani Covil Sannadhi street Kumbaconam.

14.5.17

Telephoned
14/5/17

Over

Telephone Message

From,

Registrar
University of Madras

To

M. G. R.

Can you please tell me if Mr. Sreenivasa Iyengar, father of Mr. Ramanujan is alive and whether he was or is a District munsiff.

Reply

E. B.
14. 5. 1917

Mr. Srinivasa Aiyangar is alive. He was a petty clerk on about Rs 20 under a merchant. He does not know English and was never a District Munsiff.

S. N. Aiyar
14.5.17

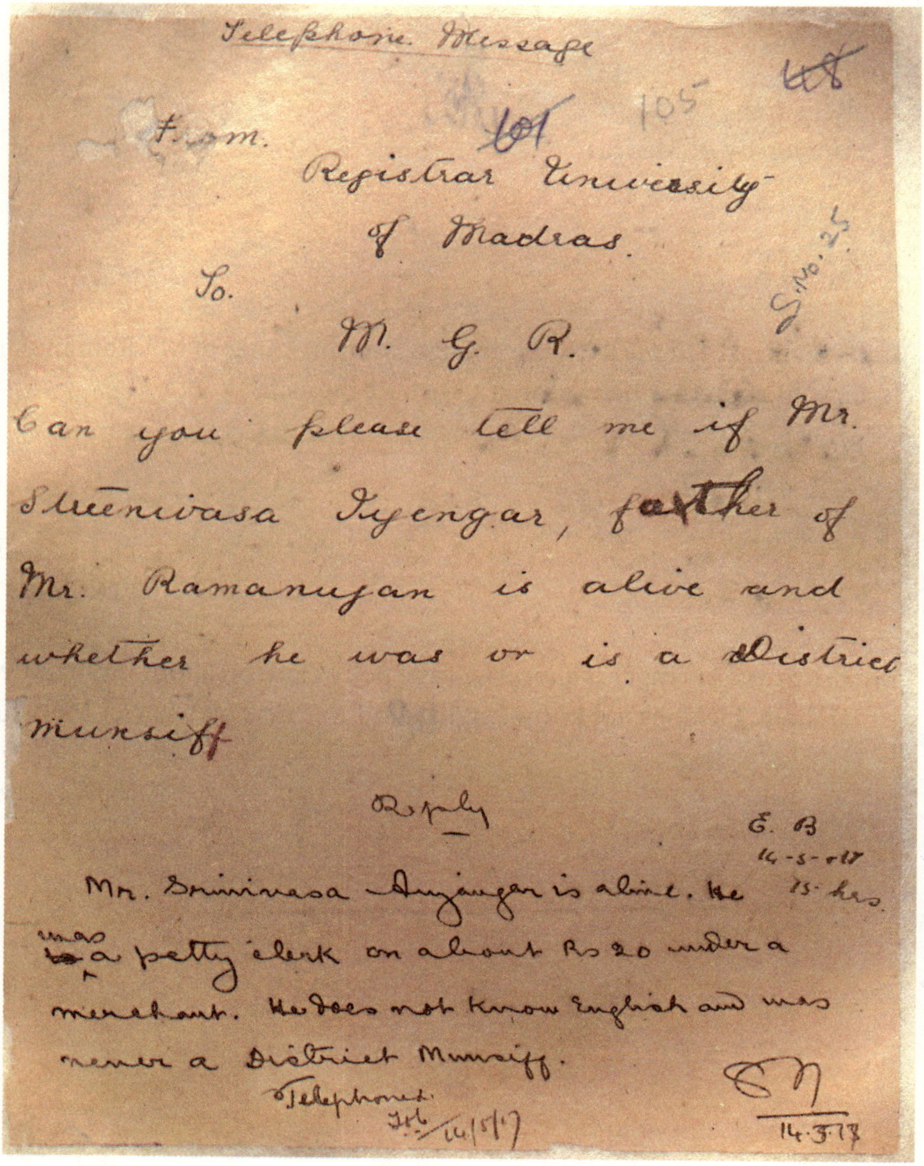

Telephone Message

From.

Registrar University of Madras.

To.

M. G. R.

Can you please tell me if Mr. Sreenivasa Iyengar, father of Mr. Ramanujan is alive and whether he was or is a District Munsiff

Reply

E. B
14-5-17
15 hrs.

Mr. Srinivasa Aiyangar is alive. He was a petty clerk on about Rs 20 under a merchant. He does not know English and was never a District Munsiff.

Telephoned 14/5/17

14.5.17

Telephone Message

From,
The Registrar
University of Madras

To,
The Office
Madras Port Trust

Can you please let me know in what year Mr. S. Ramanujan, son of Srinivasa Aiyangar was matriculated and whether he applied for the F.A or Intermediate Exam.

Reply from S. N. Aiyar

I know he is a Matriculate of this University & failed in F.A. all the subjects. I do not know the year in which he matriculated.

S. N. Aiyar
14.5.1917

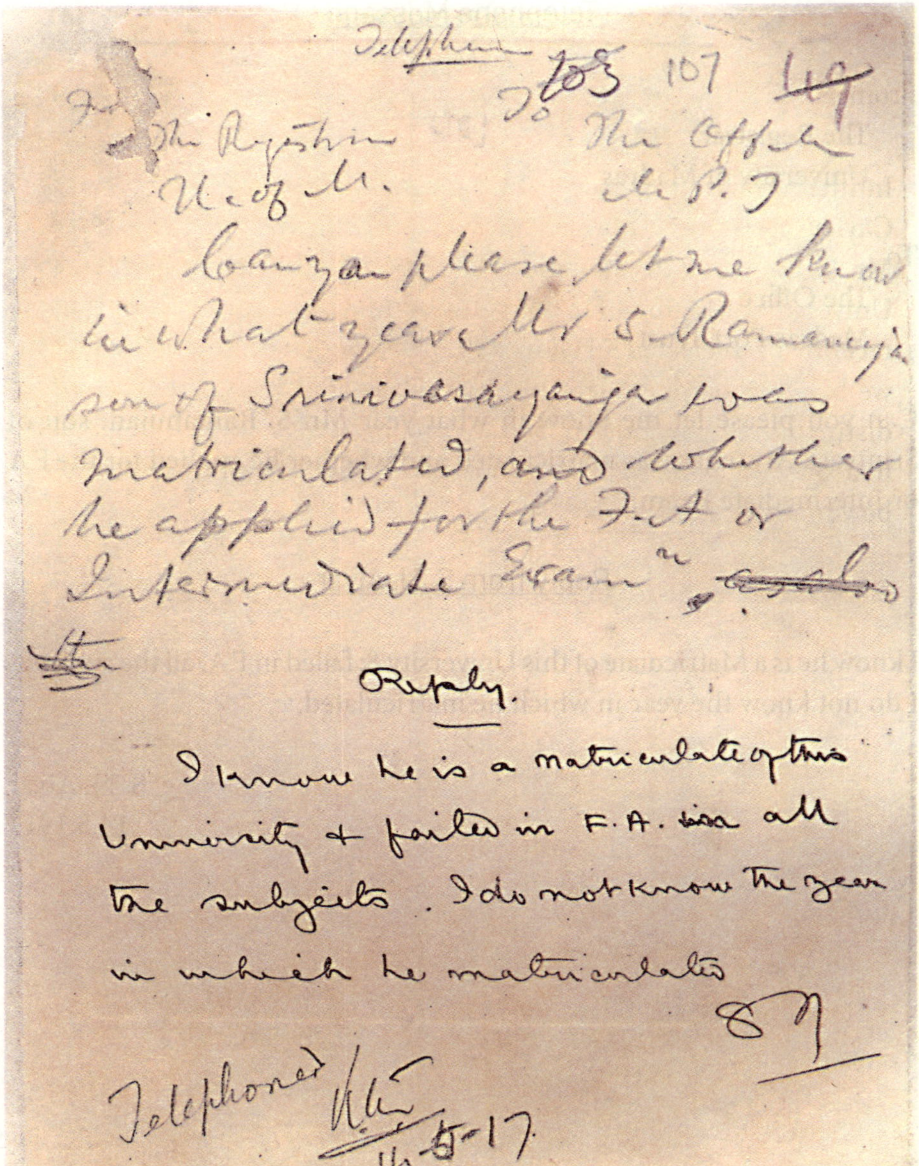

Telephone

103 107 49

From The Registrar, U. of M. To The Office[r] … P. T.

Can you please let me know in what year Mr S. Ramanujan son of Srinivasaiyangar was matriculated, and whether he applied for the F.A or Intermediate Exam".

Reply.

I know he is a matriculate of this University & failed in F.A. in all the subjects. I do not know the year in which he matriculated.

Telephoned 14-5-17.

Madras Mail

March 7th

Occasional Notes

Intimation has been received by cablegram from Mr. G. H. Hardy, the Cayley Lecturer in Mathematics at the University of Cambridge, that Mr. S. Ramanujam, the holder of a special scholarship granted by the University of Madras for the study of Mathematics at Cambridge, has recently been elected a Fellow of the Royal Society. This is the first time, we believe, that a student of the Madras University has received such distinguished recognition, and for an almost wholly self-taught scholar to achieve an F. R. S., so soon after coming under expert direction, must be very exceptional indeed.

* A writeup in the Madras Mail newspaper.

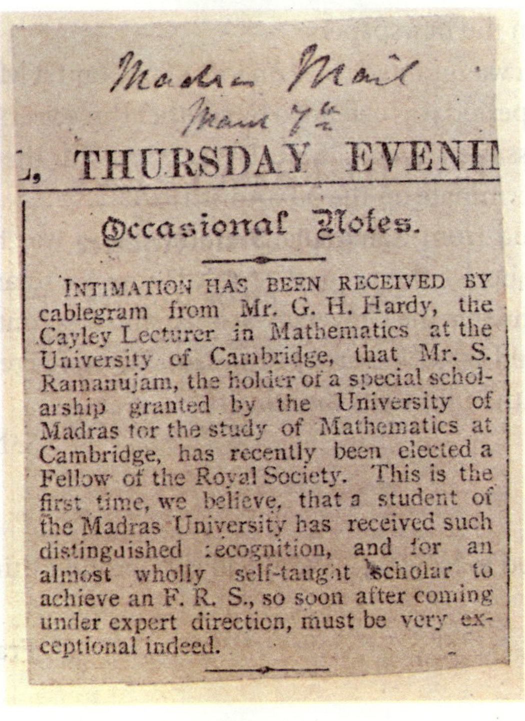

Madras Mail
March 7th

L, THURSDAY EVENI

Occasional Notes.

INTIMATION HAS BEEN RECEIVED BY cablegram from Mr. G. H. Hardy, the Cayley Lecturer in Mathematics at the University of Cambridge, that Mr. S. Ramanujam, the holder of a special scholarship granted by the University of Madras for the study of Mathematics at Cambridge, has recently been elected a Fellow of the Royal Society. This is the first time, we believe, that a student of the Madras University has received such distinguished recognition, and for an almost wholly self-taught scholar to achieve an F. R. S., so soon after coming under expert direction, must be very exceptional indeed.

Notes

1. Mr Narayana Aiyar has doubtless seen in I think in [sic] the Madras Mail of March 7th that Mr. Ramanujan has been made a Fellow of the Royal Society, one of the highest honours that can be conferred in the world of science. Sir Thomas Holland, Dr Bourne and Dr Gilbert Walker are F.R.S. and some few others in India.
2. What exactly is Mr Ramanujan's nominal connection with this office? Is there any practical use in keeping up the connection if there is one? It seems inconceivable that we should ever be of any use to him.
3. What has he now got to live on? A Madras University Scholarship, an Endowment or a grant allowance?or what?

Francis J.E.Spring
9.3.1918

Notes

1. I saw this in the newspapers.
2. Ramanujan was granted leave on loss of pay on 1st May 1913 for two years. This period was extended by another three years, the maximum limit admissible under C. S. R. His service with the Port Trust will therefore terminate on the 30th April 1918.
3. I understood from Ramanujan's mother, who was here in Madras last November at the request of the Home Secretary to the Local Government, that the University Scholarship was continued to him & that he would get a University Professorship on his return to Madras on not less than Rs 400 a month.

S. Narayana Aiyar
12. 3. 18

I am very pleased to have this. We are all very proud I think of an F. R. S.

Francis J.E.Spring
12.3.1918

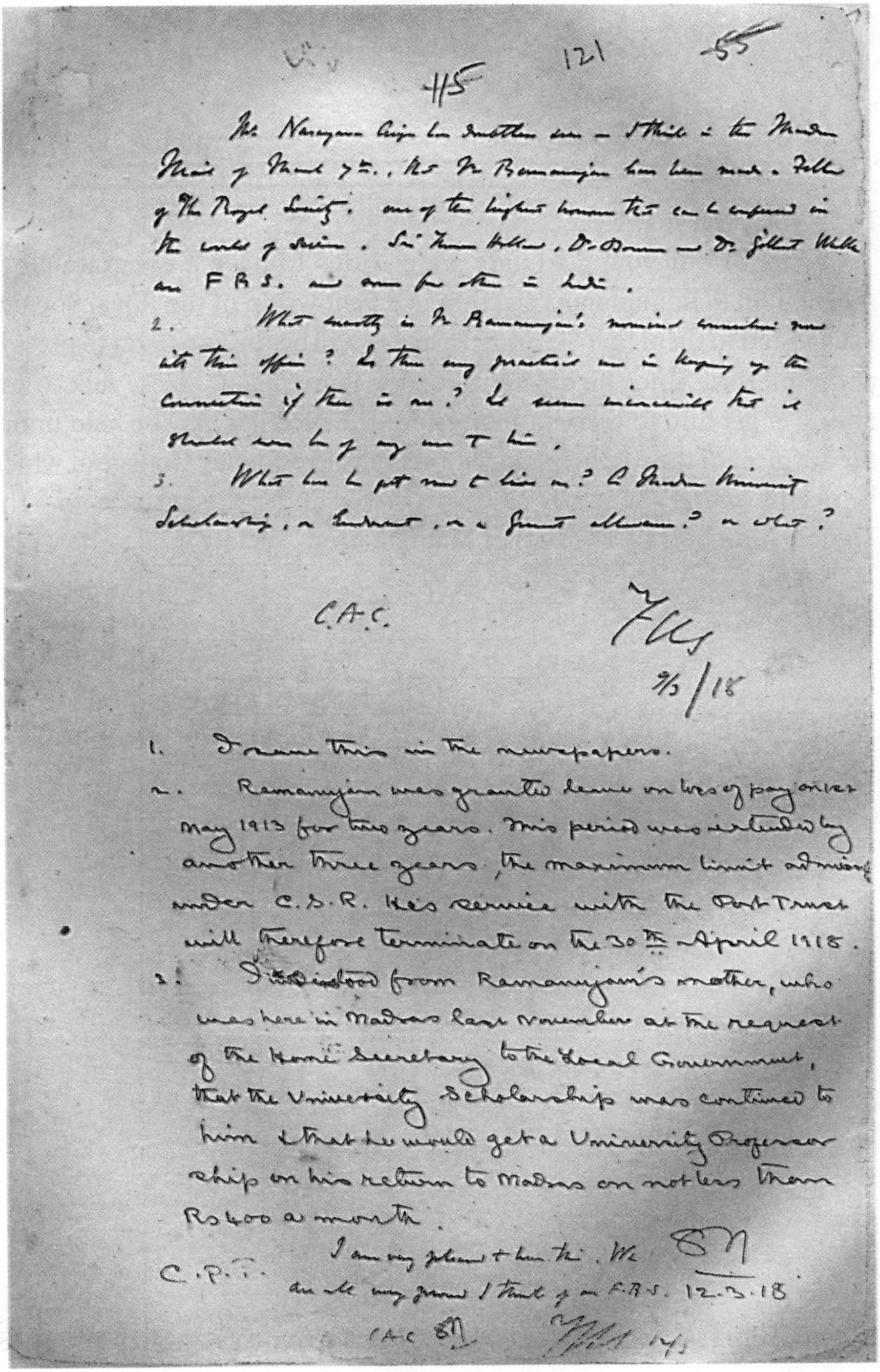

Mr Narayana Aiyar has doubtless seen — I think in the Madras Mail of March 7th — that Mr Ramanujan has been made a Fellow of the Royal Society, one of the highest honours that can be conferred in the world of science. Sir Thomas Holland, Dr Bourne and Dr Gilbert Walker are F.R.S. and some few others in India.

2. What exactly is Mr Ramanujan's nominal connection now with this office? Is there any practical use in keeping up the connection if there is one? It seems inconceivable that he should ever be of any use to him.

3. What has he got now to live on? A Madras University Scholarship, or Endowment, or a Grant allowance? or what?

C.A.C. F.J.S. 9/3/18

1. I saw this in the newspapers.

2. Ramanujan was granted leave on loss of pay since May 1913 for two years. This period was extended by another three years, the maximum limit admissible under C.S.R. His service with the Port Trust will therefore terminate on the 30th April 1918.

3. I understood from Ramanujan's mother, who was here in Madras last November at the request of the Home Secretary to the Local Government, that the University Scholarship was continued to him & that he would get a University Professorship on his return to Madras on not less than Rs 400 a month.

C.P.T. S.N. 12.3.18

I am very pleased to hear this. We are all very proud I think of an F.R.S.

CAC S.N. F.J.S. 14/3

18, Pycroft's Road
Triplicane
Madras, 17/3/1918

Dear Mr Narayana Aiyar,

Some of our young friends are anxious to have a congratulatory meeting on S. Ramanujan's election to a Fellowship of the Royal Society. I suggested to them that Sir Francis Spring will be the fit person to preside at the meeting since he did so much for Ramanujan. Please talk to Mr Spring & get him to consent to preside. The meeting may be held under the auspices of the Maths. Association of the Presidency College of which he is an honorary member or if you prefer under the auspices of "The Madras Members of The Indian Mathematical Society"

Yours Sincerely
P. V. Seshu Aiyar
Professor of Mathematical Physics
Presidency College

* Letter from P. V. Seshu Aiyar to S. Narayana Aiyar dated March 17th 1918.

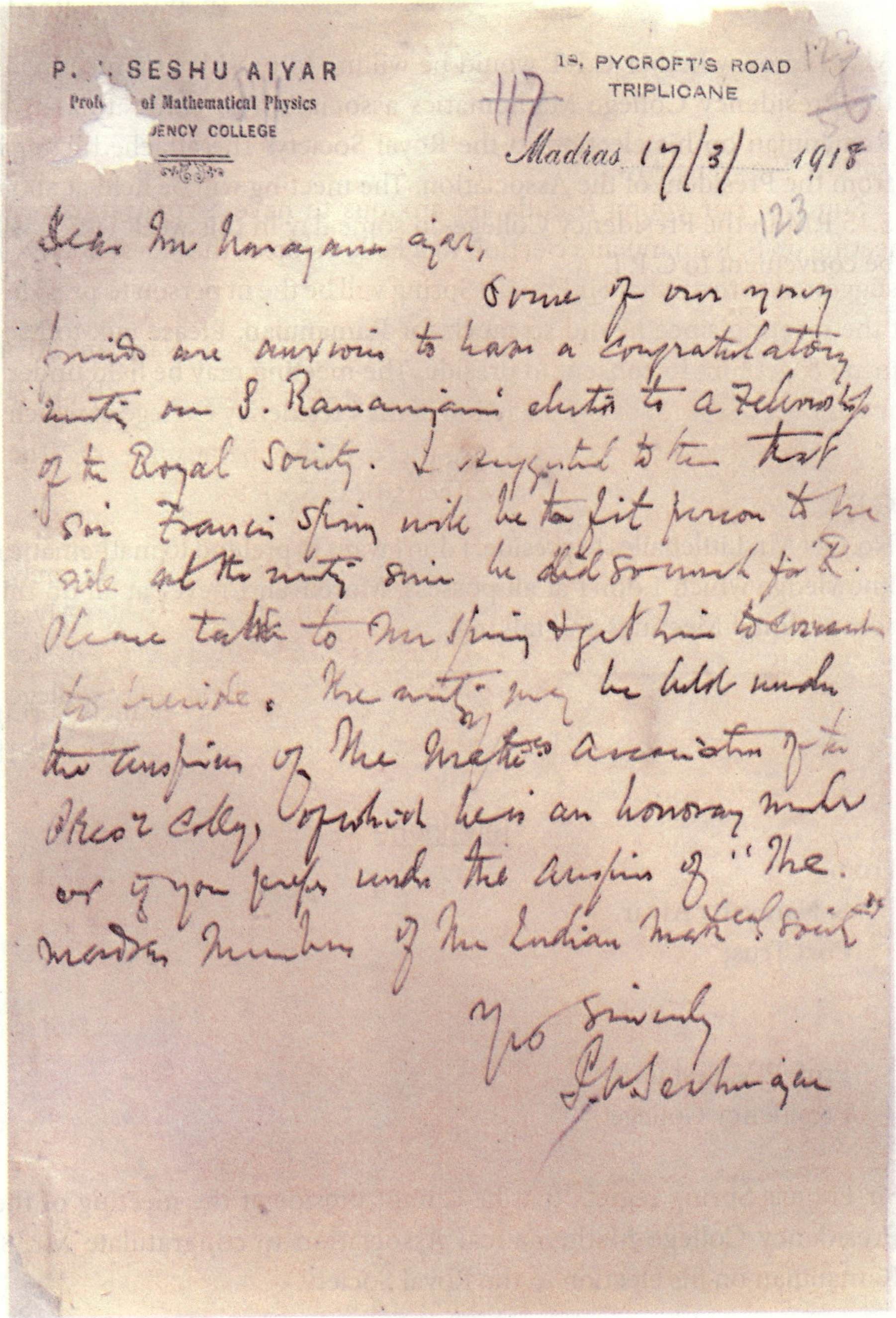

P. . SESHU AIYAR
Profe... of Mathematical Physics
...ENCY COLLEGE

1B, PYCROFT'S ROAD
TRIPLICANE

117

123

Madras 17/3/1918

Dear Mr Narayana Aiyar,

Some of our young friends are anxious to have a congratulatory meeting on S. Ramanujan's election to a Fellowship of the Royal Society. I suggested to them that Sir Francis Spring will be the fit person to preside at the meeting since he did so much for R. Please talk to Mr Spring & get him to consent to preside. The meeting may be held under the auspices of the Mathcs Association of the Presy College, of which he is an honorary member or if you prefer under the auspices of "The Madras Members of the Indian Mathl Society".

Yrs sincerely

P. V. Seshu Aiyar

Notes

May I know whether C.P.T would be willing to preside at a meeting of the Presidency College Mathematics association to congratulate Mr. Ramanujan on his election to the Royal Society. The attached letter is from the President of the Association. The meeting will be held at about 5.15 P.M in the Presidency College on some day in this week which will be convenient to C.P.T.

S. Narayana Aiyar
18.3.1918

Reply

C.P.T.
No. Get Mr. Littlehailes to preside. I don't want to pretend to mathematical knowledge which I don't at all possess. Moreover, I never at all do this sort of thing! Meetings and talking!

Francis Spring
18.3.1918

Telephone

From,
S. Narayana Aiyar
Port Trust

To,
Prof. P. V. Seshu
Presidency College

Sir Francis Spring regrets that he cannot preside at the meeting of the Presidency College Mathematical Association to congratulate Mr. S. Ramanujan on his election to the Royal Society.

S. Narayana Aiyar
18.3.1918

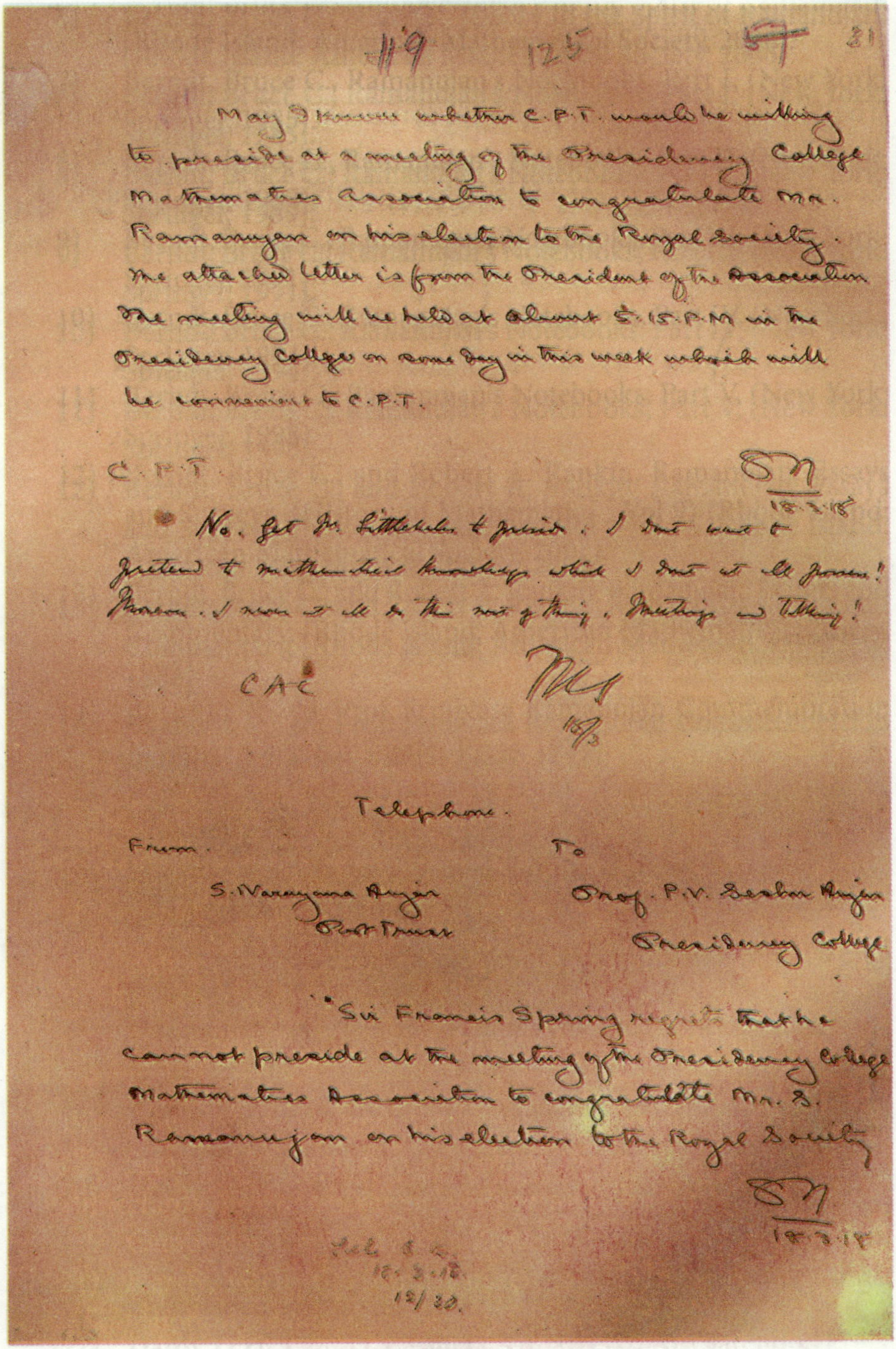

#19 125 57 31

May I know whether C.P.T. would be willing to preside at a meeting of the Presidency College Mathematics Association to congratulate Mr. Ramanujan on his election to the Royal Society. The attached letter is from the President of the Association. The meeting will be held at about 5.15 P.M. in the Presidency College on some day in this week which will be convenient to C.P.T.

S.N.
18.3.18

C.P.T.

No. Get Mr. Littlehailes to preside. I don't want to pretend to mathematical knowledge which I don't at all possess! Moreover I never at all do this sort of thing. Meetings and Talking!

CAC

[initials]
18/3

Telephone.

From.
S. Narayana Aiyar
Port Trust

To
Prof. P.V. Seshu Aiyar
Presidency College

"Sir Francis Spring regrets that he cannot preside at the meeting of the Presidency College Mathematics Association to congratulate Mr. S. Ramanujan on his election to the Royal Society.

S.N.
18.3.18

Tele. S. [illegible]
18.3.18
12/30.

Newspaper Clipping- Madras Times, dated 10.12.1918

The Statesman says: Mr. Srinivasa Ramanujan, Research student, the remarkable mathematician who was recently elected a Fellow of the Royal Society, has now been elected a Fellow of Trinity College, Cambridge.

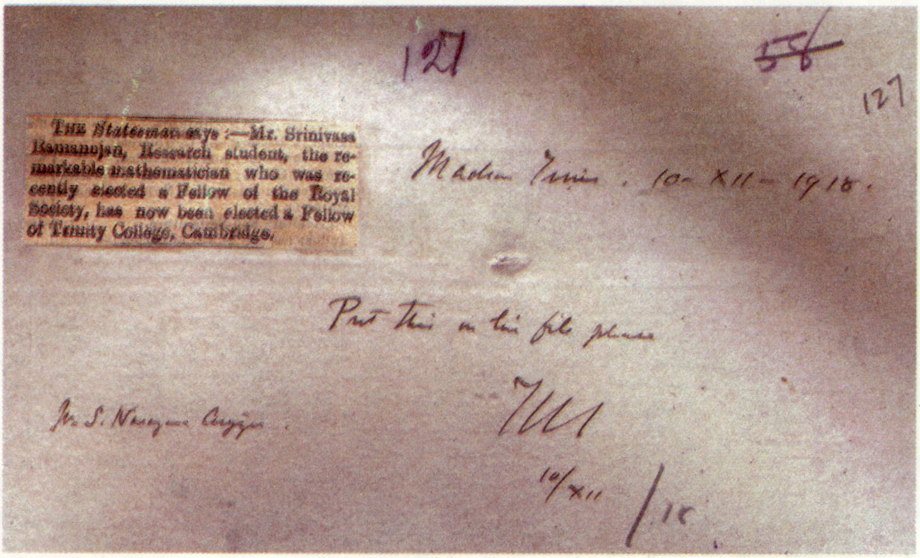

THE *Statesman* says :—Mr. Srinivasa Ramanujan, Research student, the remarkable mathematician who was recently elected a Fellow of the Royal Society, has now been elected a Fellow of Trinity College, Cambridge.

People behind Ramanujan's Success

Ramanujan's Family:

Komalatammal, Ramanujan's mother, bore a striking physical resemblance to Ramanujan, and was described in a few accounts as a astute and cultured lady[1]. Her family had a distinguished lineage, including Sanskrit scholars who had been honoured by local kings. Her father, Narayana Iyengar, was a respected official in Erode, known for his role in the district court where he took notes, summoned witnesses, and interacted with lawyers. However, when Ramanujan was around four years old, Narayana Iyengar lost his job after offending a higher official. Consequently, the family relocated to Kanchipuram, a temple city near Madras, where Narayana Iyengar managed a choultry—an annex to the temple where marriages were held and pilgrims were accommodated[2].

Ramanujan's mother, Komalatammal, sang bhajans—devotional songs—at a nearby temple. The revenue/money from her group's performances was divided equally between the temple and the singers. Given her husband's modest income of about twenty rupees per month, the extra five or ten rupees she earned from these performances were significant, and her commitment to rehearsals was unwavering.

A photograph of Komalatammal, likely taken when she was in her forties or fifties, reveals a woman, with a strong physical presence. While her hands resting lightly on the arms of her chair suggesting a certain ease, the rest of her posture—her head tilted, her eyes intensely focused, and her mouth set—conveys a sense of an underlying, restrained energy. Her overall demeanour projects a potent personal force, ready to spring into action.

---

1. Kanigal Robert : The Man who knew infinity a life of the Genius Ramanujan, Rupa & Co, 1991, pp 18.
2. Ibid pp 18, 19.

Komalatammal was an intensely passionate and strong woman, unafraid to impose her formidable personality on her interests. Throughout Ramanujan's childhood, she directed her powerful focus on him, since Ramanujan was her first child, and for a while her only child. In 1889, Komalathammal gave birth to her second son, who tragically passed away within two weeks. A daughter was born in November 1891, but she also died within three months. Two more sons were born in 1888 and 1905, named Lakshmi Narasimhan and Thirunarayanan. These two brothers remained Ramanujan's younger siblings throughout his life. In Indian culture, the mother-son relationship is highly revered, and the strong bond between Ramanujan and his mother was so significant that it was often emphasized by his biographers.

Komalatammal was actively involved in every aspect of Ramanujan's upbringing. She prepared his meals, meticulously combed his hair into a traditional tuft and sometimes adorned it with a flower. She tied his dhoti (or veshti, as it was known in Tamil), a long cloth wrapped around the waist and pulled between the legs, which was worn by nearly all men except the most Westernized. She applied the namam, a powdery caste mark, to his forehead. She accompanied him to school, where he would touch her feet—a traditional sign of respect—and seek her blessing before entering. She closely monitored his social interactions and daily schedule, made decisions for him, and even took matters into her own hands if she felt he was not receiving the appropriate treatment at school. When it came time for him to marry, she arranged the marriage without consulting her husband.

Komalatammal devoted considerable energy to her spiritual life. In Hindu families, women are often more pious and diligent in observing traditions than men. This was true for Komalatammal's family as well; her mother was reputed to have entered into hypnotic trances. Komalatammal herself was deeply devout, regularly holding prayer meetings at home, singing at the temple, and pursuing interests in astrology and palmistry. She frequently invoked the name of their family deity, the Goddess Namagiri of Namakkal, reflecting her intense devotion. One family friend described her as "an exceptionally gifted lady with psychic powers and a remarkable imagination," noting her extensive repertoire of mythological stories, including tales from the Mahabharata, and the Ramayana. In between the storytelling sessions, there would often be fervent invocations to the Goddess Namagiri.

From his mother, Ramanujan absorbed the deep traditions of his heritage, mastering the doctrines of caste and the puranas. He learned to sing religious songs, attend temple pujas, and follow dietary rules appropriate for a Brahmin boy. The family's devotion to the goddess Namagiri, consort of the lion-god Narasimha, was central to their lives. The shrine of Namagiri in Namakkal was about a hundred miles from Kumbakonam, closer to Erode, where Komalatammal's family originated. Namagiri's name was always on his mother's lips, and she took her devotion very seriously. She had prayed to Namagiri for a child after years of marriage without one, and Ramanujan's maternal grandmother, Rangammal, was a devout follower who reportedly entered trances to communicate with the goddess. She even claimed that Namagiri had once warned her of a murder plot involving local schoolteachers and had foretold that the goddess would one day speak through her daughter's son. Ramanujan grew up hearing these stories and himself attributed his mathematical talents to Namagiri. He believed that the goddess provided him with his mathematical insights, writing equations in his dreams and guiding his work.

This belief in Namagiri's influence was shared by both his grandmother and his mother, who became even more fervent in her devotion after Ramanujan's birth. Komalatammal's powerful will and intense devotion were evident in all she did, shaping Ramanujan's worldview. While his father was concerned with daily routines and practical matters, Komalatammal immersed herself in spiritual and profound influences, drawing Ramanujan into this rich inner world. When new influences emerged in Ramanujan's life, he had his mother's approval to fully embrace and follow them, guided by the example of her unwavering dedication and inner strength.

Years later, while Ramanujan was in England, he sent letters to his family that were often focused on mundane reminders to his father about maintaining the house and ensuring, for example, that the gutters did not overflow. However, he also wrote to his mother about the colossal struggle that had erupted in Europe with the onset of the First World War[1]. His

1. Letter from Ramanujan to his father and his mother (Tamil), Ramanujan Museum & Math Education Centre, Chennai.

letters were detailed, describing the scale of the conflict, the number of soldiers engaged, the extent of the battlefronts, the role of airplanes in warfare, and the contribution of Indian rajas to the British war effort. He knew that such detailed accounts would capture her interest. The bond between them was profound; they communicated effortlessly, appreciated each other's intellectual company, and shared a deep emotional connection. When Ramanujan was a child, he and his mother enjoyed playing board games such as Goats and Tigers, a strategic board game requiring intense concentration akin to chess. This shared interest in complex and logical games reflected their mutual enjoyment of intellectual challenges.

Srinivasa Iyengar, Ramanujan's father, who was twenty-four years old at the time of his son's birth and about five years older than his wife, worked as a clerk in a fabric shop, just like his own father, Kupuswamy. Srinivasa was skilled at evaluating fabrics, a talent that his employer depended on. However, despite his abilities, he struggled to advance to a better position.

Clerks like Srinivasa typically started their workdays around eight in the morning and often did not return home until well after dark, which meant long working hours. Occasionally, clerks would go home for lunch, but more often their wives would pack meals in small metal containers for them to eat at the shop. Due to the seasonal nature of the business, with weddings often scheduled in auspicious months, there were times when the shop would experience a lull, leaving clerks like Srinivasa with extended periods of inactivity.

Srinivasa's routine kept him largely absent from Ramanujan's early years. In Indian society, fathers traditionally played a minimal role in domestic life, often appearing distant, reserved, and uninvolved with their children, resulting in a formal and detached relationship, and the relationship between Ramanujan and his father followed a similar trajectory/pattern. Srinivasa was largely inconspicuous in the family narrative, his presence barely noted. Terms such as silent and insignificant and nondescript were often used by acquaintances to describe him or to denote his presence. A childhood friend of Ramanujan described him as "very quiet," while another person used the term "weightless" to capture his lack of significant presence. Even if Srinivasa had been more engaged, he would have struggled to match the formidable influence of Komalatammal on their son.

S. Janaki Ammal

In late 1908, S. Ramanujan's mother took on the significant responsibility of finding a bride for her son. During a visit to Rajendram, a village about sixty miles west of Kumbakonam, she encountered Janaki, a young girl with bright eyes who was a distant relative[1]. Impressed by Janaki, Ramanujan's mother decided to explore this potential match further. She obtained Janaki's horoscope, which is a crucial step in arranged marriages in India, and compared it with Ramanujan's horoscope, which she had drawn on the wall. After assessing their compatibility, she concluded that Janaki would be a suitable match for her son.

Janaki, born on March 21, 1899, was the fourth daughter among six children (five daughters and one son) of Rangaswamy Iyengar and Ranganayaki Ammal of Rajendram, a village near Marudur Railway Station. Janaki's mother was a friend of Ramanujan's mother, Komalatammal. During a visit to Rajendram, Komalatammal negotiated with Janaki's parents for her marriage with the 21-year-old, Ramanujan.

Discussions about the marriage began, but at that time, Janaki was only about nine years old, and her family was facing financial difficulties. Once well-off, Janaki's family had fallen on hard times and could only offer a modest dowry. Despite their financial constraints, they were eager to secure a good marriage for Janaki, who was one of five daughters.

Janaki was unaware of Ramanujan before the marriage arrangements and would not meet him until the wedding day. Ramanujan's family was conscious of his limited prospects, but his mother was adamant about proceeding with the match. Ramanujan's father, Srinivasa, was particularly unhappy with the arrangement. He felt that Ramanujan deserved a better match and was frustrated by his exclusion from the decision-making process. Previously, Srinivasa had received proposals from wealthier families, but he had been left out of those discussions. Upset by his lack of input, he chose not to attend the wedding.

The wedding took place on July 14, 1909, despite the disruptions, and Janaki and Ramanujan were married. However, Janaki did not join Ramanujan in his home until she reached puberty and completed her

1. Govil Narendra Kumar and Sharma Bhudev Mathematics Wizard, Some Glimpses into his Life and Work, Srinivasa Ramanujan, Prabhat Prakashan, 2021 pp 39.

domestic training. This marked a new chapter in Ramanujan's life as he entered married life, although his daily circumstances remained largely the same.

Janaki came of age and moved in with Ramanujan in 1912, after he secured a clerical job with the Madras Port Trust. They lived on Saiva Muthaiah Mudali Street in George Town. In May 1913, Ramanujan joined the University of Madras as its first research scholar and lived for about ten months on Hanumantharayan Koil Street, before moving to ToppuVenkatachala Mudali Street, both in Triplicane. Janaki and his mother lived with him at the latter address for a few months before Ramanujan left for England on March 17, 1914.

Ramanujan returned to India in April 1919, weakened from prolonged illness but with an esteemed reputation. Janaki joined him in Madras and cared for him until his death on April 26, 1920. During this period, Ramanujan's mother, Komalathammal, and his grandmother, Rangammal, managed the household.

Following Ramanujan's demise, Janaki returned to Rajendram with her mother after the cremation. Over the next six years, she resided with her brother in Bombay, who had become an income tax officer. Upon learning of the pension awarded to her by Madras University for relinquishing her rights to Ramanujan's papers, she briefly returned to Madras, staying with her sister in Triplicane before finding her place on Hanumantharayan Street, close to where she and Ramanujan had lived before he departed for England.

In Bombay, Janaki learned to embroider and operate a sewing machine, making a living by sewing clothes and teaching tailoring to young girls. Around 1948, she began caring for a young boy named Narayanan, whose parents were hospitalised and who himself was battling typhus. Janaki nursed him back to health, supported him in his studies, and eventually adopted him as her son when both his parents passed away. Despite brief separations for schooling, Narayanan ultimately returned to live with Janaki permanently, cementing their bond as mother and son for the rest of her life.

Janakiammal was recognized for her support of education and her philanthropic nature. She received a pension from the University of Madras since 1920, which gradually increased over the years. In the aftermath of Ramanujan's posthumous fame, Janakiammal expressed disappointment that a statue of Ramanujan had not been made.

Professor Richard Askey, responding to this, spearheaded efforts for the creation of a bronze bust of Ramanujan with the support of numerous mathematicians. A replica of the bust was presented to Janakiammal in 1985. Throughout her life, Janakiammal remained proud of her husband's legacy and the recognition that came after the 75th anniversary of Ramanujan's birth in 1962.

Janakiammal passed away on April 13, 1994, at the age of 94.

R. Ramchandra Rao

The title "Dewan" is used to denote a high-ranking official with significant financial responsibilities in an Indian state, such as a financial minister. It can also refer more broadly to any official with considerable financial duties. R. Ramachandra Rao, who held the position of Collector in Nellore, an important district headquarters located approximately 100 miles north of Madras in a rich agricultural region, was a person of such standing. In addition to his role as Collector, Rao was bestowed with the honorific "Bahadur", meaning "hero" in Hindustani. This title was often added to the names of officers and officials as a mark of respect and acknowledgment of their status.

R. Ramachandra Rao was not only a prominent administrator but also a notable figure in the field of mathematics. He was one of the founding members of the Indian Mathematical Club and played a crucial role in establishing its library by donating both, books and a monetary contribution of Rs.100. Furthermore, Rao served as the President of the Indian Mathematical Society from 1915 to 1917, demonstrating his commitment to the advancement of mathematics.

Rao, having been educated at the prestigious Presidency College in Madras, joined the provincial civil service in 1890 at the young age of nineteen. Over time, he advanced to become the Registrar of the Cooperative Credit Societies in Madras. He was then District Collector of Nellore, a sizable town with a population of approximately thirty-five thousand, located about a hundred miles up the East Coast Railway from Madras. Earlier in the same year, Rao had been honoured with the title "Dewan Bahadur"[1], an accolade similar to a British knighthood, further emphasizing his distinguished status.

1. Kanigal Robert : The Man who knew infinity a life of the Genius Ramanujan, Rupa & Co, 1991, pp 78

In addition to his administrative duties, Rao was also deeply involved in the mathematical community. He held the position of Secretary for the Indian Mathematical Society, an organization founded by Ramaswami Iyer just four years ago. Rao occasionally contributed solutions to mathematical problems published in the Society's Journal. His intelligence, affluence, and extensive network made him a pivotal figure through whom many important matters could be addressed in India.

Ramanujan visited R. Ramachandra Rao, who was a figure of considerable influence. Recognizing Ramanujan's potential and the disadvantages of keeping him in the isolated district of Nellore, Rao intervened to improve his situation. Instead of offering him a position in the local taluk office, which might have been a less fruitful opportunity, Rao sought to find Ramanujan a scholarship, despite Ramanujan's tendency to struggle with exams. Rao also made arrangements for Ramanujan to stay in Madras, agreeing to cover his living expenses.

As a result, Ramanujan began receiving monthly financial support of twenty-five rupees from Rao. Although this amount was modest, it was sufficient to alleviate Ramanujan's financial concerns and allowed him to focus on his work. This support marked a significant turning point in Ramanujan's life, enabling him to move beyond his earlier, more constrained circumstances in Kumbakonam and immerse himself in the vibrant academic environment of Madras, starting from early 1911 and continuing for the next three years.

During the year that Ramanujan was supported by Rao's generosity, he remained highly productive in his mathematical pursuits. He contributed several intriguing new problems to the Indian Mathematical Society Journal and completed a second paper. However, his lack of a permanent job began to weigh on Ramanujan. Previously, he had taken on a temporary position at the Madras Accountant General's Office, where he earned twenty rupees per month, but he only held this job for a few weeks. By early 1912, with Rao's help, Ramanujan sought to secure a new employment opportunity through Rao's influential connections, continuing his quest for a more stable position. Even afterwards, Ramachandra Rao continued to exert influence on Ramanujan almost all throughout his life.

P. V. Seshu Aiyar

Peruvemba Venkateswara Aiyar Seshu Aiyar, born in January 1872, came from a family in dire poverty. His father was a small-scale farmer, and his mother had lost her sight to smallpox. Throughout his life, Seshu Aiyar faced persistent health issues. He graduated with a Bachelor's degree from Madras Christian College in 1891, but his health deteriorated, forcing him to abandon his plans for a Master's degree. In 1893, he returned to his hometown of Palghat to serve as the Headmaster of the local high school. Shortly after, he took up a position as a Lecturer at Government College in Kumbakonam, where he taught mathematics, including a year with Ramanujan as his student.

Later, Seshu Aiyar moved to Presidency College in Madras, where he spent fifteen years teaching and eventually became a Professor of Applied Mathematics. He returned to Kumbakonam to serve as the Principal of Government College until his retirement. Aiyar was a founding member of the Indian Mathematical Society and held prominent roles, including Secretary and President.

During Ramanujan's time at Government College, Seshu Aiyar allowed Ramanujan considerable freedom in his studies, even encouraging him to explore problems in mathematics journals such as the London Mathematical Gazette[1]. Ramanujan once shared his work on infinite series with Aiyar, who described it as "ingenious and original." However, such attention was not always the norm. Ramanujan's unconventional approach to mathematics was often met with indifference or resistance. For example, a professor who lent Ramanujan a calculus book later demanded its return when it was perceived to be hindering Ramanujan's other academic work. Even Seshu Aiyar, while initially supportive, may not have been as attentive as Ramanujan later remembered, as Ramanujan himself once complained to a friend about Aiyar's "indifference."

By 1906, P. V. Seshu Aiyar had become a member of the Indian Mathematical Society and had not seen Ramanujan for about four years. In the interim, Aiyar had advanced to a position at Presidency College in Madras. When Ramanujan met him again, he came with not only his mathematical notebooks but also a recommendation from Ramaswami

1. File No. 50-60/5 A2, Ramanujan Papers, NAI, New Delhi.

Iyer. This meeting provided Ramanujan with new leads and additional letters of introduction, marking a significant step in his academic journey. Seshu Aiyar passed away in October 1935.[1]

S. Narayana Aiyar

S. Narayana Aiyar was born on December 15, 1874, in Cumbum, near Madurai in Tamil Nadu. The "S." in his name stands for Subbanarayanan, his father's name. His parents, Subbanarayanan Iyer and Lakshmi, were impoverished. Both his father and grandfather, Ananthanarayana Iyer, were Hindu priests skilled in Sanskrit and the Vedas, earning a meager living performing Hindu rituals in private homes. According to sources, their family's financial situation was so dire that NarayanaAiyar once had to share his only shirt with his elder brother during a school inspection. Despite his early hardships, he maintained a deep compassion for the underprivileged and those he worked with throughout his life. He had one older brother and three sisters.

Narayana Aiyar pursued higher education at St. Joseph's College in Trichinopoly, a leading institution in southern India at the time, where he obtained a Master's degree in mathematics. At that time, the M.A. was the highest degree available before the introduction of the Doctorate program years later. After graduating, he began teaching at St. Joseph's College, where he caught the attention of Francis Spring, then working with the railways in Trichinopoly. Spring, who later became Chairman of the Madras Port Trust and was knighted in 1911, invited Aiyar in 1905 to join the Madras Port Trust as Office Manager. Aiyar was promoted to Chief Accountant, the highest-ranking Indian position at the Port Trust, where he remained until his retirement in 1934. In recognition of his dedicated service, the British government honored him with the title "Rao Bahadur.[1]"

His background as a Brahmin priest and his M.A. in mathematics from St. Joseph's College led him to a career that involved significant administrative and financial responsibilities. At the Port Trust, he was a key figure, working closely with Sir Francis Spring, who relied heavily on him. Aiyar consistently maintained traditional Indian dress, wearing a dhoti and turban throughout his life, even as Western-style clothing became

1. File No. 78, Ramanujan Papers NAI, New Delhi.

more common among educated Indians. His adherence to traditional dress was later seen by his family as a testament to his personal strength.

Aiyar was known for his honesty, restraint, and dignified demeanour. Despite his adherence to traditional Hindu practices, he held a progressive and independent mindset. His contributions extended beyond his professional role, as he played a significant part in Ramanujan's life and career.

When Ramanujan applied for a job as a clerk in February 1912, he was hired as a Class III, Grade IV clerk at the Madras Port Trust, earning thirty rupees per month. His duties likely included verifying accounts and managing cash balances, and he occasionally substituted for other clerks. The job itself was of a modest nature, but Narayana Aiyar and Sir Francis Spring tolerated and even encouraged Ramanujan's mathematical pursuits during office hours. There are anecdotes of Ramanujan scavenging for packing paper to work on calculations or leaving mathematical results mixed with important files, which Sir Francis Spring found amusing.

Narayana Aiyar, also a member and long-time treasurer of the Indian Mathematical Society (formerly the Indian Mathematical Club), collaborated with Ramanujan extensively. They would often work late into the night, sitting with slates on the porch of Aiyar's house, with Ramanujan occasionally recording ideas that came to him in dreams. Aiyar was a respected mathematician in his own right but found Ramanujan's ability to condense complex steps into single moves challenging to follow. He often encouraged Ramanujan to break down his work into more detailed steps to make it comprehensible to others. He published two papers in the Journal of the Indian Mathematical Society, describing some of Ramanujan's chief discoveries in mathematics. Narayana Aiyar is also believed to have helped Ramanujan in drafting the first letter that the latter sent to G H Hardy. He accompanied Ramanujan to the temple of Namakkal to seek the Goddess's blessings and approval before Ramanujan left for England.

Over time, Aiyar became more than just a superior or colleague to Ramanujan; he became a mentor and friend. Aiyar believed strongly in Ramanujan's potential and advocated for him to Sir Francis Spring, helping to secure support and recognition for Ramanujan. This support marked a significant shift in Ramanujan's career, as he began to gain broader recognition within British India[1].

Narayana Aiyar's influence extended beyond his professional achievements. He was a founding member of the Indian Mathematical Society and served in various capacities, including as Assistant Secretary and Treasurer. His simplicity, dedication to traditional values, and quiet advocacy for Indian independence marked his life. Aiyar passed away on January 17, 1937. His son, N. Subbanarayanan, has poignantly documented his father's life and his relationship with Ramanujan.

Narayana Aiyar and his wife, Avibakthanayaki, had two daughters, and one son. in 1925, his son-in-law, (husband of his daughter Kamakshi) M.S. Venkataraman (1902-1967) joined the Madras Port Trust and after independence, he became the first Indian to become the Chairman of the Madras Port Trust. After assuming office, he gathered all the available papers related to Ramanujan and entrusted them to the National Archives of India[2].

Francis Spring

Sir Francis Joseph Edward Spring (1849-1933) was an Irishman who made significant contributions to India's infrastructure. He graduated from Trinity College, Dublin, and joined the Indian Civil Service in 1870, initially as a railway engineer. Spring was instrumental in developing the South Indian Railways System, a feat for which he was honoured as a Knight Commander of the Order of the Indian Empire in 1911. He had spent over three decades contributing to the development of the South Indian Railways and his notable achievements included constructing a significant railroad bridge across the Godavari River. Sir Francis was also notable for being one of the first individuals in South India to own a motorcar. He had a reputation in Madras for being an early adopter of modern technology[3].

Although he retired from active service in 1904, he chose to remain in Madras, where he took on the role of Chairman of the Madras Port Trust. At the time he joined the Madras Port Trust, he brought with him

1. File No. 78, Ramanujan Papers NAI, New Delhi.
2. File No. 50-60/50 A2 NAI, New Delhi.
3. File No. 78, Ramanujan Papers, NAI, New Delhi.

the esteemed S. Narayana Aiyar, who became a key figure in the Port Trust's operations.

By late 1912, it had become apparent at the Port Trust offices that Ramanujan possessed exceptional mathematical talent. With testimonials from influential figures such as Narayana Iyer, Ramachandra Rao, and Presidency College mathematics professor Middlemast, a question arose among British officials, including Sir Francis, about the true nature of Ramanujan's abilities. They faced a dilemma: Was Ramanujan's talent trivial or profound? Did his mathematical prowess signify the work of a genius or merely an eccentric with unconventional insights? The officials were uncertain whether Ramanujan was a minor curiosity to be dismissed or a remarkable prodigy who required careful nurturing and support. Francis Spring lobbied in support of Ramanujan and along with Narayana Aiyar helped Ramanujan to advance further in his mathematical journey.

Recognizing the need for expert evaluation, Sir Francis Spring and his colleagues decided to seek the opinion of renowned mathematicians in England. They arranged for Ramanujan to correspond with G. H. Hardy, a leading mathematician at Cambridge University. Hardy, initially skeptical, was soon astounded by Ramanujan's unconventional yet profound theorems, particularly those related to infinite series and number theory. This marked a turning point in Ramanujan's career, as Hardy extended an invitation for him to travel to Cambridge, paving the way for his eventual collaboration with British mathematicians.

Despite financial and cultural challenges, Ramanujan's supporters in India, including Spring and Narayana Iyer, worked tirelessly to secure funding and permissions for his journey. Their faith in his genius never wavered, even as others remained doubtful. Ramanujan's subsequent work in Cambridge would not only validate their belief but also revolutionize mathematics, leaving an indelible legacy. His story became a testament to the importance of recognizing and nurturing extraordinary talent, regardless of its origins.

C. L. T. Griffith

Charles Leopold Troyte Griffith, born on June 6th, 1872, was a distinguished Professor of Civil Engineering at the Madras College of Engineering. His academic background includes being an Associate

Member of the Institute of Civil Engineers, with his scientific education conducted at University College, London, from 1890 to 1892.

C. L. T. Griffith played an important role in propagating Ramanujan and his mathematical genius[1]. He sent letters to a few renowned professors such as M. J. M. Hill, who had been his professor as well, including Ramanujan's equations and sums and asking for their opinions regarding the same. According to a letter from Hill, Griffith reached out to him concerning the mathematical work of Srinivasa Ramanujan because Hill had been Griffith's mathematics professor during his time at University College, London. Although the extent of mathematical details shared with Hill remains unclear, it is known that Griffith sent Hill a copy of Ramanujan's inaugural paper, which was published in 1911 in the Journal of the Indian Mathematical Society. Additionally, Hill's comments suggest that Griffith may have also included a substantial collection of Ramanujan's unpublished results.

Gilbert Walker

Sir Gilbert Thomas Walker (1868-1958) achieved distinction as the Senior Wrangler in Part I of the Mathematical Tripos in 1889, showcasing his exceptional prowess in mathematics. He served as a Fellow of Trinity College, Cambridge from 1891 to 1904 before taking on the role of Director-General of Indian Observatories, a position he held from 1904 to 1924. Following this, he transitioned to a prominent academic role as Professor of Meteorology at Imperial College, London, from 1924 to 1935[2].

During his tenure as Director-General, Walker was based at the Observatory situated in Nungambakkam, a district of Madras. This observatory was positioned on the south bank of the River Cooum, approximately 2.5 miles from the Bay of Bengal. Walker's primary focus was on improving the forecasting of the monsoon's duration and intensity. Recognizing the critical economic importance of accurate monsoon predictions, he undertook extensive analyses by averaging surface temperatures and precipitation data from various oceanic island stations near the equator. By examining these averages over several decades,

1. File No. 78, Ramanujan Papers, NAI, New Delhi.
2. Ibid.

Walker identified a recurring 26-month oscillation, which has since been termed Walker's quasi-biennial oscillation, or simply Walker circulation.

Walker's forecasting approach was empirical; he utilized historical monthly precipitation anomalies from the past 26 months and overlaid them on mean precipitation values to predict future conditions for the next 26 months. Although this method lacked a theoretical causal framework, it was a significant improvement over existing techniques and provided valuable forecasts. he also wrote a paper "The Cold Weather Storms of Northern India".

Walker's empirical work was groundbreaking, offering early insights into the interconnected nature of atmospheric winds and laying the groundwork for future atmospheric circulation models. His contributions were so impactful that Dr. R.P. Sarker, the then Director-General of Indian Observatories, hailed Walker as "the father of monsoon studies in India."

Despite his remarkable achievements, Walker's appointment as the head of the Indian Meteorological Department in Simla came at a time when he had no formal background in meteorology. However, his reputation as a distinguished mathematician, bolstered by his recent election as a Fellow of the Royal Society, made him a promising candidate to address the pressing issue of unreliable monsoon predictions, which had stirred significant public and media concern. It was his efforts in communicating with Professor G.H. Hardy and drawing his attention to Ramanujan's work which actually led to Ramanujan moving to Cambridge in 1914 to coordinate with Prof G.H. Hardy.

Francis Dewsbury

Francis Dewsbury (1872-1946) began his education at Sedbergh School in Cumbria, before progressing to St John's College, Cambridge, where he enrolled in 1889. At Cambridge, he pursued the Law Tripos, successfully completing his studies with a Bachelor of Arts (B.A.) and a Bachelor of Laws (LL.B.) in 1892. Dewsbury then qualified as a solicitor in 1896.

From 1898 to 1903, Dewsbury worked as a schoolteacher, with his final position at Dunnheved College in Launceston, Cornwall. Following his teaching career, he transitioned to administrative roles as a district clerk for various Education Committees. His professional journey took him to India, where he served as the Registrar of the University of Madras, a position he held from 1909 until his retirement in 1924. It was during his tenure that Ramanujan got a scholarship from Madras University. Francis Dewsbury was also instrumental in sending Ramanujan to Cambridge[1].

Upon his return to England, Dewsbury's successor as Registrar, William McLean, who passed away in Glasgow on January 8, 1994, at the age of 94, noted that Dewsbury dedicated some time to assisting the University of Reading with a fundraising campaign. After this, Dewsbury settled in a house in Sedbergh, close to his former school, where he spent the remainder of his life before passing away.

E. H. Neville

Eric Harold Neville (1889-1961) began his undergraduate studies at Trinity College, Cambridge, in 1907. By 1909, he had achieved the rank of Second Wrangler in the Mathematical Tripos, demonstrating his exceptional mathematical abilities. Two years later, in 1911, he was awarded a College Fellowship. However, his Fellowship was not renewed upon its expiration, which Neville suspected was due to his pacifist views—an unpopular stance at the time with the authorities.

In 1919, Neville was appointed to the Chair of Mathematics at University College, Reading, where he remained until his retirement in 1954[2]. During his career, he was an ardent supporter of the Mathematical Association, serving as its President in 1934 and fulfilling the role of Librarian for many years. Although Neville did not produce a vast amount of mathematical work, he is particularly remembered for his influential book on Jacobian elliptic functions. In this work, he introduced a modified notation that, although it came too late for widespread acceptance, aimed to present a more logical approach to the subject.

Neville's contributions extended beyond his publications. He played a crucial role in fostering the confidence of the mathematician Srinivasa Ramanujan during Ramanujan's time in Madras. Neville and his wife were instrumental in welcoming Ramanujan to Cambridge, providing him with a supportive environment during his initial adjustment to a new country.

Neville, a former Senior Wrangler and a fellow of Trinity College,

1. File No. 78, Ramanujan Papers, NAI, New Delhi.
2. Bruce C Berndt and Robert A Rankins, Ramanujan letters and Commentary, Vol-9 American Mathematical Society and London Mathematical Society, 1995 pp 96.

arrived in Madras in the winter of 1913 to deliver a series of lectures on differential geometry. His visit also included the critical task of persuading Ramanujan to travel to England. In early January, Neville met Ramanujan at the Senate House, the university's examination hall. Over the course of several meetings, Neville was profoundly impressed by Ramanujan's notebook. When Ramanujan offered to let Neville take the notebook for further study, Neville considered it a remarkable honour, as he believed the notebook had never before been out of Ramanujan's possession.

Neville's approach, free from the prejudices Ramanujan might have encountered, and his deep appreciation for Ramanujan's work helped build a strong rapport between them. This trust enabled Neville to successfully encourage Ramanujan to move to Cambridge.

Upon Ramanujan's arrival in England, Neville and his older brother met him at the dock and drove him to 21 Cromwell Road, a residence for Indian students newly arrived in London. Unlike many Indian students who faced difficulties, Ramanujan had Neville to help him acclimate. Neville's acquaintance, A. S. Ramalingam, a young engineer from Cuddalore, also assisted Ramanujan in adjusting to life in England. After enduring the initial adjustments at Cromwell Road, Ramanujan moved to Neville's home on Chestertown Road in Cambridge, where he stayed for some six weeks.

Neville was the first Englishman to earn Ramanujan's trust and significantly eased his transition to life in England. Together with his wife Alice, Neville was known for their exceptional hospitality, providing Ramanujan with both a supportive environment and personal warmth. Their kindness and open-heartedness made a significant difference in Ramanujan's early experiences in England.

J. E. Littlewood

John Edensor Littlewood (1885-1977) was born in Rochester, Kent, but spent his early years at Wynberg near Cape Town, South Africa, where his father—an alumnus who had been the 9th Wrangler in the Mathematical Tripos in 1882—had taken up the role of headmaster at a newly established school. Littlewood returned to England in 1899 to complete his schooling at St. Paul's School in London and then matriculated at Trinity College,

Cambridge, in 1903 with an Entrance Scholarship. In 1903, he began his studies at the University of Cambridge, enrolling at Trinity College. He dedicated his first two years to preparing for the Tripos examinations, which are required for earning a bachelor's degree. By 1905, he had achieved the rank of Senior Wrangler, sharing this distinction with J. Mercer.

In the summer of 1906, Littlewood commenced his research under the guidance of E.W. Barnes. His first published paper on integral functions of order zero appeared the following year. Interestingly, Barnes suggested that Littlewood should attempt to prove the Riemann Hypothesis, although the immense difficulty and significance of the problem were not mentioned to him. Littlewood was elected a Fellow of Trinity College in 1908. He served as a Richardson Lecturer in the School of Mathematics at the University of Manchester from 1907 to 1910.

Littlewood's academic career was primarily centered in Cambridge, aside from a brief stint as a Lecturer at Manchester University between 1907 and 1910 and his service during World War I, where he worked on ballistics from 1914 to 1918. In Cambridge, he held various positions including Fellow of Trinity College, Cayley Lecturer, and from 1928 to 1951, Rouse Ball Professor of Mathematics. In 1911, he began his notable and enduring collaboration with G.H. Hardy. Together, they gained international recognition as leading figures in mathematical analysis and analytical number theory. Their expertise was highly sought after for academic appointments, and Littlewood was elected a Fellow of the Royal Society in 1916.

Littlewood also collaborated with other prominent mathematicians such as R.E.A.C. Paley, M.L. Cartwright, and A.C. Offord, Littlewood was well-acquainted with Ramanujan's work and, alongside Hardy, scrutinized the results presented in Ramanujan's first letter of January 16, 1913 to G H Hardy. According to E. Shils, Littlewood recounted that Hardy assigned him the task of updating Ramanujan on the more rigorous European mathematical methods that had emerged after Ramanujan's studies in India. Littlewood found this task exceptionally challenging, as Ramanujan's responses often overwhelmed him with original ideas, making it difficult to convey the more formal aspects of European mathematics.

Although Littlewood was only two years older than Ramanujan, his educational background was vastly different. Having been educated in England's top institutions, Littlewood was well-prepared in mathematics, with both his grandfather and father having studied at Cambridge. His father became a headmaster in South Africa, where Littlewood spent eight years. Upon returning to England at fourteen, Littlewood continued his education at St. Paul's School, where his passion for mathematics grew.

Littlewood, like Hardy, remained a bachelor and was known for his exceptional problem-solving skills. Hardy himself praised Littlewood for his ability to tackle complex mathematical problems with a unique combination of insight, technique, and power. Littlewood and Hardy first engaged intellectually in 1906 when Littlewood's early paper prompted Hardy to review it. Their professional relationship deepened when Littlewood returned to Trinity, and Hardy acknowledged his assistance in the preface to "Orders of Infinity," a book that had caught Ramanujan's attention in India.

G. H. Hardy

Godfrey Harold Hardy was born on 7 February 1877 in Cranleigh, Surrey, in England. His parents were both teachers: his father, Isaac Hardy was Bursar and Art Master, teaching geography and drawing, at Cranleigh School, while his mother, Sophia Hall, was senior mistress at Lincoln Diocesan Training College for women. Two years later, in 1879, Hardy's sister, Gertrude Edith was born.

Both parents had a strong mathematical inclination. From an early age, Hardy demonstrated a natural talent for mathematics. By the age of two, he could write numbers up to the millions, and he used to keep himself busy during church by factorizing the numbers in hymnals.

Hardy was not only talented in mathematics but also excelled in various other areas. However, his achievements were occasionally undermined by his own fragility and hesitation. He was extremely shy and self-conscious, to the point that he would sometimes find it distressing to stand in front of the entire school to receive a prize.

In July 1889, J. T. Ward, a fellow of St. John's College, Cambridge, sent a report to the headmaster at CranleighSchool regarding the results of his annual examinations for the school's upper forms. At Cranleigh, students advanced through each grade based primarily on merit rather than age;

Hardy entered the sixth form at the age of twelve. Despite being five years younger than most of his peers, Ward reported that Hardy outperformed many of them in algebra, geometry, and trigonometry. Although an older student secured first place that year, Hardy came in second.

Hardy certainly made a mark. Although Cranleigh had supported Hardy well, by age twelve, it had no further opportunities to offer. His parents, who held high hopes for their exceptionally bright son, kept an eye out for suitable scholarships. At that time, one of the most prestigious and sought-after scholarships was to Winchester, one of England's esteemed public schools and a renowned testing ground for mathematically talented students. The scholarship exam was notoriously difficult; in the 1860s, for example, 137 boys vied for just seven scholarships. Preparing for it typically involved attending a coaching school or special preparation courses. Winning this scholarship was considered the pinnacle of academic achievement for a boy. Hardy applied and, in 1890, emerged first among 102 candidates.

And so after attending Cranleigh, Hardy headed off to Winchester College for his further studies. Then in 1896, he began his studies at Trinity College, and within just two years, he placed fourth in the Mathematics Tripos. In 1898, at the age of twenty-one, Hardy's first mathematical paper was published; much like Ramanujan's early work, it was initially presented as a question, with the solution appearing in a subsequent issue. Hardy graduated in 1899 and the following year tackled Part II of the Tripos. While Part I was typically the focus of coaching and determined the Wrangler standings, Part II was known for its greater complexity and challenge. Hardy achieved the top score in Part II and was soon elected as a Fellow of Trinity.Later, Hardy aimed to reform the Tripos system, which he felt had become more of an end in itself rather than a means to an end. During his university years, he also joined the Cambridge Apostles, a secret intellectual group or society.

Hardy cited his self-study of Camille Jordan's 'Coursd'analyse de l'ÉcolePolytechnique' as a major influence, which introduced him to the more rigorous mathematical methods of continental Europe. In 1900, he passed part II of the Tripos and was appointed a Fellow of Trinity College. The following year, he earned one of the two Smith's Prizes, a prestigious award in Cambridge mathematics named after a former master of Trinity

College and regarded as the pinnacle of achievement in the field since 1769. By 1903, he had obtained his M.A., the highest degree available at English universities at the time. From 1906, he worked as a lecturer, balancing six hours of teaching per week with his research. In 1919 he left Cambridge to assume the Savilian Chair of Geometry at Oxford. He returned to Cambridge in 1931, serving as the Sadleirian Professor until 1942.

In 1903, Hardy wrote a review of Bertrand Russell's "Principles of Mathematics" for the Times Literary Supplement. Although British mathematic frequently ignored developments in other countries, Hardy took the opportunity to comment on international works through the Mathematical Gazette such as in 1903, he reviewed Einleitung in die Funktionentheorie by Stolz and Gmeiner, and in 1905, he reviewed Leçonssur les fonctions des variables réelles by Borel.

In a brief letter to the American journal Science in 1908, Hardy explained that a dominant trait would not become more common in a population over time. By assigning symbols to the probabilities of different gene types and performing simple algebra, he demonstrated that the proportion of each gene would remain stable across generations. This stability would occur if mating was random and not influenced by Darwinian natural selection, meaning dominant traits would not overshadow recessive ones, nor would recessive traits disappear. The same year, the German physician Wilhelm Weinberg also independently arrived at similar conclusions, leading to the principle being known as the Hardy-Weinberg Law. This principle had a significant impact on population genetics, being applied to the study of genetic inheritance for blood groups and rare diseases, and it is now a standard reference in scientific dictionaries and genetics textbooks.

From 1911, G.H. Hardy worked extensively with J.E. Littlewood in the fields of mathematical analysis and analytic number theory. Their collaborative efforts, including the development of the Hardy-Littlewood circle method, made significant advancements in the Waring problem and led to notable results and conditional results in prime number theory. Their work was instrumental in shaping number theory as a field of conjectures, exemplified by the first and second Hardy-Littlewood conjectures. Hardy and Littlewood's partnership is regarded as one of the most successful and renowned collaborations in mathematical history. Danish mathematician

Harald Bohr, in a 1947 lecture, noted that a colleague considered the trio of Hardy, Littlewood, and Hardy-Littlewood to be the leading English mathematicians of the time.

By 1913, when Ramanujan first sent a letter to Hardy, Hardy at the age of thirty-five, was already a renowned figure. He had been contributing to mathematical literature for fifteen years, with over a hundred papers and three books to his name. As a Fellow of Trinity College, the epicentre of Cambridge mathematics and, by extension, English mathematics, he was at the heart of the field. Having been elected to the Royal Society in 1910, Britain's most prestigious scientific institution, he was recognized as a brilliant mathematician and a significant influence on his peers. A whole mathematical school had started to form around him, and he had also served on the Council of the London Mathematical Society for three years.

Beginning in 1914, Hardy became the mentor of Indian mathematician Srinivasa Ramanujan, a relationship that has garnered much acclaim. Hardy immediately recognized Ramanujan's exceptional, though untrained, talent, and the two developed a close collaborative relationship[1]. When Paul Erdős asked Hardy about his greatest mathematical contribution, Hardy cited his discovery of Ramanujan, describing their partnership as "the one romantic incident in my life."

Hardy was a good-looking man with a finely chiseled face and ice-clear eyes. A brilliant mathematician, he was constantly assessing, evaluating, and comparing. He rated mathematicians, their work, and the books and papers they produced. An eloquent speaker, a fastidious person and scrupulously honest, he had strong opinions on everything and wasn't shy about voicing them. When a Cambridge club he was part of decided to change its official colours, Hardy wrote a six-page critique against the move. He criticized a cherished academic tradition that had lasted almost two centuries and continued to condemn it relentlessly for over twenty years. His passions, grievances, and quirks were all marked by their sharpness, consistency, and intensity. Diffident and somewhat of an eccentric character, he was "one of the most strange and charming of men," wrote Leonard Woolf. An atheist at heart, Hardy abhorred war, dogs, watches, fountain pens, politicians as a class and even the English weather. He loved sunshine and solving Times of London crossword puzzles. He was also a cricket aficionado. In fact he often included cricket

1. Letter from G.H. Hardy to S. Ramanujan 1913, File No. 78 NAI, New Delhi.
2. Newspapers Clipping, NAI, New Delhi.

metaphors in his math papers.

G.H. Hardy is most renowned for his contributions to number theory and mathematical analysis. His 1940 essay, "A Mathematician's Apology," is celebrated as one of the most profound reflections on the nature of mathematics, written for a general audience. He died on 1st December, 1947.

Hardy's collected papers were published by Oxford University Press. The novel "The Indian Clerk" (2007) by David Leavitt explores Hardy's life at Cambridge, including his discovery of and collaboration with Srinivasa Ramanujan.

Close Friends

E. Vinayaka Rao was born on 14 July 1891 in Tanjore, as the eldest son of Sri S. EkanathaRao and Smt. Chandrakantha, also known as Meenakshi Bai. He attended Kumbakonam Town High School for boys and later graduated from Pachaiyappa's College in Madras. As a student at the University of Madras, he was highly distinguished and spent some time as a tutor at Pachaiyappa's College. Subsequently, he pursued legal studies at the Law College in Madras and became a practicing lawyer at the Madras High Court. In his legal career, he worked alongside prominent figures such as Sir C.P. Ramaswamy Iyer and Sir Alladi Krishnaswamy Iyer.

Vinayaka Rao was also a member of the Apollonius Circle, an intellectual group that included Ramanujan. It is likely that Ramanujan and Vinayaka Rao interacted during Ramanujan's time as students at Pachaiyappa's College. Their correspondence indicates a shared enthusiasm for mathematics and a connection with the mathematics community at the college, including both students and teachers[1].

A.S. Ramalingam was born on 26 August 1891. In 1910, he enrolled as a student at King's College, University of London, and earned a B.Sc. in civil engineering in 1913. Despite his focus on scientific subjects, he also had a profound interest in religion. After graduating, he worked as an engineer for the North Staffordshire Railway before joining the 6th Royal Fusiliers Division of the British Army in Dover. During his military service, he became known as A.S. Ram.

Ramanujan met Alampadi Subbaraya Ramalingam (1891-1953) at the Indian Students Hostel at 21 West Cromwell Road in London shortly

1. Letter from S. Ramanujan to Vinayaka Rao, 11 June 1914, Ramanujan Museum and Math Education Centre, Chennai.

after arriving in England in 1914. It seems they did not encounter each other again until Ramanujan was confined to nursing homes. From their subsequent letters, it is evident that Ramalingam, known as Ram, was a deeply caring friend who was very concerned about Ramanujan's well-being and health. Ramalingam shared some information about himself in a letter to Hardy, which has been further supplemented from other sources.

In August 1918, the Secretary of State for India appointed Ramalingam as Assistant Engineer in the Imperial Service. By the time he retired in March 1944, he had attained the position of Executive Engineer. Ramalingam returned to India in August or September 1918, nearly a year before Ramanujan's return. The lack of any recorded meetings between Ramanujan and Ram in India led to the mistaken belief that Ram had perished during the sea voyage back to India. However, the actual reason for their lack of contact was that Ram was stationed far from Madras, working for the Public Works Department in Bengal. Ramalingam passed away in Madras on 6th May 1953.

Last Days and Legacy

In February 1919, Ramanujan started the process of his return to India and to start with he got his passport done. The age recorded in has passport was 30 years with profession marked as Research Student[1]. In the passport Ramanujan's physique was visibly altered and he looked weak and ill. His ship landed in Bombay on March 1919. The Madras Mail and the Madras Times printed reasonably long articles on Ramanujan, on March 29th and March 30th respectively.

A detailed and extensive account of Ramanujan's life was printed in the Madras Times, on April 6th, 1919. It become known later through a letter dated 15th February 1921, that Francis Spring and S.N. Aiyar were the two authors of this article.

A few memos from the Madras Port Trust contain discussions about a certain sum of money, one hundred and three rupees, twelve annas and eight pies, which were credited to Ramanujan's Provident Fund account.

After ailing for over one year in India, Ramanujam passed away in April, 1920. The Madras Mail of April 26th, 1920 carried news of Ramanujan's death.

Letters were exchanged between Francis Spring, Narayana Aiyar and Ramachandra Rao in relation to writing a chapter on Ramanujan. G. H. Hardy had asked Francis Spring to write and he in turn asked for help from S. N. Aiyar and Ramachandra Rao.

On 18th August 1925, Professor Bertram Martin Wilson FRSE who was an English mathematician best known for his role as a co-editor of Srinivasa Ramanujan's Collected Papers, alongside G. H. Hardy and P. V. Seshu Aiyar, wrote a letter to Professor Seshu Aiyar regarding the same and the challenges he and Hardy are encountering.

The Wealth & Welfare, August 1st, 1947, carried an article on Ramanujan written by S. Krishnan, describing Ramanujan's life in great detail.

1. Passport of S. Ramanujan, Ramanujan Museum and Math Education Centre, Chennai.

Two newspaper articles in The Hindu, one on December 11th, 1947, and the second one on January 25th, 1948 talk about G. H. Hardy. The first one mentions the death of Hardy, his achievements and his iconic collaboration with Ramanujan. The second one descibes Ramanujan and his life in detail.

An article appeared in The Hindu, April 18th, 1948, describing how tributes were paid to the late distinguished mathematician, Ramanujan and a portrait of his was unveiled by a Mr. S. A. Vaneswar, Accountant-General, Madras.

On June 13th, 1948, an article was published in The Mail, paying tribute to Ramanujan and unveiling of his portrait at the Madras Port Trust office by Mr. S. Venkataraman, acting Chairman. The artist behind the portrait, Mr. P. Kothandapani was presented with a silver plate.

In August 1947, the Chairman of the Madras Port Trust (CPT) decided to commission a portrait of S. Ramanujan and install it in the CPT chamber. On 17th April 1948, Mr. S. A. Vaneswar, the Accountant General of Madras, unveiled the portrait and delivered a remarkable lecture on Ramanujan's life and contributions.

On 22nd November 1948, The Hindu published an article titled, 'Tribute to Late S. Ramanujam'. And on December 24th, 1949, the Hindu brought out another article on Ramanujan with the heading, 'American Tribute to Late Ramanujam'.

Srinivasa Ramanujan's brief, yet remarkable life was characterized by exceptional brilliance and enduring mathematical contributions, particularly in number theory, infinite series, and continued fractions. Despite his tragically short lifespan, Ramanujan's profound insights and innovative approach left an indelible mark on the field, earning him a revered status among the most distinguished mathematicians. Hailing from the modest town of Erode, India, Ramanujan's innate mathematical prowess emerged early in his life, propelling him on a captivating trajectory that continues to fascinate and inspire mathematicians worldwide.

Srinivasa Ramanujan's legacy was cut short at the tender age of 32, leaving behind a profound impact on the mathematical world. His untimely demise in 1920 stirred deep sorrow within the mathematical community, particularly evident during a poignant moment at a meeting of the Mathematical Society in London on June 10th of that year. There, amidst heavy hearts, the Society's President solemnly acknowledged the loss felt by all in Ramanujan's passing. A speech was delivered, commemorating Ramanujan's extraordinary mathematical contributions, which had left an indelible mark on the discipline. Notably, G. H. Hardy, his esteemed collaborator, penned a poignant obituary for Nature, capturing the essence of Ramanujan's genius. Neville later expanded upon Hardy's tribute, crafting a more comprehensive homage for the Proceedings of the London Mathematical Society. The profound impact of Ramanujan's work was also recognized, across the Atlantic, in America, with the American Mathematical Monthly dedicating ample space to recounting his remarkable journey and mathematical achievements. Despite his brief sojourn on this earth, Ramanujan's mathematical brilliance continues to inspire and captivate mathematicians, ensuring his enduring legacy for generations to come.

A few months following Ramanujan's passing, his sixty-five-year-old father fell ill and was brought to the Pycroft's Road residence of Narayana Iyer. There, Komalatammal and Narayana Iyer's wife cared for him until November, when he passed away in the very house where Ramanujan and Narayana Iyer had spent countless hours delving into mathematics.

Meanwhile, Komalatammal struggled to overcome the grief of losing her son. After seven years of no communication, in August 1927, she penned a letter to Hardy, enlisting the help of a scribe or family friend to convey her thoughts from Tamil to English. In her letter, she updated Hardy on her sons' progress—Lakshmi Narasimhan had passed his Intermediate examination and worked for the post office, while Tirunarayanan had graduated from Presidency College with a B.A. degree earlier that year.

Most of the letter addressed the family's financial struggles, their modest pensions, and Komalatammal's hardships. She appealed to Hardy to intervene with the government and the India Office in London to secure high-ranking positions for her sons in the post office department. Whether Hardy acted upon her request or not, Tirunarayanan did eventually become an assistant postmaster, while Lakshmi Narasimhan's life was cut short prematurely.

Ramanujan's mathematical breakthroughs continue to shape ideas and present puzzles for modern mathematicians. His extensive body of work, spanning nearly 3,900 discoveries, includes numerous groundbreaking findings that have sparked entirely new branches of mathematics. This substantial contribution attests to his exceptional intellect. The Ramanujan Journal, dedicated to the fields of mathematics influenced by his work, stands as a tribute to his unforgettable influence in the Indian history.

The narrative surrounding Ramanujan's Notebooks is a testament to resilience, dedication, and an unyielding quest for knowledge that spanned decades and engaged numerous individuals. Initially driven by the ambition to prove a single formula, Ramanujan's journey led him to discover countless others, prompting the inception of his notebooks as a means to document his findings. As recounted by his friend Neville, the genesis and evolution of Ramanujan's notebooks were rooted in his college years from 1904 to 1907, particularly during his study of Carr's Synopsis, laying the foundation for the reputation he would later acquire.

The earliest known version of Ramanujan's notebooks, believed to have been compiled around his departure from Pachaiyappa's College in 1907, filled over two hundred large pages with formulas spanning singular moduli, hypergeometric series, and continued fractions. Beyond mere scribblings, this "first" notebook was meticulously organized into distinct chapters, each dedicated to specific topics and featuring consecutively numbered theorems. Reflective of Ramanujan's meticulous nature, it hinted at a deliberate effort for formal presentation, possibly aimed at aiding his job-seeking endeavors. Remarkably error-free, Ramanujan had diligently corrected most mistakes during the recording process, showcasing his attention to detail.

Driven by the desire to validate the theorems in Carr's book, Ramanujan quickly outstripped his mentor's teachings. Through relentless experimentation, he explored uncharted mathematical territories, unveiling new theorems daily and recognizing the necessity of recording them. Although his work primarily resided in the realm of "pure" mathematics, with practical applications largely unexplored, Ramanujan's commitment to documenting his discoveries remained steadfast.

Working in isolation from mainstream mathematicians and without access to contemporary mathematical literature, Ramanujan developed his theories independently. This isolation led to a distinctive characteristic in modern academic references to his work, often prefaced with phrases like

"In Ramanujan's notation" or "Expressing Ramanujan's idea in standard notation."

Before departing for England, Ramanujan had meticulously documented his research results in three notebooks between 1903 and 1914, which he used to demonstrate his mathematical prowess to potential benefactors. These notebooks were carefully organized by him, with the first notebook comprising 16 chapters across 134 pages, the second being a revised, expanded version containing 21 chapters across 252 pages, and the third containing 33 pages of unorganized material. Despite carrying these notebooks to Cambridge, Ramanujan admitted in a letter to a friend that he had little time to explore them during his five-year stay abroad.

Upon returning to India, Ramanujan, though plagued by illness and largely confined to his bed, continued his mathematical pursuits. His habit of working on a slate before transferring final results to paper or notebooks was well-known, and upon his death, a vast quantity of notes was handed over to the University by his family. Ramanujan's brother painstakingly compiled handwritten narratives detailing his remarkable life and achievements, further cementing his legacy.

Ramanujan's notebooks continued to make their way through the academic world even after his death. Three days after he passed away, his brother informed Professor Hardy that all of Ramanujan's manuscripts had been given to the University of Madras. On August 30, 1923, the Registrar, Francis Drewsbury, sent a significant portion of these materials to G. H. Hardy, who was supposed to forward them to G.N. Watson, professor of Pure Mathematics at the University of Birmingham. However, the notebooks remained unlocated until 1976, when the American mathematician George E. Andrews discovered a "lost" notebook containing over six hundred mathematical formulas during a visit to Trinity College. This notebook is believed to have been written in the final year of Ramanujan's life.

This discovery sparked renewed interest in Ramanujan's work, with mathematicians around the world analysing and proving the theorems and conjectures contained within his notebooks. In 1987, the centenary of his birth, numerous conferences were held worldwide to celebrate his contributions to mathematics and discuss recent developments inspired by his work.

The University of Madras played a crucial role in preserving Ramanujan's legacy. Having intended during his lifetime to establish a Mathematics Chair and invite Ramanujan to occupy it, the University acquired all his papers, including the notebooks, after his death. Despite bureaucratic hurdles, the University eventually made photostat copies of the notebooks and distributed them, with one set lost in an air disaster in 1949.

Efforts to publish Ramanujan's notebooks faced delays until 1957 when the Tata Institute of Fundamental Research, with financial assistance from the Sir Dadabhai Naoroji Trust, published a facsimile edition. This publication marked a significant milestone in mathematical scholarship, making Ramanujan's insights accessible to researchers worldwide.

The remarkable journey of Ramanujan's notebooks underscores the enduring value of his contributions and the collective effort to preserve his genius for future generations. Despite the challenges and setbacks encountered along the way, the eventual publication of his notebooks has furthered the lasting impact of a mathematical prodigy whose work continues to inspire mathematicians worldwide. The sheer volume of Ramanujan's work, many of which were original and some that pioneered new branches of mathematics, is a testament to his genius.

Ramanujan, despite his limited formal education, left behind a legacy marked by remarkable intuition, ground-breaking discoveries, and enduring mathematical enigmas. His story unfolds as a tale of unparalleled mathematical genius, inspiring and challenging mathematicians to this day.

The mathematical community, along with the University of Madras, mourned his death deeply. Among the earliest memorials was an oil painting of Ramanujan, crafted using the only available likeness from his passport. This portrait was unveiled by Sir K Srinivasa Ayyangar, the Vice-Chancellor of the University of Madras, in 1922. Another depiction, based on a group photograph taken in Cambridge, adorned the walls of the University of Madras. Hardy's book of 1940 also featured a photograph of Ramanujan, sourced from the physicist S Chandrasekharan FRS.

In 1930, admirers of Ramanujan within the Indian Mathematical Society established the Ramanujan Prize, funded by a sum of Rs 18,000. Administered by the University of Madras, the prize aimed to recognize outstanding papers contributed to the field of mathematics. The inception of this prize saw only two contenders in its inaugural year: S Chandrasekharan and Kosambi. Following a rigorous assessment by the Board of Assessors, it was decided to divide the prize equally between the two competitors.

The establishment of the Ramanujan Institute for Advanced Study in Mathematics traces back to the Ramanujan Institute of Mathematics, founded on January 26, 1950, by Alagappa Chettiar as a memorial to the mathematician. Initially governed by the Asoka Charitable Trust, the Institute faced financial challenges, leading to its eventual takeover by the University of Madras in May 1957. Under the University's stewardship, the Institute evolved into a prominent centre for mathematical study. The transition period saw the amalgamation of the Department of Mathematics and the Ramanujan Institute of Mathematics, forming a centre for the advanced study in mathematics named the "Ramanujan Institute for Advanced Study in Mathematics" (RIASM).

In tribute to Ramanujan's legacy, a museum was established within the institute's premises, with funding sourced from various channels, including the National Board for Higher Mathematics and the Ministry of Culture and Tourism. Substantial financial support from the Ministry of Human Resource Development further propelled the museum's growth and research endeavours. Initiated with a grant from UGC Special Assistance for Equipment, and with assistance from the Vikram A. Sarabhai Community Science Centre in Ahmedabad, a Mathematical Laboratory was inaugurated within the institute. This endeavour facilitated the development of multiple mathematical models, which were subsequently showcased in numerous events, including refresher courses organized by the Academic Staff College of the University of Madras, the Silver Jubilee conference of the Association of Mathematics Teachers of India held in Madras during January 10-13, 1991, and the Science Exhibition held at the National Institute of Technology, Tiruchirapalli in July 1991. These models have since been lent for display in several schools in and around Chennai. Eventually, the Mathematical Laboratory transitioned into a permanent museum, named the Ramanujan Museum.

In honour of Ramanujan's seventy-fifth birthday in 1962, the Indian Postal Department issued a special postage stamp featuring his portrait. This milestone was accompanied by numerous celebrations and tributes across India, including the All India Radio station in Madras, that chose to broadcast a discussion about Ramanujan. As part of the festivities commemorating Ramanujan's seventy-fifth birthday, his alma mater, The Town High School in Kumbakonam, dedicated one of its main halls as the Ramanujan Hall. Concurrently, an exhibition showcasing Ramanujan's Archives, which were under the possession of the University of Madras, took place in connection with this event.

The narrative of Ramanujan is not merely one of mathematical success; it is also a tale of the resilience and determination of the human spirit. His ascent from humble beginnings in India to becoming a Fellow of the Royal Society and an iconic figure at Cambridge serves as a powerful testament to the limitless possibilities inherent in a curious and devoted mind. As we delve into the enigmas of the cosmos, the legacy of Srinivasa Ramanujan will continue to shine as a source of motivation, symbolising the elegance and profundity of mathematics.

No. 239960

PASSPORT

Mr. Arthur James Balfour. Member of His Britannic Majesty's.------Party Council—Member of the -----of Head- --Member of Parliament.-------His Majesty's Principal Secretary of State for Foreign Affairs.

Request and require in the Name of His Majesty all those whom it may concern to allow

Mr. Srinivasa Ramanujan

To pass freely without let or hindrance and to afford <u>him</u> *every assistance and protection of which* <u>he</u> *may stand in need.*

Given at Foreign Office London
<u>24th</u> *day of* <u>February 1919</u>

Sign. Arthur James Balfour

This passport is valid for two years only from the date of its issue. It may be removed for four further periods of two years each after which a new passport will be required.

<u>DESCRIPTION OF BEARER</u>

Age-30
Profession-Research Student
Place and date of birth-Erode, India. Dec. 1888
Maiden Name if widow or married woman travelling singly
Height-5 feet 6 inches
Forehead-Medium
Eyes-Normal
Nose-Broad
Mouth-Normal
Chin-Normal
Colour of Hair-Black
Complexion-Olive
Face-Oval
Any special peculiarities- Small pox marks
National Status-British. India. Born Subject. Hindu Brahamin. Son of Mr. Srinivasa Aiyanagar of Kumbakonam, Tanjore

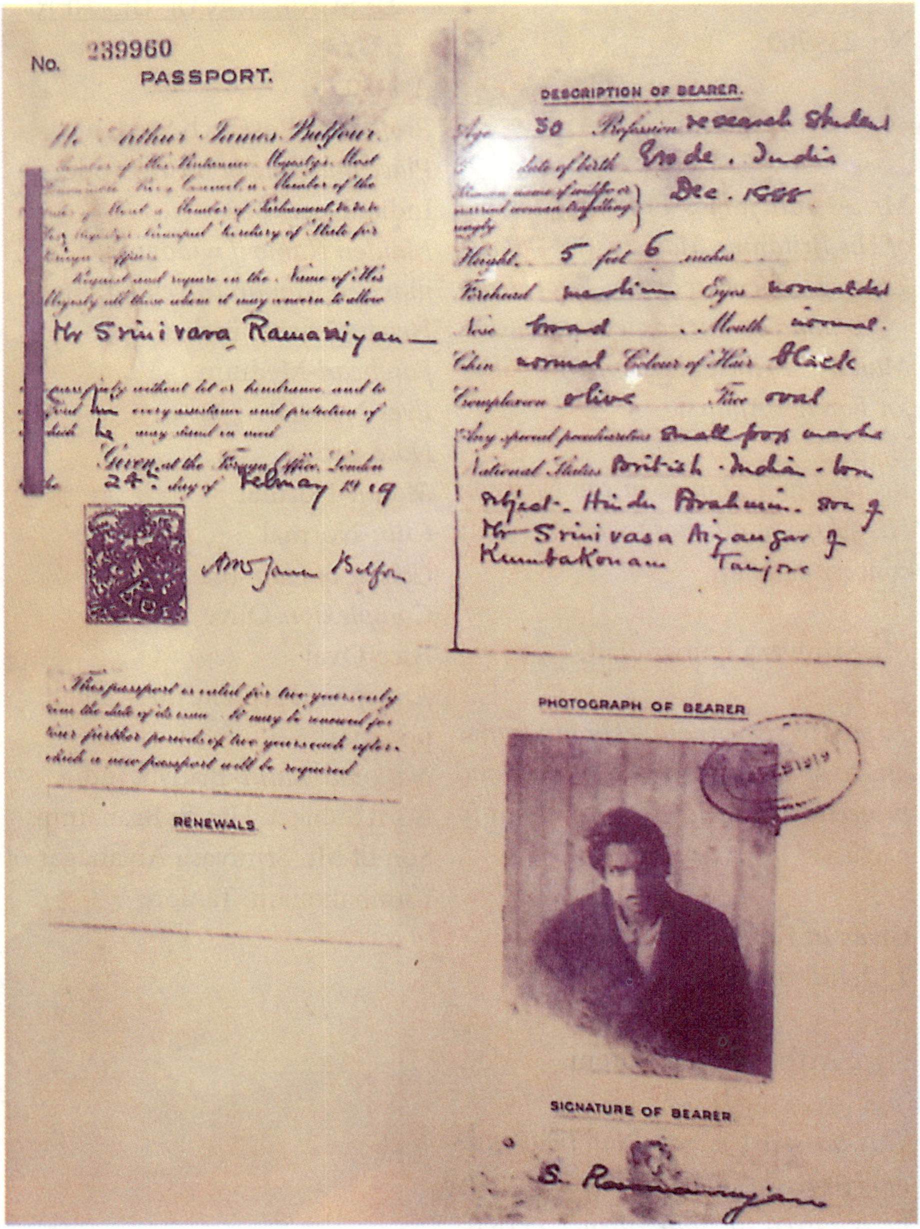

No. 239960

PASSPORT.

Request and require in the Name of His Majesty all those whom it may concern to allow

Mr Srinivasa Ramanujan —

to pass freely without let or hindrance and to afford him every assistance and protection of which he may stand in need.

Given at the Foreign Office, London the 24th day of February 1919

A. J. Balfour

This passport is valid for two years only from the date of its issue.

RENEWALS

DESCRIPTION OF BEARER.

Age 30 Profession research Student

Place and date of birth Erode, India Dec. 1888

Height 5 feet 6 inches

Forehead medium Eyes normal

Nose broad Mouth normal.

Chin normal Colour of Hair Black

Complexion olive Face oval

Any special peculiarities small pox marks

National Status British India - born subject - Hindu Brahmin. son of Mr Srinivasa Aiyangar of Kumbakonam Tanjore

PHOTOGRAPH OF BEARER

SIGNATURE OF BEARER

S. Ramanujan

THE MADRAS MAIL

Saturday Evening, March 29th, 1919.

MR. S. RAMANUJAM.

We have received the following from the Registrar of the University:-

Mr. S. Ramanujan, F. R.S., who was recently elected to a Fellowship at Trinity College, Cambridge, is not, and has never been, a Government State Scholar, but for the last six years has been in receipt of special scholarships granted to him by the Syndicate of the University of Madras from the University funds. The facts of his case are briefly as follows:-

In February, 1913, the Director-General of Observatories, Sir Gilbert Walker, drew the attention of the Syndicate to the mathematical work of Mr. S. Ramanujam, at that time a clerk in the Accounts Department in the Madras Port Trust and previously an undergraduate of the Madras University. In March of the same year Mr. Arthur Davies, the Secretary to the Madras Students Advisory Committee, forwarded a letter from the Secretary for Indian students in London, also inviting enquiry into the work of Mr. Ramanujam on a suggestion made by a tutor of Trinity College, Cambridge, with whom Mr. Ramanujam had been in correspondence. Mr. Arthur Davies added that Mr. Ramanujam was unwilling to leave India.

The Board of Studies in Mathematics recommended a special scholarship of Rs. 75 per mensem to enable Mr. Ramanujam to devote his whole time to the study of Mathematics. As there were no University Regulations enabling the Syndicate to grant this scholarship, a reference was made to the Government for the necessary permission to do so. This permission was received and Mr. Ramanujam was offered and accepted a scholarship tenable from the 1st May of that year, 1913. This scholarship was paid from the University Fee Fund.

In the early part of the following year Mr. E. H. Neville, a Fellow of the Trinity College Cambridge, visited Madras as a special lecturer in Mathematics, and interested himself in Mr. S. Ramanujam's work, upon which he reported to the Syndicate and suggested that Mr. Ramanujam should be afforded all opportunity of being trained in modern methods and of coming into contact with European scholars. Mr. R. Littlehailes, then Professor of Mathematics in the Presidency College, also at the same time recommended to the Syndicate that that Mr. Ramanujam, who had overcome his unwillingness to leave India, should be sent to Trinity College, Cambridge, by means of a special scholarship of £250 a year. The Syndicate decided to adopt Mr. Littlehailes' suggestion and requested the Government's permission to utilise for this purpose part of the balances of the grant previously made to the University to provide Vacation Lectures to teachers. The Government sanctioned the appropriation, from this University fund, of a sum not exceeding Rs. 10,000 for a period of two years, free passage and outfit. Mr. Ramanujam accepted the scholarship and proceeded to Cambridge in March of the same year. Two years later, in 1916, this scholarship was extended for another year, and again in 1917 and for a third time in 1918, the necessary funds being provided, with the permission of the Government, from the same source.

In March last the Syndicate communicated to the Senate its intention to make a further grant to Mr. Ramanujam of £250 a year for five years from April next, together with his expenses, on approved journeys to and from Europe, in the hope that this would sufficiently supplement the amount of his Fellowship to enable him to pay visits to India and also to keep in touch with Western Mathematicians. The Senate accepted an allocation, in the University Budget, for this purpose, of Rs. 5,000 for the ensuing year. The sanction of the Government to the appropriation of this sum from the grant above, mentioned is awaited.

Mr. Ramanujam, who has been very ill in England, arrived in India by the S.S. Negoya on the 27th instant. Mr. G. H. Hardy, F.R.S., who periodically reported to the Syndicate of the University of Mr. Ramanujam's condition and work and has befriended him in every possible way, describes Mr. Ramanujam in one of his letters as being "in some respects the most remarkable mathematician in the world."

The Madras Mail

SATURDAY EVENING, MAR. 29, 1919.

MR. S. RAMANUJAM.

We have received the following from the Registrar of the University:—

Mr. S. Ramanujam, F. R. S., who was recently elected to a Fellowship at Trinity College, Cambridge, is not, and has never been, a Government State Scholar, but for the last six years has been in receipt of special scholarships granted to him by the Syndicate of the University of Madras from the University funds. The facts of his case are briefly as follows:—

In February, 1913, the Director-General of Observatories, Sir Gilbert Walker, drew the attention of the Syndicate to the mathematical work of Mr. S. Ramanujam, at that time a clerk in the Accounts Department in the Madras Port Trust and previously an undergraduate of the Madras University. In March of the same year Mr. Arthur Davies, the Secretary to the Madras Students' Advisory Committee, forwarded a letter from the Secretary for Indian students in London, also inviting enquiry into the work of Mr. Ramanujam on a suggestion made by a tutor of Trinity College, Cambridge, with whom Mr. Ramanujam had been in correspondence. Mr. Arthur Davies added that Mr. Ramanujam was unwilling to leave India.

The Board of Studies in Mathematics recommended a special scholarship of Rs. 75 per mensem to enable Mr. Ramanujam to devote his whole time to the study of Mathematics. As there were no University Regulations enabling the Syndicate to grant this scholarship, a reference was made to the Government for the necessary permission to do so. This permission was received and Mr. Ramanujam was offered and accepted a scholarship tenable from the 1st May of that year, 1913. This scholarship was paid from the University Fee Fund.

In the early part of the following year Mr. E. H. Neville, a Fellow of Trinity College, Cambridge, visited Madras as a special lecturer in Mathematics, and interested himself in Mr. Ramanujam's work, upon which he reported to the Sydicate and suggested that Mr. Ramanujam should be afforded an opportunity of being trained in modern methods and of coming into contact with European scholars. Mr. R. Littlehailes, then Professor of Mathematics in the Presidency College, also at the same time recommended to the Syndicate that Mr. Ramanujam, who had overcome his unwillingness to leave India, should be sent to Trinity College, Cambridge, by means of a special scholarship of £250 a year. The Syndicate decided to adopt Mr. Littlehailes' suggestion and requested the Government's permission to utilise for this purpose part of the balances of the grant previously made to the University to provide Vacation Lectures to teachers. The Government sanctioned the appropriation, from this University fund, of a sum not exceeding Rs. 10,000 for a period of two years, free passage and outfit. Mr. Ramanujam accepted the scholarship and proceeded to Cambridge in March of the same year. Two years later, in 1916, this scholarship was extended for another year, and again in 1917 and for a third time in 1918, the necessary funds being provided, with the permission of the Government, from the same source.

In March last the Syndicate communicated to the Senate its intention to make a further grant to Mr. Ramanujam of £250 a year for five years from April next, together with his expenses, on approved journeys to and from Europe, in the hope that this would sufficiently supplement the amount of his Fellowship to enable him to pay visits to India and also to keep in touch with Western Mathematicians. The Senate accepted an allocation, in the University Budget, for this purpose, of Rs. 5,000 for the ensuing year. The sanction of the Government to the appropriation of this sum from the grant above mentioned is awaited.

Mr. Ramanujam, who has been very ill in England, arrived in India by the s.s. *Nagoya* on the 27th instant. Mr. G. H. Hardy, F.R.S., who periodically reported to the Syydicate of the University of Mr. Ramanujam's condition and work and has befriended him in every possible way, describes Mr. Ramanujam in one of his letters as being "in some respects the most remarkable mathematician in the world."

This does not seem to me to go far enough in satisfying legitimate public interest in a man whose mathematical genius may yet do great things for the world and has been already by the highest world authority in such matters, been fully recognised by the F.R.S.

So will Mr. S. Narayana Aiyar please send me the office papers relating to Mr. Ramanujan and after looking through them and seeing what further information I want I will have a talk with Mr. N.A..and will write a further article for the press.

C.A.C

Francis Spring
29th March 1919

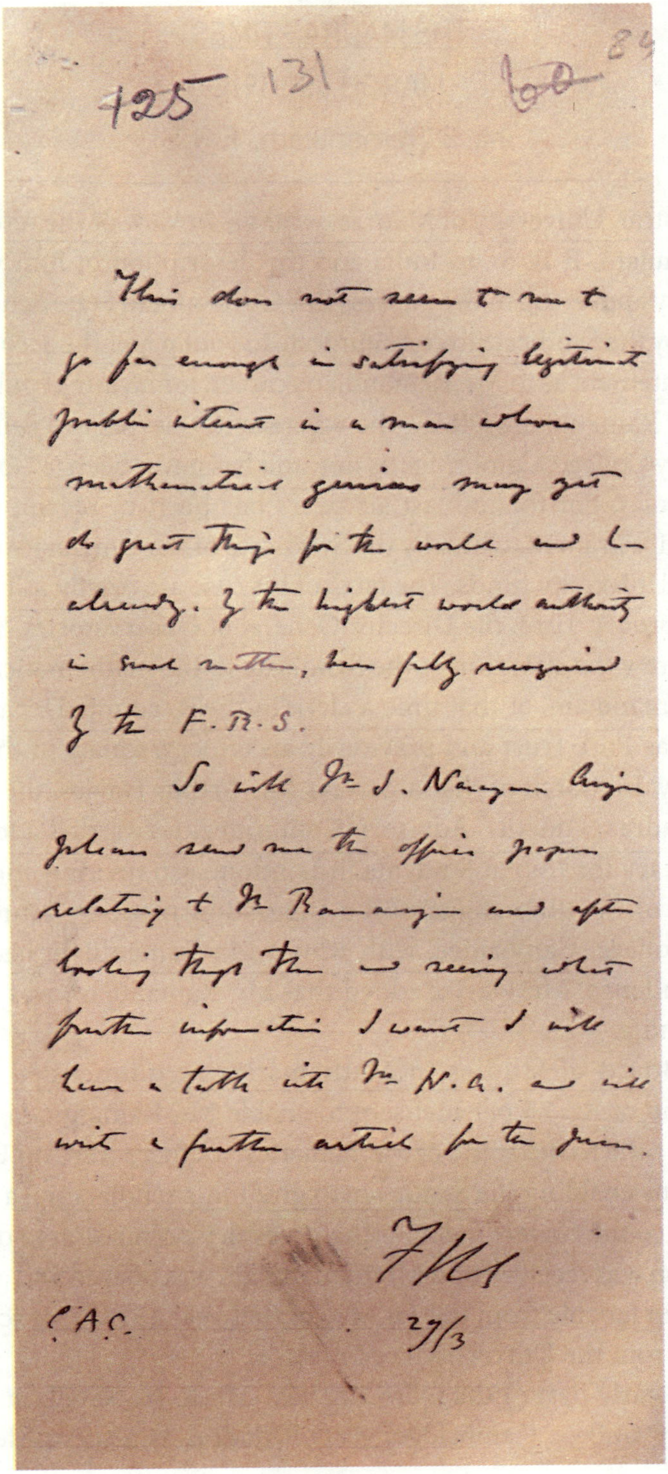

125 131 100 84

This does not seem to me to go far enough in satisfying legitimate public interest in a man whose mathematical genius may yet do great things for the world and has already, by the highest world authority in such matters, been fully recognised by the F.R.S.

So will Mr S. Narayana Aiyar please send me the official papers relating to Mr Ramanujan and after looking through them and seeing what further information I want I will have a talk with Mr N.A. and will write a further article for the press.

FJS

C.A.C. 27/3

THE MADRAS TIMES

MARCH 30th, 1919

Mr. S. Ramanujam, F. R. S.

The Registrar, University of Madras, writes :- In view of the return of Mr. S. Ramanujam, F. R. S., to India and the description of him which has been lately appearing in the papers "as a Government State Scholar", I am directed by the Syndicate to communicate to your paper the accompanying official statement as to Mr. Ramanujan's career, for favour of publication:-

Mr. S. Ramanujam, F.R.S., who was recently elected to a Fellowship at the Trinity College, Cambridge, is not, and has never been, a Government State Scholar, but for the last six years has been in receipt of special scholarships granted to him by the Syndicate of the University of Madras from the University funds. The facts of his case are briefly as follows:-

In February, 1913, the Director General of Observatories, Sir Gilbert Walker, drew the attention of the Syndicate to the mathematical work of Mr. S. Ramanujam, at that time a clerk in the Accounts Department in the Madras Port Trust and previously an undergraduate of the Madras University. In March of the same year Mr. Arthur Davies, the Secretary to the Madras Students' Advisory Committee, forwarded a letter from the Secretary for Indian Students in London, also inviting enquiry into the work of Mr. Ramanujam on a suggestion made by a tutor of the Trinity College, Cambridge, with whom Mr. Ramanujam had been in correspondence. Mr. Davies added that Mr. Ramanujam was unwilling to leave India.

The Board of Studies in Mathematics recommended a special scholarship of Rs. 75 per mensem to enable Mr. Ramanujam to devote his whole time to the study of Mathematics. As there were no University Regulations enabling the Syndicate to grant this scholarship, a reference was made to the Government for the necessary permission to do so. This permission was received and Mr. Ramanujam was offered and accepted a scholarship tenable from the 1st May of that year 1913. This scholarship was paid from the University Fee Fund.

In the early part of the following year Mr. E. H. Neville, a Fellow of the Trinity College Cambridge, visited Madras as a special lecturer in

Mathematics, and interested himself in Mr. S. Ramanujam's work, upon which he reported to the Syndicate and suggested that Mr. Ramanujam should be afforded an opportunity of being trained in modern methods and of coming into contact with European scholars. Mr. R. Littlehailes, then Professor of Mathematics in the Presidency College, also at the same time recommended to the Syndicate that that Mr. Ramanujam, who had overcome his unwillingness to leave India, should be sent to Trinity College, Cambridge, by means of a special scholarship of £250 a year. The Syndicate decided to adopt Mr. Littlehailes' suggestion and requested the Government's permission to utilise for this purpose part of the balances of the grant previously made to the University to provide Vacation Lectures to teachers. The Government sanctioned the appropriation, from this University fund, of a sum not exceeding Rs. 10,000 for a period of two years, free passage and outfit. Mr. Ramanujam accepted the scholarship and proceeded to Cambridge in March of the same year. Two years later, in 1916, this scholarship was extended for another year, and again in 1917 and for a third time in 1918, the necessary funds being provided, with the permission of the Government, from the same source.

In March last the Syndicate communicated to the Senate its intention to make a further grant to Mr. Ramanujam of £250 a year for five years from April next, together with his expenses, on approved journeys to and from Europe in the hope that this would sufficiently supplement the amount of his Fellowship to enable him to pay visits to India and also to keep in touch with Western Mathematicians. The Senate accepted an allocation, in the University Budget, for this purpose, of Rs. 5,000 for the ensuing year. The sanction of the Government to the appropriation of this sum from the grant above, mentioned is awaited.

Mr. Ramanujam, who has been very ill in England, arrived in India by the S.S. Nagoya on the 27th instant. Mr. G. H. Hardy, F.R.S., who periodically reported to the Syndicate of the University of Mr. Ramanujam's condition and work and has befriended him in every possible way, describes Mr. Raamanujam in one of his letter as being "in some respects the most remarkable mathematician in the world."

THE MADRAS TIMES. MARCH 30. 1919.

Mr. S. Ramanujam, F. R. S.

The Registrar, University of Madras, writes:—In view of the return of Mr. S. Ramanujam, F. R. S., to India and the description of him which has been lately appearing in the papers "as a Government State Scholar," I am directed by the Syndicate to communicate to your paper the accompanying official statement as to Mr. Ramanujam's career, for favour of publication:—

Mr. S. Ramanujam, F. R. S., who was recently elected to a Fellowship at the Trinity College, Cambridge, is not, and has never been, a Government State Scholar, but for the last six years has been in receipt of special scholarships granted to him by the Syndicate of the University of Madras from the University funds. The facts of his case are briefly as follows:—

In February, 1913, the Director-General of Observatories, Sir Gilbert Walker, drew the attention of the Syndicate to the mathematical work of Mr. S. Ramanujam, at that time a clerk in the Accounts Department in the Madras Port Trust and previously an undergraduate of the Madras University. In March of the same year Mr. Arthur Davies, the Secretary to the Madras Students' Advisory Committee, forwarded a letter from the Secretary for Indian Students in London, also inviting enquiry into the work of Mr. Ramanujam on a suggestion made by a tutor of the Trinity College, Cambridge, with whom Mr. Ramanujam had been in correspondence. Mr. Davies added that Mr. Ramanujam was unwilling to leave India.

The Board of Studies in Mathematics recommended a special scholaship of Rs. 75 per mensem to enable Mr. Ramanujam to devote his whole time to the study of Mathematics. As there were no University Regulations enabling the Syndicate to grant this scholarship, a reference was made to the Government for the necessary permission to do so. This permission was received and Mr. Ramanujam was offered and accepted a scholarship tenable from the 1st May of that year 1913. This scholarship was paid from the University Fee Fund.

In the early part of the following year Mr. E. H. Neville, a Fellow of the Trinity College, Cambridge, visited Madras as a special lecturer in Mathematics, and interested himself in Mr. Ramanujam's work, upon which he reported to the Syndicate and suggested that Mr. Ramanujam should be afforded an opportunity of being trained in modern methods and of coming into contact with European scholars. Mr. R. Littlehailes,

RAS TIMES. SUND

then Professor of Mathematics in the Presidency College, also at the same time recommended to the Syndicate that Mr. Ramanujam, who had overcome his unwillingness to leave India, should be sent to Trinity College, Cambridge, by means of a special scholarship of £250 a year. The Syndicate decided to adopt Mr. Littlehailes' suggestion and requested the Government's permission to utilise for this purpose part of the balances of the grant previously made to the University to provide Vacation Lectures to teachers. The Government sanctioned the appropriation, from this University fund, of a sum not exceeding Rs. 10,000 for a period of two years, free passage and outfit. Mr. Ramanujam accepted the scholarship and proceeded to Cambridge in March of the same year. Two years later, in 1916, this scholarship was extended for another year, and again in 1917 and for a third time in 1918, the necessary funds being provided, with the permission of the Government, from the same source.

In March last the Syndicate communicated to the Senate its intention to make a further grant to Mr. Ramanujam of £250 a year for five years from April next, together with his expenses on approved journeys to and from Europe in the hope that this would sufficiently supplement the amount of his Fellowship to enable him to pay visits to India, and also to keep in touch with Western mathematicians. The Senate accepted an allocation, in the University Budget, for this purpose, of Rs. 5,000 for the ensuing year. The sanction of the Government to the appropriation of this sum from the grant above mentioned is awaited.

Mr. Ramanujam, who has been very ill in England, arrived in India by the ss. *Nagoya* on the 27th instant. Mr. G. H. Hardy, F. R. S., who periodically reported to the Syndicate of the University on Mr. Ramanujam's condition and work and has befriended him in every possible way, describes Mr. Ramanujam in one of his letters as being "in some respects the most remarkable mathematician in the world."

Write up on Ramanujan by Francis Spring and S. Narayana Aiyar

Mr. Ramanujan, F.R.S

In the belief that Madras Presidency may well be proud to have produced perhaps the greatest - within certain definite lines - pure mathematician of this or any age, we venture to day to offer to our readers such notes as we have been able to collect, showing how S. Ramanujan obtained recognition, in spite of many unfavourable surroundings, and so has been enabled, as explained in the note by the Registrar, Madras University, which we published on March 30th to offer to the world the fruit of his marvellous genius. The notes for this article have chiefly been collected from papers in possession of the Madras Port Trust.

Mr. Ramanujan is a native of Kumbakonam in the Tanjore District of Madras Presidency. He was born in 1888 of poor, and so far as English goes, illiterate parents, of the Vaishnava sect of Brahmins. His father whose name is Sreenivasa Iyengar lives at 17, Sarangpani Coil Sannadhi Street, Kumbakonam. He has two of his younger brothers of 20 and 11 years of age living. Three sisters died while young. In the year 1900, when in his 12th year, he found himself progressing in his mathematical studies faster than his teacher could carry him. A mathematical friend of his gives the following terse note of his studies at this period.

Arithmetic and Geometric series. [Trigonometry(copied Loney's II part) sine, cosine series and not the ratios] 1902 learnt from another how to solve cubic equations. Solved biquadratic equation independently by resolving into two quadratic factors. 1903 Attacked evolving quintic equation and failed. Beginning of 1904 began to investigate the series. 1 1/2, 1/3....... and calculated Eular's constant in a regular series and also to 15 places of decimals, and also Bernoulli's numbers without knowing that these existed. Developed summation of series and subsequently learnt that this was Only integral calculus. Then learnt what was differentiation and integration.

Was curious to know what Trigonometry was. So he borrowed from a student a Trigonometry. This happened to be part II of Loney's. He went through the whole book and was this fortunate to learn at the outset that sine, cosine and other functions represented algebraic series and not the ratios as is generally taught to young school boys.

At the end of 1904 at the age of 16 he passed the Madras University matriculation and joined Kumbakonam College in the intermediate class, going through the 1st year course. Taking, however, undue interest in mathematics to the sacrifice of other subjects, he failed to secure promotion to the 2nd year course. In 1905, he was afflicted with an illness, but not withstanding this, he in that year investigated much of what is known as "hypergeometric series". At the end of 1905 and during 1906 he investigated the relation of many integrals and series, learning only subsequently that these investigations of his related to what are called Elliptic Functions. In 1906, he joined Pachiappa's College and for 3 months read in the 1st year course of the college. Unhappily, at this stage, having fallen seriously ill again, he was obliged to discontinue his college studies. In December 1907, however, he appeared privately for the First Arts Examination and had the distinction of failing in all the subjects, doubtless, as the result of his illness. In 1908, he developed "continued fractures" and investigated "divergent series". In the following year, he underwent a severe surgical operation and was completely prostrated for nearly 12 months. In 1910, he developed relations among Elliptical Modular equations. In 1911 he went in search of mathematicians in the hope of their appreciating his work and got in touch, inter alia, with Mr. V. Ramaswami Aiyar, Professor Ross of the Christian College, Professor of Middlemast of the Presidency College, and last not least, Mr. Ramachandra Rao, Collector of Nellore and now Dewan Bahadur, and Secretary to Government. This last gentleman paid his boarding fees in Madras for nearly a year, and throughout up to the present date, has been his kind and faithful friend.

At this stage, there began Mr. Ramanujan's connection with the Port Trust, which has led to the recognition and the facilities of which he had made such wonderful use. Supported by Mr. S.W. Middlemast and by S. Narayana Aiyar, M.A., now Chief Accountant, Madras Port Trust, and himself a fine mathematician, he applied for a small billet in the Trust's Accounts Department. The former gentleman wrote of him "He is a young man of quite exceptional capacity in mathematics and exceptionally in work related to numbers." The latter wrote of him as "a mathematical genius". Thereupon, he found himself appointed as accounts clerk on Rs. 25 per mensem from 1st of March 1912. Eight months later, Mr. C. L. T. Griffith, then professor of Engineering in Madras Engineering College, wrote to Sir Francis Spring as follows :-

You have in your office as an accountant on Rs. 25 a young man named S. Ramanujan, who is a most remarkable mathematician. He may be a very poor accountant, but I hope you will ensure that he is kept happily employed until something can be done to make use of his extraordinary gifts. I am writing to one of the leading Mathematical professors at home about him and sending copies of some of Ramanujan's papers and results. Our Mathematics professor here says that very few people could follow or criticise his work. It is of course far beyond my scope, but I happen to know who is at work in the same line at home, and I hope to get instructions as to what this fellow ought to do.

If there is any real genius in him, he will have to be provided with money for books and with leisure, but until I hear from him, I don't feel sure that it is worthwhile spending much time or money on him.

Dr. Bourne F.R.S., at that time Director of Public Instruction, Madras, was next communicated with. Up to that date, no intimation seemed to have reached Dr. Bourne from any of the schools in which Ramanujan had attempted to study. So it may, truly perhaps, be said that had his discovery depended on the Madras educational Department, the poor struggling student might never have got a chance to offer to the world what he has since given it, and the first mathematicians of the age who have been glad to publish it. Meanwhile, Mr. Griffith had enlisted the interest of Mr. W. Graham, I. C. S. , Accountant General, Madras, and a good mathematician, indeed a very high "wrangler", - since alas; killed in command of his battery at the French front, whose letter reached Sir Francis Spring under cover of a note from Mr. Griffith. Mr. Griffith's letter and its enclosure from Mr. Graham ran as follows:-

Mr. Griffith's letter

I enclose the letter re Ramanujan, which Graham has kind enough to send me. He says the man has brains, but may be of the calculating boy type; but, like the other mathematician here, modestly disclaims the power of criticizing R's work.

R. seems to have seen Mr.Middlemast already, and he also appears to be unable to criticize.

I think I was right in writing to Professor Hill in London and we must wait for his opinion, which I hope to get during January.

Mr. Graham's letter.

Ramanujan came to see me to-day (27-11-1912) He seems to have done a great deal of work in one particular branch of calculus, and from the way he has done it he must have considerable mathematical aptitude. He has read no mathematics at all except calculus, apparently, and it is possible his brain are akin to those of the calculating boy.

I should say, however, that if he had the training, mathematics of a certain kind - algebra, Differential Equations, Hydrodynamics, and Calculus - i.e., pure theory and development of algebraic functions - juggling with symbols it has been called - would have become very easy to him.

Whether he has the stuff of great mathematicians or not I do not know. He gave me the impression of having brains. His original work is an interesting development of work already done - but interesting only to the purist. However, I am not the best qualified to judge.

Middlemast's opinion must be valued.

The next thing of any importance to happen was the arrival from England of two successive letters both dated December 1912, from Mr. M. J. M. Hill of University College, London University. These letters which are perhaps rather technical for reproduction here, gave useful advice, chiefly in the direction of insisting on rigid proofs, step by step, instead of conclusions being jumped at which, however correct, had been reached intuitively or sub-consciously, without any intentional or deliberate working out of the intermediate stages. The receipt of these letters was a great assistance to Mr. S. Narayan Aiyar, under whom Mr. Ramanujan was carrying on his humble clerical account duties. In insisting on the filling up of the requisite intermediate steps by way of rigid proof instead of flying to conclusions, however correct they might prove to be, Mr. Hill recommended to use, particularly of Bromwich's Theory of Infinite Series published by Macmillan. This letter of Professor Hill's reached Sir Francis Spring with the following note from Mr. Griffith and was passed on Mr. S. Narayan Aiyar, Mr. Ramanujan's constant friend and mathematical advisor.

I enclose Professor Hill's last letter, re, Ramanujan, will you read it and hand it on to him. I have written to Mr. Ramachandra Rao, collector of Nellore, and asked him to buy this book mentioned and give it to Ramanujan.

The fact that Professor Hill is prepared to consider Ramanujan's Elliptical Functions even though the proofs may not be of that logical completeness that is demanded nowadays shows that it is possible that the "intuitive results" may be of interest. All the same Ramanujan's ought to his utmost to make his proofs complete.

At this stage, a letter dated 8th Feb, 1913 was received from Professor G. H. Hardy of Trinity College and Cayley Lecturer in Mathematics at the University of Cambridge, fully appreciative of the specimen of Mr. Ramanujan's work, which has been sent home to him by Mr. S. Narvayana Aiyar, but entrusting a rigid proof of the theorems. At the same time, Professor Hardy wrote to Mr. Mallet of the India Office to prevail upon Ramanujan to go over to Cambridge. Mr. Mallet communicated with Mr. Arthur Davies, then Secretary to the Student Advisory Board. Mr. Davis wrote in his turn to the Madras anniversary. On Feb 13, Dr. Gilbert Walker, F. R. S., happened to be at the Madras Harbour in connection with observatory matters and Sir Francis Spring took the opportunity to get Mr. Narayana Aiyar to produce some of the work. This was pronounced on most favourably by Dr. Walker, who advised that it should be sent to Professor Hardy, who was probably be found to be able to judge of it at its true value and also promised at the instance of Mr. S. Narayana Aiyar to write the University of Madras recommending Ramanujan to a research scholarship. The next thing to happen was the receipt of a letter from Mr. Hanumantha Rao, asking Mr. Narayana Aiyar to be present at the meeting of Board of Studies of the University to decide what it was possible to do to help Mr. Ramanujan. As stated in the note already published, University of Madras offered Mr. Ramanujan a Rs. 75 scholarship to aid him in continuing his studies and this was accepted on the 12th April 1913, whereupon the Port Trust gave him 3 years leave with the option of returning on the cessation of the scholarship. At this stage, there came a letter from Mr. Arthur Davies to say that he was conveying to Mr. Mallet of the India office the news of the grant of the scholarship and that he hoped some good might come of it from Cambridge. Mr. Littlehailes next came on the scene and Mr. Narayan Aiyar took Ramanujan to see this gentleman, (now Director of Public Instruction, Madras, a well-known mathematician). On 5th Feb 1914, Mr. Francis Spring wrote as follows to His Excellency, the Governor's Private Secretary.

If I understand right, His Excellency has the Educational portfolio. So I am anxious to interest him in a matter which I presume will come before him within the next few days - a matter which under the circumstances is, I believe, very urgent. It relates to the affairs of a clerk of my office named S. Ramanujan who, as I think His Excellency has already heard from me, is pronounced by very high Mathematical authorities to be a mathematician of a new and high, if not transcendental, order of genius.

A few months ago, the Madras University gave S.Ramanujan a scholarship to enable him to fill certain gaps in his education which operated to prevent his conceiving his conceptions to the outside world. Meanwhile, during the last 8 or 9 months, various mathematicians in the first rank in Cambridge, Shimla, and Madras have had before them selections from his work and have pronounced upon them in terms of the very highest eulogy.

Just now, as probably His Excellency is aware, a Mr. Neville, who I think is a Senior Wrangler and a fellow of Trinity, Cambridge, has been in Madras giving a series of lectures on certain phases of the higher mathematics to Honours students and others interested. Under a mandate from Cambridge he has interested himself greatly in Ramanujan and there is every reason to hope that he may be persuaded to go to Cambridge for a year or two so that under expert guidance, not only the way the fruits of his genius be given to the world, but also we may hope his own fame, future usefulness, and personal prosperity may be secured - matters probably quite impossible if he remained in a backwater like Madras for the rest of his life.

I now come to the point where His Excellency may perhaps be able to interfere with advantage. Last evening, I learnt from Mr. Littlehailes and others that the University Syndicate has decided, subject to sanction of the Government, to set aside a sum of Rs. 10,000 in order to secure Ramanujan's visit to England for a couple of years. Messrs. Littlehailes and Neville begged me to intercede with His Excellence with a view to speedy confirmation of the action of the University Syndicate. But I wish to make it quite clear that I write under no mandate from the Syndicate but merely as a private individual interested in my own employee, Ramanujan, as well as in Mathematics.

Mr. Arthur Davies will doubtless arrange for the voyage to England

and that Ramanujan's orthodoxy may be maintained unimpaired. Mr. Neville assures me that he will meet him on his arrival in London and conduct him personally to Cambridge and that when there he will entrust himself personally in his welfare, generally and in all matters of Brahman orthodoxy, so that he may return to India without any loss of esteem of his caste men.

I myself am very far from being a Mathematician enough to express adequately what has been said to me by several who are fully qualified to express an opinion on the subject of the potential value to Science of the new line or thought in which Ramanuja's investigations lie. I am assured, however, by those who ought to know what I am talking about, that they may conceivably be epoch-making and as such well worthy of financial support at the hands of Madras University.

Needless to say, Professor Hardy and other high mathematicians may be trusted to give Ramanujan the fullest credit in the scientific world for his work. My reason for saying anything so obvious as this is that I am told that certain of his Indian friends have been suggesting to him that all that the scientists of England desire to steal his ideas- obviously an utterly impossible suggestion with men of their class.

The result was that His Excellency Lord Pentland expressed cordial sympathy with the proposal that the University should provide Ramanujan with the means of continuing his studies at Cambridge and expressing a desire to do all that was possible to assist in the matter.

About the beginning of March 1914, Mr. Ramanujan was prevailed upon the Sir Francis Spring to accept a scholarship of Rs. 10,000 from Madras University in order to continue his studies in the more favourable Cambridge atmosphere and with the help of Mr. Arthur Davies, in caste matters and so on, he embarked, on the 17th March in the SS Nevasa, from Madras for England, and in May 1914 he went into residence in Trinity College, Cambridge in order to read with Mr. Hardy, Mr. Littlewood and Mr. E. H. Neville. The last gentleman, a Fellow of Trinity College, Cambridge had been in Madras as a special lecturer in Mathematics during the cold weather of 1914 and was most kind in helping Mr. Ramanujan on his arrival in England. Mr. Hardy wrote:-

The first I knew of him was about 15 months ago. He wrote to me explaining who he was, and sent a large number of mathematical theorems which he had proved. There were great, many very remarkable results. His theorems were all in pure mathematics, particularly in the theory of numbers and the theory of elliptic functions. While many of them were quite new, others had been anticipated by writers of whom he had never heard and of whose work he was quite innocent. That is a very wonderful thing; he discovered for himself a great number of things which the leading mathematicians of the last hundred years, such as Cauchy and Jacobi, had added to the knowledge of school men.

Meanwhile, the scholarship term was coming to an end and then arose a question of the continuance of his studies in Cambridge, whereupon on receipt of a letter from Mr. Ramanujan Sir Francis Spring wrote as follows to the Registrar of Madras University.

The accompanying papers refer to Mr. S. Ramanujan, in whom I am interested if for no other reason than that he was discovered while working as a clerk in my office. The papers have reached me from my office manager, Mr. S. Narayan Aiyar, M.A.L.T., who himself a good mathematician, was chiefly interested in bringing Mr. Ramanujan into notice.

In the interests of India's reputation as the birthplace of some good mathematicians of which Mr. Ramanujan is, I am assured, one of the most remarkable. I hope it may be possible for the University to ensure the uninterrupted continuance of the studies, but chiefly of his original research work at Cambridge, by promising him the enjoyment of his present scholarship up to the end of March 1918.

The syndicate will, I have no doubt, give the matter their best consideration.

The reply was as follows:-

In reply to a letter dated December 15, 1915, I have the honour to state that the University of Madras has requested sanction for the allocation of funds for the extension of the scholarship to Mr. S. Ramanujan for another year, i.e., to the end of March 1917. Your letter and enclosures will be placed before the Syndicate for orders. The Syndicate has been given to understand that it is quite possible for Mr. Ramanujan to become independent of a scholarship before the expiry of this extension. If this proves not to be the case a further extension can be considered at a later date. In the meantime it will be difficult for the Syndicate to consider the question of providing for a return of Mr. Ramanujan to India next year, in the absence of any representation on the point from him or from those connected with his work at Cambridge. Possibly Mr. Narayan Aiyar may be able to furnish the Syndicate with more detailed information on the matter.

This was replied as follows,

1. With reference to the concluding portion of the letter No. 7923, dated 16th December 1915, from the University Registrar, I attach an extract from Mr. S. Ramanujan's letter dated 11th November 1915.
2. He wants to arrive in Madras in April 1916 and to stay with his family during May and June, returning to England in July. If his scholarship is to end in March 1917, that leaves him only 8 or 9 months more of study at Cambridge. If he is to compete for the Fellowship mentioned by Mr. Hardy in October 1916, and if he is successful and the continuance to him of the Madras University Scholarship will not be necessary.
3. If the question of providing for the return to the Indian next year can be considered only after a formal representation from him, I will write to him to put it in the formal application through the University authorities there. But I doubt if there is enough time for this formal representation.

Sd. S Narayan Aiyar,
20th December 1915,

Mr. S. RAMANUJAN, F.R.S.

In the belief that Madras Presidency may well be proud to have produced perhaps the greatest -- within certain definite lines -- pure mathematician of this or any age, we venture to-day to offer to our readers such notes as we have been able to collect, showing how Mr. S. Ramanujan obtained recognition, in spite of many unfavourable surroundings, and so has been enabled, as explained in the note by the Registrar, Madras University, which we published on March 20th, to offer to the world the fruits of his marvellous genius. The notes for this article have chiefly been collected from papers in the possession of the Madras Port Trust.

Mr. S. Ramanujan is a native of Kumbakonam in the Tanjore District of Madras Presidency. He was born in [illegible] of poor and so far as English goes, illiterate parents, of the Vaishnava sect of Brahmins. His father whose name is Sreenivasa Aiyengar lives at 17, Sarangapani Coil Sannadhi Street, Kumbakonam. He has two of his younger brothers of 20 and 14 years of age living. Three sisters died while young. In the year 1900, when in his 13th year, he found himself progressing in his mathematical studies faster than his teacher could carry him. A mathematical friend of his gives the following terse notes of his studies at this period.

Arithmetic and Geometric series. [Trigonometry (copied Loney's II part) sine, cosine series and not the device.] 1902 learnt from another how to solve cubic equations. Solved biquadratic equation independently by resolving into two quadratic factors. 1903 Attacked solving quintic equation and failed. Beginning of 1904 began to investigate the series. 1 + ½ + 1/3 ... and calculated Euler's constant in a regular series and also to 15 places of decimals, and also Bernoulli's numbers without knowing that these existed. Developed summation of series and subsequently learnt that this was [illegible]

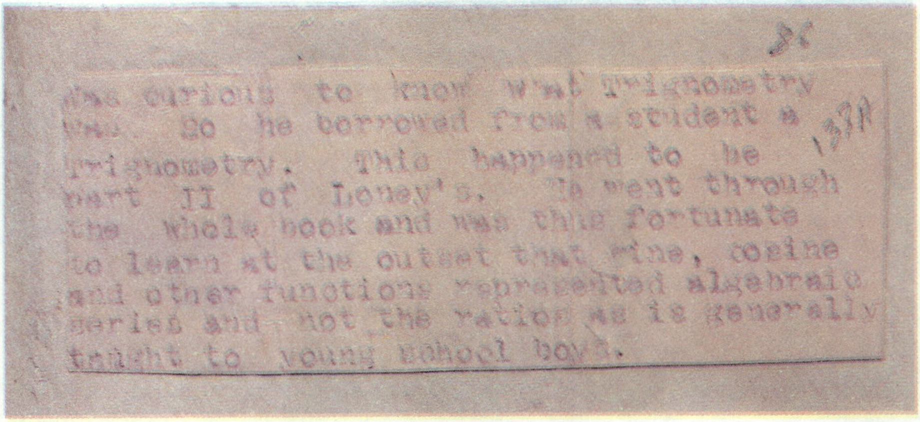
was curious to know what Trignometry was. So he borrowed from a student a Trignometry. This happened to be part II of Loney's. He went through the whole book and was thus fortunate to learn at the outset that sine, cosine and other functions represented algebraic series and not the ratios as is generally taught to young school boys.

only integral calculus. Then learnt what was differentiation and integration.

At the end of 1904 at the age of 16 he passed the Madras University Matriculation and joined Kumbakonam College in the Intermediate class, going through the 1st year course. Taking, however, undue interest in mathematics to the sacrifice of other subjects he failed to secure promotion to the 2nd year course. In 1905 he was afflicted with an illness, but notwithstanding this, he in that year investigated much of what is known as "hypergeometric series". At the end of 1905 and during 1906 he investigated the relation of many integrals and series, learning only subsequently that these investigations of his related to what are called Elliptic Functions. In 1906 he joined Pachiappa's College and for 3 months read in the 1st year course of that College. Unhappily, at this stage, having fallen seriously ill again, he was obliged to discontinue his college studies. In December 1907, however, he appeared privately for the First Arts Examination and had the distinction of failing in all the subjects, doubtless, as the result of his illness. In 1908 he developed "continued fractions" and investigated "divergent series". In the following year he underwent a severe surgical operation and was completely prostrated for nearly twelve months. In 1910 he developed relations among Elliptical Modular equations. In 1911 he went in search of mathematicians in the hope of their appreciating his work, and got in touch, inter alia, with Mr. V. Ramaswami Aiyar, Professor Ross of the Christian College, Professor Middlemast of the Presidency College, and last not least, Mr. R. Ramachandra Row the Collector of Nellore and now Dewan Bahadur and Secretary to Government. This last gentleman paid his boarding fees in Madras for nearly a year, and throughout up to the present date has been his kind and faithful friend.

At this stage there began Mr. Ramanujam's connection with the Port Trust which has led to the recognition and the facilities of which he has made such wonderful use. Supported by

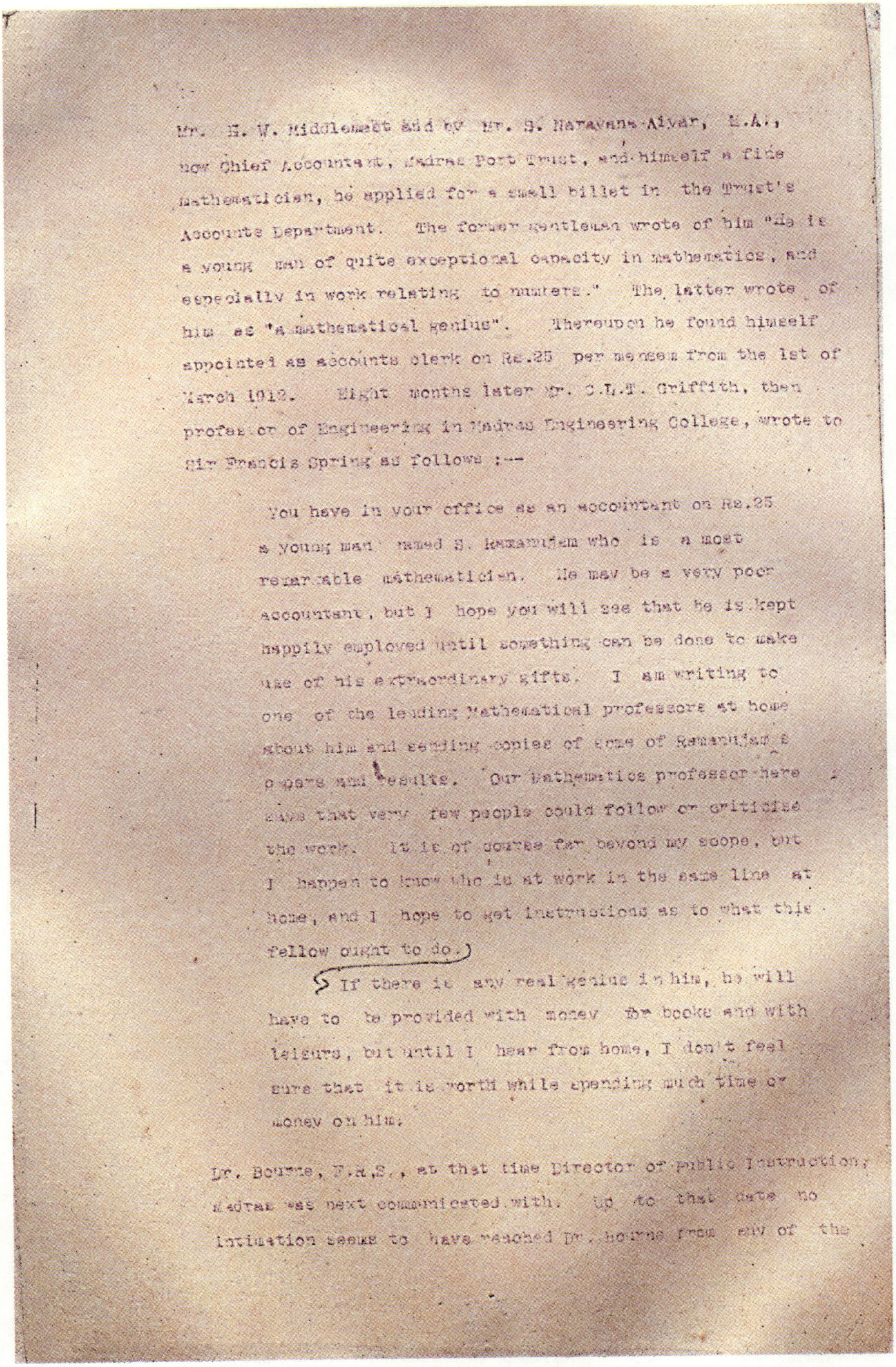

Mr. E. W. Middlemast and by Mr. S. Narayana Aiyar, M.A., now Chief Accountant, Madras Port Trust, and himself a fine mathematician, he applied for a small billet in the Trust's Accounts Department. The former gentleman wrote of him "He is a young man of quite exceptional capacity in mathematics, and especially in work relating to numbers." The latter wrote of him as "a mathematical genius". Thereupon he found himself appointed as accounts clerk on Rs.25 per mensem from the 1st of March 1912. Eight months later Mr. C.L.T. Griffith, then professor of Engineering in Madras Engineering College, wrote to Sir Francis Spring as follows :--

> You have in your office as an accountant on Rs.25 a young man named S. Ramanujam who is a most remarkable mathematician. He may be a very poor accountant, but I hope you will see that he is kept happily employed until something can be done to make use of his extraordinary gifts. I am writing to one of the leading Mathematical professors at home about him and sending copies of some of Ramanujam's papers and results. Our Mathematics professor here says that very few people could follow or criticise the work. It is of course far beyond my scope, but I happen to know who is at work in the same line at home, and I hope to get instructions as to what this fellow ought to do.
>
> If there is any real genius in him, he will have to be provided with money for books and with leisure, but until I hear from home, I don't feel sure that it is worth while spending much time or money on him.

Dr. Bourne, F.R.S., at that time Director of Public Instruction, Madras was next communicated with. Up to that date no intimation seems to have reached Dr. Bourne from any of the

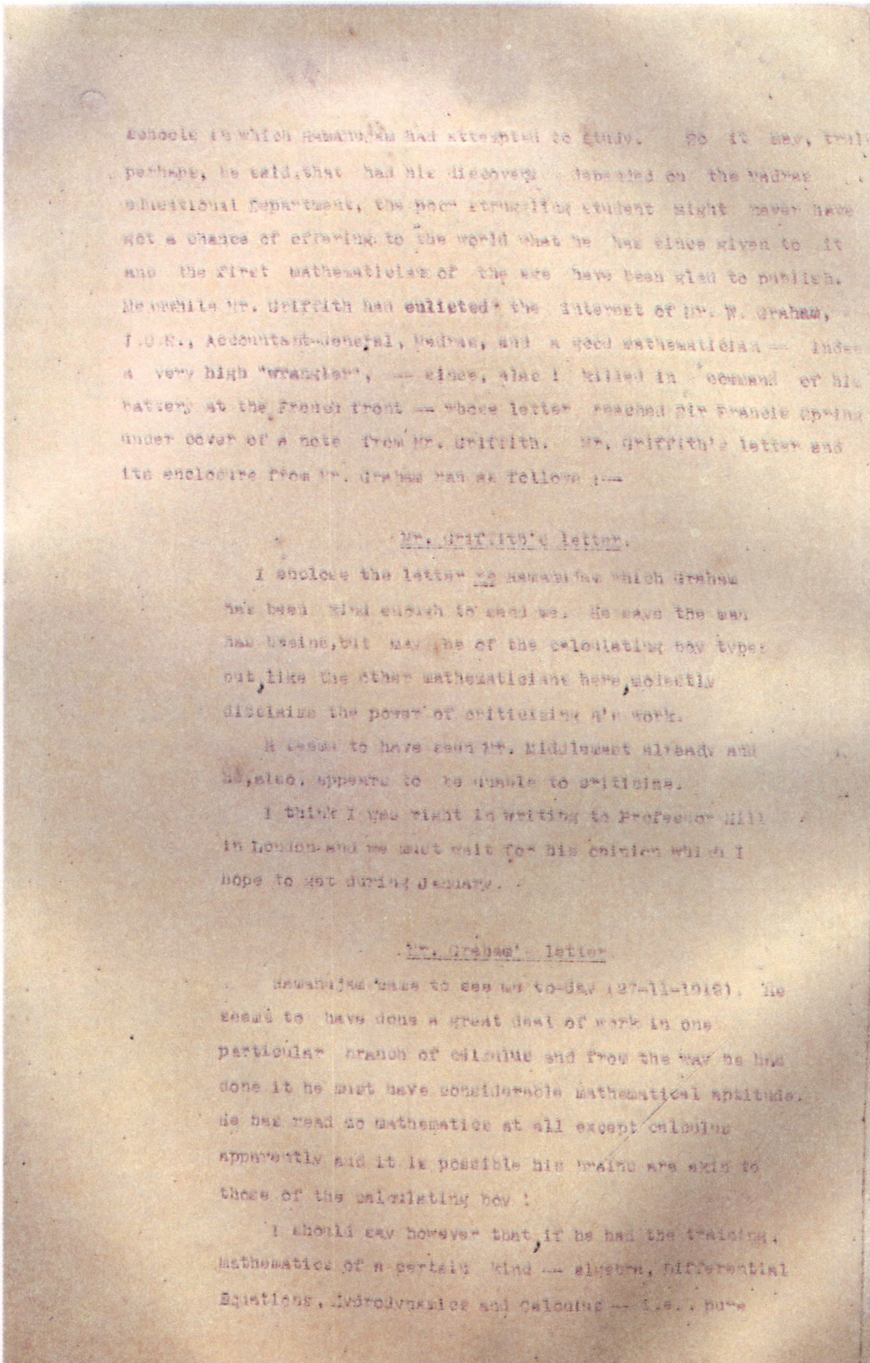

schools in which Ramanujan had attempted to study. So it may, truly perhaps, be said, that had his discovery depended on the Madras Educational Department, the poor struggling student might never have got a chance of offering to the world what he has since given to it and the first mathematicians of the age have been glad to publish. Meanwhile Mr. Griffith had enlisted the interest of Mr. W. Graham, I.C.S., Accountant-General, Madras, and a good mathematician — indeed a very high "Wrangler", — since, alas ! killed in command of his battery at the French front — whose letter reached Sir Francis Spring under cover of a note from Mr. Griffith. Mr. Griffith's letter and its enclosure from Mr. Graham ran as follows :—

Mr. Griffith's letter.

I enclose the letter re Ramanujan which Graham has been kind enough to send me. He says the man has brains, but may be of the calculating boy type: but, like the other mathematicians here, modestly disclaims the power of criticising his work.

He seems to have seen Mr. Middlemast already and he, also, appears to be unable to criticise.

I think I was right in writing to Professor Hill in London and we must wait for his opinion which I hope to get during January.

Mr. Graham's letter

Ramanujan came to see me to-day (27-11-1912). He seems to have done a great deal of work in one particular branch of calculus and from the way he had done it he must have considerable mathematical aptitude. He has read no mathematics at all except calculus apparently and it is possible his brains are akin to those of the calculating boy !

I should say however that, if he had the training, mathematics of a certain kind — algebra, Differential Equations, Hydrodynamics and Calculus — i.e., pure theory and development of algebraic functions -- juggling with symbols it has been called -- would have become very easy to him.

Whether he has the stuff of great mathematicians or not I do not know. He gave me the impression of having brains. His original work is an interesting development of work already done -- but interesting only to the purist. However I am not the best qualified to judge.

Littlewood's opinion would be of value.

The next thing of any importance to happen was the arrival from England of two successive letters both dated December 1912 from Mr. W.H.W. Hill of University College, London University. These letters which are perhaps rather technical for re-production here, gave useful advice, chiefly in the direction of insisting on rigid proofs, step by step, instead of conclusions being jumped at which, however correct, had been reached intuitively or sub-consciously, without any intentional or deliberate working out of the intermediate stages. The receipt of these letters was a great assistance to Mr. S. Narayana Aiyar, under whom Mr. Ramanujam was carrying on his humble clerical account duties, in insisting on the filling up of the requisite intermediate steps by way of rigid proof instead of flying to conclusions, however correct they might prove to be. Mr. Hill recommended the use, particularly, of Bromwich's Theory of Infinite Series published by Macmillan. This letter of Professor Hill's reached Sir Francis Spring with the following note from Mr. Griffith and was passed on to Mr. S. Narayana Aiyar, Mr. Ramanujam's constant friend and mathematical adviser.

> I enclose Professor Hill's last letter re Ramanujam. Will you read it and send it on to him. I have written to Mr. Ramachandra Rao, Collector of Bellary, and asked him to buy the book mentioned and give it to Ramanujam.

The fact that Professor Hill is prepared to

theorems. At the same time Professor Hardy wrote to Mr. Mallet of the India Office to prevail upon Ramanujan to go over to Cambridge. Mr. Mallet communicated with Mr. Arthur Davies, then Secretary to the Students' Advisory Board. Mr. Davies wrote in his turn to the Madras University. On February 13th Dr. Gilbert Walker, F.R.S., happened to be at Madras Harbour in connection with observatory matters and Sir Francis Spring took the opportunity to get Mr. Narayana Aiyar to produce some of the work. This was pronounced on most favourably by Dr. Walker who advised that it should be sent to Professor Hardy who would probably be found to be able to judge of it at its true value and also promised at the instance of Mr. S. Narayana Aiyar, to write to the University of Madras recommending Ramanujan to a research scholarship. The next thing to happen was the receipt of a letter from Mr. Hanumantha Rao asking Mr. Narayana Aiyar to be present at a meeting of the Board of Studies of the University to decide what it was possible to do to help Mr. Ramanujan.

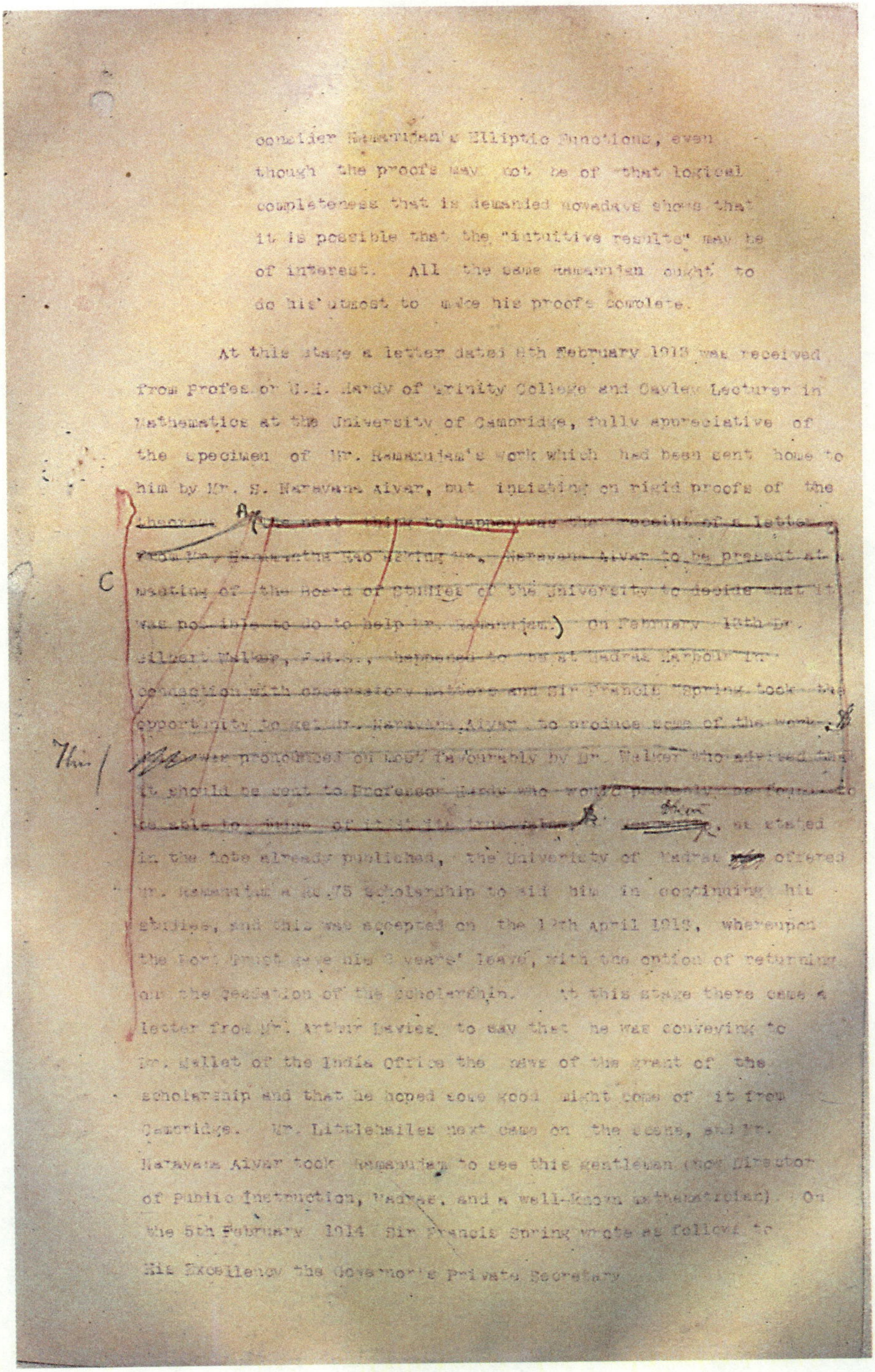

consider Ramanujan's Elliptic Functions, even though the proofs may not be of that logical completeness that is demanded nowadays shows that it is possible that the "intuitive results" may be of interest. All the same Ramanujan ought to do his utmost to make his proofs complete.

At this stage a letter dated 8th February 1913 was received from Professor G.H. Hardy of Trinity College and Cayley Lecturer in Mathematics at the University of Cambridge, fully appreciative of the specimen of Mr. Ramanujam's work which had been sent home to him by Mr. S. Narayana Aiyar, but insisting on rigid proofs of the ~~theorems. (The next thing to happen was the receipt of a letter from Mr. Ramanatha Rao asking Mr. Narayana Aiyar to be present at meeting of the Board of Studies of the University to decide what it was possible to do to help Mr. Ramanujam.) On February 13th Dr. Gilbert Walker, F.R.S., happened to be at Madras Harbour in connection with observatory matters and Sir Francis Spring took the opportunity to get Mr. Narayana Aiyar to produce some of the work. It was pronounced on most favourably by Dr. Walker who advised that it should be sent to Professor Hardy who would probably be found to be able to judge of it at its true value.~~ As stated in the note already published, the University of Madras offered Mr. Ramanujam a Rs.75 scholarship to aid him in continuing his studies, and this was accepted on the 12th April 1913, whereupon the Port Trust gave him 2 years' leave, with the option of returning on the cessation of the scholarship. At this stage there came a letter from Mr. Arthur Davies to say that he was conveying to Mr. Mallet of the India Office the news of the grant of the scholarship and that he hoped some good might come of it from Cambridge. Mr. Littlehailes next came on the scene, and Mr. Narayana Aiyar took Ramanujam to see this gentleman (now Director of Public Instruction, Madras, and a well-known mathematician). On the 5th February 1914 Sir Francis Spring wrote as follows to His Excellency the Governor's Private Secretary

If I understand right, His Excellency has the Educational portfolio. So I am anxious to interest him in a matter which I presume will come before him within the next few days — a matter which under the circumstances is, I believe, very urgent. It relates to the affairs of a clerk of my office named S. Ramanujan who, as I think His Excellency has already heard from me, is pronounced by very high Mathematical authorities to be a Mathematician of a new and high, if not transcendental, order of genius.

A few months ago the Madras University gave S. Ramanujan a scholarship to enable him to fill certain gaps in his education which operated to prevent his conveying his conceptions to the outside world. Meanwhile during the last 8 or 9 months various mathematicians in the first rank in Cambridge, Simla and Madras have had before them selections from his work and have pronounced upon them in terms of the very highest eulogy.

Just now, as probably His Excellency is aware, a Mr. Neville, who, I think, is a Senior Wrangler and a Fellow of Trinity, Cambridge, has been in Madras giving a series of lectures on certain phases of the higher Mathematics to Honours students and others interested. Under a mandate from Cambridge he has interested himself greatly in Ramanujan and there is every reason to hope that he may be persuaded to go to Cambridge for a year or two so that under expert guidance not only may the fruits of his genius be given to the World but also, we may hope, his own fame, future usefulness and personal prosperity may be secured — matters probably quite impossible if he remained in a backwater like Madras for the rest of his life.

I now come to the point where His Excellency may perhaps be able to interfere with advantage. Last evening I learnt from Mr. Littlehailes and others that the University Syndicate had decided, subject to sanction of Government, to set aside a sum of Rs.10,000 in order to secure Ramanujan's visit to England for a couple of years. Messrs. Littlehailes and Neville begged me to intercede with His Excellency with a view to the speedy confirmation of this action of the University Syndicate. But I wish to make it quite clear that I write under no mandate from the Syndicate but merely as a private individual interested in my own employee, Ramanujan, as well as in Mathematics.

Mr. Arthur Davies will doubtless arrange for the voyage to England and that Ramanujan's orthodoxy may be maintained unimpaired. Mr. Neville assures me that he will meet him on his arrival in London and conduct him personally to Cambridge, and that when there he will interest himself personally in his welfare, generally and in all matters of Brahman orthodoxy, so that he may return to India without any loss of the esteem of his caste men.

I myself am very far from being Mathematician enough to express adequately what has been said to me by several who are fully qualified to express an opinion on the subject of the potential value to Science of the new line of thought in which Ramanujan's investigations lie. I am assured however, by those who ought to know what I am talking about, that they may conceivably be epoch-making, and as such well worthy of financial support at the hands of the Madras University.

According to many, Professor Hardy and other high mathematicians may be trusted to give Ramanujan the fullest credit in the scientific world for his work. My reason for saying all this so obvious as

this

> this is that I am told that certain of his Indian friends have been suggesting to him that all that the Scientists of England desire is to steal his ideas — obviously an utterly impossible suggestion with men of their class.

The result was that His Excellency Lord Pentland expressed cordial sympathy with the proposal that the University should provide Ramanujan with the means of continuing his studies at Cambridge and expressing a desire to do all that was possible to assist in the matter.

About the beginning of March 1914 Mr. Ramanujan was prevailed upon by Sir Francis Spring to accept a scholarship of Rs.10,000 from the Madras University in order to continue his studies in the more favourable Cambridge atmosphere, and with the help of Mr. Arthur Davies in caste matters and so on, he embarked from Madras on the 17th March in the S.S. Nevasa for England, and in May 1914 he went into residence in Trinity College, Cambridge, in order to read with Mr. Hardy, Mr. Littlewood and Mr. E.H. Neville. The last gentleman, a Fellow of Trinity College, Cambridge, had been in Madras as a special lecturer in Mathematics during the cold weather of 1914 and was most kind in helping Mr. Ramanujan on his arrival in England. Mr. Hardy wrote :—

> The first I knew of him was about fifteen months ago. He wrote to me explaining who he was, and sent a large number of mathematical theorems which he had proved. There were a great many very remarkable results. His theorems were all in pure mathematics, particularly in the theory of numbers and the theory of elliptic functions. While many of them were quite new, others had been anticipated by writers of whom he had never heard, and of whose work he was quite innocent. That is the wonderful thing ; he discovered for himself a great number of things which the leading mathematicians of the last hundred years, such as Cauchy and Jacobi, had added to the knowledge of schoolmen

Meanwhile the scholarship term was coming to an end and then arose a question of the continuance of his studies in Cambridge, whereupon, on receipt of a letter from Mr. Ramanujan Sir Francis Spring wrote as follows to the Registrar of Madras University.

The accompanying papers refer to Mr. S. Ramanujam in whom I am interested if for no other reason than that he was discovered while working as a clerk in my office. The papers have reached me from my Office Manager, Mr. S. Narayana Aiyar, M.A.L.T., who, himself a good mathematician, was chiefly interested in bringing Mr. Ramanujam into notice.

In the interests of India's reputation, as the birthplace of some good mathematicians of which Mr. Ramanujam is, I am assured, one of the most remarkable. I hope it may be possible for the University to ensure the uninterrupted continuance of his studies, but chiefly of his original research work, at Cambridge, by promising him the enjoyment of his present scholarship up to the end of March 1918.

The Syndicate will, I have no doubt, give the matter their best consideration.

The reply was as follows :-

In reply to your letter dated December 15, 1916, I have the honour to state that the University of Madras has requested sanction for the allocation of funds for the extension of the scholarship to Mr. S. Ramanujam for another year, *i.e.*, to the end of March, 1917. Your letter and enclosures will be placed before the Syndicate for orders. The Syndicate has been given to understand that it is quite possible that Mr. Ramanujam may become independent of a scholarship before the expiry of

this

this extension. If this proves not to be the case a further extension can be considered at a later date. In the meantime it will be difficult for the Syndicate to consider the question of providing for a return of Mr. Ramanujan to India next year, in the absence of any representation on the point from him or from those connected with his work at Cambridge. Possibly Mr. Narayana Aiyar may be able to furnish the Syndicate with more detailed information on the matter

This was replied to as follows :—

With reference to the concluding portion of letter No.7023 dated the 16th December 1915 from the University Registrar, I attach an extract from Mr. S. Ramanujan's letter dated 11th November 1915.

2. He wants to arrive in Madras in April 1916 and to stay with his family during May and June, returning to England in July. If his scholarship is to end in March 1917 that leaves him only 8 or 9 months more for study at Cambridge. If he is to compete for the Fellowship mentioned by Mr. Hardy in October 1916 and if he is successful the continuance to him of the Madras University scholarship will not be necessary.

3. If the question of providing for his return to India next year can be considered only after a formal representation from him I will write to him to put in a formal application through the University authorities there. But I doubt if there is enough time for this formal representation.

Sd. S. Narayana Aiyer.
20th December 1915

Forwarded to the Registrar of Madras University in reply to his letter No.7023 dated the 16th December 1915.

20th December 1915. Sd. Francis J.E. Spring

Forwarded to the Registrar of Madras University in reply to his letter no. 7923, dated 18th December 1915.

Sd. Francis, J. E. Spring
20th December 1915

Later, on the 17th January 1916, the Syndicate of Madras University, with sanction of Government, decided to continue the scholarship for another year and on the 18th October 1916, the Port Trust gave him a further year's leave. Early in 1918 the wonderful news was received that Mr. S. Ramanujan has been elected a Fellow of the Royal Society, the highest honour attainable in Science amongst the English race, thereby only confirming the correctness of his backer's diagnosis. Later, towards the end of 1918, it was announced that he had been elected as a Fellow of Trinity College, Cambridge, whereupon Sir. Francis Spring made over his Madras University Fellow cap and gown to be offered by Mr. Narayan Aiyar to Mr. Ramanujan in the pretty certain event of his being made a Fellow of Madras University on his return to India - feeling highly honoured, he says, in so doing. Full details of the University Scholarship granted to Mr. Ramanujan will be found in the Registrar's Note, which we published on 30th March.

Mr. Ramanujan arrived in India in the SS Nagoya last week, (27 March 1919) and it remains to be seen what his future is to be. Unhappily, he is reported as not being in the best of health, but his many friends and admirers cannot but hope that his return to his Motherland, to his parents, to his friends of his early manhood, and to those who, in the small Madras, scientific world admire his work, even if unable to assimilate much of it - may have the effect of restoring him completely to health and of the world being given further instalments of the results of his wonderful genius. Somebody indeed wrote of him from Cambridge that since Newton there has been nobody his equal - then which, needless to say, there can be no higher eulogy.

*Same article was published in the newspaper the Madras Times on 6th April 1919.

Later, on the 17th January, 1916, the Syndicate of Madras University with sanction of Government decided to continue the scholarship for another year and on the 18th October 1916 the Port Trust gave him a further year's leave. Early in 1918 the wonderful news was received that Mr. S. Ramanujam had been elected a Fellow of the Royal Society, the highest honour attainable in science amongst the English race, thereby fully confirming the correctness of his backers' diagnosis. Later, towards the end of 1918, it was announced that he had been elected a Fellow of Trinity College, Cambridge, whereupon Sir Francis Spring made over his Madras University Fellow cap and gown to be offered by Mr. Narayana Aiyar to Mr. Ramanujam in the pretty certain event of his being made a Fellow of Madras University on his return to India — feeling highly honoured, he says, in so doing. Full details of the University Scholarships granted to Mr. Ramanujam will be found in the Registrar's note which we published on March 20th.

(27th March 1919) Mr. Ramanujam arrived in India in the S.S. "Nagoya" last week and it remains to be seen what his future is to be. Unhappily, he is reported as not being in the best of health, but his many friends and admirers cannot but hope that his return to his motherland, to his parents, to the friends of his early manhood and to those who in the small Madras scientific world admire his work — even if unable to assimilate much of it — may have the effect of restoring him completely to health and of the world being given further instalments of the results of his wonderful genius. Somebody indeed wrote of him from Cambridge the since Newton there has been nobody his equal —' than which, needless to say, there can be no higher eulogy.

Office of the Chairman, Madras Port Trust

Madras, 23rd October 1919
No. A. 7728

From,
THE CHIEF ACCOUNTANT,
MADRAS PORT TRUST,

To,
Mr. S. Ramanujam, B.A., F.R.S.,
17, SarangapaniKoilsannidhi Street
Kumbakonam.

Memo

Mr. S. Ramanujam is informed that there is a sum of Rs. 103-12-8* standing to the credit of his Provident Fund account with the Port Trust. This sum will be paid to him by a cheque on the Bank of Madras on his furnishing a stamped receipt for the amount.

S. Narayana Aiyar
C.A.C.
21.2.1919

* Rs. 103-12-8: One hundred and three, annas twelve and paisa eight.
Chetpet

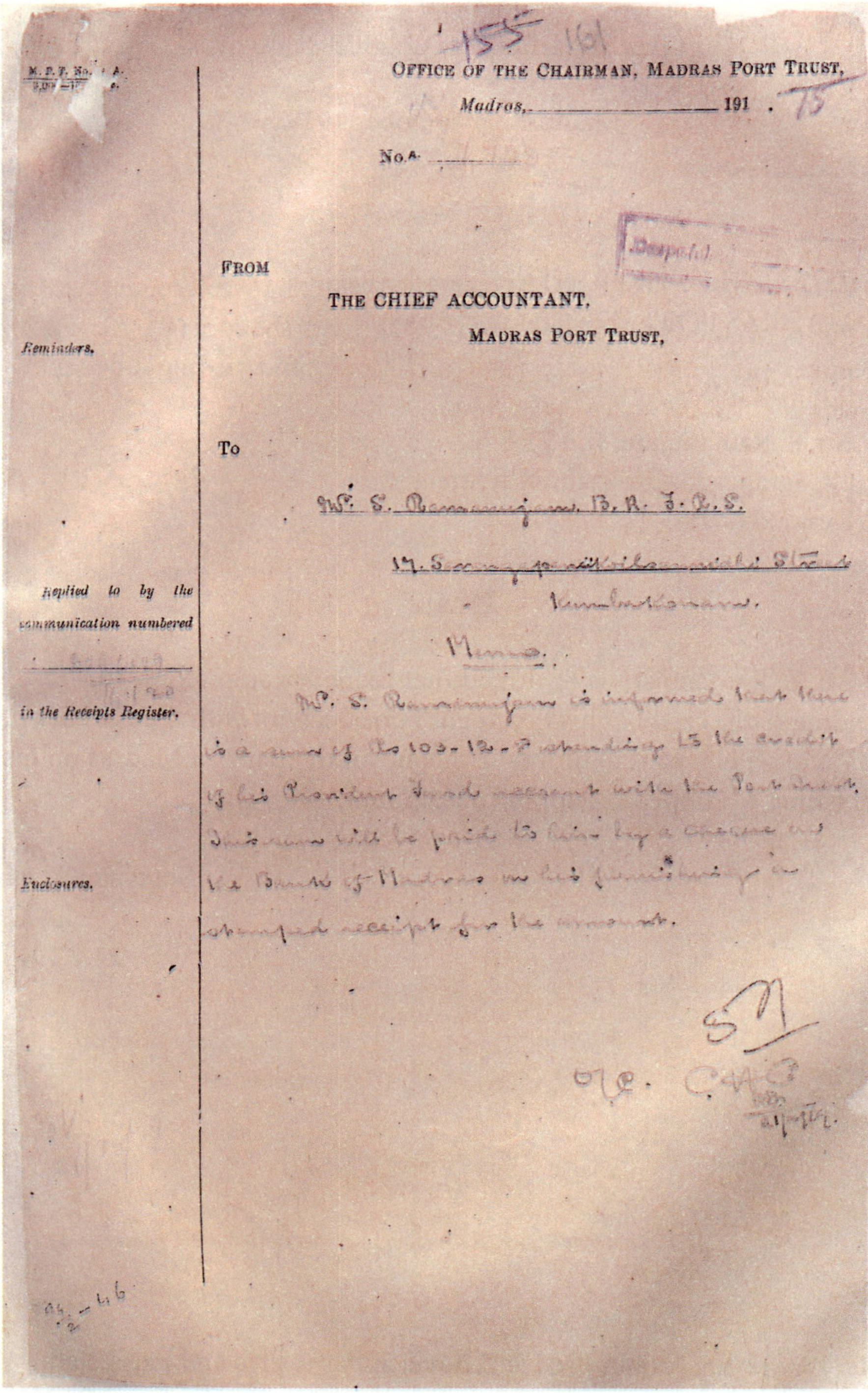

OFFICE OF THE CHAIRMAN, MADRAS PORT TRUST,

Madras, ______________ 191 .

FROM

THE CHIEF ACCOUNTANT,

MADRAS PORT TRUST,

Reminders.

To

Mr. S. Ramanujan, B.A. F.R.S.

17. Sarangapanikoilsannidhi Street

Kumbakonam.

Replied to by the communication numbered

in the Receipts Register.

Memo.

Mr. S. Ramanujan is informed that there is a sum of Rs 103-12-7 standing to the credit of his Provident Fund account with the Port Trust. This sum will be paid to him by a cheque on the Bank of Madras on his furnishing a stamped receipt for the amount.

Enclosures.

12.1.1920

To

The Chief Accountant
Madras Port Trust

Sir,

With reference to your Memo No. 7728 A D/23-10-19 I request you to be good enough to send by the bearer of this letter the sum (Rs. 103-12-8) of Rupees One hundred and three, annas twelve and pies eight being my Provident Fund contribution and subscription.

I have the honour to be,

Sir,
Your most obedient servant,
S. Ramanujan

* Letter from S. Ramanujan to Chief Accountant Madras Port Trust regarding his Provident Fund dated January 12, 1920, NAI, New Delhi.

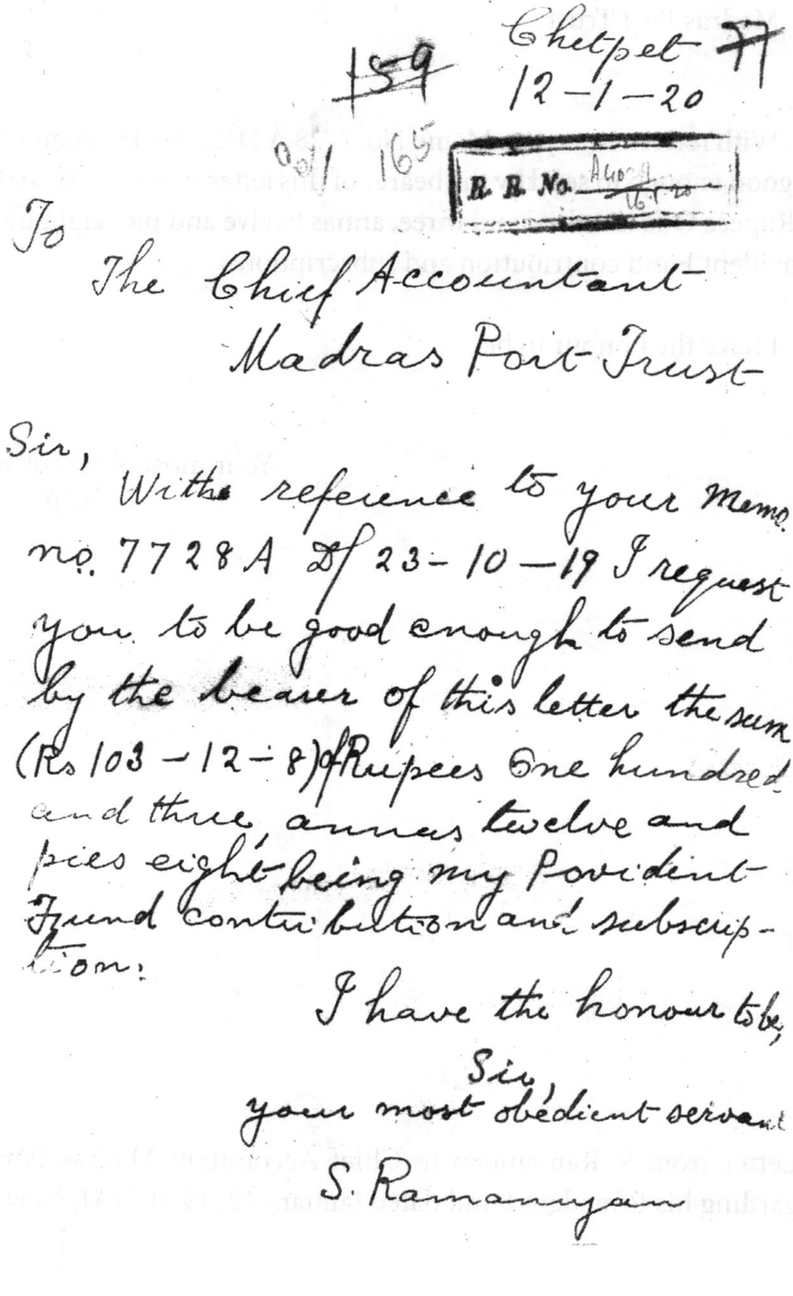

159 Chetpet 77
12-1-20

165 R. R. No. A409 16-1-20

To
The Chief Accountant
Madras Port Trust

Sir,

With reference to your Memo. no. 7728 A D/ 23-10-19 I request you to be good enough to send by the bearer of this letter the sum (Rs 103 - 12 - 8) of Rupees One hundred and three, annas twelve and pies eight being my Provident Fund contribution and subscription.

I have the honour to be,
Sir,
your most obedient servant
S. Ramanujan

Office of the Chairman

Madras Port Trust
Madras, Jan 1920
No. A. 7728

From,
THE CHIEF ACCOUNTANT,
MADRAS PORT TRUST,

To,
Mr. S. Ramanujam, B.A., F.R.S.,
'Kudsia'. Harrington Road
Chetpet, Madras

Memo

With reference to his letter dated 12-1-1920, a cheque for Rs. 103.12.8 being the amount due to him in final settlement of his Provident Fund account with the Madras Port Trust is forwarded herewith. He is requested to acknowledge the receipt of the cheque.

S. Narayana Aiyar
C.A.C.
20.1.1920

Enclosures.One cheque.

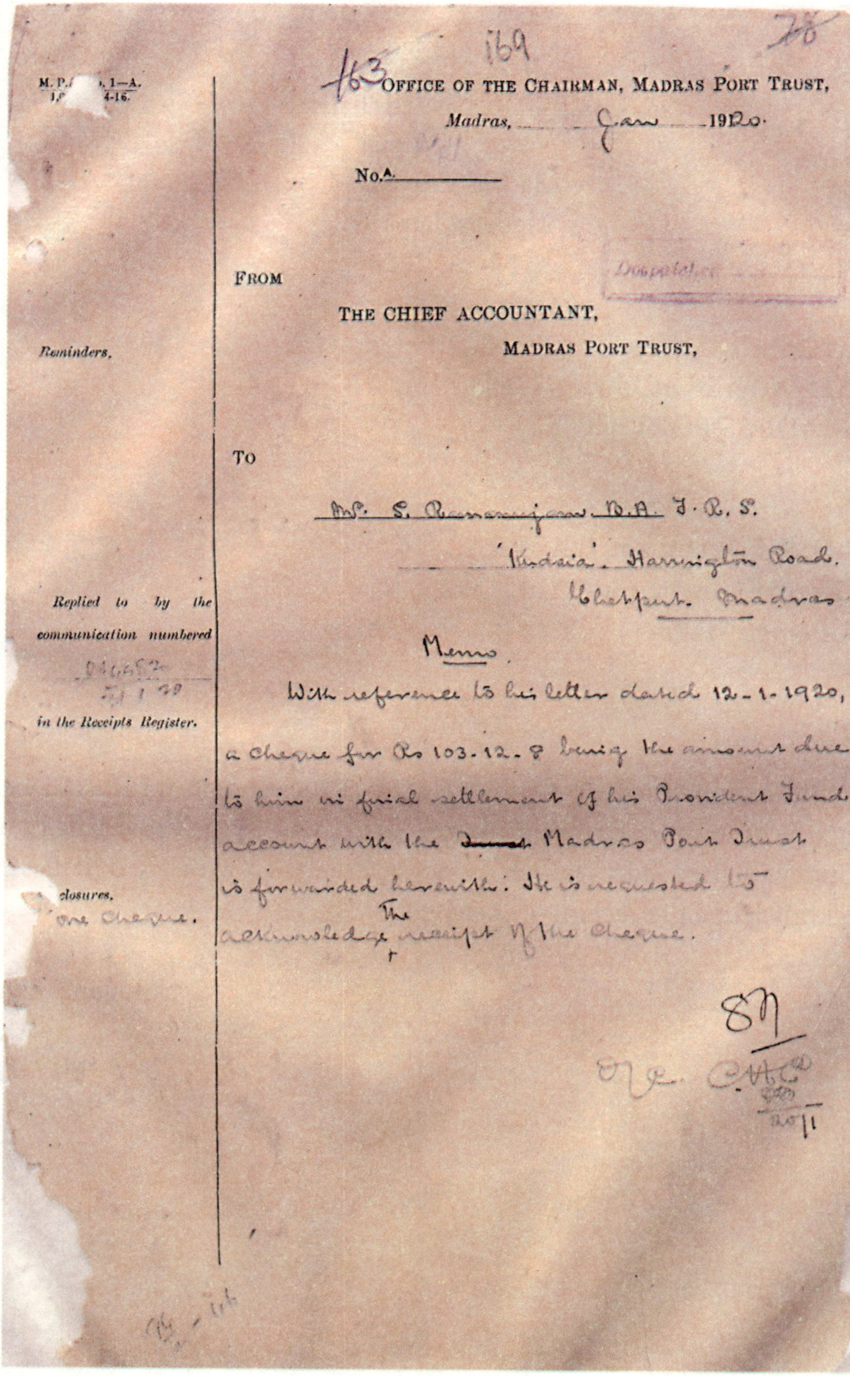

163 169 78

OFFICE OF THE CHAIRMAN, MADRAS PORT TRUST,

Madras, Jan 1920.

No. A.

FROM

THE CHIEF ACCOUNTANT,
MADRAS PORT TRUST,

Reminders.

TO

Mr. S. Ramanujan B.A. F.R.S.
'Kudsia', Harrington Road,
Chetput, Madras

Memo.

With reference to his letter dated 12-1-1920, a cheque for Rs 103-12-8 being the amount due to him in final settlement of his Provident Fund account with the ~~Trust~~ Madras Port Trust is forwarded herewith. He is requested to acknowledge the receipt of the cheque.

Replied to by the communication numbered 016652 21-1-20 *in the Receipts Register.*

Enclosures. One cheque.

SN

O.V. C.A.

20/1

<u>Office of the Chairman</u>
Madras Port Trust
Madras, Jan 1920
No. A. 7728

From,

THE CHIEF ACCOUNTANT,
MADRAS PORT TRUST,

To,

Mr. S. Ramanujam, B.A., F.R.S.,
'Kudsia'. Harrington Road
Chetpet, Madras

<u>Memo</u>

With reference to this office letter No. 11028A dated 20th January 1920 forwarding to him a cheque for Rs. 103-12-8, Mr. S. Ramanujam is requested to acknowledge the receipt of the cheque at an early date.

S. Narayana Aiyar
C.A.C.
27.1.1920

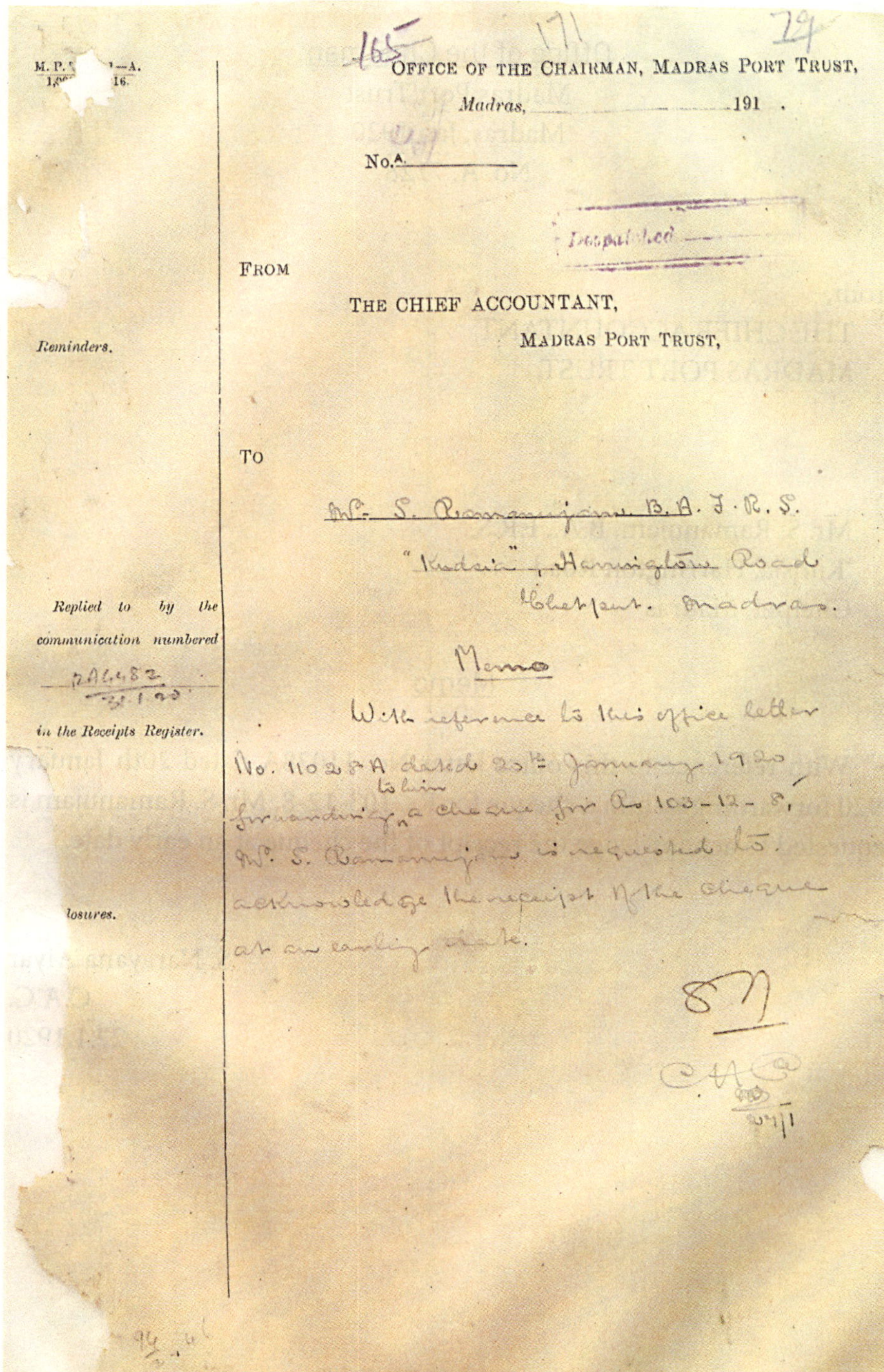

165 171 79

M. P. [illegible]—A.
1,[illegible] 16.

OFFICE OF THE CHAIRMAN, MADRAS PORT TRUST,

Madras, ... 191 .

No. A.

Despatched

FROM

THE CHIEF ACCOUNTANT,
MADRAS PORT TRUST,

Reminders.

TO

Mr. S. Ramanujan B.A. F.R.S.
"Crynant", Harrington Road
Chetpet. Madras.

Memo

With reference to this office letter No. 11028 A dated 20th January 1920 forwarding to him a cheque for Rs 103-12-8, Mr. S. Ramanujan is requested to acknowledge the receipt of the cheque at an early date.

S N

Replied to by the communication numbered [illegible] *in the Receipts Register.*

[Enc]losures.

THE MADRAS MAIL

MONDAY EVENING

April 26, 1920

We regret to record the death this morning at his residence at Chetpet of Mr. S. Ramanujam, F.R.S., who returned to India in March last year as he had been very ill in England. He was born in 1888 of a very poor Brahmin family of Kumbakonam and early in his school career gave promise of exceptional mathematical talent. Mr. Ramanujam entered the service of the Madras Port Trust and there he found recognition of his extraordinary talent, which secured for him facilities for exclusive devotion to research work in higher mathematics, of which he has made such wonderful news. Sir Francis Spring, Mr. Littlehailes, and the late Mr. E. W. Middlemast were instrumental in securing him special scholarships from the Syndicate of the Madras University, with which he proceeded to England. He entered Trinity College, Cambridge, where he attracted the attention of some of the foremost mathematicians of the day, one of whom wrote that Ramanujam discovered for himself a great number of things which the leading mathematicians of the last 100 years had added to the knowledge of schoolmen. In recognition of his exceptional genius for mathematics, he was elected a Fellow of the Royal Society, a much coveted distinction. His death at the age of 32 years will be deplored by the learned world, both in India and England.

* The newspaper article records the death of S. Ramanujan. And a brief writeup about his life, published in the Madras Mail dated April 26, 1920.

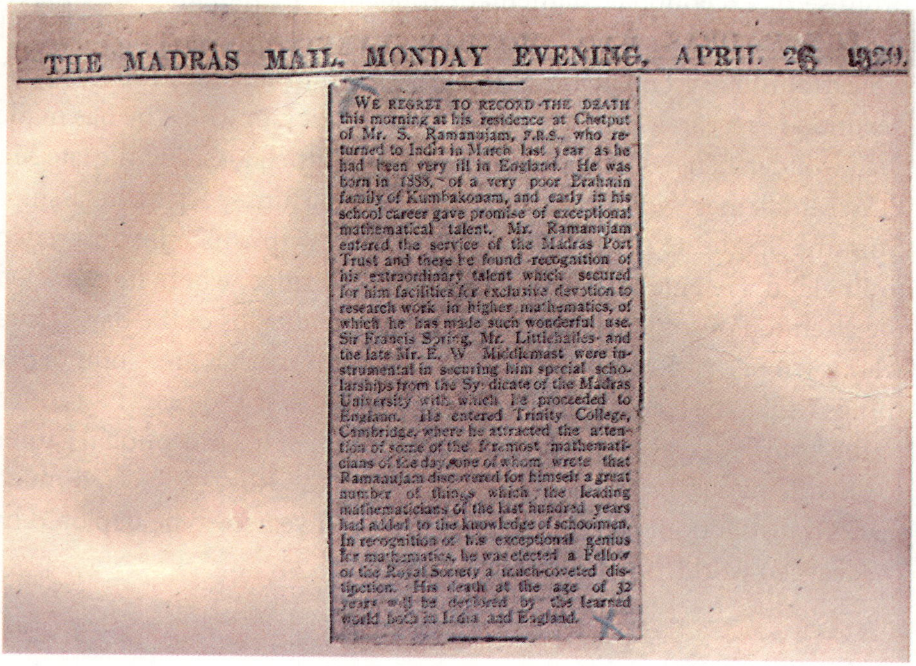

THE MADRAS MAIL, MONDAY EVENING, APRIL 26, 1920.

WE REGRET TO RECORD THE DEATH this morning at his residence at Chetput of Mr. S. Ramanujam, F.R.S., who returned to India in March last year as he had been very ill in England. He was born in 1888, of a very poor Brahmin family of Kumbakonam, and early in his school career gave promise of exceptional mathematical talent. Mr. Ramanujam entered the service of the Madras Port Trust and there he found recognition of his extraordinary talent which secured for him facilities for exclusive devotion to research work in higher mathematics, of which he has made such wonderful use. Sir Francis Spring, Mr. Littlehailes and the late Mr. E. W. Middlemast were instrumental in securing him special scholarships from the Syndicate of the Madras University with which he proceeded to England. He entered Trinity College, Cambridge, where he attracted the attention of some of the foremost mathematicians of the day, one of whom wrote that Ramanujam discovered for himself a great number of things which the leading mathematicians of the last hundred years had added to the knowledge of schooimen. In recognition of his exceptional genius for mathematics, he was elected a Fellow of the Royal Society a much-coveted distinction. His death at the age of 32 years will be deplored by the learned world both in India and England.

15.2.1921
8, Chester Terrace,
Eaton Square,
London S.W.

Dear Narayana Aiyar,

I wrote suggesting to Professor Hardy that he and I should write a chapter about our poor friend Ramanujan for the information of Mathematicians throughout the World. He has now replied welcoming the suggestion and promising to write the mathematical part if I would write the biographical part. All I have to go is in the article which you helped me to write that appeared in the Madras Times of April 6th 1919. In many respects this is redundant and in others inadequate and it would help me very much and would be a fitting tribute to our friend's great genius if you, and if possible also Mr R. RamachandraRao, could at once send me any additional notes that occur to you both.

I say "at once" because Mr Hardy wants the Notice to appear in the London Mathematical Society's Proceedings Vol. 19. He says "about March or April". So if you can put a few notes together quickly, there may be time, even if we have to print them of as an Appendix.

There is some question about printing all Ramanujan's papers. But did not the Madras University buy the copyright of them by an annuity to his mother?

A few notes, which surely Mr. Ramachandra Rao could furnish of Ramanujan's last few months of life after his return to Madras would be interesting. Also any notes you can give in regard to his preservation of his Brahminical "Orthodoxy" in matters of food, avoidance of "defilement" and so on.

I would like very much to get the life records of this wonderful genius as complete as practicable. They are certain to be of high interest to the entire scientific world.

My very kind regards to old friends. I hope you keep well and your family circle also.

Yours sincerely
Francis J.E. Spring

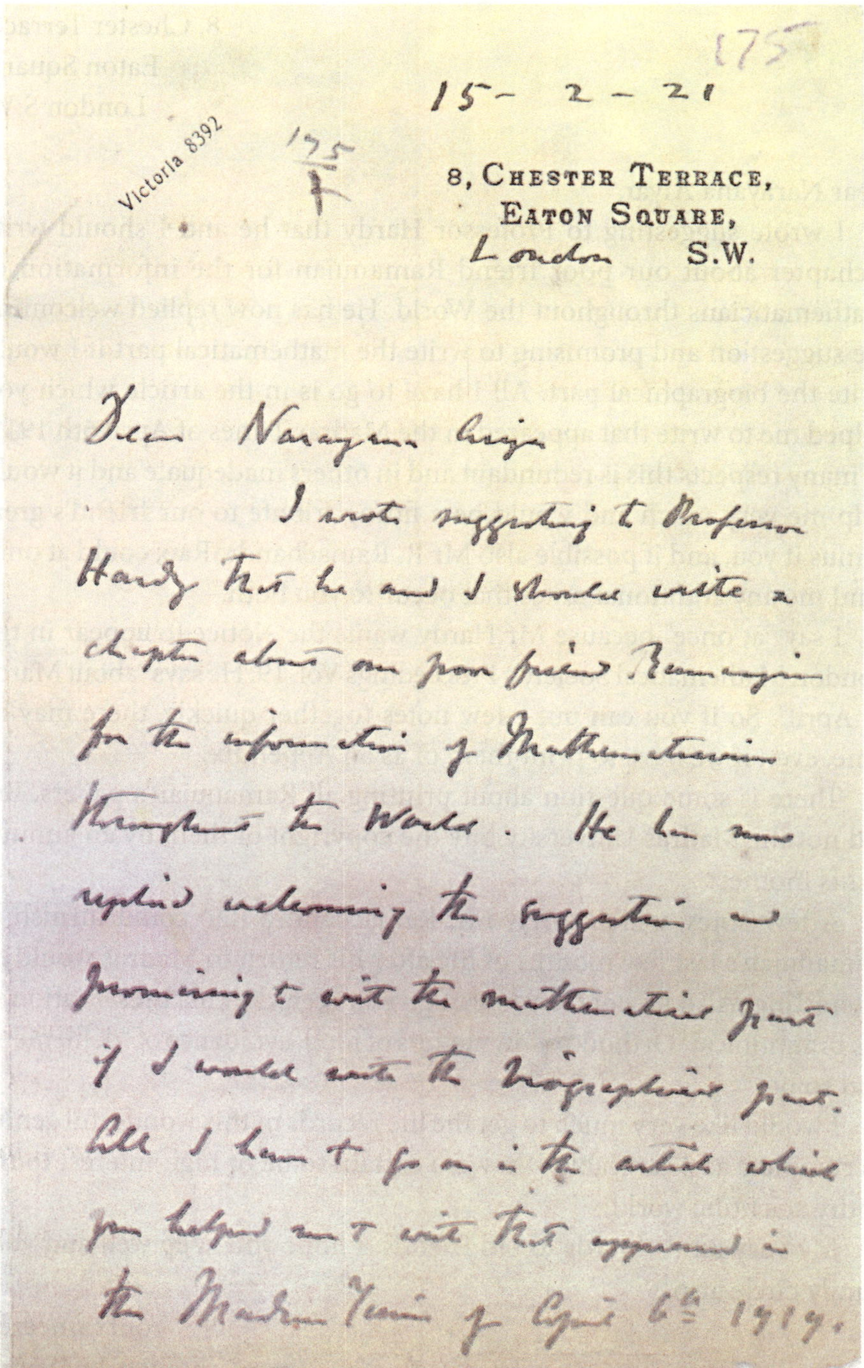

175

15-2-21

Victoria 8392

175
F

8, CHESTER TERRACE,
EATON SQUARE,
London S.W.

Dear Narayana Aiyar

I wrote suggesting to Professor Hardy that he and I should write a chapter about our poor friend Ramanujan for the information of Mathematicians throughout the World. He has now replied welcoming the suggestion and promising to write the mathematical part if I would write the biographical part. All I have to go on is the article which you helped me to write that appeared in the Madras Times of April 6th 1919.

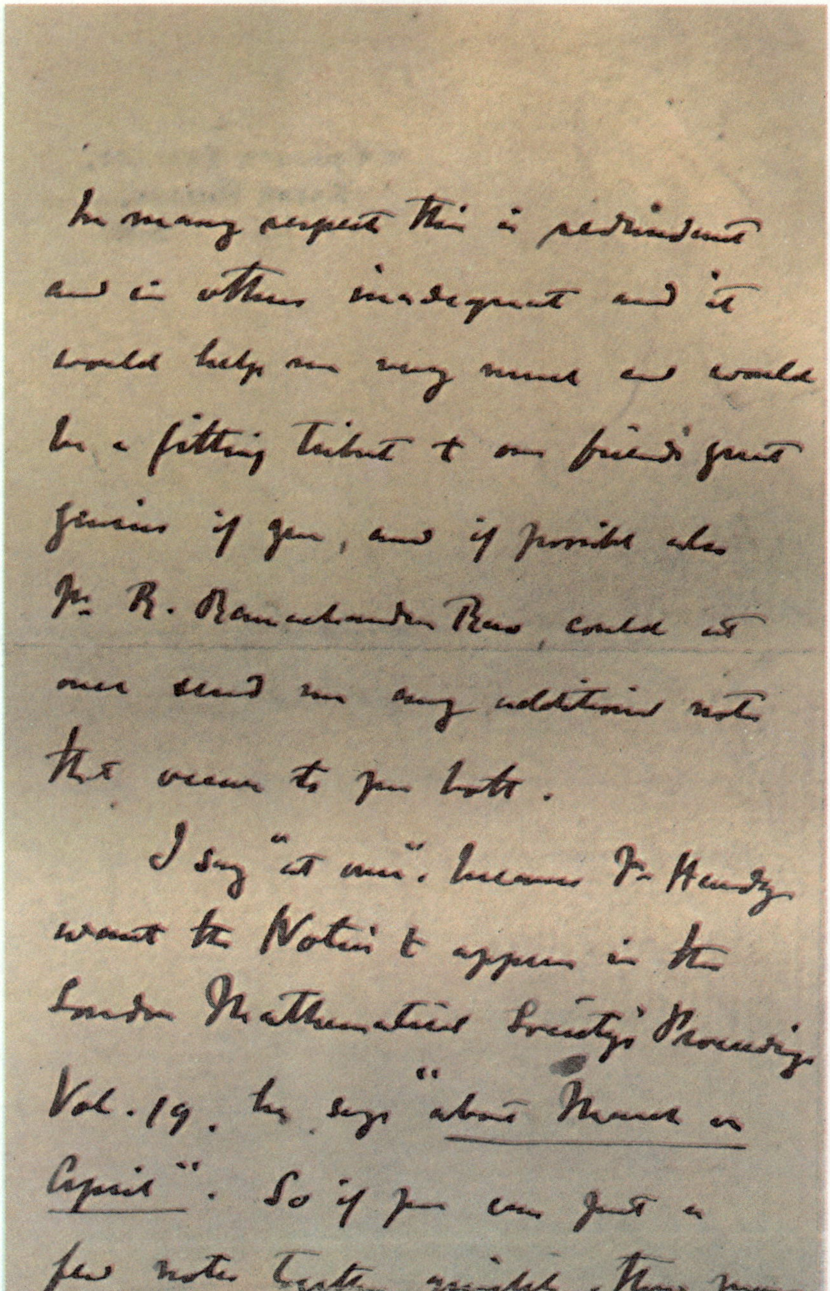

In many respects this is redundant and in others inadequate and it would help me very much and would be a fitting tribute to our friend's great genius if you, and if possible also Mr R. Ramachandra Rao, could at once send me any additional notes that occur to you both.

I say "at once" because Mr Hardy wants the Notice to appear in the London Mathematical Society's Proceedings Vol. 19. He says "about March or April". So if you can put a few notes together quickly. There may

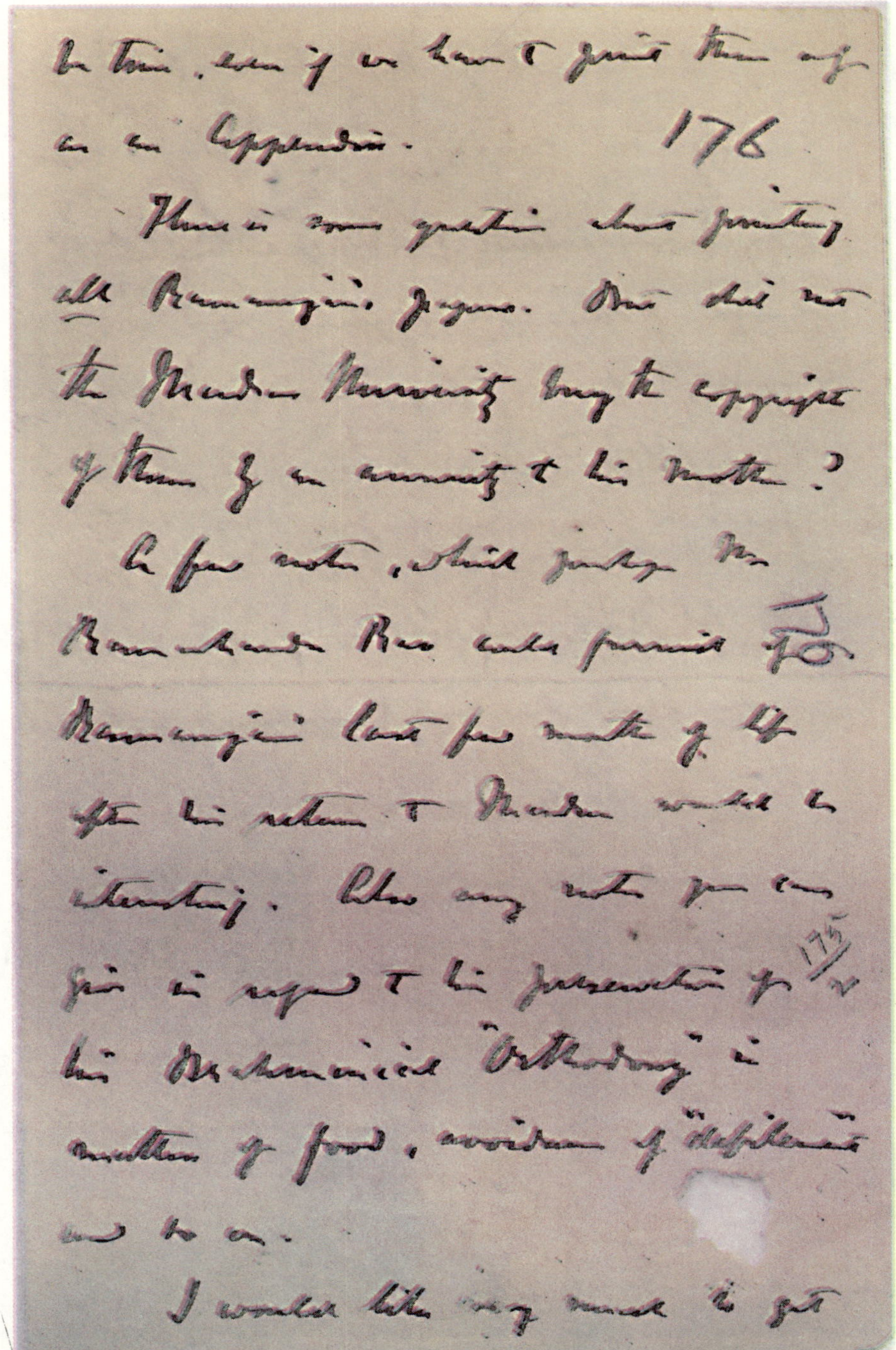

be true, even if we have to print them only as an Appendix.

There is some question about printing all Ramanujan's papers. Why shd not the Madras University buy the copyright of them by an annuity to his mother?

A few notes, which perhaps Mr Ramachandra Rao could furnish of Ramanujan's last few months of life after his return to Madras would be interesting. Also any notes you can give in regard to his preservation of his Brahminical "Orthodoxy" in matters of food, avoidance of "defilement" and so on.

I would like very much to get

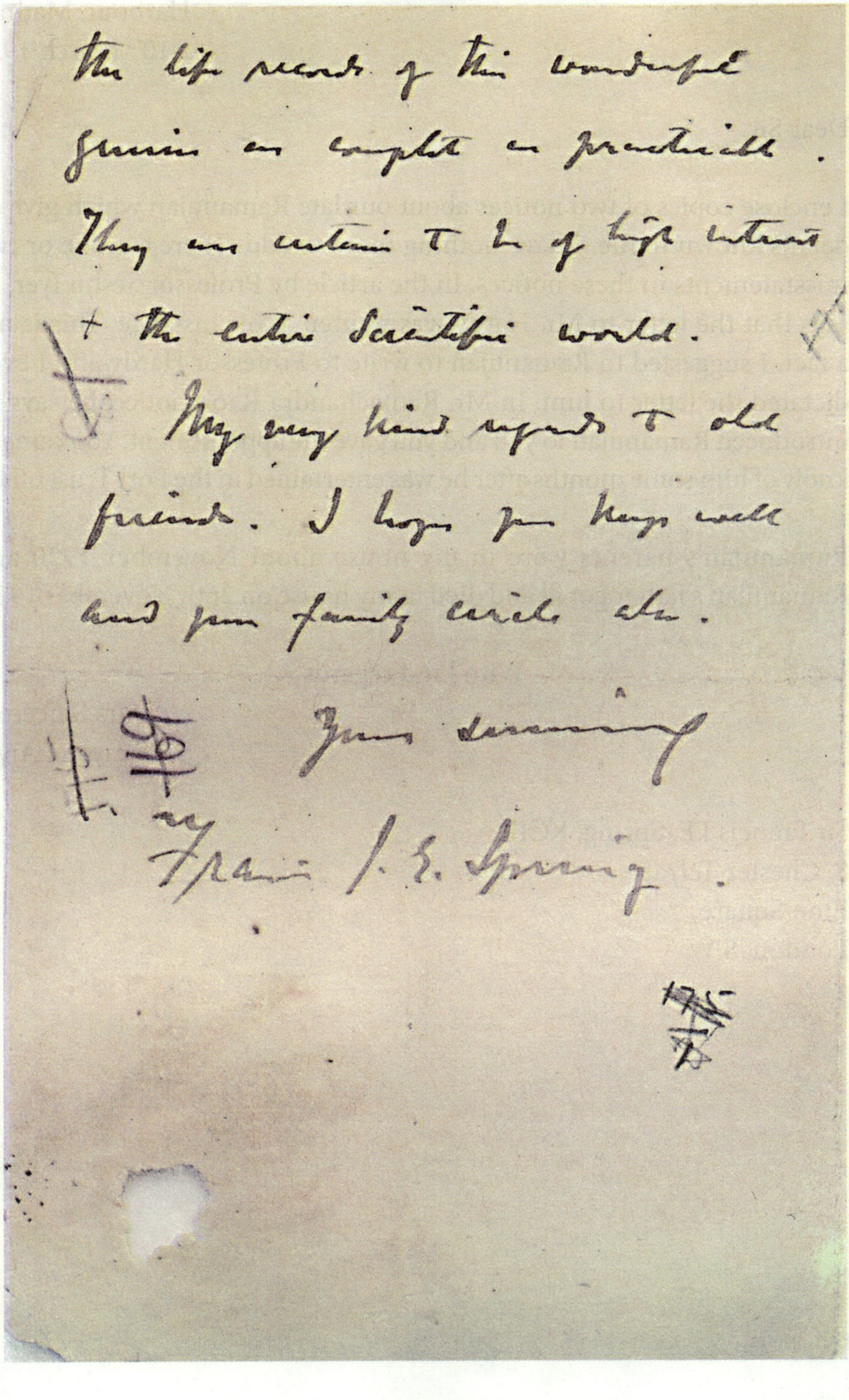

the life record of this wonderful genius as complete as practicable. They are certain to be of high interest to the entire Scientific world.

My very kind regards to old friends. I hope you keep well and your family circle also.

Yours sincerely

Francis J. E. Spring.

Harbour, Madras,
10th March 1921

Dear Sir,

I enclose copies of two notices about our late Ramanujan which give all details known to me. I have nothing more to add. There are one or two misstatements in these notices. In the article by Professor Seshu Iyer, he says that the letter to Mr. Hardy was written at his instance. This is not a fact. I suggested to Ramanujan to write to Professor Hardy and I even dictated the letter to him. In Mr. Ramachandra Rao's notice, he says he introduced Ramanujan to you and you gave the appointment. You came to know of him some months after he was entertained in the Port Trust office.

Ramanujan's parents were in my house about November 1920 and Ramanujan's father got ill and died in my house on 26th November 1920.

With kind regards,

Yours Sincerely,
S. Narayana Aiyar

Sir Francis J.E. Spring, KCIE,
8, Chester Terrace,
Eton Square,
London, S.W.

Harbour, Madras,

10th March 1921.

[De]ar Sir,

I enclose copies of two notices about our late Ramanujan which give all details known to me. I have nothing more to add. There are one or two misstatements in those notices. In the article by Professor Seshu Aiyar he says that the letter to Mr. Hardy was written at his instance. This is not a fact. I suggested to Ramanujan to write to Professor Hardy and I even dictated the letter to him. In Mr. Ramachandra Rao's notice he says he introduced Ramanujan to you and you gave the appointment. You came to know of him some months after he was entertained in the Port Trust Office.

Ramanujan's parents were in my house about November 1920 and Ramanujan's father got ill and died in my house on 26th November 1920.

With kind regards,

Yours sincerely,

Sir Francis J.E.Spring, K.C.I.E.,
8, Chester Terrace,
Eaton Square,
London, S.W.

Mont du vere
Ootacamund
1st July, 1921

From,

R Ramachandra Rao

Dear Sir,

I have been asked by the University of Madras to compile a sketch of the late Ramanujan's life and career.

Can you please let me know all you know, with full details of his Madras life, Sir Francis Spring's assistance etc. also about his mannerisms etc. while in Madras.

Yours Sincerely,
R. Ramachandra Rao

* Letter from Ramachandra Rao regarding details of Ramanujan dated July 1, 1921.

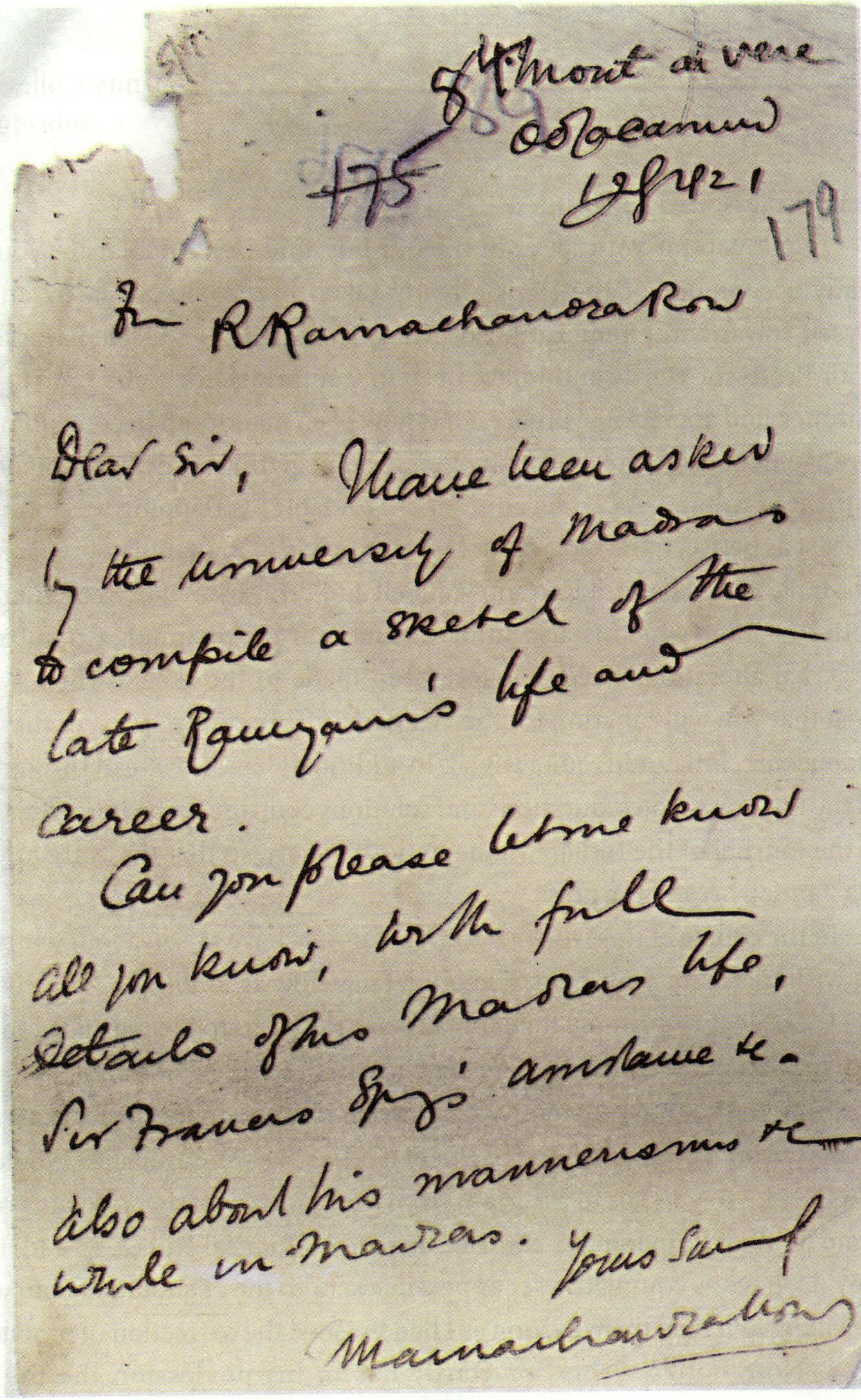

8 Mount de Vere
Ootacamund
19/2/21

179

To R. Ramachandra Rao

Dear Sir, I have been asked by the University of Madras to compile a sketch of the late Ramanujan's life and career.

Can you please let me know all you know, with full details of his Madras life, Sir Francis Spring's assistance &c. also about his mannerisms &c while in Madras. Yours Sincerely

[illegible]

18 August 1925

Trinity College,
Cambridge

Dear Professor Aiyar,

Thank you for your letter of the 8th July, and in particular for your ready acceptance of the steps already taken by Professor Hardy and myself towards the publication of Mr S. Ramanujan's collected works. Both Professor Hardy and I have been in Cambridge for some time this summer, and appreciable progress has now been made both in concluding arrangements with the University Press and in getting ready the contents of the first volume. A certain amount of avoidable overlapping was found to exist as between the biographical sketch of Mr. S. Ramanujan prepared by Mr. R. Ramachandra Rao and yourself and Professor Hardy's obituary notice of him (which is also to be included in the volume): a number of verbal alterations have therefore been made to the sketch which we trust that you will sanction for the avoidance of repetition. Most of these changes are, I may add, quite trivial. In addition I have now read through all the memoirs, notes, questions and solutions contributed by Ramanujan to the Journal of the Indian Mathematical Society, so that these are now substantially ready for press.

In the course of this work a number of points have arisen about which we wish to ask for your help. These I detail below as follows:—

1. So far as re-printing Ramanujan's contributions to the Journal of the Indian Mathematical Society are concerned, the Press will be able to do this from the volumes themselves. But when it comes to the correction of proofs it would be extremely convenient if off-prints were available. Would you then be so good as to ascertain from the Society whether offprints of some or all of Ramanujan's contributions to its Journal still exist, and, if they do, have as complete a set as possible sent to me . I should of course be willing to return them as soon as I had finished the correction of proofs.

2. Note-books. Professor Hardy has in his possession the four manuscript note-books sent to him by the Registrar of the University of Madras. These are, I understand, copies of Ramanujan's own note-books. He also had earlier one original note-book, but returned this to the University of Madras at their request. He now finds, on examining the copies more closely that they appear to omit some things which he remembers to have seen in the original volume. Would it then, in view of all this, be possible to recover from the University of Madras the note-book which he returned so that it may be collated with the ones we have. If this is possible would you kindly direct that the note-book be sent straight to Professor Hardy.

3. Guarantee. I notice that in your letter you kindly offer to use your influence with the authorities of the University of Madras if it is found necessary to have stronger financial support in order to complete publication. I think that it is now quite clear that our present guarantees are more than sufficient to ensure publication of the first volume. But unless that sells rather unexpectedly rapidly it is very likely that more money will be required to guarantee the second volume; if this proves to be the case we shall certainly be glad of your good offices with the University of Madras.

4. Frontispiece to volume. It is obviously fitting that the volume of collected memoirs should have, as frontispiece, a photograph of Ramanujan. The best photograph of which we know is the one reproduced in Vol. XI of the Journal of the Indian Math. Soc., showing head and shoulders and with academic dress. I have failed, after enquiry at all the Cambridge photographers, to find any trace of this photograph, or, rather, of the group of which it formed part, and so am forced to conclude either that they have missed it or that it was not taken in Cambridge at all. Would you therefore kindly find out for us from where the photograph from which that illustration was reproduced was obtained? If it was in India would you then have the negative if possible (rather than a print or reproduction) sent direct to the Cambridge University Press here, — telling them who it is? If, on the other hand, it was obtained from England would you let me know the name and address of the photographer, and I will obtain the negative for the Press.

These four points cover all of importance that has arisen between Professor Hardy and myself as calling for consultation with you. Thanking you once again,

I remain,

Yours Truly,
B.M. Wilson

If you happen to know Professor N.M. Shah you might be so good as to give him my very kind regards when next you meet him. He and I were contemporaries at Trinity and took the Tripos together.

B.M.W.

* Letter from B.M. Wilson to P.V. Seshu Aiyar about publishing of Ramanujan's work. In the post script Wilson is enquiring about N.M.Shah. Nagindas Maneklal Shah received First Class Honours in Part I (1917) and Part II (1919) of the Mathematical Tripos, as did B.M. Wilson. He received his BA in 1919 and MA in 1923 from Cambridge University. Shah and Wilson coauthored a paper that was published in 1919, Ramanujan and Math Education Centre Chennai.

18th August, 1925.

Trinity College,
Cambridge

Dear Professor Aiyar,

Thank you for your letter of the 8th July, and in particular for your ready acceptance of the steps already taken by Professor Hardy and myself towards the publication of Mr. S. Ramanujan's collected works. Both Professor Hardy and I have been in Cambridge for some time this summer, and appreciable progress has now been made both in concluding arrangements with the University Press and in getting ready the contents of the first volume. A certain amount of avoidable overlapping was found to exist as between the biographical sketch of Mr. S. Ramanujan prepared by Mr. R. Ramachandra Rao and yourself and Professor Hardy's obituary notice of him (which is also to be included in the volume): a number of verbal alterations have therefore been made to the sketch which we trust that you will sanction for the avoidance of repetition. Most of these changes are, I may add, quite trivial. In addition I have now read through all the memoirs, notes, questions and solutions contributed by Ramanujan to the Journal of the Indian Mathematical Society, so that these are substantially ready for press.

In the course of this work a number of points have arisen about which we wish to ask for your help. These I detail below as follows:—

1. So far as re-printing Ramanujan's contributions to the Journal of the Indian Mathematical Society is concerned, the Press

will be able to do this from the volumes themselves. But when it comes to the correction of proofs it would be extremely convenient if off-prints were available. Would you then be so good as to ascertain from the Society whether offprints of some or all of Ramanujan's contributions to its Journal still exist, and, if they do, have as complete a set as possible sent to me. I should of course be willing to return them as soon as I had finished the correction of proofs.

2. Note-books. Professor Hardy has in his possession the four manuscript note-books sent to him by the Registrar of the University of Madras. These are, I understand, copies of Ramanujan's own note-books. He also had earlier one original note-book, but returned this to the University of Madras at their request. He now finds, on examining the copies more closely that they appear to omit some things which he remembers to have seen in the original volume. Would it then, in view of all this, be possible to recover from the University of Madras the note-book which he returned so that it may be collated with the ones we have. If this is possible would you kindly ~~direct~~ that the note-book be sent straight to Professor Hardy.

3. Guarantee. I notice that in your letter you kindly offer to use your influence with the authorities of the University of Madras if it is found necessary to have stronger financial

support in order to complete publication. I think that it is now quite clear that our present guarantees are more than sufficient to ensure publication of the first volume. But unless that sells <u>rather</u> unexpectedly rapidly it is very likely that more money will be required to guarantee the second volume; if this proves to be the case we shall certainly be glad of your good offices with the University of Madras.

4. <u>Frontispiece to volume</u>. It is obviously fitting that the volume of collected memoirs should have, as frontispiece, a photograph of Ramanujan. The best photograph of which we know is the one reproduced in Vol. XI of the Journal of the Indian Math. Soc., showing head and shoulders and with academic dress. I have failed, after enquiry at all the Cambridge photographers, to find any trace of this photograph, or, rather, of the group of which it formed part, and so am forced to conclude either that they have missed it or that it was not taken in Cambridge at all. Would you therefore kindly find out for us from where the photograph from which that illustration was reproduced was obtained? If it was in India would you then have <u>the negative</u> if possible (rather than a print or reproduction) sent direct to the Cambridge University Press here, — telling them who it is? If, on the other hand, it was obtained from England would you let me know the name and address of the photographer, and I will obtain the negative for the Press.

These four points cover all of importance that has

arisen between Professor Hardy and myself as calling for consultation with you. Thanking you once again &,

I remain,

Yours Truly,

B. M. Wilson.

If you happen to know Professor N. M. Shah you might be so good as to give him my very kind regards when next you meet him. He and I were contemporaries at Trinity and took the Tripos together.

B. M. W.

WEALTH & WELFARE

August 1st, 1947

SRINIVASA RAMANUJAM: INDIA'S GREAT MATHEMATICIAN

By S. KRISHNAN--(F.P.J.)

Born of humble parents, and bred up and educated in conditions of extreme penury, Srinivasa Ramanujam wrung admiration and applause from mathematicians all over the world. Without even the University degree of B.A. he was elected Fellow of the Trinity College, Cambridge and of the Royal Society, He had an extraordinary insight into algebraic formulae and transformations of infinite series, and solved problems which, in the words of Prof. G. H. Hardy, his " Guru" and collaborator "have taken the finest mathematicians in Europe a hundred years to solve and of which the solution is incomplete even to-day."

Like Keats, Shelley and other geniuses, Ramanujam died a premature death Just when he had been initiated by Prof. Hardy into a regular and graduated course of mathematics, which could have given an impetus to his erratic and extraordinary genius, he died in 1920 at the early age of thirty-three.

Here is a brief life sketch of this mathematical prodigy as his life and career are not as well known in India as they deserve to be.

Born of Poor Parents

Ramanujam's father belonged to the Tanjore District, He was a "Gumastha " (petty accountant to a cloth merchant). He and his wife lived an orthodox religious life. Of these parents. Ramanujam was born on 22nd December 1887. In 1892 he was sent to school, and his school career was devoid of any outstanding brilliance, However, he displayed extreme devotion to mathematics. It is said that he mastered trigonometry in his school days and derived the Eulers' Theorems.

In 1903 by chance he got a copy of "Car's Synopsis of Pure Mathematics" which stimulated his mathematical genius. From then his real career was assured - that of a mathematician. From then until his death he 'lisped in figures, for the figures came.' He dreamt of mathematical figures and symbols; they were his constant companions. His imagination was busy conjuring up and establishing relations between them.

In December 1903 he passed the Matriculation Examination. In January 1904 he joined the Government College, Kumbakonam. His excessive preoccupation with mathematics proved his undoing. Mathematics proved a jealous and exacting mistress, she bade him forsake the other subjects completely. No. wonder, therefore, that he failed in the Junior B.A. Examination. From 1904 to 190 he strove unsuccessfully to complete his B.A. Course

Recognition by University

Rananujam was married in 1909. This as also the poverty of his family forced him to seek immediate employment. After a long struggle he secured a clerkship in the Madras Port Trust Office on a salary of Rs. 30 per mensem. Fortunately enough influential gentlemen soon came to know of his startling and marvellous flair for mathematics and were loth to let him rot as a clerk. They moved high quarters and the Madras University was persuaded to award Ramarujam a scholarship of Rs. 75 per mensem for two years.

At his friend's suggestions Ramanujam opened in 1919 a regular correspondence with Mr. G HI. Hardy, a fellow of the Trinity College, Cambridge, himself a mathematician of great repute. Hardy was convinced of the originality of Ramanujam and prevailed upon him to proceed to Cambridge. Hardy, was able to persuade the Madras University authorities to award Ramanujam a scholarship of £250 a year with free passage to England and adequate outfit allowance.

Grounding in Mathematics

On 17th March 1914, Ramanujam sailed for England reaching there in April. Hardy could find out that Ramanujam's solution of intricate mathematical problems was based more upon intuition, deduction, or call it what we will, than upon a regular and systematic study of Mathematics. He, therefore, set about imparting to Ramanujam a thorough grounding in all the branches of mathematics. The collaboration of Hardy and Ramanujam that commenced then was a fruitful one inasmuch as it has left behind valuable papers on problems contributed to mathematical journals in England and Europe,

Fame and Death

In February 1918, Ramanujan was elected a Fellow of the Royal Society in recognition of his worthy contributions to mathematics . The Cambridge University also honoured him by electing him in October 1918 a Fellow of the Trinity College. This Fellowship gave him a prize of £250 a year for 6 years with no duties or conditions. The Madras University did not lag behind; it granted him an allowance of £250 a year for 5 years from Ist April 1919.

However, Ramanujam was not destined to continue his career as a mathematician without carping care and pinching poverty, against which so much provision was generously made by the Madras and Cambridge Universities. He caught tuberculosis during his stay in England. He left England for India on 27th February 1919, landed at Bombay on 27th March 1919 and arrived at Madras on 22nd April 1919. Medical treatment was given to him in vain. He died on 26th April 1920 at Chetpet, a suburb of Madras.

A large-sized portrait of Ramanujam adorns the walls of the Madras University library. A contemporary pen-picture describes him as 'having a big head, with large forehead and long wavy dark hair and sharp, bright, dark eyes.' He was intensely religious, strictly observing religious rites even in England.

An Honoured Place

It is useless to conjecture what more discoveries Ramanujam would have made in the realms of mathematics with his innate ability, and knowledge gathered at Cambridge if he had been granted by Providence a longer life. The discoveries he was able to make within the all-too-short-span of his life are remarkable. His name occupies an honoured place in any recent history of mathematics. He was yet another concrete example to the world of the fact that India does not lack in geniuses in any walk of life or knowledge. .

*Article by S. Krishnan published in the paper Wealth & Welfare on 1st August 1947.

for tobacco. The "Elizabethan era might be better named the beginning of the smoking era," wrote Barrie in "My Lady Nicotine." Of course there were dissenters. Smoking offended them. It was not in keeping with the times. But the voice of the dissenter was lost in smoke. And tobacco was something to be taxed. Cardinal Richelieu discovered that in France in 1624

Tobacco has done many other things besides providing solace and revenue. It has stirred the blood of moralists; It has been the theme of preachers; It has inspired poets. composers, artists and novelists. Its very history is a literature in itself.

To smoke or not to smoke is to no longer an issue. The big question that tobacco poses today is this: Will the nations again smoke the pipe of peace?

SRINIVASA RAMANUJAM: INDIA'S GREAT MATHEMATICIAN

By S. Krishnan—(F.P.J.)

Born of humble parents, and bred up and educated in conditions of extreme penury, Srinivasa Ramanujam wrung admiration and applause from mathematicians all over the world. Without even the University degree of B.A. he was elected Fellow of the Trinity College, Cambridge and of the Royal Society. He had an extraordinary insight into algebraic formulae and transformations of infinite series, and solved problems which, in the words of Prof. G. H. Hardy, his "Guru" and collaborator, "have taken the finest mathematicians in Europe a hundred years to solve and of which the solution is incomplete even to-day."

Like Keats, Shelley and other geniuses, Ramanujam died a premature death. Just when he had been initiated by Prof. Hardy into a regular and graduated course of mathematics, which could have given an impetus to his erratic and extraordinary genius, he died in 1920 at the early age of thirty-three.

Here is a brief life sketch of this mathematical prodigy as his life and career are not as well-known in India as they deserve to be.

Born of Poor Parents

Ramanujam's father belonged to the Tanjore District. He was a "Gumastha" (petty accountant to a cloth merchant). He and his wife lived an orthodox religious life. Of these parents Ramanujam was born on 22nd December 1887. In 1892 he was sent to school, and his school career was devoid of any outstanding brilliance. However, he displayed extreme devotion to mathematics. It is said that he mastered trigonometry in his school days and derived unaided the Eulers' Theorems.

In 1903 by chance he got a copy of "Carr's Synopsis of Pure Mathematics" which stimulated his mathematical genius. From then his real career was assured—that of a mathematician. From then until his death he 'lisped in figures, for the figures came.' He dreamt of mathematical figures and symbols; they were his constant companions. His imagination was busy conjuring up and establishing relations between them.

In December 1903 he passed the Matriculation Examination. In January 1904 he joined the Government College, Kumbakonam. His excessive preoccupation with mathematics proved his undoing. Mathematics proved a jealous and exacting mistress; she bade him forsake the other subjects completely. No wonder, therefore, that he failed in the Junior B.A. Examination. From 1904 to 190' he strove unsuccessfully to complete his B.A. Course.

Recognit. n by University

Ramanujam was married in 1909. This as also the poverty of his family forced him to seek immediate employment. After a long struggle he secured a clerkship in the Madras Port Trust Office on a salary of Rs. 30 per mensem. Fortunately enough influential gentlemen soon came to know of his startling and marvellous flair for mathematics and were loth to let him rot as a clerk. They moved high quarters and the Madras University was persuaded to award Ramanujam a scholarship of Rs. 75 per mensem for two years.

At his friend's suggestions Ramanujam opened in 1919 a regular correspondence with Mr. G. H. Hardy, a fellow of the Trinity College, Cambridge, himself a mathematician of great repute. Hardy was convinced of the originality of Ramanujam and prevailed upon him to proceed to Cambridge. Hardy was able to persuade the Madras University authorities to award Ramanujam a scholarship of £ 250 a year with free passage to England and adequate outfit allowance.

Grounding in Mathematics

On 17th March 1914, Ramanujam sailed for England reaching there in April. Hardy could find out that Ramanujam's solution of intricate mathematical problems was based more upon intuition, deduction, or call it what we will, than upon a regular and systematic study of Mathematics. He, therefore, set about imparting to Ramanujam a thorough grounding in all the branches of mathematics. The collaboration of Hardy and Ramanujam that commenced then was a fruitful one inasmuch as it has left behind valuable papers on problems contributed to mathematical journals in England and Europe.

Fame and Death

In February 1918, Ramanujam was elected a Fellow of the Royal Society in recognition of his worthy contributions to mathematics. The Cambridge University also honoured him by electing him in October 1918 a Fellow of the Trinity College. This Fellowship gave him a prize of £ 250 a year for 6 years with no duties or conditions. The Madras University did not lag behind; it granted him an allowance of £ 250 a year for 5 years from 1st April 1919.

However, Ramanujam was not destined to continue his career as a mathematician without carping care and pinching poverty, against which so much provision was generously made by the Madras and Cambridge Universities. He caught tuberculosis during his stay in England. He left England for India on 27th February 1919, landed at Bombay on 27th March 1919 and arrived at Madras on 22nd April 1919. Medical treatment was given to him in vain. He died on 26th April 1920 at Chetput, a suburb of Madras.

A large-sized portrait of Ramanujam adorns the walls of the Madras University library. A contemporary pen-picture describes him as 'having a big head, with large forehead and long wavy dark hair and sharp, bright, dark eyes.' He was intensely religious, strictly observing religious rites even in England.

An Honoured Place

It is useless to conjecture what more discoveries Ramanujam would have made in the realms of mathematics with his innate ability, and knowledge gathered at Cambridge if he had been granted by Providence a longer life. The discoveries he was able to make within the all-too-short-span of his life are remarkable. His name occupies an honoured place in any recent history of mathematics. He was yet another concrete example to the world of the fact that India does not lack in geniuses in any walk of life or knowledge.

Printed by Mr. G. Raghavan at the Huxley Press, 114, Armenian Street, G.T., Madras Q. H. M. S. 180-C. and Published by Mr. K. Sundararajiengar, 3, Somasundaram Street, Thyagarayanagar, Madras.

Note

MR. S. RAMANUJAM, F.R.S.

The late Mr. S. Ramanujam, F.R.S., was first appointed as a clerk in the Trust's Accounts Department on Rs.25/- per mensem from the 1st March 1912. Finding exceptional mathematical talents in him the Late Rao Bahadur S. Narayana Ayyar, with the help of the Hon'ble Sir Francis Spring, then Chairman of the Trust, secured for Ramanujam a monthly research scholarship of Rs.75/- from the University of Madras to aid him to devote his whole time to the studies of mathematics in Trinity College at Cambridge. He was granted leave on loss of pay till his work in England was finished. Early in 1918 in recognition of his exceptional genius for mathematics, Mr. Ramanujam was elected a Fellow of the Royal Society, the highest honour attainable in science among the English race and thereby fully confirmed the correctness of the opinion of late Rao Bahadur S. Narayana Ayyar, who was solely responsible to usher Ramanujam to the mathematical world. Later he was also elected a Fellow of the Trinity College, Cambridge.

A reference is invited to the following publications put up below wherein his remarkable talents in mathematics have been eulogised by eminent men and journalists :-

1. "Wealth and Welfare" – 1st August 1947.
2. "RAMANUJAM - "Twelve Lectures on subjects suggested by his life and work" – By Mr. G. H. Hardy, Professor of pure Mathematics in the University of Cambridge.
3. "The Great Mathematicians" By H. W. Turnbull, F.R.S. Professor of Mathematics in the University of St. Andrews (pages 122-124).

After returning to India in March 1919 he was very ill and died on the 26th April 1920.

It is understood that a portrait of the late Mr. Ramanujam, F.R.S., will be exhibited in the Accountant General's Office where he was to be offered an appointment. As a past member of the Trust's Accounts Department attaining remarkable world wide fame in mathematics it is only in the fitness of things that a portrait of the late F.R.S. should adorn the walls of the Chief Accountant's room, I understand that a copy of his portrait can be spared for this purpose by Major M.S. Venkataraman, Ag. C.P.T.

C.P.T. 's permission is requested to have the portrait of the late Mr.Ramanujam, F.R.S, put up in the Chief Accountant's room.

C.A.C.
28.8.1947

C.A.C.
Is board's permission necessary

C. P. T.

No please. CPT's permission is sufficient and the portrait will be put up in my room. If approved, I shall discuss details for unveiling the portrait with Major Venkataraman, Ag. CPT, in due course.

C. P. T.
2.9.1947

Approved

C.P.T

MR. S. RAMANUJAM F.R.S.

The late Mr. S. Ramanujam, F.R.S., was first appointed as a clerk in the Trust's Accounts Department on Rs.25/- per mensem from the 1st March 1912. Finding exceptional mathematical talents in him the late Rao Bahadur S.Narayana Ayyar, with the help of the Hon'ble Sir Francis Spring, then Chairman of the Trust, secured for Ramanujam a monthly research scholarship of Rs.75/- from the University of Madras to aid him to devote his whole time to the studies of mathematics in Trinity College at Cambridge. He was granted leave on loss of pay till his work in England was finished. Early in 1918 in recognition of his exceptional genius for mathematics, Mr. Ramanujam was elected a Fellow of the Royal Society, the highest honour attainable in science among the English race and thereby fully confirmed the correctness of the opinion of late Rao Bahadur S.Narayana Ayyar, who was solely responsible to usher Ramanujam to the mathematical world. Later he was also elected a Fellow of the Trinity College, Cambridge.

A reference is invited to the following publications put up below wherein his remarkable talents in mathematics have been eulogised by eminent men and journalists :-

1. "Wealth and Welfare" - 1st August 1947.

2. "RAMANUJAM - Twelve Lectures on subjects suggested by his life and work" - By Mr.G.H.Hardy, Professor of pure mathematics in the University of Cambridge.

3. "The Great Mathematicians" By H.W. Turnbull, F.R.S., Professor of Mathematics in the University of St.Andrews (pages 122 - 124).

After returning to India in March 1919 he was very ill and died on the 26th April 1920.

It is understood that a portrait of the late Mr. Ramanujam, F.R.S., will be exhibited in the Accountant General's Office where he was to be offered an appointment. As a past incumbent of the Trust's Accounts Department attaining

remarkable

- 2 -

remarkable world wide fame in mathematics it is only in the fitness of things that a portrait of the late F.R.S. should adorn the walls of the Chief Accountant's room. I understand that a copy of his portrait can be spared for this purpose by ~~C.P.T.~~ Major M. S. Venkataraman, Ag. C.P.T.

C.P.T's permission is requested to have the portrait of the late Mr. Ramanujam, F.R.S., ~~exhibited~~ put up in the Chief Accountant's room.

C.P.T.

C.A.C.
28-8-1947.

MADRAS PORT TRUST
29 AUG 1947
ACCOUNTS DEPARTMENT

C.A.C.
Is Board's permission necy.

28.8.47

No Sir. C.P.T.'s permission is sufficient as the portrait will be put up in my room. If apprd, I shall discuss details for unveiling the portrait with Major Venkataraman, Ag. C.P.T., in due course.

C.P.T.

21/8/47

C.P.T. approves

SA(P)
pl speak
31/8/47

Speech

Mr. Chairman, Ladies and Gentlemen,

We are assembled here today to honour the memory of a great mathematician, the late S. Ramanujam, and to commemorate this happy occasion by installing his portrait in this office where he worked for some time during 1912-13.Mr. Ramanujam was born in 1888 and died very young on 26th April, 1920 at the age of 33. His was a life of devotion and sacrifice in the cause of the great science of mathematics. Inspite of adverse circumstances and difficulties, he devoted his noble time and energies to building up his monumental work in mathematics. He had studied up to F.A. and in his own language "he was prevented from pursuing his studies further owing to several untoward circumstances". This is what he said in his application dated 9-2-1912 to the Chief Accountant, Madras Port Trust for a clerk's post in this office. He went on to say that he had, however, been devoting all his time to mathematics and developing the subject. He was appointed as an accounts clerk on Rs. 25/- P.M..and joined his post on 1-3-1912. The fact that he had no training or higher education in mathematics at all shows that he was a self-taught man and that his great work in the field of higher mathematics was entirely his own, without outside help or training. It's a mystery how he could tackle unsolved intricate theories and problems in mathematics and solve them on his own initiative and resource without even a short term of training or research work in the fundamentals of higher mathematics. At the time, he joined service in this office in March 1912, The recommendation that got him the job was that he was a young man of quite exceptional capacity in mathematics and especially in the theory of numbers. In fact, he had already written several papers giving his solution to several unsolved problems.

Mr. Ramanujam's work and genius were noted by the late Rao Bahadur S. Narayana Iyer, retired Chief Accountant, Madras Fort Trust and a great mathematician himself and Honorary Secretary of the Indian Mathematical Society at the time. It was mainly due to the late Narayana Iyer's initiate and personal interest that Mr. Ramanujam was taken into the Port Trust service and thereafter with the active help of the then Chairman, Madras Port Trust, Sir Francis Spring, the Madras University and the Local Government were prevailed upon to give necessary financial assistance to enable Ramanujan to go to Cambridge and work with Professor Hardy,

Professor Neville and Professor Littlewood. He stayed in England for about 5 years from 1914 to 1919, during which period he was acclaimed on all hands as one of the greatest mathematicians of the time. He was made a Fellow of the Royal Society in 1918, the highest honour attainable in science. Later in the same year, he was elected a Fellow of Trinity College, Cambridge. In the height of his fame and popularity, he had to return to India in March 1919 due to failing health and shortly thereafter he died on 26-4-1920. His noble life was spent in the cause of mathematics and he has left behind him a very rich heritage of which any country may justly be proud. It is in the fitness of things that we should keep his sacred memory always green and fresh and I trust that his noble portrait adorning this office will be a perennial source of inspiration to one and all.

Though the proposal to install Mr. Ramanujam's portrait in this office has been uppermost in the minds of us all, it took concrete shape recently when Major M. S. Venkataraman, Traffic Manager and Acting Chairman, Madras Port Trust kindly offered to present a nice portrait for being put up in this office. On behalf of the members of the Accounts Department, I feel most grateful to Major Venkataram for his valuable gift of a portrait and for his having kindly consented to preside over this function today and to unveil the portrait in spite of his varied engagements.

It is now my pleasant duty to request major Venkatraman to kindly unveil the portrait of the late S. Ramanujam F.R.S, one of the greatest mathematicians of this age.

Chief Accountant, Madras Port Trust

Mr.Chairman, Ladies and Gentlemen,

We are assembled here today to honour the memory of a great mathematician, the late S.Ramanujam and to commemorate this happy occasion by installing his portrait in this office where he worked for some time during 1912-13. Mr.Ramanujam was born in 1888 and died very young on 26th April 1920 at the age of 33. His was a life of devotion and sacrifice in the cause of the great science of mathematics. Inspite of adverse circumstances and difficulties, he devoted his noble time and energies to building up his monumental work in mathematics. He had studied upto F.A. and in his own language "he was prevented from pursuing his studies further owing to several untoward circumstances." This is what he said in his application dated 9-2-1912 to the Chief Accountant, Madras Port Trust, for a clerk's post in this office. He went on to say that he had however, been devoting all his time to mathematics and developing the subject. He was appointed as an Accounts Clerk on Rs.25/- P.M. and joined his post on 1-3-1912. The fact that he had no training or higher education in mathematics at all shows that he was a self taught man and that his great work in the field of higher mathematics was entirely his own, without outside help or training. It is a mystery how he could tackle unsolved intricate theories and problems in mathematics and solve them on his own initiative and resource without even a short term of training or research work in the fundamentals of higher mathematics. At the time, he joined service in this office in March 1912, the recommendation that got him the job was that he was a young man of quite exceptional capacity in mathematics and especially in the theory of numbers. In fact, he had already written several papers giving his solutions of

-2-

199

of several unsolved problems.

Mr.Ramanujam's work and genius were noted by the late Rao Bahadur S.Narayana Iyer, retired Chief Accountant, Madras Port Trust and a great mathematician himself and Honorary Secretary of the Indian Mathematical Society at the time. It was mainly due to the late Narayana Iyer's initiate and personal interest that Mr.Ramanujam was taken into the Port Trust service and thereafter with the active help of the then Chairman, Madras Port Trust Sir Francis Spring, the Madras University and the Local Government were prevailed upon to give necessary financial assistance to enable Ramanujam to go to Cambridge and work with Prof.Hardy, Prof.Neville and Prof.Littlewood. He stayed in England for about 5 years from 1914 to 1919, during which period he was acclaimed on all hands as one of the greatest mathematicians of the time. He was made a Fellow of the Royal Society in 1918 the highest honour attainable in Science, later in the same year he was elected a Fellow of the Trinity College Cambridge. In the height of his fame and popularity, he had to return to India in March 1919 due to failing health and shortly thereafter he died on 26-4-1920. His noble life was spent in the cause of mathematics and he has left behind him a very rich heritage of which any country may justly be proud. It is in the fitness of things that we should keep his sacred memory always green and fresh and I trust that his noble portrait adorning this office will be a perennial source of inspiration to one and all.

Though the proposal to instal Mr.Ramanujam's portrait in this office has been uppermost in the minds of us all, it took concrete shape recently when Major M.S. Venkataraman, Traffic Manager and Acting Chairman, Madras Port Trust kindly offered to present a nice

portra.

-3-

portrait for being put up in this office. On behalf of the Axxxx members of the Accounts Department, I feel most grateful to Major Venkataraman for his valuable gift of a portrait and for his having kindly consented to preside over this function today and to unveil the portrait inspite of his varied engagements.

It is now my pleasant duty to request Major Venkataraman to kindly unveil the portrait of the late S.Ramanujam F.R.S. one of the greatest mathematicians of this age.

Chief Accountant, Madras Port Trust.

THE HINDU

SUNDAY, APRIL 18, 1948

TRIBUTE TO GENIUS OF RAMANUJAN

Portrait unveiled

Tributes were paid to the genius of the late Mr.. S. Ramanujan, the great Indian Mathematician, by several speakers at a meeting held under the auspices of the Accountant-General's Office Recreation Club to unveil his portraits at the Garrison Theatre, Fort St. George, Madras, last evening, Mr. S. A. Vaneswar, Accountant-General, Madras, was in the chair.

Mr. P. Narayanan welcomed the gathering.

Mr. Vaneswar unveiling the portrait stated that the late Ramanujan by his profound and far-reaching discoveries and by his characteristic originality had so woven his name into the fabric of world history that for all times his name would conjure up in the mathematical world thoughts of deep and intense veneration. The Accountant-General's Office was proud to be associated with a prodigy like Ramanujan who served for some years in that office.

Mr. N. Narayanaswami speaking next gave a short sketch of Ramanujan's brief but phenomenal career and cited the tribute paid to his genius by Pandit Jawaharlal Nehru in his book "The Discovery of India"

Mr. C. V. Rangachari also spoke. Mr. K. Nagabhushanam proposed a vote of thanks.

* Press Clippings, The Hindu, Dated April 18, 1948.

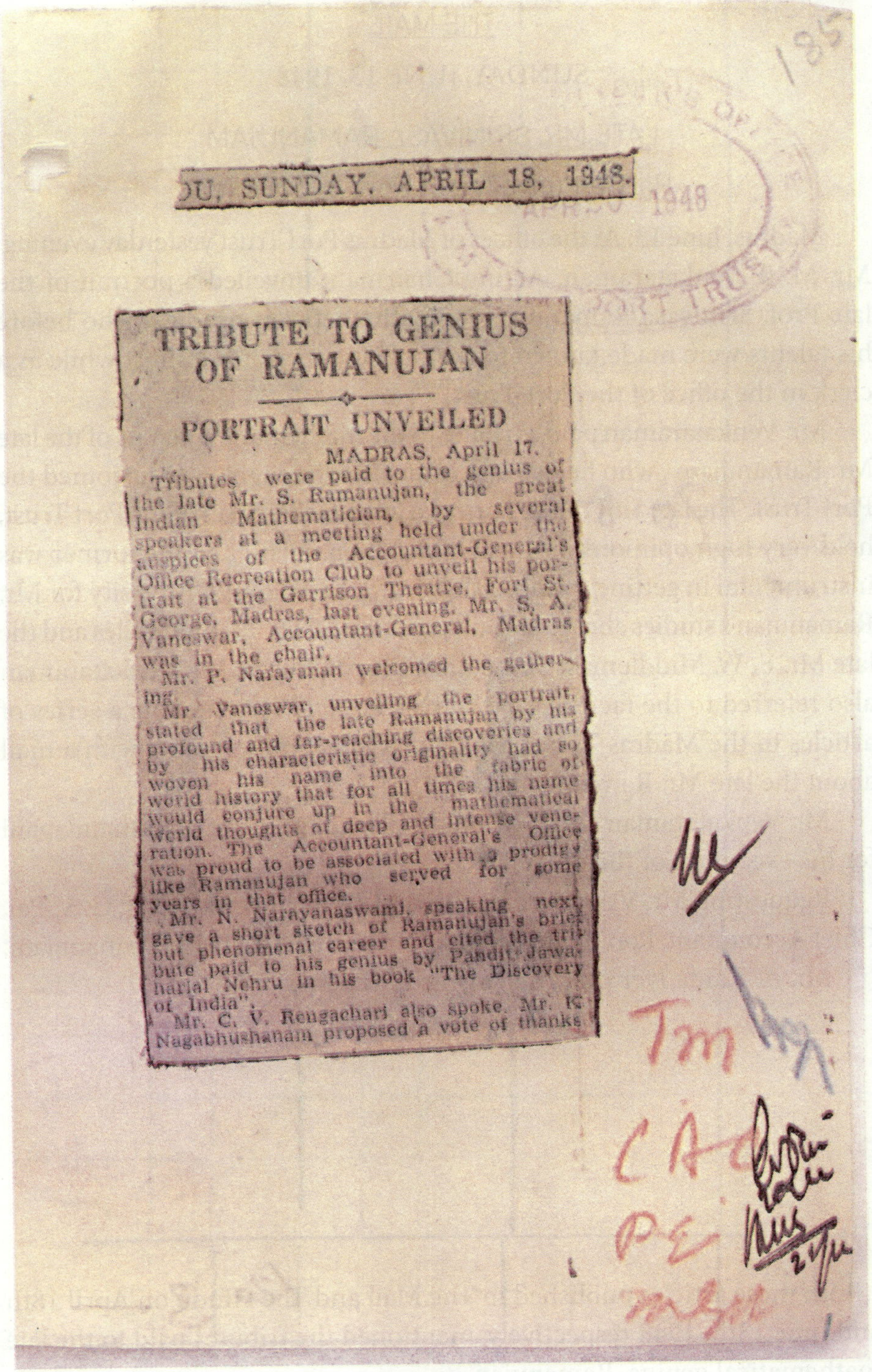

DU, SUNDAY, APRIL 18, 1948.

TRIBUTE TO GENIUS OF RAMANUJAN

PORTRAIT UNVEILED

MADRAS, April 17.

Tributes were paid to the genius of
the late Mr. S. Ramanujan, the great
Indian Mathematician, by several
speakers at a meeting held under the
auspices of the Accountant-General's
Office Recreation Club to unveil his por-
trait at the Garrison Theatre, Fort St.
George, Madras, last evening. Mr. S. A.
Vaneswar, Accountant-General, Madras
was in the chair.

Mr. P. Narayanan welcomed the gather-
ing.

Mr. Vaneswar, unveiling the portrait,
stated that the late Ramanujan by his
profound and far-reaching discoveries and
by his characteristic originality had so
woven his name into the fabric of
world history that for all times his name
would conjure up in the mathematical
world thoughts of deep and intense vene-
ration. The Accountant-General's Office
was proud to be associated with a prodigy
like Ramanujan who served for some
years in that office.

Mr. N. Narayanaswami, speaking next,
gave a short sketch of Ramanujan's brief
but phenomenal career and cited the tri-
bute paid to his genius by Pandit Jawa-
harlal Nehru in his book "The Discovery
of India".

Mr. C. V. Rengachari also spoke. Mr. K
Nagabhushanam proposed a vote of thanks

THE MAIL

SUNDAY, JUNE 13, 1948

LATE MR. SRINIVASA RAMANUJAM

Portrait unveiled at Port Trust Office

Madras, June 13: At the offices of Madras Port Trust yesterday evening, Mr. M. S. Venkataraman, Acting Chairman, unveiled a portrait of the late Prof. Srinivasa Ramanujam,, a mathematician prodigy, who before his talents were made known to the public, served for a short while as a clerk in the office of the Port Trust.

Mr. Venkataraman paid a tribute to the mathematical genius of the late Mr. Ramanujam , who he has said came into limelight after he joined the Port Trust. The late Sir Francis Spring, a former chairman of the Port Trust, held very high opinions of the late Mr. Ramanujan, and the former was instrumental in getting a scholarship from the Madras University for Mr. Ramanujan's studies abroad through the help of Mr. R. Little Hales and the late Mr. E. W. Middlemast of the Presidency College. Mr. Venkataraman also referred to the fact that the late Sir Francis Spring wrote a series of articles in the Madras Times, which was now amalgamated with a mail about the late Mr. Ramanujam.

Mr. Venkataraman also presented a silver plate to Mr. P. Kothandapani for his execution of the portrait.

Requesting Mr. Venkataraman to unveil the portrait of Mr. G. V. Pai, Chief Accountant, Port Trust, traced the career of the late Mr. Ramanujam.

Mr. A. Rama Iyer proposed a vote of thanks.

* Both these articles published in The Mail and The Hindu on April 18th and June 13th, 1948 respectively, mentioned the tributes paid to the late mathematical genius, Ramanujan.

THE MAIL

SUNDAY, JUNE 13, 1948

Late Mr Srinivasa Ramanujam

Portrait unveiled at Port Trust Office

MADRAS, June 13: At the offices of the Madras Port Trust yesterday evening, Mr M. S. Venkataraman, acting Chairman, unveiled a portrait of the late Prof. Srinivasa Ramanujam a mathematical prodigy, who before his talents were made known to the public, served for a short while as a clerk in the offices of the Port Trust.

Mr Venkataraman paid a tribute to the mathematical genius of the late Mr Ramanujam who he said, came into limelight after he joined the Port Trust. The late Sir Francis Spring, a former Chairman of the Port Trust, held very high opinions of the late Mr Ramanujam and the former was instrumental in getting a scholarship from the Madras University for Mr Ramanujam's studies abroad through the help of Mr R. Littlehailes and the late Mr E. W. Middlemast of the Presidency College Mr Venkataraman also referred to the fact that the late Sir Francis Spring wrote a series of articles in the Madras Times which was now amalgamated with The Mail about the late Mr Ramanujam.

Mr Venkataraman also presented a silver plate to Mr P. Kothandapani for his execution of the portrait.

Requesting Mr Venkataraman to unveil the portrait, Mr G. V. Pai, Chief Accountant, Port Trust, traced the career of the late Mr Ramanujam.

Mr A. Rama Ayyar proposed a vote of thanks.

THE HINDU

MONDAY, NOVEMBER 22, 1948

TRIBUTE TO LATE S. RAMANUJAM

Tributes to the late S. Ramanujam were held at a meeting in the Chintadripet High School this morning in connection with the celebration of the "Ramanujam Day".

Sir M. S. Venkataraman, Traffic Manager, Madras Port Trust, addressing the meeting said that it was given to the last Sir Francis Spring, Chairman of the Madras Port Trust, to discover the mathematical genius of a young Ramanujam who was employed as a clerk in the offices of the Trust in 1912. Within three months of his joining the office the then Manager of the Port Trust, Mr. Narayana Aiyar, himself a good mathematician, noticed Ramanujam's interest in mathematics and brought it to the notice of the authorities. No time was lost in securing for the young prodigy a scholarship to prosecute his studies at the Cambridge University where Ramanujam worked along with Hardy and Neville. Ramanujam returned to India in 1919 but did not live long after, and passed away in 1920, in his 32nd year. He had, however, left posterity a good collection of his researches to profit by.

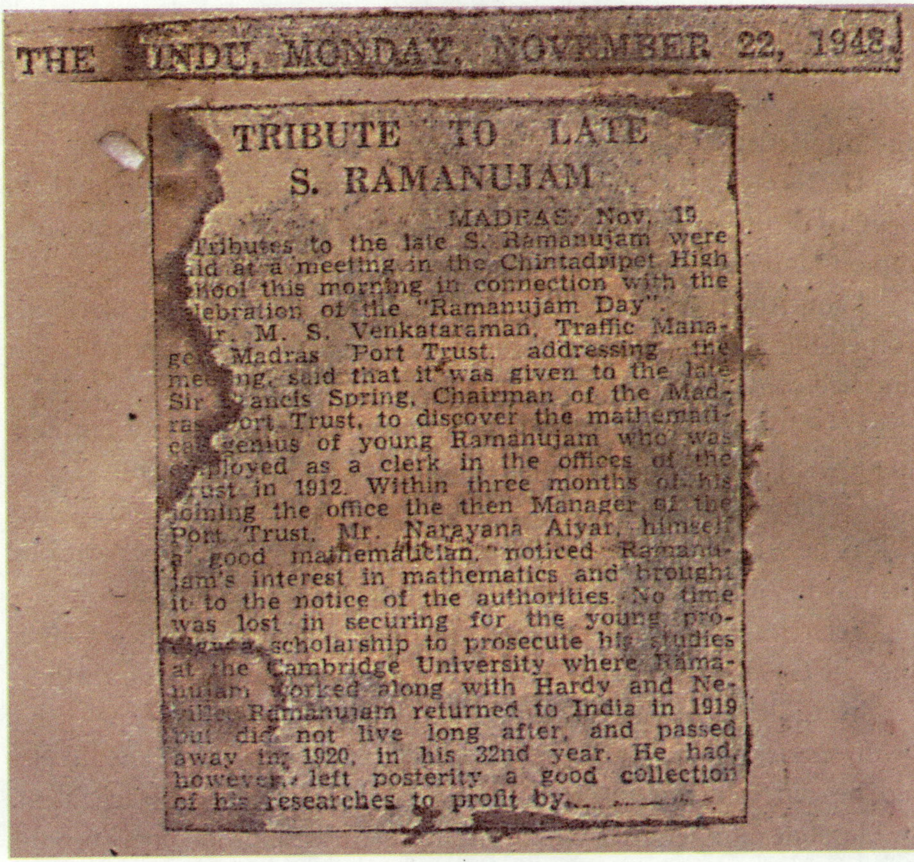

THE [illegible]INDU, MONDAY, NOVEMBER 22, 1948

TRIBUTE TO LATE S. RAMANUJAM

MADRAS, Nov. 19

Tributes to the late S. Ramanujam were [illegible]aid at a meeting in the Chintadripet High [illegible]chool this morning in connection with the [illegible]lebration of the "Ramanujam Day".

[illegible]r. M. S. Venkataraman, Traffic Manage[illegible] Madras Port Trust, addressing the me[illegible]ng, said that it was given to the late Sir [illegible]ancis Spring, Chairman of the Madra[illegible] [illegible]ort Trust, to discover the mathematica[illegible] genius of young Ramanujam who was [illegible]ployed as a clerk in the offices of the [illegible]rust in 1912. Within three months of his joining the office the then Manager of the Port Trust, Mr. Narayana Aiyar, himself a good mathematician, noticed Ramanujam's interest in mathematics and brought it to the notice of the authorities. No time was lost in securing for the young pro[illegible] a scholarship to prosecute his studies at the Cambridge University where Ramanujam worked along with Hardy and Neville. Ramanujam returned to India in 1919 but did not live long after, and passed away in 1920, in his 32nd year. He had, however, left posterity a good collection of his researches to profit by.

THE HINDU

SATURDAY, DECEMBER 24, 1949.

AMERICAN TRIBUTE TO LATE RAMANUJAM

The late Dr. Srinivasa Ramanujam, F.R.S., was by far the most remarkable mathematician that India had ever produced. He was a great genius and few could ever hope to reach his eminence for another 200 or 300 years, observed Dr Marshall H. Stone, Professor of Mathematics of the University of Chicago in an interview with Globe last evening.

Dr. Stone further observed that Dr. Ramanujam represented the symbol of the great tradition in mathematics in India. He was world famous and his work was original in character, he added.

Many American mathematicians, Dr. Stone continuing said, had found something new in his researches which they had not discovered before and had come to recognize his genius.

Dr. Stone remarked that India to-day had also many eminent mathematicians, who were unfortunately not very well-known.

Dr. Stone next made a reference to the genius of Dr. S. Chandrasekhar, F. R. S. he said, “We are proud to have him in our faculty there. We regard his stay in America as a gain to our continent.”

Referring to the future of mathematics in India, Dr. Stone remarked that the Government as well as philanthropists should aid its growth.

In addition to the teaching of this subject, Dr. Stone felt, that “Universities should also conduct first class research.” They should also aid, he said, in the discovery of new mathematics and encourage talents to blossom into geniuses by providing them with ample opportunities for research and study.

“I am confident” Dr. Stone said in conclusion, “that India will make a great name in the field of mathematics”. – Globe

THE HINDU, SATURDAY, DECEMBER 24, 1949.

AMERICAN TRIBUTE TO LATE RAMANUJAM

MADRAS, Dec. 21.

The late Dr. Srinivasa Ramanujam, F.R.S., was by far the most remarkable mathematician that India had ever produced. He was a great genius and few could ever hope to reach his eminence for another 200 or 300 years, observed Dr. Marshall H. Stone, Professor of Mathematics of the University of Chicago, in an interview with *Globe* last evening.

Dr. Stone further observed that Dr. Ramanujam represented the symbol of the great tradition in mathematics in India. He was world famous and his work was original in character, he added.

Many American mathematicians, Dr. Stone continuing said, had found something new in his researches which they had not discovered before and had come to recognize his genius.

Dr. Stone remarked that India to-day had also many eminent mathematicians, who were unfortunately not very well-known.

Dr. Stone next made a reference to the genius of Dr. S. Chandrasekhar, F.R.S. He said, "We are proud to have him in our faculty there. We regard his stay in America as a gain to our continent".

Referring to the future of mathematics in India, Dr. Stone remarked that the Government as well as philanthropists should aid its growth.

In addition to the teaching of this subject, Dr. Stone felt, that "Universities should also conduct first class research". They should also aid, he said, in the discovery of new mathematics and encourage talents to blossom into geniuses by providing them with ample opportunities for research and study.

"I am confident", Dr. Stone said in conclusion, "that India will make a great name in the field of mathematics".—Globe.

THE HINDU

THURSDAY, DECEMBER 11, 1947.

DEATH OF PROF. G. H. HARDY

Distinguished Pure Mathematician,

London, (by Air Mail)

Professor G. H. Hardy, F.R.S., died at Cambridge on December 1. His death recalls the achievements of S. Ramanujan, the first Indian fellow of the Royal Society. Professor Hardy, in collaboration with that remarkable but self-taught Indian mathematician, produced some brilliant treatises on the theory of numbers.

Ramanujan's work was first appreciated in 1913 when he sent a letter enunciating more than 100 theorems to Professor G. H. Hardy. Although not all the theorems were accurate, Hardy recognized the genius of his correspondent and arranged for Ramanujan to go up to Trinity College, Cambridge, of which he became the first Indian Fellow. To Hardy's great grief, Ramanujan died in 1920.

Prof. Hardy, perhaps the greatest pure mathematician of his day, often worked in realms into which few were able to follow him (on non-differential functions, etc.) But his brilliant textbook, "A Course in Pure Mathematics", which was published in 1908 and ran into a number of editions, is widely known. His most original work was done in the analytical theory of numbers and allied subjects.

Born in 1877, Professor Hardy had a distinguished career at the University, where he was a contemporary of Sir James Jeans, and his reputation had become worldwide even before he left Cambridge. In 1919, he became Savilian Professor of Geometry at Oxford, with a fellowship at New College, and later lectured in U.S. universities. In 1931, he returned to the Sadleirian Chair of Pure Mathematics at Cambridge, and a fellowship at Trinity.

An expert tennis player in his time, and a devotee of cricket.(he had all averages at his fingertips). Hardy, nevertheless, personified the popular idea of the absent-minded professor. A brilliant conversationalist, he had a lively sense of humor, and once produced a booklet, "A Mathematician's Apology", which, to the day of readers from many facilities, challenged anyone to dispute the unique qualities of utter uselessness possessed by pure mathematicians.

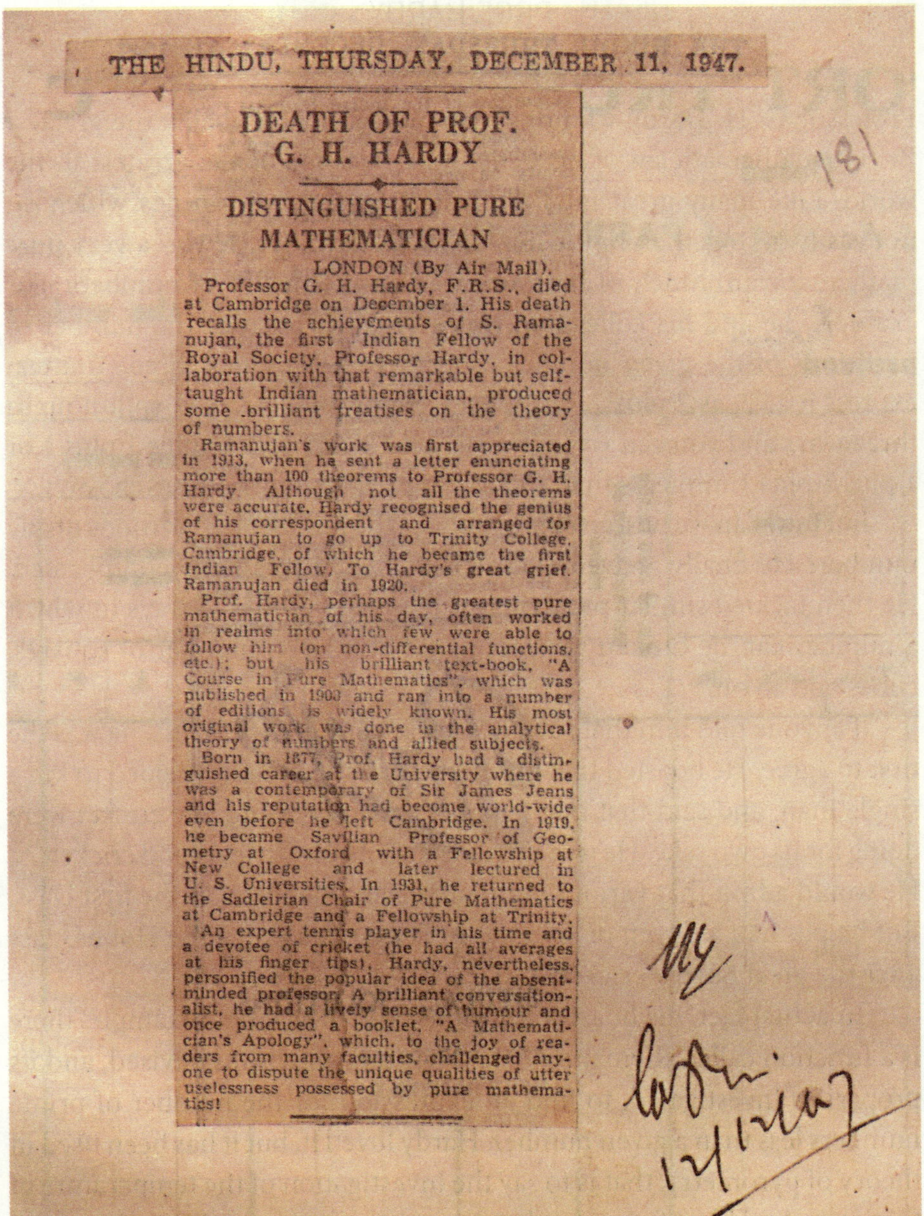

THE HINDU, THURSDAY, DECEMBER 11, 1947.

DEATH OF PROF. G. H. HARDY

DISTINGUISHED PURE MATHEMATICIAN

LONDON (By Air Mail).

Professor G. H. Hardy, F.R.S., died at Cambridge on December 1. His death recalls the achievements of S. Ramanujan, the first Indian Fellow of the Royal Society. Professor Hardy, in collaboration with that remarkable but self-taught Indian mathematician, produced some brilliant treatises on the theory of numbers.

Ramanujan's work was first appreciated in 1913, when he sent a letter enunciating more than 100 theorems to Professor G. H. Hardy. Although not all the theorems were accurate, Hardy recognised the genius of his correspondent and arranged for Ramanujan to go up to Trinity College, Cambridge, of which he became the first Indian Fellow. To Hardy's great grief, Ramanujan died in 1920.

Prof. Hardy, perhaps the greatest pure mathematician of his day, often worked in realms into which few were able to follow him (on non-differential functions, etc.); but his brilliant text-book, "A Course in Pure Mathematics", which was published in 1908 and ran into a number of editions is widely known. His most original work was done in the analytical theory of numbers and allied subjects.

Born in 1877, Prof. Hardy had a distinguished career at the University where he was a contemporary of Sir James Jeans and his reputation had become world-wide even before he left Cambridge. In 1919, he became Savilian Professor of Geometry at Oxford with a Fellowship at New College and later lectured in U. S. Universities. In 1931, he returned to the Sadleirian Chair of Pure Mathematics at Cambridge and a Fellowship at Trinity.

An expert tennis player in his time and a devotee of cricket (he had all averages at his finger tips), Hardy, nevertheless, personified the popular idea of the absent-minded professor. A brilliant conversationalist, he had a lively sense of humour and once produced a booklet, "A Mathematician's Apology", which, to the joy of readers from many faculties, challenged any-one to dispute the unique qualities of utter uselessness possessed by pure mathematics!

THE HINDU

SUNDAY, JANUARY 25, 1948.

PROF. HARDY

Prof. J. B. S. Haldane, F.R.S.

Professor G. H. Hardy who died last month, was probably the greatest British mathematician of his generation and one of the greatest in the world. Like many great men, he held views and did things which do not easily go together, in the lives of ordinary men. He was a very pure mathematician. Much of his work was on the theory of numbers. For example, he and his colleagues tackled the problem of the number of partitions of the given number. Consider the number three. You can express it as 2, as 2 plus 1, or 1 plus 1 plus 1, that is to say, split it up in three ways and you can write it as 4 3 plus 1. 2 plus 2 , 2 plus 1 plus 1,or 1 plus 1 plus 1 minus 1, that is to say five ways and five in seven ways.

But how can we find an expression for the number of partitions of any number? He finally arrived at the formula, which is fairly complicated. He then tackled similar problems such as the number of ways in which a number can be broken up into a sum of a given number of squares, cubes and so on.

If anyone told him that such work was completely useless, he was the first to agree. He boasted that his mathematics had never helped to kill a single man, and said that mathematics was something like cricket were doing for its own sake. He was an intense admirer of cricket and cricketers. He would admit that various mathematicians had been in the first class. But he put half a dozen or so of them in what he called the Hobbs class after the great Surrey cricketer.

In actual fact, his boast was unique. To take a single example, there is a function called Riemann's Zeta function, which was devised, and its properties investigated, to find an expression for the number of prime numbers less than a given number. Hardy loved it, but it has been used in theory of pyrometry, that is to say the investigation of the temperature of furnaces. And blast furnaces play a very important part in modern war.

Even cricket has its social function. For example, in spite of the strong resentment aroused by Larwood's bowling, it has certainly cemented friendship between Britain and Australia; and the prowess of Indian and West India cricketers has made some Englishmen, who would not otherwise have done so, resent members of darker coloured races. Hardy's pure mathematics had a social function of this kind. In 1913, an unknown Indian clerk, Ramanujam, sent him a letter containing about a hundred mathematical theorems. Hardy got him over to England and he became the first Indian Fellow of Trinity College, Cambridge and later of the Royal Society. Unfortunately, he got tuberculosis. As he lay dying of it, Hardy visited him. He asked Hardy for the number of his taxi cab. Hardy replied "1729, not a particularly interesting number." "What?" replied Ramanujan, "don't you realise that it is the smallest number which can be expressed in two different ways as the sum of two cubes?" (10^3 plus 9^3 or 12^3 plus 1^3), or so the story goes. Hardy is alleged to have said that Ramanujan was on terms of personal friendship with every number less than 10,000.

In spite of this attitude to his profession, which many readers of this article will regard as futile and reactionary, Hardy was a staunch opponent of what he regarded as injustice and superstition, a Socialist and a trade unionist. I remember him making a recruiting speech for the National Union of Scientific Workers, which was a trade union up to 1927, and, as the Association of Scientific Workers, is one again. He argued that science and mathematics were worth doing for their own sake. But he went on to say that although our jobs were very different from a coal miner's, we are much closer to coal miners and the capitalists. At least we and the miners were both skilled workers, not exploiters of other people's work, and if there was going to be a line-up, he was with the miners.

The idea of art for art's sake or mathematics for mathematicians' sake is an incomplete idea. But this is very much better than the idea of art for money's sake or mathematician or engineering's sake, no matter how the engineering is to be used, if you really believe in art for art's sake, you will soon want to change things so that everyone who wants can get a chance to practise art and to enjoy it. That means working for a society where everyone has the necessary leisure and means, in fact, for socialism. That was as far as G. H. Hardy got.

The next state is reached when the artist realised that his art can become a weapon for socialism and can be all the better for it. Men like William Morris, Alan Bush, and in his early plays Bernard Shaw got to this stage. It is certainly harder for a mathematician to do so because mathematics only appeals to the emotions of a few people, and can only be used directly for socialism after socialism has been won.

Though I disagree with Hardy's attitude, I regard it as one-sided rather than wholly wrong. It is right that every skilled worker should take pride in his or her work, particularly when it is not done to increase someone else's profit. Hardy spent his life devising intellectual tools which he tried out of the easiest material to hand namely "pure" numbers. Other people have used these tools for the study of mechanical systems as the telephones, and living ones, such as brains.

To take an example from my own work, I have just used part of the theory of the partitions of number to analyse family records to see whether on an average, certain diseases occur more often among the later-born members of a family than the earlier ones. I happen to be one of them who find an intense aesthetic pleasure in mathematics quite apart from the applications. I quite realise that this is not enough, but I also realize that those who enjoy it most are likely to do it best, so I do not feel that Hardy's attitude was wholly wrong, and I mourn a man whom not only I liked personally, but whose writings gave me some of the emotions which others derive from classical music, - D. & G. N.

THE HINDU, SUNDAY, JANUARY 25, 1948.

Prof. HARDY

By Prof. J. B. S. Haldane, F.R.S.

PROFESSOR G. H. HARDY, who died last month, was probably the greatest British mathematician of his generation, and one of the greatest in the world. Like many great men, he held views and did things which do not easily go together in the lives of ordinary men. He was a very pure mathematician. Much of his work was on the theory of numbers. For example, he and his colleagues tackled the problem of the number of partitions of a given number. Consider the number three. You can express it as 3, as 2 plus 1, or as 1 plus 1 plus 1, that is to say, split it up in three ways. Four can be written as 4, 3 plus 1, 2 plus 2, 2 plus 1 plus 1, or 1 plus 1 plus 1 plus 1, that is to say in five ways, and five in seven ways.

But how can we find an expression for the number of partitions of any number? He finally arrived at the formula, which is fairly complicated. He then tackled similar problems, such as the number of ways in which a number can be broken up into a sum of a given number of squares, cubes, and so on.

If anyone told him that such work was completely useless, he was the first to agree. He boasted that his mathematics had never helped to kill a single man, and said that mathematics was something like cricket, worth doing for it's own sake. He was an intense admirer of cricket and cricketers. He would admit that various mathematicians had been in the first class. But he put half a dozen or so of them in what he called the Hobbs class, after the great Surrey cricketer.

In actual fact his boast was untrue. To take a single example, there is a function called Riemann's Zeta function, which was devised, and its properties investigated, to find an expression for the number of prime numbers less than a given number. Hardy loved it. But it has been used in the theory of pyrometry, that is to say the investigation of the temperature of furnaces. And blast furnaces play a very important part in modern war.

Even cricket has its social functions. For example, in spite of the strong resentment aroused by Larwood's bowling, it has certainly cemented friendship between Britain and Australia; and the prowess of Indian and West India cricketers has made some Englishmen, who would not otherwise have done so, respect members of darker-coloured races.

Hardy's pure mathematics had a social function of this kind. In 1913 an unknown Indian clerk, Ramanujam, sent him a letter containing about a hundred mathematical theorems. Hardy got him over to England, and he became the first Indian Fellow of Trinity College, Cambridge, and later of the Royal Society. Unfortunately he got tuberculosis. As he lay dying of it, Hardy visited him. He asked Hardy for the number of his taxicab. Hardy replied: "1729, not a particularly interesting number." "What", replied Ramanujam, "don't you realise that it is the smallest number which can be expressed in two different ways as the sum of two cubes?" (10^3 plus 9^3 or 12^3 plus 1^3), or so the story goes. Hardy is alleged to have said that Ramanujam was on terms of personal friendship with every number less than 10,000.

In spite of this attitude to his profession, which many readers of this article will regard as futile and reactionary, Hardy was a staunch opponent of what he regarded as injustice and superstition, a Socialist and a trade unionist. I remember him making a recruiting speech for the National Union of Scientific Workers which was a trade union up to 1927, and, as the Association of Scientific Workers, is one again. He argued that science and mathematics were worth doing for their own sake. But he went on to say that although our jobs were very different from a coalminer's, we were much closer to coalminers than to capitalists. At least we and the miners were both skilled workers, not exploiters of other people's work, and if there was going to be a line-up he was with the miners.

The idea of art for art's sake or mathematics for mathematics' sake is an incomplete idea. But it is very much better than the idea of art for money's sake, or mathematics for engineering's sake, no matter how the engineering is to be used. If you really believe in art for art's sake you will soon want to change things so that everyone who wants can get a chance to practise art and to enjoy it. That means working for a society where everyone has the necessary leisure and means, in fact for socialism. That was as far as G. H. Hardy got.

The next stage is reached when the artist realises that his art can become a weapon for socialism, and be all the better for it. Men like William Morris, Alan Bush and in his early plays, Bernard Shaw, got to this stage. It is certainly harder for a mathematician to do so, because mathematics only appeals to the emotions of a few people, and can only be used directly for socialism after socialism has been won.

Though I disagree with Hardy's attitude, I regard it as one-sided rather than wholly wrong. It is right that every skilled worker should take pride in his or her work, particularly when it is not done to increase someone else's profits. Hardy spent his life devising intellectual tools, which he tried out on the easiest material to hand, namely "pure" numbers. Other people have used these tools for the study of mechanical systems such as telephones, and living ones, such as brains.

To take an example from my own work. I have just used part of the theory of the partitions of numbers to analyse family records to see whether, on an average, certain diseases occur more often among the later-born members of a family than the earlier ones. I happen to be one of those who find an intense aesthetic pleasure in mathematics quite apart from its applications. I quite realise that this is not enough. But I also realise that those who enjoy it most are likely to use it best. So I do not feel that Hardy's attitude was wholly wrong, and I mourn a man whom not only I liked personally, but whose writings gave me some of the emotions which others derive from classical music.—*D. & G. N.*

Select Bibliography

1. Interviews/ Discussions

   1) Shri A. Balasubramaniyam, Head Master, Town Higher Secondary School, Kumbkonam, dated- 20th May 2024
   2) Shri A T B Bose, Secretary of Ramanujan Museum & Math Education Centre, Chennai, dated- 21st May 2024
   3) Shri Sunil Paliwal, IAS, Chairman, Madras Port Trust, Chennai, dated- 22nd May 2024
   4) Shri M. Pitchaimani, Director, Ramanujan Institute for Advanced Study in Mathematics, University of Madras, Chennai, dated- 22nd May 2024
   5) Shri I. K. Lenin Tamil Kovan, FAS, Executive Director, Tamil Nadu Science & Technology Centre, Chennai, dated- 23rd May 2024

2. Books/ Journals

   1) Alladi, Krishnaswami, Ramanujan's Place in the World of Mathematics: Essays Providing a Comparative Study, (New Delhi: Springer India, 2012).
   2) Andrews, G. E., R. A. Askey, B. C. Berndt, K. G. Ramanathan, and R. A. Rankin, eds., Ramanujan Revisited, (Boston: Academic Press, 1988).
   3) Andrews, G. E., The Theory of Partitions, (Reading: Addison-Wesley, 1976).
   4) Askey, R. A., "Beta integrals in Ramanujan's Papers, his unpublished work and further examples," Ramanujan Revisited, (G. E. Andrews et al.,eds.), (Boston: Academic Press, 1988).
   5) Banerjee, Swapan, Ramanujan & Ancient Indian Mathematicians, (California: Createspace Independent Publishing Platform, 2019).

6) Berndt, Bruce C., Number Theory in the Spirit of Ramanujan, (Rhode Island: American Mathematical Society, 2006).
7) Berndt, Bruce C., Ramanujan's Notebooks, Part I, (New York: Springer, 1985).
8) Berndt, Bruce C., Ramanujan's Notebooks, Part II, (New York: Springer, 1989).
9) Berndt, Bruce C., Ramanujan's Notebooks, Part III, (New York: Springer, 1991).
10) Berndt, Bruce C., Ramanujan's Notebooks, Part IV, (New York: Springer, 1994).
11) Berndt, Bruce C., Ramanujan's Notebooks, Part V, (New York: Springer, 1998).
12) Berndt, Bruce C., and Robert A. Rankin, Ramanujan: Essays and Surveys, (History of Mathematics : Vol 9) (Rhode Island: American Mathematical Society, 2001).
13) Berndt, Bruce C., and Robert A. Rankin, Ramanujan: Letters and Commentary, (Rhode Island: American Mathematical Society, 1995).
14) Bharathi, R., ed. Prof. Srinivasa Ramanujan Commemoration Volume, (Chennai: Jupiter Press, 1974).
15) Bollobas, B., Littlewood's Miscellany, (Cambridge: Cambridge University Press, 1986).
16) Burkill, J.C., Dictionary of Scientific Biography, (New York: Charles Scribner's Sons, 1971).
17) Candelpergher, Bernard, Ramanujan Summation of Divergent Series, (Cham: Springer, 2017).
18) Davenport, H., Collected Papers, Vol. III, (London: Academic Press, 1977).
19) Govil, Narendra, and Bhu Dev Sharma, Mathematics Wizard Srinivasa Ramanujan, (New Delhi: Prabhat Prakashan, 2021).
20) Hardy, G.H., A Course of Pure Mathematics, (Cambridge: Cambridge University Press, 1908).
21) Hardy, G.H., Bertrand Russell and Trinity, (Cambridge: Cambridge University Press, 1942).
22) Hardy, G.H., Collected Papers, Vol. 1, (Oxford: Clarendon Press, 1966).

23) Hardy, G.H., Collected Papers, Vol. 2. (Oxford: Clarendon Press, 1967).

24) Hardy, G.H., Collected Papers, Vol. 4, (Oxford: Clarendon Press, 1969).

25) Hardy, G.H., Collected Papers, Vol. 5, (Oxford: Clarendon Press, 1972).

26) Hardy, G.H., Collected Papers, Vol. 6, (Oxford: Clarendon Press, 1974).

27) Hardy, G.H., Collected Papers, Vol. 7, (Oxford: Clarendon Press, 1979).

28) Hardy, G. H., Ramanujan: Twelve Lectures on Subjects Suggested by his Life & Work, (Cambridge: Cambridge University Press, 1940).

29) Kanigel, Robert, The Man who knew Infinity: A life of the Genius Ramanujan, (New York: Washington Square Press, 1991).

30) Littlewood, J. E., A Mathematician's Miscellany, (London: Methuen & Co. Ltd, 1953).

31) Nagarajan, K. R., and T. Soundararajan, eds. Srinivasa Ramanujan, 1887-1920 : A Tribute, (Chennai: Macmillan India, 1988).

32) Rajagopalan, K. R., Srinivasa Ramanujan (Chennai: Sri Aravinda-Bharati, 1988).

33) Ram, Suresh, Srinivasa Ramanujan, (New Delhi: National Book Trust, 1972).

34) Ramanujan, Srinivasa, Collected Papers of Srinivasa Ramanujan, ed. by, G. H. Hardy, P. V. Seshu Aiyar and B. M. Wilson, (Cambridge : Cambridge University Press, 2015).

35) Ramanujan, Srinivasa, Notebooks. Vols. 1, 2, (Bombay: Tata Institute of Fundamental Research, 1957).

36) Ramanujan, Srinivasa, The Lost Notebook and Other Unpublished Papers, (Berlin : Springer, 1988).

37) Ranganathan, S. R., Ramanujan : The Man & the Mathematician, (Bombay: Asia Publishing House, 1967).

38) Rao, K. Srinivasa, Srinivasa Ramanujan : Life and Work of a Natural Mathematical Genius, Swayambhu, (Singapore : Springer Nature, 2021).

39) Salwi, Dilip M., S. Ramanujan : The Mathematical Genius, (New Delhi: Rupa Publications, 2004).

40) Venkateswaran, T. V., Kanitha Methai Ramanujan (in Tamil), (Chennai: Bharathi Puthakalayam, 2012).

3. Articles/Journals

1) Aiyar, S. N., "The distribution of primes," Journal of Indian Mathematical Society 5, (1913), 60-61.

2) Aiyar, P. V. Seshu., "The late Mr. S. Ramanujan. B.A., F.R.S.," Journal of Indian Mathematical Society 12, (1920), 81-86.

3) Andrews, G. E., "An introduction to Ramanujan's 'Lost' Notebook," American Mathematical Monthly 86 (1979), 89-108. Andrews, G. E., "On the theorems of Watson and Dragonette for Ramanujan's mock theta functions," American Journal of Mathematics 88, (1966), 454-490.

4) Andrews, G. E., B. C. Berndt, L. Jacobsen, and R. L. Lamphere, "The continued fractions found in the unorganized portions of Ramanujan's notebooks," Memoirs of American Mathematical Society 99, (1992), 477.

5) Birch, B. J., "A look back at Ramanujan's Notebooks," Mathematical Proceedings of the Cambridge Philosophical Society 78, (1975), 73-79.

6) Bollobas, B., "Ramanujan—A Glimpse of his Life and his Mathematics," The Cambridge Review, (1988), 76-80.

7) Hardy, G. H., "A Chapter from Ramanujan's note-book," Proceedings of the Cambridge Philosophical Society (2) 21, (1923), 492-503.

8) Hardy, G. H., "A formula of Ramanujan." Journal of London Mathematical Society 3 (1928), 238-240.

9) Hardy, G. H., "A formula of Ramanujan in the theory of primes." Journal of London Mathematical Society 12, (1937), 94-98.

10) Hardy, G.H., "Obituary, S. Ramanujan." Nature 105, (June 17, 1920), 494-495.

11) Hardy, G. H., "Srinivasa Ramanujan," Proceedings of the London Mathematical Society (2) 19, (1921), xl-lviii.

12) Hardy, G. H "Some formulae of Ramanujan," Proceedings of the London Mathematical Society (2) 22, (1924), xii-xiii.
13) Neville, E. H. "The Late Srinivasa Ramanujan," Nature 106, No. 2673, (January 1921), 661-662.
14) Rao, R. Ramachandra, "In Memoriam S. Ramanujan, B.A., F.R.S.," Journal of Indian Mathematical Society 12, (1920), 87-90.

4. Archives Material
1) S. Ramanujan Papers, Acc no. 78, NAI, New Delhi
2) File no. 50-63/50 A2, Ministry of Education, 1950, NAI, New Delhi
3) File no. IR4/ 20275/ 81/ S, Vol I, MPT Office, Secy Department, IR Section, 1981, Madras Port Trust, Chennai
4) File no. IR4/ 20275/ 81/ S, Vol II, MPT Office, Secy Department, IR Section, 1981, Madras Port Trust, Chennai
5) File no. IR4/ 20275 (F)/ 81/ S, Vol I, MPT Office, Secy Department, IR Section, 1981, Madras Port Trust, Chennai
6) Horoscope of S. Ramanujan, Ramanujan Museum & Math Education Centre, Chennai
7) Letter from G H Hardy to Ramanujan, 26th March 1913, Ramanujan Museum & Math Education Centre, Chennai
8) Letter from G H Hardy to Ramanujan, Ramanujan Museum & Math Education Centre, Chennai
9) Letter from Ramanujan to Vinayaka Rao, 11th June 1914, Ramanujan Museum & Math Education Centre, Chennai
10) Letters from Ramanujan to his Mother Komalatammal (in Tamil), 11th September 1914, Ramanujan Museum & Math Education Centre, Chennai
11) Letters from Ramanujan to his Father Srinivasa Aiyangar (in Tamil), 17th November 1914, Ramanujan Museum & Math Education Centre, Chennai
12) Letter from Ramanujan to C N Ganapathy Iyer, 17th December 1914, Ramanujan Museum & Math Education Centre, Chennai
13) Letter from Ramanujan to Vinayaka Rao, 24th March 1915, Ramanujan Museum & Math Education Centre, Chennai

14) Letter from Ramanujan to Vinayaka Rao, 10th September 1915, Ramanujan Museum & Math Education Centre, Chennai
15) Certificate of Candidate to Election, 18th December 1917, Ramanujan Museum & Math Education Centre, Chennai
16) Passport of S. Ramanujan, February 1919, Ramanujan Museum & Math Education Centre, Chennai
17) Letter from B M Wilson to Professor Seshu Aiyar, 18th August 1925, Ramanujan Museum & Math Education Centre, Chennai

5. Surveys
1) Town Higher Secondary School, Kumbakonam
2) Ramanujan Museum & Math education Centre, Chennai
3) Madras Port Trust, Chennai
4) University of Madras, Chennai
5) Ramanujan Institute for Advanced Study in Mathematics, University of Madras, Chennai
6) Tamil Nadu Science & Technology Centre, Chennai

Abbreviations

1. N.A.I.- National Archives of India
2. Sd.- Signed
3. US- Under Secretary
4. M. of Edu.- Ministry of Education
5. US (A)- Under Secretary (Archives)
6. Ag.- Acting
7. Intd.- Intended
8. F.J.E.S.- Francis Joseph Edward Spring
9. S.N.- Subbanarayanan Narayana Aiyar
10. C.A.C.- Chairman of the Account Committee or Chief Accounts Clerk
11. C.P.T.- Chairman of the Port Trust
12. Mensen- every month/ by the month
13. Esq.- Esquire
14. K.C.I.E.- Knight Commander of the most Eminent Order of the Indian Empire
15. C.B.- Cecil Bernard Cotterell
16. F.R.S.- Fellow of the Royal Society
17. F.A.- First Arts
18. M.R.Ry- Maharaja Rajashry- approximately translated respected (Shri) king (Raja) of great kings (Maharaja)
19. G.H.Hardy- Godfrey Harold Hardy
20. S.S.- Steamship
21. F.R.S.E – Fellowship of the Royal Society of Edinburgh

Index

N

O

P

R